A People's History of London

A People's History of London

Lindsey German and John Rees

VERSO
London • New York

First published by Verso 2012
© Lindsey German and John Rees 2012

1 3 5 7 9 10 8 6 4 2

Verso
UK: 6 Meard Street, London W1F 0EG
US: 20 Jay Street, Suite 1010, Brooklyn, NY 11201
www.versobooks.com

Verso is the imprint of New Left Books

ISBN-13: 978-1-84467-855-6

British Library Cataloguing in Publication Data
A catalogue record for this book is available from the British Library

Library of Congress Cataloging-in-Publication Data

German, Lindsey.
A people's history of London / Lindsey German and John Rees.
   p. cm.
Includes bibliographical references.
 ISBN 978-1-84467-855-6 -- ISBN 978-1-84467-914-0 (ebook)
1. London (England)--History. 2. London (England)--Social conditions. 3. Social
reformers--England--London--History. 4. Dissenters--England--London--History. I.
Rees, John, 1957- II. Title.
 DA677.1.G47 2012
 942.1--dc23

2012010609

Typeset in Bembo by Hewer Text UK Ltd, Edinburgh
Printed and bound by CPI Group (UK) Ltd, Croydon, CR0 4YY

Contents

Acknowledgements

This book has obscure origins in an idea that David Shonfield once suggested for a 'Radical Walks in Britain' guide. We suggested it to Tariq Ali, and then we all forgot about it for a couple of years. Tariq recalled the plan and transmuted it into an offer to write this book. Tom Penn, Leo Hollis and Dan Hind at Verso have made it happen. We are grateful to all of them. We are indebted to Neil Faulkner, who knows a lot about most things and something about everything; we have plundered his knowledge without restraint. Dominic Alexander's knowledge of the medieval world was put at our service and the relevant chapter would clearly be poorer without it. David Shonfield provided many insights and suggestions as he read the draft. Our long-time comrades and friends at the Stop the War Coalition, Chris Nineham, Andrew Murray, and Andrew Burgin read and commented on the whole book with their usual kindness and perspicacity. Kate Connolly was generous with her marvellous work on the Suffragette movement and Peter Morgan supplied the Oscar Wilde story. Jane Shallice, Feyzi Ismail, Mike Simons, Paul Cunningham and John Westmoreland have all been generous with encouragement and suggestions along the way. We are very grateful to all of them.

John Rees
Lindsey German
London, 5 November 2011

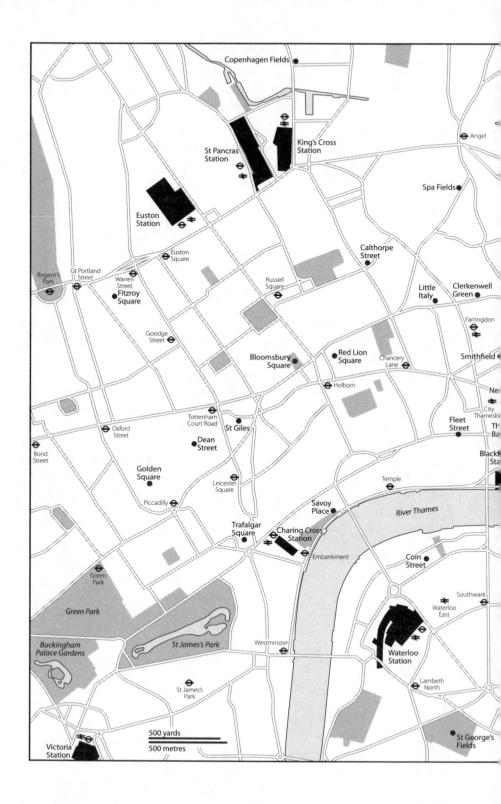

Copenhagen Fields

St Pancras Station

King's Cross Station

Angel

Spa Fields

Euston Station

Calthorpe Street

Regent's Park

Gt Portland Street

Warren Street

Euston Square

Russell Square

Little Italy

Clerkenwell Green

Fitzroy Square

Farringdon

Goodge Street

Bloomsbury Square

Red Lion Square

Chancery Lane

Smithfield

Oxford Street

Tottenham Court Road

St Giles

Holborn

Ne

City Thameslin

Bond Street

Dean Street

Fleet Street

Th Ba

Golden Square

Leicester Square

Blackf Sta

Piccadilly

Temple

Savoy Place

River Thames

Trafalgar Square

Charing Cross Station

Green Park

Embankment

Coin Street

Green Park

Southwark

Waterloo East

Buckingham Palace Gardens

St James's Park

Westminster

Waterloo Station

Lambeth North

St James's Park

500 yards

500 metres

Victoria Station

St George's Fields

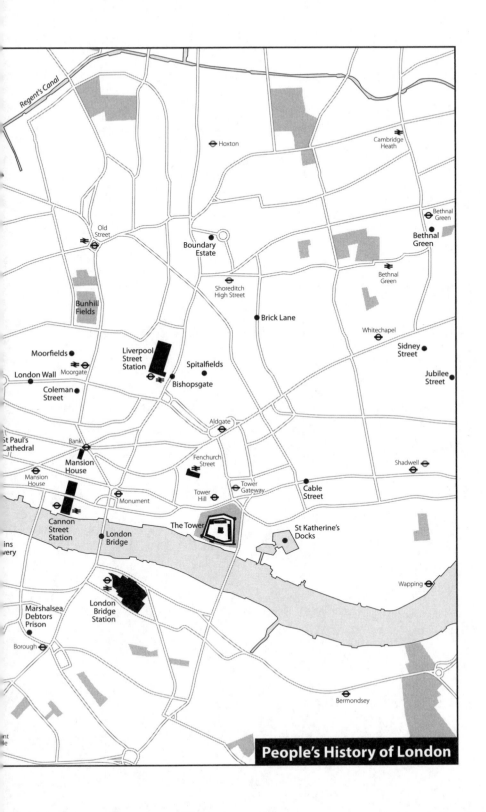

People's History of London

Introduction

Joshua Virasami is twenty-one years old, black, and 'born and bred' a Londoner. He grew up in West London and, like most of his fellow students, was working to pay his way through college. His job was in Costa Coffee at Heston motorway service station on the M4. But on 15 October 2011 Josh wasn't at work or college. He was in one of the oldest parts of his home city, the original site of the Roman Temple to Diana, the church-yard at St Paul's Cathedral. He was about to have a remarkable day.

Josh and some thousands of others were at St Paul's because it was the advertised starting point for a demonstration. The protestors intended to occupy the London Stock Exchange – hence the name 'Occupy LSX'. But the police prevented them from doing so, and in the game of cat and mouse that followed through the streets of the City of London the demonstrators took their last stand back where they started: on the steps of St Paul's Cathedral. There an impromptu rally took place and a tent city began to take shape.[1] The protest grabbed the attention of the media, partly because it was one of many similar protests in eighty countries around the world, partly because it sparked a political crisis in the Church of England over whether the permanent protest camp that sprang up around the Cathedral should be forcibly removed. Not all of Josh's fellow protestors will have been aware of it as they struggled to resist the attempts by the police to remove them that evening, but many other radicals over many centuries had stood where they now stood.

In the stillness of that night at St Paul's, after the tents were erected, it was possible to imagine that the tolling of the bell was not that of the modern Cathedral but the sound of the Great Bell of the Jesus Tower, a free-stand-ing bell tower in the courtyard of the medieval Cathedral, summoning the citizens of London to the one of the thrice yearly folkmoots at St Paul's Cross, the open-air pulpit. Attendance was compulsory until the fourteenth century and here papal bulls, news of military victories or royal marriages,

---

1   Joshua Virasami to John Rees, personal communication.

excommunications and proclamations were read out. News of the victory of Agincourt was read on the Cathedral steps. William Tyndale's English translation of the Bible was burnt here, so were the works of Martin Luther. Martyred Bishops Ridley and Latimer preached here. St Paul's Cross was only removed by order of Parliament in 1643 during the English Revolution.

Josh's seventeenth-century precursors, the apprentices of the City of London, were at the heart of the mass mobilizations that made the English Revolution. The 'apron youths', as the Leveller leader John Lilburne called them, would swarm St Paul's Churchyard. They were looking for print. By the time of the English Revolution St Paul's churchyard was a hive of political radicalism, the very centre of the printing industry. The houses around the Churchyard contained stationers' premises, including printing presses. Booths around the Cathedral itself sold the pamphlets and newsbooks that were pouring from the presses in unprecedented numbers. The printed declarations of the Agitators in the New Model Army could be bought here. So could the pamphlets of the Levellers. So could the revolutionary works of John Milton, resident around the corner in Aldersgate Street. The nave of the Cathedral was used as a cavalry barracks for Cromwell's army, and the statues of Charles I and his father, which had stood in Inigo Jones's portico, were destroyed by troopers. The Levellers had particular reason to remember St Paul's Churchyard: one of their heroes, Robert Lockyer, was executed by a firing squad of musketeers for mutiny there in 1649.

It is unlikely that one of the actors in the drama of the Occupy movement, Canon Chancellor Giles Fraser, was not aware of this history. Long before he resigned as a result of his defence of the Occupy movement's right to remain outside St Paul's he was based in St Mary's Putney, the venue for the great 'Putney debates' in which the Levellers and their allies in the New Model Army confronted Cromwell over the future direction of the revolution in 1647. He remains a supporter of the Leveller Association.

In the late 1830s the first great working-class movement, the Chartists, adopted an unusual agitational strategy: mass attendance at Sunday sermons. St Paul's Cathedral was one of their targets. On Sunday 11 August 1839, some 500 Chartists assembled in West Smithfield and marched to St Paul's. They wore, as protestors still do today, ribbons in their buttonholes to show support for the cause. At first they refused to take off their hats as they entered the Church but 'after some remonstrance from the Vergers, they submitted'.[2]

Not all protests at St Paul's have been as peaceful as the Chartists or the Occupy movement. In 1913 the Suffragettes planted a bomb under the bishop's throne in the Cathedral. It failed to explode because the clockwork

---

2   J. Ashton, *Gossip in the First Decade of Victoria's Reign* (Bremen, 2010), p. 107.

arming mechanism had been wound in the wrong direction. *The Morning Post* for 8 May 1913 reported that 'there is no doubt in the minds of the authorities that the contrivance was designed and placed there by someone associated with the militant Suffragist movement', since it was 'carefully wrapped in brown paper and in part of the recent issue of the militant news-paper *The Suffragette*'. In the light of this careful police work there was, of course, outrage. The bishop of London preached a sermon in which he gave 'our thanks to Almighty God for taking care of His own Cathedral (cries of "Amen") against the machinations of some miscreant who tried to wreck it last night . . . it was only an accident that the lever was turned by mistake to the right instead of the left . . . and therefore, we know that those who set themselves to do the Devil's work often even cannot do that right.'

An unusual amount of London's history has happened in and around St Paul's. But there is barely a street in inner London that cannot tell at least one tale like this. Here we set out to capture just some of this past. Partly we try to do this through describing the social circumstances of the poor and the working class in London down the centuries. But this is not in the first instance a social history; it is mainly the story of London as a theatre of political activism, told, as much as is possible, with a focus on the lives, actions and words of the actors themselves. Why does London have such a history of radicalism?

LONDON AND GOVERNMENT

The things that make London a centre of wealth and power have also made it a centre of dissent and radicalism. As the home of national government, London is the focal point for protest. This has made London politics pecu-liarly volatile. In Roman times London was a seat of imperial government and from then on, with the exception of the Saxon period, it has been the site from which the national and international power of the nation's ruling classes has been projected. Any seat of government and power will dictate much of the political discourse in the city. As a result the city's churches and chapels, mosques and synagogues, coffee houses, taverns, meeting halls, parks and squares have all acted as hotbeds of dissent.

Controlling a city the size of London requires a high degree of repres-sion and regulation. The historian E. P. Thompson describes how by the late eighteenth century 'the British people were noted throughout Europe for their turbulence, and the people of London astonished foreign visitors by their lack of deference'.[3] Those who controlled the wealth and power

---

3 E. P. Thompson, *The Making of the English Working Class* (London, 1982), p. 66.

of the city ensured that those who did not were aware of the penalties for infringement of legal codes. Repression was met by resistance.[4] Prisons loomed large in the popular imagination, especially Newgate (which met the same fate at a similar time to the Paris Bastille, but with rather different political consequences). It was very easy to get into prison if you were poor, and pretty easy to be hanged. 'In the years between the Restoration and the death of George III the number of capital offences was increased by about 190 . . . no less than sixty-three of these were added in the years 1760–1810.'[5] By the mid nineteenth century there were the beginnings of a modern police force, aimed at preventing at least some crime from taking place, and centrally involved with the protection of property. Their role, and that of the law more generally, seems to have remained constant from that time on – up to and including the student protests of 2010 and the London riots of 2011.

London government is not only the national government, however. London politics has long had a peculiarity that no other city in England can boast: the City's own local government exists alongside the national government. And London local government is not just any local government. The modern all-London authority rules the richest and most populous city in the nation. The older government of the City of London, roughly the 'square mile' of the modern financial centre, arose from the elders of the city that King Alfred established when he repopulated the area within the old Roman walls. This 'council' developed into the medieval City administration which came to represent the commercial interests of the traders and manufacturers of the area, chiefly the interests of the richest of them. City government was not, even at the very beginning, all of London's government. It did not exercise power outside the City walls. Westminster, growing from 1066 as the centre of national government, was obviously beyond its power. So too was Southwark, facing it on the south bank of the Thames just across London Bridge. And the areas which grew up beyond the walls, the Tower Hamlets in the east, the ribbon development along the Strand towards Charing Cross and Westminster to the west, were also beyond City jurisdiction. Even within the walls, the City authorities had powers over some aspects of life but not others – and where City 'liberties' began and ended was a matter of repeated conflict with the Crown and the national government.

This relationship between Crown and City was not always contentious; quite often they needed each other. Monarchs needed City money, and the

---

4   See Thompson, *Making of the English Working Class,* pp. 64–6. Also in general see P. Linebaugh, *The London Hanged* (London, 1991); C. Hill, *Liberty against the Law* (London, 1996).
5   Thompson, *Making of the English Working Class*, p. 65.

City needed a stable and effective national government that could control the environment in which money was made from trade, manufacture and commerce. But if the City was never really democratic in the modern sense it did at least, for long periods, have a more representative structure than the national state. And when conflicts over City rights and liberties did erupt with the Crown, wider social forces might find themselves with the political space to mount a more serious challenge to the status quo, both in the City itself and in the nation as a whole. Such was the case in the revolt of William Longbeard, in the Peasants' Revolt of 1381, during the English Revolution and in the Wilkesite reform movement of the eighteenth century.

Once the franchise widened in 1832, the site of struggle between Londoners and government changed. The creation of the London County Council in 1889 (which still excluded London counties such as Middlesex and Essex) and the rise of borough councils meant that conflict between local government and national administration took on a popular form that was impossible when the City was the main repository of local power in the capital. The successor to the LCC, the Greater London Council, became the focus for one of the great contests between central government and London authority in the 1980s. Ken Livingstone's Labour administration's confrontation with the Thatcher government led in 1986 to the Tories completely abolishing any London-wide local government – probably the greatest single destruction of London's local government since Edward I humiliated the City in the late thirteenth century. Only in 2000 was the Greater London Authority, with its elected mayor and assembly, established by referendum as a new all-London authority, although with fewer powers than its predecessor.

A WORKING CITY

London does more than many capitals: it combines a centre of national and local government with a financial centre, a port, and a vast retail and entertainment hub. Goods were imported and exported from Roman times, and work grew up around related trades. For most of its history London has been pre-eminently an international port: within living memory many of its jobs were still connected with the river, the realm of dockers, stevedores, lightermen, warehousemen, shipbuilders and seafarers.

In addition, the streets of the city of London and many of its old buildings reflect its trading origins in the profusion of drapers, fishmongers, ironmongers, butchers, bookbinders, cordwainers, candlemakers, tailors, carpenters. Before the industrial revolution, London was a city of buyers and sellers, of workers in the 'trades'. Nevertheless, the artisans were highly protective of their trades and employed apprentices who usually lived in the masters' houses for long years until they had learned the skills. From the English Revolution the artisans and more especially their apprentices played a prominent role in London organization and politics. Time and again, carpenters, shoemakers and tailors took the lead in political organization. Francis Place, the great figure of the eighteenth-century reform movement, was a tailor in the Charing Cross Road. Thomas Hardy, one of the founders of Chartism, was a boot-maker in Piccadilly. The Spitalfields silk-weavers and their apprentices 'had long been noted for their anti-authoritarian turbulence'.[6]

The Industrial Revolution and the subsequent development of an industrial working class took place for the most part away from London. But while the workshop of the world developed outside the capital, its goods had to be traded on an unprecedented scale. These goods helped to create the financial wealth of London, to expand its port and to give impetus to the railway building which so transformed London's geography. London was a huge importer city, gathering in from the empire an increasing array of goods. The port offered a particularly dramatic spectacle. The young Friedrich Engels wrote in the 1840s:

> I know nothing more imposing than the view which the Thames offers during the ascent from the sea to London Bridge. The masses of buildings, the wharves on both sides, especially from Woolwich upwards, the countless ships along both shores, crowding ever closer and closer together, until, at last, only a narrow passage remains in the middle of the river, a passage through which hundreds of steamers shoot by one another; all this is so vast, so impressive, that a man cannot collect himself, but is lost in the marvel of England's greatness before he sets foot upon English soil.[7]

By 1880, as the author of early tourist guides, Fritz Baedeker, said: 'Nothing will convey to the stranger a better idea of the vast activity and stupendous wealth of London than a visit to the warehouses, filled to overflowing with interminable stores of every kind of foreign and colonial products.'[8]

London's port was a cradle of radicalism and dissent. The vast number of jobs created on and around the river, the centrality of the docks to commercial life, and the huge mixture of races and cultures which came to London on ships from across the world, all contributed to a consciousness

---

6   Thompson, *Making of the English Working Class*, p. 75.
7   F. Engels, *The Condition of the Working Class in England* (Moscow, 1973), p. 63.
8   Quoted in A. Briggs, *Victorian Cities* (London, 1963), p. 318.

formed by living in the city itself. The East End of London, formed out of the docks and their industrial hinterland, peopled by immigrants both from within the rest of Britain and from China, Russia, Germany and Ireland, has a special place in that history. Time after time the Tower Hamlets such as Limehouse and Stepney feature in the history of London: the Levellers organized here in Wapping, the biggest strike waves in London were here, Communist and left-wing MPs were elected here. The river was the boundary of other radical areas: Southwark and Lambeth to the south, and further upstream Battersea, a notorious site of industrial radicalism.

While London workplaces were often small, they could still be organized. The London tailors struck in 1889, linking up West Enders with their East End counterparts. The dock strikes of 1889 and 1911 brought together workers from different firms and across trades. The bus workers of the 1930s organized across the whole city's workforce, as do the tube workers in the twenty-first century. The gas workers unionized the big gas employers throughout the East End and westwards to areas such as Battersea in 1889. The newspaper printers organized in and around Fleet Street – this concentrated handful of streets contained as many printing works and as much machinery as factories in many industrial towns.

Out of this organization came ideas of collective change to achieve greater social and political equality. The early shoots of ideas about equality for all, audacious notions of free love, and protests against property first surfaced in the English Revolution. William Godwin, Mary Wollstonecraft and William Blake returned to them during the French Revolution, and the ideas of utopianism took hold in London in the 1820s and 30s. It was only late in the nineteenth century, in the early 1880s, that socialism was properly reborn. While the socialists played a big part in free-speech agitation against the police and in organizing the unemployed, the real success of socialists and radicals came with the fight for the new unions. All the major strikes centrally involved political figures – the radical journalist Annie Besant in the match girls' strike which began the strike wave in Bow in 1888, John Burns, Will Thorne and Tom Mann in the dockers' action, Eleanor Marx with the gas workers and other major disputes of 1889. The battle for the new unions in 1888–89 was much stronger and more powerful in London than anywhere else in the country. The strikes of the unskilled London workers in those years wrote a new page of working-class history, and their organization led to the establishment of the two main general workers' unions, which today are the GMB and Unite. A sign of the success of the movement was the election of the Scottish socialist Keir Hardie as MP for West Ham. John Burns was also elected for Battersea in 1892.

Women have become an increasingly visible part of left-wing, working-class politics in London. Even at the end of the nineteenth century and beginning of the twentieth, the importance of London for the 'new woman' – educated, self-reliant and emancipated – was becoming clear. The big city gave young women the space and freedom to develop away from family or the confines of village or small-town life. This privilege was initially felt only by middle-class women, but increasingly at least some working-class women who were branching into white-collar work gained some of this benefit. Single women benefited from London's public spaces – not just shopping streets, parks and gardens, libraries and public halls, but public transport, especially the Underground, which gave women opportunities for social interaction unknown by previous generations. Women trained as typists, schoolteachers and clerks. Women today are a growing part of the London working class; it is impossible to study the working class without seeing women.

What the working class looks like today is very different and London probably has the most varied working class in terms of race and nationality of anywhere in the world. The generations of Afro-Caribbeans and Asians who played such a big part in building unions in transport, health and the manufacturing industries such as Ford have been joined by militants from across the world – and most of the overt barriers to entering certain trades have broken down (although invisible and institutional barriers still remain). Successive generations have asserted their right to live and work in Britain and to be treated equally; in a sense, the riots of 1981 marked the young black working class demanding an end to racism and to be accepted as part of society. While divisions of race, nationality and gender remain real and can sometimes be exacerbated, the common experience of class in London is a powerful countervailing factor.

THE MOB AND THE POLITICS OF THE CITY

London's mob, a term for the mass crowd which assembles in London over a wide variety of issues, was capable of laying siege to Parliament, demonstrating, rioting and attacking the rich. The mob was also a means of communication where news and information seem to spread like wildfire. The term 'mob' comes from the Latin term *mobile vulgus*, coined in the eighteenth century to describe the labouring poor. Peter Linebaugh has suggested that it could be translated as 'movement', which has less pejorative overtones and places it in the context of protest.[9] The campaign in the mid eighteenth century in support of John Wilkes and his attempts to be re-elected as an MP, while king and Parliament did their best to stop him, saw repeated mobilization of the mob, their cry being 'Wilkes and Liberty'. There was a complex

---

9   Linebaugh, *The London Hanged*, p. 38.

relationship between the mob and sections of the upper and middle classes, some of whom at least partly licenced and tolerated it for their own political ends: 'the Londoners who mobbed the carriages and broke the windows of the Great knew ... that they were acting under licence.'[10]

Most famous of the actions of the eighteenth-century 'mob' were the Gordon riots of 1780, shortly before the impact of the French Revolution on London helped to change the nature of protest. The threat to privilege and property that erupted across the channel in 1789 shook the British ruling class, and over the next four years events frightened them even further as the French monarchy and aristocracy were overthrown and executed. 'Church and King' mobs were licenced by magistrates and clergy to attack supporters of the revolution, although in London they never took off. Repressive laws were aimed at crushing dissent. The French wars and this period of repression of politics marked a watershed. Never again did the city's political elite unleash the mob to behave in this way. By the early nineteenth century the city's aldermen and politicians could not risk the assault on property and the rule of law that the mob threatened, hence the establishment of a London police force. But the mob did not entirely disappear, resurfacing with the demonstrations in 1886 and 1887, when window smashing in Pall Mall frightened the extremely wealthy ruling class with the threat of a rising by the poor. The mob took to the streets in the mass strikes of 1888 and 1889, and in the great unrest of 1910–14. This time however it was channelled into a growing and militant labour movement. It surfaced again in the 1930s with the great demonstrations of the jobless, many of which turned into riots when attacked by the police.

In 1981 young black Londoners (along with their counterparts elsewhere in the country) rose up against racism and oppression, rioting in Brixton and being joined by white youth in these most working class of areas. In 1990 the mass demonstration against the Poll Tax turned into a riot across central London, which, along with general non-payment of the tax, succeeded in getting rid of Margaret Thatcher as well as the tax itself. The student demonstrations at the end of 2010 showed many of the characteristics of the traditional mob. Large numbers of young and relatively poor people gathered quickly, since the use of new media allowed them to communicate from the furthest suburbs to central London, thus breaking down some of the logistical difficulties presented by the geographical spread of London; they expressed an unrelenting opposition to the government and elite, and targeted hated buildings (Tory HQ and the Treasury).

In the summer of 2011, the riots which erupted across London were denounced by politicians and media as the actions of a criminal mob, or

10   Thompson, *Making of the English Working Class*, p. 78.

'feral youth' as they were described. Criminality could not explain many of the actions, however: they started with the death of a young black man shot by the police in Tottenham, spreading to Hackney where police harassment was a major issue. The shops which were targeted were mostly chain stores, much of the looting was one-off opportunism, symbols of expensive consumerism such as a Notting Hill restaurant were attacked, and those who responded to questions about their motives repeatedly expressed anger about lack of a future, unemployment, inequality, racism and police harassment.

RICH AND POOR

London's mixture of extreme poverty and exploitation, the expansion of working-class districts especially in the East End, the radicalism of the intellectuals who tended to congregate there and who developed alternative ways of thinking, like the women who pioneered the figure of the 'New Woman', all combined to create a sympathetic atmosphere for socialist and radical ideas. London also became a seedbed for municipal socialism, with the settlements, housing schemes, education pioneers and health radicals all creating an infrastructure upon which Londoners still rely today.

London's radicalism has not traditionally been based, as in other British cities such as Manchester or Glasgow, on strong industrial organization with large concentrations of workers. It has rather relied on its sheer size and on its capacity to centralize dissent by virtue of its targets. The fact most frequently commented on by visitors to London since its earliest days is the immensity of the place. The Roman city was the largest in the country. After it was rebuilt in the early Middle Ages it became, again, the largest urban area in Britain. Soon it would become the largest city in Europe. Until the 1950s it was one of the three largest cities in the world, alongside New York and Tokyo. Its population grew from half a million in 1750 to a million by the dawn of the nineteenth century. A hundred years later, it stood at 6 million, the hub of an empire on which 'the sun never set'. Numbers peaked in 1939 at nearly 9 million, and, despite quite dramatic falls in the second half of the twentieth century, the population of London is now almost 8 million again.[11] The geographical mass of Greater London (the term was recognized long before it became an official government entity in the 1960s) spreads out across the entire map of south-eastern England.

London's size alone suggests an impersonality and lack of community which would seem to work against radicalism. So too would its pace of

11   Available online at demographia.com.

life: the speed with which people move around, the hurrying crowds, the callousness often noted at the centre of the city, all give it an air of unfriendliness, even cruelty, remarked on especially by outsiders.

It is also a city of phenomenal wealth. The scale of the wealth today, as of the poverty which is its opposite, is greater than at any time since the eighteenth century when plantation owners flaunted the riches created out of chattel slavery. It is impossible to ignore this wealth throughout central London and in its richer inner residential areas. There are many other parts of London where it is impossible to believe that such riches exist. The poverty in the eastern half of inner London boroughs is on a par with anywhere else in Britain, and many inhabitants rarely leave their local areas.

Yet London is almost unique in the proximity with which rich and poor live together.

> It is hard to find social statistics as extreme and environments as different but so close together as are found within the hearts of London and New York. The intertwining of rich and poor neighbourhoods is far greater in the centres of these two cities than anywhere else in the rich world.[12]

All of the elements which contribute to the alienation of so many from London are also the source of much of its radicalism. London's size in relation to the rest of Britain gives its working class and poor a clout which, when they care to use it, has a major political impact. The impersonality of the city forces its inhabitants to come together in all sorts of different ways to try developing community, organization and civil society so as to alleviate some of the worst features of city life. And the wealth of the London rich is a source of daily resentment for the vast majority of those inhabitants who help to produce that wealth. It is they who ensure that a city of this size continues to function, but who are rewarded by levels of inequality which are all the more staggering since they are in such contrast to the riches on display.

There may be as many discontinuities as continuities between the Roman city and today's metropolis. Indeed, as we shall see, there is not even a physical continuity of the same inhabited area which lasts over that span of time. But there are nevertheless some long periods where similar patterns of development are identifiable, long-term causes which explain the shape of the city and the nature of its radicalism.

The London of the twenty-first century is reproducing the conditions that gave rise to radical and socialist ideas in the past. Glittering skyscrapers

---

12   D. Dorling, *Injustice: Why Social Inequality Persists* (Bristol, 2011), p. 288.

are transforming the London horizon more quickly than ever before. The city is moving east again, creating a huge pool of poverty bordered by wealth in the City, Canary Wharf and the new Olympic development in Stratford. But this is only the most visible form of the inequality that is growing across the metropolis.

Going by most measures, indeed, London has more than its fair share of disadvantage compared with the rest of Britain. In 2011 over one million Londoners lived in low-income families where at least one adult is working. That figure has increased by 60 per cent over the last decade. Housing costs are a critical factor in explaining why London has the highest poverty rates of all England's regions. Taking housing into account, the poverty rate in London is 28 per cent, compared to 22 per cent in the rest of England. Again, the gap has grown in the last decade. Nearly 50 per cent of young adults are paid less than the London Living Wage. The unemployment rate among young people is at its highest level for nearly twenty years (23 per cent) and rising. Despite, on average, being better qualified than young people in the rest of England, young Londoners are more likely to be unemployed.

Inequality in London is staggering. The poorest 50 per cent have less than 5 per cent of financial or property wealth. The richest 10 per cent have 40 per cent of income wealth, 45 per cent of property wealth and 65 per cent of financial wealth. Babies born in Southwark, Croydon, Haringey and Harrow are twice as likely to die before their first birthday as those born in Bromley, Kingston and Richmond. Adults in Hackney are twice as likely to die before the age of sixty-five as those in Kensington & Chelsea.[13] 'As a rule of thumb, life expectancy falls by one year for each stop that is travelled east from Westminster on the Jubilee line.'[14]

As the 2012 Olympics open, motorcades of dignitaries, politicians, company CEOs and celebrities will sweep through East London on the specially cleared executive super-highway to Stratford that is only open to them. A few yards away, in damp and overcrowded blocks of flats, Black, white, and Asian workers will be preparing to go to work, if they are lucky, in jobs that pay a pittance. Perhaps they will be serving coffee to, or clearing up after, those very same people. For centuries in London such contrasting conditions have produced riots and radicalism, strikes and socialism. That history is unlikely to be over.

---

13   T. MacInnes, A. Parekh, P. Kenway, *London's Poverty Profile 2011* (New Policy Institute, 2011), p. 7.
14   Greater London Authority Information (London, 2008), available online at london.gov, p. 77.

I

Origins

Llyn Din: the City of the Lake.

Celtic origin of Londinium

LONDINIUM

London was established by invaders: the Romans. There were pre-Roman
settlements in the Thames valley, including in the area of modern London,
but it was not until after the Roman invasion of AD 43 that a large urban
area was settled. After landing on the Kent coast, the II Augusta, XIV
Gemina, XX Valeria, and IX Hispana legions crossed the Thames at the
same point before breaking into separate units as they continued north and
west, almost unopposed at first. There were two subsequent, and decisive,
battles, both of which the Romans won. London was born as a military
supply base.

Londinium became established as a Roman trading centre over the
following two decades. Its location had some natural advantages. It was at
the furthest point inland where the Thames was still a tidal river, and therefore was readily accessible for sea-going ships; yet it was also the eastern-
most point where it was possible to cross the river easily. At some point in
the second century AD the Romans were the first to bridge the Thames, at
the site of the modern London Bridge. Here on the south bank of the river
– what would become Southwark – there then lay two large islands with
minor channels of the Thames flowing south of them. On the ground that
rose above the surrounding marshes it was possible to build approach roads,
like that from the already important town of Canterbury. The north bank,
on the hills that would come to be known as Ludgate Hill and Cornhill,
provided raised ground on which buildings could be safely constructed.

London was an advantageous location for a Roman settlement for
other reasons. Londinium gave the Roman army access to corn from
the rich farmland nearby. Fairly powerful tribes in the surrounding area

had submitted to Roman rule whereas tribes in the West, Wales and, later, the North were actively hostile. The Thames itself was also a major attraction, for in the ancient world water connected more than it separated people. Within a decade of the invasion quays were being established along the Thames, and soon perhaps 10,000 people lived in the area between the crossing to Southwark and the western side of the Walbrook River, now vanished underground, but which entered the Thames near modern-day Cannon Street station. On the south side of the crossing, granaries, bakeries and workshops sprang up. The Roman historian Tacitus admired the teeming settlement, 'crowded with merchants and goods'.

The native Britons' first significant contribution to the history of London was to destroy it. In AD 60, seventeen years after the Roman invasion, the Iceni tribe swept out of their territory in the East Anglian heartland, destroying the Roman city of Colchester (Camulodunum) and then London. The Iceni had good reasons for their hostility. Following the invasion, the Romans had not conquered the Iceni but made a pact with their king, Prasutagus. On his death, however, Roman policy hardened towards them, a fact even Tacitus could hardly disguise. Tacitus records that Prasutagus 'in the course of a long reign had amassed considerable wealth', which he left in his will 'to his two daughters and the emperor in equal shares'. This Prasutagus thought would be enough to secure 'the tranquility of his kingdom and his family'. In a masterpiece of understatement, Tacitus says 'The event was otherwise'.

> His dominions were ravaged by the centurions; the slaves pillaged his house, and his effects were seized as lawful plunder. His wife, Boudicca, was disgraced with cruel stripes; her daughters were ravished, and the most illustrious of the Icenians were, by force, deprived of the positions which had been transmitted to them by their ancestors. The whole country was considered as a legacy bequeathed to the plunderers. The relations of the deceased king were reduced to slavery.
>
> Exasperated by their acts of violence, and dreading worse calamities, the Icenians had recourse to arms.[1]

Boudicca (Boadicea is a later corruption) made an alliance with 'neighbouring states, not as yet taught to crouch in bondage', who, says Tacitus, 'pledged themselves, in secret councils, to stand forth in the cause of liberty'.

---

1 'Description by Tacitus of the Rebellion of Boudicca (AD 60–61)', *Athena Review*, vol.1, no.1, adapted from A. Murphy, *Works of Tacitus* (1794), Chapter 31. Available online at athenapub.com.

We have some sense of the feelings that motivated the Iceni from Tacitus's account of Boudicca's speech at a later stage of the same campaign:

> Boudicca, in a [chariot], with her two daughters before her, drove through the ranks. She harangued the different nations in their turn: 'This,' she said, 'is not the first time that the Britons have been led to battle by a woman. But now she did not come to boast the pride of a long line of ancestry, nor even to recover her kingdom and the plundered wealth of her family. She took the field, like the meanest among them, to assert the cause of public liberty, and to seek revenge for her body seamed with ignominious stripes, and her two daughters infamously ravished. From the pride and arrogance of the Romans nothing is sacred; all are subject to violation; the old endure the scourge, and the virgins are deflowered. But the vindictive gods are now at hand. A Roman legion dared to face the warlike Britons: with their lives they paid for their rashness . . .'[2]

After Boudicca's victory at Colchester the Roman general Suetonius was forced to march to London, but then decided to abandon it as indefensible. The first Londoners pleaded with Suetonius to stay, but he refused and 'the signal for the march was given'. In consequence Boudicca's forces sacked an unresisting London and burnt it to the ground. The city was devastated, its destruction so comprehensive that today modern archeologists find in nearly every site a layer of charred remains up to half a metre thick, on both sides of the Thames.

London was at this time the nerve centre of a new regime of state taxation and colonial land dispossession that enraged the indigenous peasantry, as testified by the Boudiccan revolt.[3] The final victory, though, lay with the Romans. Legions returning from Wales defeated Boudicca at a battle in the Midlands, after which she took her own life by drinking poison. The Romans returned to London and set about rebuilding it, although serious construction would not begin for another decade. Ironically, it was another foreigner, Gaius Julius Alpinus Classicianus, a member of the Gallic aristocracy and a brilliant administrator, who began rebuilding London. It was AD 75 before the forum-basilica was begun. But at the end of the first century AD London was the largest town on the British Isles. About AD 200 the stone wall which was to mark out the city limits for the next 1,500 years was constructed, stretching from what is now the site of the Tower of London to the Fleet River, near Blackfriars. Gates were made

---

2   Ibid.
3   N. Faulkner, *Rome: Empire of the Eagles* (London, 2008), p. 197.

at Bishopsgate, Newgate, and Ludgate. The existing Aldgate was incorporated into the wall.[4]

THE DECLINE OF LONDINIUM AND
THE RISE OF LUNDENWIC

In the second century AD, London prospered and grew as an imperial and trade hub. But in the following one hundred years growth was thrown into reverse. The Roman Empire was overextended, defending long frontiers against increasingly powerful enemies. Earlier in Roman history, wars of conquest had meant inflows of treasure and slaves. Later, as the frontiers became permanent borders, like Hadrian's Wall, the empire became dependent on internal resources. Higher taxes replaced the spoils of war, and forced labour was imposed on peasants as the supply of slaves dried up. The imperial state siphoned wealth away from towns to support the army.

In AD 200 Britannia was divided in two. One half, Britannia Inferior, was ruled from York, the other half, Britannia Superior, was ruled from London. This diminished the city as an administrative centre. In addition, falling tidal levels in the Thames meant that quays had to be built further out into the river, which didn't help trade. Moreover, significant trade was being diverted to northern ports, much of it en route to the army mainly based on Hadrian's Wall. Infighting among would-be Emperors (and Britain was for a period part of a breakaway Empire in northern Europe no longer connected to Rome) further diminished the city's ability to sustain earlier growth.

Londinium declined during the third and fourth centuries, as public buildings were not repaired and the private houses of the elite were too expensive to maintain. The population shrank, and much of the townscape was reduced to dereliction and filth. A change of name – from Londinium to Augusta (meaning 'Imperial') – could not alter the reality: the empire and its cities were in decline as an all-powerful state centralized resources in a desperate struggle to keep the 'barbarians' out. It was a struggle that the Romans abandoned in relation to Britain around AD 400. London by then was little more than ruins and waste ground.[5]

In the early fifth century Angles and Saxons from northern Germany settled in southern Britain. To the west of the deserted Roman city were the Middle Saxons (hence Middlesex), to the east the Eastern Saxons (hence Essex). They spoke a Germanic language that they called 'Englisc'.

---

4 See J. Black, *London: A History* (Lancaster, 2009), pp. 11–30, S. Inwood, *A History of London* (London, 1998), pp. 13–38, C. Ross and J. Clark, *London, The Illustrated History* (London, 2011), pp. 26–32, 50–4.
5 See N. Faulkner, *The Decline and Fall of Roman Britain* (Stroud, 2004), pp. 169–248.

Urban living had collapsed, and these newcomers were mostly engaged in settled agriculture. But slowly some new large settlements did appear. Around 730 the chronicler Bede was describing the 'metropolis of the East Saxons' as 'an emporium for many nations coming by land and sea'. Excavations over many years have revealed that the site Bede was referring to lay immediately west of the walled Roman city of Londinium – its core remains are now underneath Fleet Street, the Strand and Trafalgar Square. This is where the Saxon trading town was built. Contemporary documents refer to this town as Lundenwic. In Anglo-Saxon, the 'wic' ending meant 'market', or to use Bede's Latin equivalent, 'emporium'.

Lundenwic extended from the western edge of the Roman city round the riverbank south and west to Westminster, and as far north as Oxford Street: excavations at the Royal Opera House revealed nearly sixty buildings along one street. Lundenwic benefited from a shallow beach on the Thames. The Strand is both a synonym for beach and marks the higher tidal reach of the Thames at this time. It was a better place for ships to dock than the old decaying quays of Londinium. But Lundenwic was close enough to the old Roman centre to make use of the network of Roman roads. Pottery, glass and metalwork from northern France and the Rhineland, millstones from Germany and amber from the Baltic have all been found in Lundenwic. So too have English wool and evidence of weaving and metal working. But Lundenwic was, after more than 200 years, destined to disappear. From the end of the eighth century Viking sea raiders, Danes and Norwegians, began to attack Britain. North Sea trade was disrupted and the Vikings attacked Lundenwic in 842 and 851. In 865 the Great Army of the Danish Vikings began a campaign which subdued the kingdoms of Northumbria, East Anglia and most of Mercia. In 871–72 the Danish army wintered in London. By 877 only King Alfred's West Saxons were outside Danish control.

THE RISE OF LUNDENBURG

King Alfred is perhaps best known for his lack of culinary ability. But he has a greater claim to fame as the figure who re-established London on the site of the old, deserted location within the Roman walls. Alfred's advance to London came after his fortunes had reached their lowest ebb. After years of warfare against the Danes, Alfred was surprised at the royal stronghold of Chippenham in Wiltshire while celebrating Twelfth Night in 878. Fleeing southwest, he took refuge in the Somerset levels where, according to legend, he burnt the cakes.

Alfred rallied his forces in Wessex, defeated the Danes at the battle of Ethandun (possibly at Westbury) and besieged them until they surrendered at Chippenham. The Danish King Guthrum converted to Christianity, and the Danes left Wessex. Within a decade Alfred had become strong enough to conclude a treaty with Guthrum that divided up the old kingdom of Mercia. The boundary between Alfred's kingdom and the Danelaw, as Guthrum's territory was now called, ran along the Thames and up the valley of the River Lea to the east of the old Roman city.

Practically the only change within the old city since the Romans left was the establishment of a church called St Paul's on Ludgate Hill, built in 604 by Mellitus, bishop of the East Saxons. This wooden building burned down in 675 and was rebuilt ten years later. Alfred needed London as a border fortress: the *Anglo-Saxon Chronicle*, begun on Alfred's instructions and maintained until the middle of the twelfth century, records his decision to rebuild the city in 886: 'King Alfred fortified the city of London [*gesette Lunden burg*, in the original]'. The city was then given into the control of Alderman Ethelred, 'to hold it under him'.[6]

Under Ethelred, Lundenburg (or Lundenburh) was rebuilt east of St Paul's with new blocks of streets on a grid system. A new dock was built called Ethelred's Hithe (now Queenshithe). The Saxon town of Lundenwic became fields once more, remembered in the name Aldwych, the 'old town'. South of the river, where graveyards had earlier replaced the Roman urban area, development took place: Southwark is first mentioned around 915 as *Suthringa geweorche*, the fortified work of the men of Surrey. Indeed fortification north and south of the Thames was still very necessary, as conflict with the Danes, never long subdued, erupted once more.

Alfred died around 900. However, it took another 116 years before the power of the Danes in England was such that a Danish King, Cnut, became accepted as King of all the English. Londoners had already reached a separate peace with Cnut, and had bought off invaders during the preceding wars by the payment of Danegeld. This continued as a regular levy, and in 1018 London was taxed 10,500 pounds in silver: one eighth of the total burden placed upon the nation, an indicator that London was again the wealthiest and largest town in the country. And although the abbey had existed since the eighth century, it was under Cnut that Westminster began to develop on what was then Thorney Island in the Thames, at the western tip of Lundenwic. Cnut was possibly the first monarch to reside at Westminster and it is here, tradition has it, that he ironically demonstrated the limits of royal power by commanding the incoming tidal wash of the Thames to retreat.

Perhaps if Cnut or his successors Harold Harefoot and Harthacnut had

---

6   *The Anglo-Saxon Chronicle*, Part 2: AD 750–919, Online Medieval and Classical Library Release #17, available at omacl.org.

lived longer, his reign might have marked out a very different path for Britain's history, in joint sovereignty with Scandinavian countries. 'Anglo-Saxon freedom' was not all myth. 'Freemen' had obligations of military service, but also the rights of security of property and protection under the law. The Domesday Book accordingly distinguishes between serfs and freemen. But Cnut's heirs died early and the survivor of the Wessex dynasty, Edward the Confessor, was recalled from exile in Normandy to take the throne in 1043.

From then on, Norman nobles took an increasing interest in England. When Edward died in 1066 the Witan, a group of about sixty lords and bishops, met to decide who would become the next king of England. They chose Harold, the son of Earl Godwin of Wessex, over William of Normandy, to whom Harold had previously promised the throne. The Norman invasion and the Battle of Hastings reversed that decision.

So began the Norman conquest of London, the last hostile foreign invasion the capital has endured to date. Centuries later, in the English Revolution, Levellers would complain that 'the Norman Yoke' had robbed 'free-born Englishmen' of their rights. Perhaps they were inventing less, and remembering more, than modern historians have been willing to allow.

2

Lords, Lollards, Heretics and Peasants in Revolt

I am the saviour of the poor.

William Longbeard

THE 'COMMUNE' OF LONDON

Westminster Abbey was consecrated in 1065, but the first monarch to be crowned there did not last twelve months. Harold Godwinson, Earl of Wessex, lost his life the following year at the Battle of Hastings. Despite his victory, William of Normandy knew that he couldn't control England without occupying London. As the twelfth-century *Song of the Battle of Hastings* had it: 'London is a great city, overflowing with forward inhabitants and richer in treasure than the rest of the kingdom. Protected on the left side by its walls, on the right side by the river, it neither fears its enemies nor dreads being taken by storm.' And indeed William could not conquer London by storm. An assault on London Bridge failed, and so William laid waste to Southwark and the countryside for miles around. He did, however, eventually gain the City but not without meeting opposition:

> Upon entering the city some scouts, sent ahead, found many rebels determined to offer every possible resistance. Fighting followed immediately and thus London was plunged into mourning for the loss of her sons and citizens. When the Londoners finally realized that they could resist no longer, they gave hostages and surrendered themselves and all they possessed to the most noble conqueror and hereditary lord.[1]

---

1 William of Jumieges 16(37) in E. M. C. Van Houts (ed. and trans.), *The Gesta Normannorum Ducum of William of Jumieges Orderic Vitalis, and Robert of Torigni,* vol. 2 (Oxford, 1995), p. 171.

William was crowned in Westminster Abbey on Christmas Day 1066. The London that William now ruled was already the largest and richest city in his kingdom, the centre of national and international trade, but it was not the political or royal capital. William's need to guard himself 'against the fickleness of the vast and fierce population' led to the construction of three towers: Baynard's Castle, Montfichet Tower and the White Tower. The first two were later demolished, but the limestone White Tower still dominates the Tower of London, surrounded now by the walls added in the thirteenth century.

The City government that would come to dominate the affairs of the capital was still embryonic. There would be no mayor for 100 years and the two sheriffs, royal appointees responsible for delivering tax to the Crown, were named the leading officials. But the City was already divided into twenty-four wards, and the aldermen who would represent them on the City's governing council were beginning to appear. The trade guilds and fraternities were also in formation.

An important opening episode in the City of London's long struggle with the Crown followed the death of Henry I in 1135. The succession was disputed between Henry's daughter Matilda and Henry's nephew, Stephen of Blois. The powerful group of nobles backing Stephen got their way, but at the cost of plunging the nation into nearly twenty years of civil strife. Chroniclers describe this period as one in which 'Christ and his saints were asleep', while Victorian historians called it simply 'The Anarchy'.

Stephen's base of support was in south-east England, but the Crown was too weak to impose order. This gave the City of London an unusual moment of leverage. In Stephen's time of greatest danger, while held captive in Winchester by Matilda in 1141, he obtained the support of London by granting it virtual commune status. This is the closest the City came to being a self-governing urban confederation able to collect its own taxes and choose its own officials on the European model. In return, when Matilda tried to have herself crowned queen while she held Stephen captive, the masses of London rose and attacked her and her supporters at their pre-coronation feast. They were driven from the City and Londoners also provided the arms to free Stephen from his captivity in Winchester. The commune status of London was reasserted in 1191.

London first began to express its independence from the Crown in the twelfth century. This was, of course, nothing resembling democracy but rather the ability of the aldermen to select their own sheriff following the model of city states, like those in northern Italy. But the concessions that the City was able to extract from weak or cash-strapped monarchs fell far short of the ideal. Italian Republics or the communes found in Flanders and the Rhineland were widespread in the feudal period, but not in England.

They were based on a pledge of allegiance among citizens that released them from aristocratic or royal control. This pact offered a completely different form of social coexistence: a 'community of equals' governed by a social contract.[2] London never achieved this status, but its struggle for autonomy was a feature of the conflicts with the Crown in the twelfth and thirteenth centuries. What the London elite wanted was the liberty to appoint their own administrative leader, run their own legal system, gather their own taxes, and regulate their own trade. Even powerful monarchs might be minded to grant some of these wishes, if they thought it would enhance London's prosperity and therefore their own income.

London's would-be governing classes only began to achieve some autonomy in the reigns of King Richard I and King John, between 1189 and 1216. Richard's absence in Palestine gave the City the chance to ally with John against Richard's unpopular deputy, William Longchamp, Constable of the Tower. In return for supporting John's claim to rule in Richard's absence, London's aldermen were given the right to choose a mayor. On Richard's return, however, the City refused to back John's attempt to take the throne in 1194. Yet when he eventually became king in 1199, and upon payment of a gift of 1,500 marks, he allowed the commune to stand. For the further sum of 3,000 marks the City was permitted to elect its own sheriff.

Paradoxically, King John's defeat by the barons who forced him to sign Magna Carta in June 1215 at Runnymede was the event that finally institutionalized the concessions he had made to the City years before. In order to buy London's loyalty against the barons, John granted the City a new charter in May 1215 that introduced the principle of an annually elected mayor. But a minority of the City sided with the barons and, despite John's concessions, opened the gates to the barons a few days later. This allowed the barons to use the City as a base for their negotiations with the king, and as a result the City's 'ancient liberties and customs' were inscribed in Magna Carta itself. From now on the sheriffs were elected by the City oligarchy and increasingly subordinate to the mayor. And the mayor was elected from among the aldermen each October at a gathering of the 'commonalty', those who had gained by inheritance, purchase, or apprenticeship the right to name the 'citizen' or 'freeman' of the City. From now on, mayor and aldermen became increasingly responsible for the law in the City.

This was obviously not democracy in the modern sense, since it excluded apprentices, masterless men, wage labourers, the poor in general and women in total. But neither was it a complete sham, for these excluded classes were not as numerous as they are now, and the 'citizens' represented a broad

---

2   P. Anderson, *Passages from Antiquity to Feudalism* (London, 1996), p. 194.

swathe of the population, many of whom were not part of the traditional feudal ruling class. These layers came to form the Common Council of the City, which the aldermen were likely to consult on matters of importance. By the fourteenth century the members of the Council were elected by wards and, sometimes, guilds. Although it may have been used earlier, the Guildhall was from the twelfth century the meeting place of City administration, such as it was. In 1411 the hall was rebuilt on a grander scale, and much of the original remains visible in the modern building.

The London oligarchy which ran this system was rich from land, commerce and trade, and royal patronage. They owned shops and tenements, warehouses and quays, urban and rural manors. They were traders, but not exclusively so and not in a single commodity – that would come later. As some trades and businesses prospered and others faltered, so power migrated from one section of the elite to another. But we should be careful of concluding that these interests always put the City elite at odds with the Crown. The City wanted self-government, but it also needed an economic and a foreign policy that suited its interests, and this was something that only the Crown could provide. Moreover, the Crown was a market in its own right and most members of the London elite profited directly from royal contracts and employment. Over half the sheriffs and aldermen between 1200 and 1340 whose interests can be identified held posts in the Royal Exchequer or the Royal Wardrobe, were royal suppliers or contractors, or were in some other way in Crown service.[3]

There were always, however, underlying tensions in the relationship between Crown and City. And at certain moments the voice of the citizens, and sometimes of the popular mass below them, could exploit these tensions with movements and demands of their own. One such moment was seized by William Longbeard.

THE REBELLION OF WILLIAM LONGBEARD

William Longbeard's 1196 revolt is little studied by historians, but it is an early example of a class revolt in English history, and it was no accident that it happened in London.[4] Longbeard's true name was William fitz Osbern and he seems to have been a member of London's elite: 'in origin of the most noble citizens of London'. He was possibly a lawyer and seems to have taken part in the Third Crusade, which again suggests a relatively

---

3   S. Inwood, *A History of London* (London, 1998), p. 62.
4   We are indebted to Dominic Alexander for allowing us to use his remarkable recovery of William Longbeard's story, Chapter 7 of *The Hermit and the Crowd* (forthcoming).

high social rank. Nevertheless, in the early stages of the revolt – which may have lasted for over a year – he appealed to the king to lift the burden of taxation on the poor. Longbeard's complaint in particular was against the 'insolence of the rich and powerful' and their plans to place the tax burden upon the poor. A contemporary chronicler, Roger of Howden, records that 'the rich men, sparing their own purses, wanted the poor to pay everything', and notes that William Longbeard 'becoming sensible of this, being inflamed by zeal for justice and equity ... became the champion of the poor, it being his wish that every person, both rich as well as poor, should give according to his property and means, for all the necessities of the state.'[5]

Longbeard's campaign began with his discovery of the Court's plan to increase the burden of taxation on the poor. His followers, at least to begin with, seem to have been drawn from both the poor and the 'middling people'. They were bound together by the taking of some sort of oath. William of Newburgh records that some 52,000 citizens were organized in Longbeard's conspiracy, 'the names of each being, as it afterwards appeared, written down'. Dominic Alexander considers these numbers vastly exaggerated, but Longbeard's organization does seem to have been on an impressive scale. Certainly this initial phase of revolt was enough to provoke the nobles' 'indignation' against this agitator. This may have been Longbeard's motivation in crossing the Channel to France to see Richard I, in a bid to gain royal approval for his actions. He seems to have succeeded, since it is reported that on his return to London, Longbeard behaved 'as if under the countenance of the royal favour'.[6]

It remained standard practice up to and including the start of the English Revolution for those rebelling against authority to claim that they were doing so in the name of the monarch. But Longbeard's use of this stratagem may have had specific meaning at this moment. When Richard I came to the throne, he granted London extensive self-government after Henry II had limited it severely. 'So the London elite, those families providing the Mayor and Aldermen, had only just attained a degree of self-government. The liberties granted by the King to London were new and could have been revoked, so Longbeard may have been trying to play the London elite and the King against each other.'[7]

---

5   See the account of William of Newburgh, *Historia rerum anglicarum*, in R. Howlett (ed.), *Chronicles of the Reigns of Stephen, Henry II and Richard I*, Rolls Series 82 (London, 1964), Vol. 1, pp. 466–73. The translation is by Joseph Stevenson from *The History of William of Newburgh* (1856, reprinted Llanerch, 1996), pp. 652–6.

6   Alexander, *The Hermit and the Crowd*, pp. 6–7.

7   Ibid., p. 7.

Archbishop Hubert Walter had other ideas: he 'was clearly intent on bringing royal power' to repress Longbeard. Walter took action to suppress 'rumours', and also took hostages from wealthy Londoners to enforce quiescence. It seems this crackdown divided Longbeard's supporters, silencing some of the better-off, and that Longbeard responded by appealing more directly to popular forces; Roger of Wendover's account highlights the political organization that the rebellion entailed. Longbeard 'in contempt of the king's majesty, convoked assemblies of people, and binding many to him by oath at their meetings' he at last 'raised a sedition and disturbance in St Paul's church'. William of Newburgh records what Longbeard said to his audiences:

> I am the saviour of the poor. Oh poor, who have experienced the heaviness of rich men's hands, drink from my wells the waters of the doctrine of salvation, and you may do this joyfully; for the time of your visitation is at hand. For I will divide the waters from the waters. The people are the waters. I will divide the humble and faithful people from the haughty and treacherous people: I will separate the elect from the reprobate, as light from darkness.[8]

Dominic Alexander comments on this remarkable speech, 'He, or Newburgh for him, is directly associating the "poor" with the saved and the powerful with the damned. If still in the eleventh century *"pauperes"* could refer simply to the religious, here economic categories have fully invaded spiritual ones. Newburgh presumably intends his readership to understand the shocking social meaning of the message.'[9] Longbeard reacted to Hubert's intervention by 'convoking public meetings by his own authority, in which he arrogantly proclaimed himself the king or saviour of the poor', according to Newburgh.[10]

Longbeard's message was popular, and his following substantial. Archbishop Walter's strategy was to wait until he was apart from his followers and surprise him. Two 'noble citizens' thus watched for a time when he was 'unattended by his mob', now that 'the people out of fear for the hostages had become more quiet'. In due course, on the orders of the Archbishop, they seized their opportunity to make an arrest. Longbeard and his party resisted, and in the struggle one of his assailants was killed with his own weapon. After the fight Longbeard's party took refuge in St Mary-le-Bow, in the heart of the City. The Archbishop now laid siege to

---

8   William of Newburgh, *Historia rerum anglicarum*, p. 469, quoted by Alexander, p. 2.

9   Alexander, *The Hermit and the Crowd*, p. 2.

10   Newburgh in ibid., p. 8.

the troop and even took the sacrilegious action of breaking the sanctuary of the Church and setting it ablaze.[11]

The fire forced Longbeard's group from the Church and, as he emerged, a relative of the assailant who had died in the original attack lunged at Longbeard and 'cut open his belly with a knife'.[12] All of the group were subsequently condemned to death by the king's court, on the direction of Archbishop Walter. Longbeard was dragged from the Tower by horses to Tyburn, where he and his nine followers were all hanged. 'In this yere was one William with the long berde taken out of Bowe churche and put to dethe for herysey', recorded the *Chronicle of the Grey Friars of London*.[13] Others of his followers had to give hostages to the Archbishop as guarantors of good behaviour.

The Longbeard rebellion was over. But there is evidence that his reputation and ideas lived on in popular memory. And Longbeard's rebellion was not the last, nor the greatest, challenge to feudal authority.

JEWS IN MEDIEVAL LONDON

The first sizeable Jewish immigration into Britain came with William the Conqueror in 1066. They were moneylenders from Rouen. As Christians were forbidden to lend money, Jews played this critical role in medieval society, not least for the Crown. In return they were supposed to enjoy royal protection. Both moneylending and the protection of the monarch were likely to make Jews, at particular times, the target of popular hostility. This was stoked by their designation as 'Christ-killers', and by the ideology that underpinned the Crusades from the late eleventh to the late thirteenth century.

The Jews settled around Jew Street (now Old Jewry) and Cheapside. Until 1177 the only Jewish cemetery was in Cripplegate. From the middle of the twelfth century the rise of Italian banking houses gave the monarchs an alternative – Christian – source of finance. It was Richard I's coronation that occasioned the first series of pogroms against Jews. Elders who came to pay their respects to the new king at Westminster unwittingly sparked a riot that left thirty Jewish families dead. John Stow records looting of the Jewish community in London during the Barons' Wars, 1199–1216. In 1215 the Pope enacted a decree that all non-Christians (that is, Muslims and Jews) should have to wear distinguishing clothing to prevent them mingling with

---

11   Ibid., pp. 8–9.
12   Newburgh, p. 470, cited by Alexander, p. 9.
13   'The Chronicle of the Grey Friars: Richard I', *Chronicle of the Grey Friars of London*, Camden Society Old Series, vol. 53 (1852), p. 1. Available online at british-history.ac.uk.

Christians. In 1262 a London mob attacked a synagogue at Lothbury in the heart of the City, killing 700 people. In 1282 the Bishop of London was ordered to destroy all synagogues in his diocese.

In 1275 Edward I issued the Statute of Jewry which prohibited Jews from charging interest on loans and ruled, on pain of forfeit, that they must collect all outstanding debts by the following Easter. The new Statute also made it law that all Jews from the age of seven had to wear a yellow felt badge six inches long and three inches wide. A poll tax of 3 pence was imposed on every Jew over the age of 12 years. Finally the Jews were ordered out of England. On 18 July 1290 every Jew was told to leave the country. About 16,000 Jews were forced to flee.

Jews were not the only 'aliens' who were the victims of the prejudice generated by the economic contradictions of medieval society. These paradoxes were ultimately rooted in the social structure defended by elites, but they could not help but affect the lives of ordinary Londoners. Consequently there could be a popular dimension to prejudice, although it was rarely universal or uncontested. Besides Jews there were many other trading communities in medieval London. Italian merchants could be found around modern day Lombard Street and excavations at One Poultry found a large tenement let to merchants from Lucca, Tuscany, in 1355. The site of Cannon Street station was once a walled enclave of German traders from the Hanseatic League, who had arrived in London in the mid-1200s. We know of the Flemish community and the peasants who invaded London in 1381 singled them out as a result of the trade wars that had been raging in the preceding period. One account reminds us that they suffered along with the elites as targets of the Revolt: 'on Corpus Christi day, was the rising of Kent and Essex, and they ware called Jake Strawes men, and came to London, and ... went to the tower of London, and there toke out sir Simon Beuerle (Sudbury) Archbishop of Canterbury and Chancellor of England ... and divers other, and beheaded them at the Tower Hill, and slew many Flemings and other men.'[14]

THE CITY AND THE CROWN

Division between City and Crown also gave space to popular revolt in the thirteenth century. In 1245 Henry III's establishment of two new fairs in Westminster, outside City jurisdiction, directly affecting trade and his repeated meddling with London government angered the City oligarchy.

14   From: 'The Chronicle of the Grey Friars: Richard II', *Chronicle of the Grey Friars of London*: Camden Society Old Series, vol. 53 (1852), pp. 6-9. Available at british-history.co.uk. Date accessed: 27 June 2011. We have modernized the spelling of some words in this quotation.

In the 1260s his polices of granting access to London markets to foreign traders, heavy taxation and royal favouritism further annoyed the City.

The first we know of St Paul's Cross, the preaching cross and open-air pulpit in front of St Paul's Cathedral, is in 1236 when a king's justice convened a folkmoot, or general assembly of the people, to proclaim Henry III's desire that London should be well governed. In 1259 a second meeting at St Paul's Cross was more divisive when Londoners were summoned to swear allegiance to Henry. They did so, but only because the army held the gates of the city. Later they reassembled on the same spot and swore allegiance to Simon de Montfort, whose baronial challenge to Henry became the trigger for popular mobs to take to the London streets, besieging Henry's Queen Eleanor in the Tower. One alderman was aghast at the intervention of the popular movement:

> This mayor ... has so pampered the City populace, that, styling themselves the 'Commons of the City', they had obtained the first voice in the City. For the Mayor, in doing all that he had to do, acted and determined through them, and would say to them, − 'Is it your will that so it shall be' and then, if they answered 'Ya, Ya', so it was done. And on the other hand, the aldermen, or chief citizens were little or not at all consulted on such a matter.[15]

The defeat of de Montfort's revolt ended the popular movement. Henry III's heir Prince Edward had a hand in the subsequent punishment of the City, and when he succeeded to the throne in 1272 he remodelled City government. Edward I finished the inner wall of the Tower begun by his father, and added an outer wall. This did not prevent a fresh outbreak of disorders in 1284, when a leading member of the Goldsmiths' Company was killed in St Mary-le-Bow, the site of Longbeard's last stand the century before. That and the riot at Newgate prison a year later gave Edward the pretext for an even harsher set of penal codes, and, when the mayor and aldermen protested, he replaced them with a royal warden. In 1289 a final humiliation was visited on the City: a royal treasurer was sent into Guildhall to take control of City finances.

This long night of exclusion for the City elite lasted through most of the reign of Edward II; some of its powers were returned in the charters granted in 1319 and in 1327, the year that Edward III came to the throne.

Much of Edward III's reign was peaceable in the City of London, if bloody on the fields of the Hundred Years War. But in the late 1300s the relationship between the City and the Crown was becoming unstable once

---

15   Alderman Arnold fitz Thedmar, quoted in Inwood, *History of London*, p. 64.

again. The debts of the Hundred Years War hung heavily around the neck of the monarchy and the glorious victories of the English archers, at Crécy in 1346 and Poitiers a decade later, were fading from memory. But one aspect of the battles of the mid-century did perhaps linger in the minds of the men who fought in France. Those battles had meant that 'the prestige of the armoured feudal cavalry had received its death blow', because the longbow 'placed the trained peasant archer on terms of equality with his lord, robbing the latter of his main claim to special consideration, his position as a specialist in war'.[16]

For much of his reign Edward III held sway over the City of London, even when unpopular policies like selling licences to Italian merchants raised royal revenues at domestic merchants' expense. But as the king grew old, the City began to flex its muscles. The 'good Parliament' of 1376, as part of a wider purge of those loyal to the Crown, impeached three aldermen who were allies of the king. Power increasingly fell into the hands of the king's son, the duke of Lancaster, John of Gaunt. At first he placated powerful London wool merchants by re-establishing the monopoly practice whereby English wool was only to be traded on favourable terms through Calais, then an English possession, the so-called Calais staple.

John of Gaunt also feted the rogue but popular member of the Court of Aldermen, John de Northampton. In doing so he set in train a three-way search for alliances in the City. The mayor and aldermen, fearing John of Gaunt's alliance with Northampton, did their own deal with him. This required them to accede to Northampton's demand that the Common Council be elected by the misteries or guilds, the craft organizations, rather than the wards, and that it be consulted by the aldermen twice a quarter. Thus the infighting among the elite paved the way for changes to the way London worked, and to the City constitution, that had radical implications for the future.

The following year, 1377, the tables turned again. Edward III died and Richard II, at barely eleven years old, became king. Meanwhile John of Gaunt remained the de facto ruler of the country, and was no lover of the City's liberties. When it was rumoured that he intended to bring the City under royal control, a mob attacked his Savoy Palace, sited on the Strand with gardens running down to the Thames and one of the grandest palaces in Europe. It was an ominous foretaste of events during the revolt four years later. But John of Gaunt pressed on: in 1377 the Gloucester Parliament withdrew the concessions of the previous year and enabled Italian merchants to trade directly between Genoa and Southampton, thus

---

16   A. L. Morton, *A People's History of England* (London, 1979), p. 113.

revoking the monopoly of the Calais staple. The City was prepared to pay the Crown handsomely for this entitlement to be returned to them, but the Italian merchants' pockets were deeper. Moreover, French naval strength constituted a threat to English merchant trade with which John of Gaunt seemed incapable of dealing. By the time the Peasants' Revolt exploded a few years later, there were some among the City elite that looked on it with some sympathy, at least in its opening phases.[17] As contemporary chronicler Canon Henry Knighton recorded, 'During this crisis, the commons held the peaceful duke of Lancaster as their most hated enemy of all mortal men and would certainly have destroyed him immediately if they had found him . . .'.[18]

THE PEASANTS' REVOLT

The greatest revolt of the feudal era in England took place in 1381. It was essentially a rural rising but the source of the trouble, as the peasant insurrectionists realized, lay in the capital; and it was to London they came to get redress. Wages had been rising because of the labour shortage created by the Black Death. All figures are estimates in this period, but the plague killed perhaps a third of London's population of 45,000 when it first struck the city in 1349. There were further outbreaks in 1361 and 1368. However, the authorities attempted to depress wages to pre-Black Death levels by imposing the Statute of Labourers, that sought not only to reduce pay but also to prevent labourers from moving out of their locality and to ban day-labour in favour of a yearly contract. In addition the poll tax of 1380 was the latest of three such taxes raised since 1377; but the 1380 tax was three times higher – one shilling for every man and woman over the age of fifteen. It was, as one unknown poet wrote, a tax that 'has tenet [harmed] us alle'. And, as with Margaret Thatcher's poll tax in the 1980s, tens of thousands disappeared from the tax roll to avoid payment long before the revolt flared into the open.

The revolt began in Brentwood, Essex, on 30 May 1381 as a Royal Commission arrived to assess evasion of the third poll tax, and lasted through the first half of June. The uprisings spread rapidly, partly as a result of deliberate organization by the rebels and partly as a result of the use of feast days and other traditional moments of collective celebration, as well as the meetings of manorial courts and the visitation of royal justices, as occasions to spread dissension. The 'hue and cry' would be sent out and church

---

17   Inwood, *History of London,* pp. 74–7; D. Jones, *Summer of Blood: The Peasants' Revolt of 1381* (London, 2010), pp. 20–2.
18   Quoted in Jones, *Summer of Blood,* p. 33.

bells rung to summon the rebels. John Ball, one of the leaders of the revolt, is said to have written:

> John Ball greeteth you all
> And doth to understand he hath rung your bell,
> Now with might and right, will and skill,
> God speed every dell.[19]

Surviving letters from John Ball to his supporters cryptically encourage the commons while urging them to disciplined, collective action. He urges them to stand 'together in God's name', to 'chastise well Hob the Robber' and to observe one leader rather than act individually. Ball uses code to communicate with fellow rebel leaders. He is 'John Schep', while others include 'John Nameles', 'John the Miller', 'John Carter', 'John Trewman' and 'Piers Plowman'.

Ball certainly had a previous record of opposition to authority, as noted by Jean Froissart – the remarkable French historian and sometime employee of the queen of England whose chronicle provides one of the greatest, if hostile, accounts of the rising.[20] Froissart was deeply committed to the notion of medieval chivalry, and acutely sensitive to any affront to authority. Speaking of the peasants, he tells us:

> These unhappy people of these said countries began to stir, because they said … they were neither angels nor spirits, but men formed to the similitude of their lords, saying why should they then be kept so under like beasts; the which they said they would no longer suffer, for they would be all one, and if they laboured or did anything for their lords, they would have wages therefor as well as other.[21]

---

19   Quoted in E.Vallance, *A Radical History of Britain* (London, 2010), p. 55.
20   Froissart's *Chronicles* are not the only major account of the Peasants' Revolt. Thomas Walsingham, monk of St. Albans (*Historia anglicana, Chronicon Angliae*); Henry Knighton, Augustinian canon of St Mary-of-the-Meadows, Leicester (*Chronicon*); the Benedictine author of *Anonimalle Chronicle* (from St Mary's, York); a chronicler of Westminster (*Chronicon Westmonasteriense*) also recount the stages of the rebellion in detail. They all represent the events as 'dangerously revolutionary and damaging to the body politic'. These accounts are often contradictory. We have relied on Froissart for the basic outline of events, but signalled in footnotes some of the important moments where other chroniclers give different accounts. See J. M. Dean (ed.), *Literature of Richard II's Reign and the Peasants' Revolt: Introduction* (originally published in Dean (ed.), *Medieval English Political Writings*, Michigan, 1996).
21   J. Froissart, *The Chronicles of Froissart*, translated by John Bourchier, Lord Berners, pp. 61–2. Available online at fordham.edu.

John Ball was a former priest and Froissart records that he would 'often-times on the Sundays after mass, when the people were going out of the minster, to go into the cloister and preach, and made the people to assemble about him, and would say thus:

> Ah, ye good people, the matters goeth not well to pass in England, nor shall not do till everything be common, and that there be no villains nor gentlemen, but that we may be all united together, and that the lords be no greater masters than we be.

Ball questioned why some were kept in servitude when we 'all come from one father and one mother, Adam and Eve'. He asked how the aristocracy could show that 'they be greater lords than we be'. As the Church was the main ideological institution of feudal society, all social conflict was addressed in theological terms, and clerics like Ball were educated men equipped to give political leadership. And some of them stood close enough to the people to share their grievances. There is an unmistakable economic content to Ball's words when he says:

> They are clothed in velvet and camlet furred with grise, and we be vestured with poor cloth: they have their wines, spices and good bread, and we have the drawing out of the chaff and drink water: they dwell in fair houses, and we have the pain and travail, rain and wind in the fields; and by that that cometh of our labours they keep and maintain their estates: we be called their bondmen, and without we do readily them service, we be beaten; and we have no sovereign to whom we may complain, nor that will hear us nor do us right.

Ball's solution was to 'go to the king, he is young, and shew him what servage we be in, and shew him how we will have it otherwise, or else we will provide us of some remedy'. He was confident that 'if we go together, all manner of people that be now in any bondage will follow us to the intent to be made free; and when the king seeth us, we shall have some remedy, either by fairness or otherwise'.[22]

This is all of a piece with John Ball's most famous saying, the rhetorical question that suggested an absence of class difference in Eden: 'When Adam delved and Eve span, who was then the gentleman?' The message made John Ball popular: 'wherefore many of the mean people loved him, and such as intended to no goodness said how he said truth; and so they

---

22   Ibid., pp. 62–3.

would murmur one with another in the fields and in the ways as they went together, affirming how John Ball said truth.'

The archbishop of Canterbury, however, did not love him. When he heard what Ball was preaching he 'caused him to be taken and put in prison a two or three months to chastise him'. But this was useless, because 'when this John Ball was out of prison, he returned again to his error, as he did before'. Froissart concludes: 'it had been much better at the beginning that he had been condemned to perpetual prison or else to have died, rather than to have suffered him to have been again delivered out of prison.'[23]

Ball seems to have had particular appeal in London. Froissart records that 'of his words and deeds there were much people in London informed, such as had great envy at them that were rich and such as were noble; and then they began to speak among them and said how the realm of England was right evil governed, and how that gold and silver was taken from them by them that were named noblemen: so thus these unhappy men of London began to rebel . . .'. Froissart even suggests that it was Londoners that 'sent word to the foresaid countries that they should come to London and bring their people with them, promising them how they should find London open to receive them and the commons of the city to be of the same accord', although it seems unlikely that the revolt was actually stirred up by the metropolis.[24] At any rate it was the surrounding counties, especially Essex and Kent, that rose up in revolt with John Ball, Wat Tyler and Jack Straw at their head.[25]

A huge mass of rebels, some 60,000 in Froissart's exaggerated estimate, now converged on London.[26] And, as English peasants were accustomed to do, they bore arms – often the very same bows that had proved so effective at Crécy and Poitiers. The rebels caught up with the king's mother on her way back from a pilgrimage, but she was unharmed. Having collected greater numbers in Canterbury and Rochester, the marchers arrived at Blackheath in South East London. There they took the family of one Sir John Newton hostage and sent him to Richard II, who was at the Tower of London with his courtiers. Sir John apologized profusely for the message he bore, which was a clear summons to the king to meet the rebels. Richard was forced to agree. 'In the morning on Corpus Christi day King Richard

---

23   Ibid.

24   Ibid., p. 63.

25   It is unclear whether 'Jack Straw' was merely a pseudonym used by Wat Tyler (and others) or whether he was indeed another individual leader of the revolt. John Ball also used the alias 'John Trewman' on occasion.

26   Although another contemporary account, by Thomas Walsingham, puts the number of 'commons and rustics' at 100,000. See Jones, *Summer of Blood*, p. 69.

heard mass in the Tower of London, and all his lords, and then he took his barge with the earl of Salisbury, the earl of Warwick, the earl of Oxford and certain knights, and so rowed down along the Thames to Rotherhithe, whereas was descended down the hill a ten thousand men to see the king and to speak with him.'

But the threat of the crowd was too terrifying for Richard to disembark as the rebels wanted. When the mob handed over a list of those they wanted executed, Richard refused this demand also. He would not even speak with them, and returned to the Tower, which ignited the anger of the crowd, and 'they cried all with one voice, "Let us go to London".' As they moved towards London Bridge they pulled down the houses of the courtiers and the rich and broke open the Marshalsea prison. Finding the gates of the bridge closed the rebels threatened to take the city by storm, but Londoners inside the gates put their heads together, saying 'Why do we not let these good people enter into the city? They are your fellows, and that that they do is for us.' The gates were opened and the Peasants' Revolt poured into the capital through Aldgate, where Geoffrey Chaucer had his lodgings.[27]

According to Froissart, the following day a crowd of some 20,000 followed John Ball, Wat Tyler and Jack Straw towards Westminster. Along the Strand they came to the Savoy Palace of the hated John of Gaunt, one of the main inspirers of the poll tax. The crowd – much more determined than it had been four years earlier – broke into the opulent residence and pillaged it, killing John of Gaunt's servants. Then it was set on fire. At the same time the anger built up over many years was also spent in killing Flemish immigrants and those associated with the Italian merchants: 'they brake up divers houses of the Lombards and robbed them and took their goods at their pleasure, for there was none that durst say them nay.' Wat Tyler got his revenge on a rich merchant who had ill-treated him in the past, parading his severed head on spear-point.[28]

When they got to Westminster the rebels broke open the prison. They then surged back to the Tower to confront the king. That night the crowd assembled at St Katherine's in front of the Tower of London, 'saying how they would never depart thence till they had the king at their pleasure'. Richard was advised by 'his brethren and lords and by Sir Nicholas Walworth, mayor of London, and divers other notable and rich burgesses, that in the night time they should issue out of the Tower and enter into the city, and so to slay all these unhappy people, while they were at their rest

---

27   Froissart, *Chronicles*, pp. 69–70; Vallance, *Radical History of Britain*, p. 60. See also Dean, *Literature of Richard II's Reign*.
28   Froissart, *Chronicles*, p. 71.

and asleep'. But the plan was not acted upon for fear it might provoke an even more extensive rising of the 'commons of the city'.

The embattled royal party then decided that if force was not yet possible, fraud should be attempted. 'The Earl of Salisbury and the wise men about the king said: "Sir, if ye can appease them with fairness, it were best and most profitable, and to grant them everything that they desire, for if we should begin a thing the which we could not achieve, we should never recover it again, but we and our heirs ever to be disinherited."' The following day when the crowd at St Katherine's began 'to cry and shout, and said, without the king would come out and speak with them, they would assail the Tower and take it by force, and slay all them that were within', Richard decided that he would have to speak to them. He 'sent to them that they should all draw to a fair plain place called Mile-end . . . and there it was cried in the king's name, that whosoever would speak with the king let him go to the said place, and there he should not fail to find the king'.[29]

The king's party rode out of the Tower hoping to reach Mile End Green. But 'as soon as the Tower gate opened . . . then Wat Tyler, Jack Straw and John Ball and more than four hundred entered into the Tower and brake up chamber after chamber'. When they came on the archbishop of Canterbury, the 'chief chancellor of England', 'these gluttons took him and strake off his head'. Three others met the same fate 'and these four heads were set on four long spears . . . to be borne before them through the streets of London and at last set them a-high on London bridge, as though they had been traitors to the king and to the realm'. The crowd also broke into the bedroom of the king's mother and – in an eerie precursor to the incident during the student demonstrations of 2010, when Prince Charles's wife Camilla was poked with a placard pole in their car in central London – the peasants poked the princess with a stick and asked her for a kiss, though she suffered no worse.[30]

At Mile End Green the King came face to face with 'three-score thousand men of divers villages and of sundry countries in England'. Wisely the King spoke to them 'sweetly', addressing them as 'ye good people' and asking 'what lack ye? what will ye say?' The reply was straightforward: 'We will that ye make us free for ever, ourselves, our heirs and our lands, and that we be called no more bond nor so reputed.'

In this remarkable, unique confrontation between bondsmen and their overlord, the king replied: 'Sirs, I am well agreed thereto. Withdraw you home into your own houses and into such villages as ye came from, and

---

29 Ibid., pp. 71–2.
30 Ibid., pp. 72–3. Other accounts claim that the storming of the Tower happened immediately after the meeting at Mile End, rather than just before it as Froissart claims. See Vallance, *Radical History of Britain*, p. 66.

leave behind you of every village two or three, and I shall cause writings to be made and seal them with my seal, the which they shall have with them, containing everything that ye demand'. The king also agreed to 'pardon everything that ye have done hitherto, so that ye follow my banners and return home to your houses.'

Some were satisfied with the undertakings that Richard gave them. But 'Wat Tyler, Jack Straw and John Ball said, for all that these people were thus appeased, yet they would not depart so'; according to Froissart, some 30,000 stayed with them.[31]

The following day Wat Tyler, Jack Straw and John Ball assembled with some 20,000 at Smithfield, then the site of a horse market, and told the crowd that they had done 'nothing as yet'. According to Froissart the plan was to take control of London. He records the crowd being told: 'These liberties that the king hath given us is to us but a small profit: therefore let us be all of one accord and let us overrun this rich and puissant city.' We cannot know how this scheme would have fared for at this moment, seemingly by accident, the king and a party of forty horsemen came into the area in front of the abbey of Saint Bartholomew. In Froissart's account, when Wat Tyler saw the king he told his supporters, 'Sirs, yonder is the king: I will go and speak with him. Stir not from hence, without I make you a sign; and when I make you that sign, come on and slay all them except the king; but do the king no hurt, he is young, we shall do with him as we list and shall lead him with us all about England, and so shall we be lords of all the realm without doubt.' Tyler then rode out and asked the king if he saw his supporters ranged behind him. He told Richard that this mass were sworn to him in 'faith and truth, to do all that I will have them'.

There then followed an exchange about the letters which the king had promised he would send to the counties freeing the peasants. But as this discussion took place Tyler 'cast his eye' on a squire in the king's party that seems to have been an old enemy. He demanded that the king tell the squire to 'Give me thy dagger.' The king instructed him to do so, and Tyler then demanded that he 'Give me also that sword.' This was refused, and in the ensuing squabble the king 'began to chafe and said to the mayor: "Set hands on him."' The mayor drew his sword and 'strake Tyler so great a stroke on the head, that he fell down at the feet of his horse, and as soon as he was fallen, they environed him all about, whereby he was not seen of his company. Then a squire of the king's alighted, called John Standish, and he drew out his sword and put it into Wat Tyler's belly, and so he died.'[32]

---

31   Froissart, *Chronicles*, p. 74.
32   Ibid., p. 79. Again, other accounts of this incident differ, some claiming that Wat Tyler tried to rush the king and giving Standish's Christian name as Ralph, not John. See Vallance, *Radical History of Britain*, pp. 69–70.

Tyler's supporters, on realizing that their leader had been killed, 'arranged themselves on the place in manner of battle, and their bows before them', as their forebears had done at Crécy and Poitiers. Richard rode out to confront them alone. He said: 'Sirs, what aileth you? Ye shall have no captain but me: I am your king: be all in rest and peace.' This seems to have been enough to divide the rebellion. Some began to 'wax peaceable and to depart', others did not. But now the king's loyalists from the City began to arrive, and the balance of forces turned against the rebels. The king knighted John Standish, Tyler's assassin, and two others and sent them to demand that the banners and letters freeing the bondsmen be returned, and that the crowd disperse. The gambit worked, and Richard tore up the letters granting freedom to the peasants. 'Thus these foolish people departed, some one way and some another', writes Froissart, 'and the king and his lords and all his company right ordinately entered into London with great joy.' John Ball and Jack Straw were caught and beheaded. Their heads, with Wat Tyler's, were displayed on London Bridge. Richard II told his mother, 'I have this day recovered mine heritage and the realm of England, the which I had near lost.'[33]

The Peasants' Revolt did not end with the defeat in London. Related revolts occurred at St Albans (beginning 14 June), Bury St Edmunds (14 June), Norfolk (14 June), and Cambridgeshire and Huntingdonshire (15–17 June). On 15 June the townsfolk of Cambridge rioted against the University, particularly attacking Corpus Christi College. By the end, 'all England south and east of a line drawn from York to Bristol had risen.'[34] Not even the eventual defeat of the whole revolt could return Richard's kingdom to its condition before the Black Death. As the historian Gerald Harriss says, 'political society had always lived in fear of social revolution, and in 1381 it peered into the abyss and took heed.'[35] Although there was retribution by the ruling class, and the attempts to tamp down wages continued, the poll tax passed by Parliament in 1382 was to be levied only on landowners. By 1389, justices of the peace had gained the power to set local pay scales. Wages rose steadily, and by the end of the century they were at a historic high. Increasingly peasants held their land not in return for servile duties but on payment of rent. Landlords who lived from rent, yeoman farmers who paid it, and free wage-labourers (unable to find that rent) were becoming more widespread.

---

33   Froissart, *Chronicles*, p. 81.
34   Morton, *People's History of England*, p.125.
35   Quoted in Vallance, *Radical History of Britain*, p. 77.

THE MURMURINGS OF THE LOLLARDS

The rise of the Wycliffe heresy coincided with the Peasants' Revolt. John Wycliffe was born in Yorkshire around 1330 and became a leading theologian at Oxford just as strains within the English church itself, and between that Church and Rome, were becoming more visible. In London in 1312 the mayor and aldermen complained that the monasteries and other religious landlords around the City paid nothing toward the upkeep of the City wall and defences, despite raking in a third of all the City's rental income and owning, by some estimates, almost two-thirds of the land. The Church hierarchy was seen by many as corrupt, worldly and incapable of giving spiritual guidance, and in defiance barbers, cordwainers and other artisans were opening their shops on Sundays. In 1468 shoemakers defied a Papal Bull which directed them to stop Sunday trading, saying that 'the pope's curse was not worth a fly'.[36]

The Black Death removed a good number of priests, as many high-ranking clergy fled the stricken areas. This meant that in order to bury the dead and perform marriages and baptisms, new untrained clergy emerged. These people often owned no land and lived in poverty. The orthodox Christian view was that man was sinful and all his privations were directed by God, but some of the new clergy – and John Ball is a representative figure in this context – felt the pain of the peasants. Ball's religious standpoint was evangelical, and he talked to his audience directly.

This new fervour coincided with John Wycliffe's attack on Rome. The English Church paid too much money to the pope, in Wycliffe's view. He opposed the Church hierarchy and justified this belief with a 'true reading' of the Bible. Even more heretically, he believed the Bible should be printed in English: 'Englishmen learn Christ's law best in English. Moses heard God's law in his own tongue; so did Christ's apostles.' This was a revolutionary view, because religion could now be used for the people instead of against them. The Church authorities responded by declaring: 'By this translation, the Scriptures have become vulgar, and they are more available to lay, and even to women who can read, than they were to learned scholars, who have a high intelligence. So the pearl of the gospel is scattered and trodden underfoot by swine.'[37]

Wycliffe appealed to a wider public by presenting his views to Parliament and having them printed in a tract, accompanied by additional notes and explanations. In March 1378, after the Parliament had met, he was hauled

36   M. Honeybourne quoted in Inwood, *History of London*, p. 144. See also p. 145.
37   'John Wycliffe', christianhistorytoday.com.

to the Palace of Lambeth to answer for his views. The proceedings had barely begun before an angry crowd gathered with the aim of protecting him from persecution. Two years later – the year of the Peasants' Revolt – Wycliffe and his followers were dismissed from Oxford, but this merely created an evangelical corps that preached throughout the country. In 1382 the crowd again interrupted the Synod at Blackfriars when it discussed Wycliffe's doctrines. The London supporters of Wycliffe were sophisticated enough to support his views despite the fact that they detested his patron, John of Gaunt. Although London was not as important a centre of support for Wycliffe as Oxford, it was said that 'Londoners began to grow insolent beyond measure . . . they not only abominated the negligence of the curates but detested their avarice.'[38]

Wycliffe died in 1384, leaving the first English-language Bible to be completed by his associate, John Purvey. Such was the impact of Wycliffe's teachings that thirty years later they were condemned by the Council of Constance as heretical; his body was exhumed from its resting place in his parish of Lutterworth, and burnt. The ashes were eventually scattered into the river Swift, but, as Thomas Fuller recorded: 'This brook conveyed them to the Avon, the Avon to the Severn; the Severn to the narrow seas; they into the main Ocean; and thus the ashes of Wycliffe were the emblem of his doctrine, which is now dispersed the whole world over.'[39] Yet it was less the current of the tides and more the activity of Wycliffe's followers, armed with the unique weapon of the Wycliffe Bible, that spread his message.

Wycliffe's followers were known as Lollards and were strongest in the counties around London, Kent, Sussex and Essex. The origin of the term is disputed, but its most likely root is the Dutch word for 'mummer', related to the word 'lullaby': it refers to the Lollards' habit of talking or singing in a low voice to, as their persecutors said, 'conceal heretical principles or vicious conduct under a mask of piety.'[40] In May 1394 the Lollards presented a petition to Parliament which struck at the roots of corruption in the Church, blaming 'conformity with the precedents of Rome' for 'Faith, Hope and Charity' leaving the national Church. It lambasted the 'English priesthood derived from Rome' for 'pretending a power superior to angels'. It attacked idolatry in terms that would become part of mainstream Puritanism and echo in the debates of the English Revolution. And it insisted on the separation of Church and state: 'the joining of the offices of prince and bishop, prelate and secular judge, in the same person, is plain

---

38   See Inwood, *History of London,* p. 146.
39   See C. Hampton (ed.), *A Radical Reader: The Struggle for Change in England, 1381–1914* (Harmondsworth, 1984), p. 73.
40   Ibid., p. 74.

mismanagement and puts the kingdom out of the right way.' It also offered the view that 'the taking away of any man's life, either in war or in courts of justice, is expressly contrary to the New Testament.'[41]

By the early fifteenth century the state was engaged in severe repression of Lollardy, including, for the first time, burning lay-heretics at the stake. In 1414 there was an attempted Lollard rising in London in response to the arrest on Twelfth Night of 'certain persons called Lollards, at the sign of the Axe, without Bishop's Gate'. Sir John Oldcastle, friend of King Henry V and a model for Shakespeare's Falstaff, was already being held in the Tower for Lollardy. He escaped and tried to raise an insurrection which involved the kidnap of the king. The plan failed, and Oldcastle was executed alongside some thirty-eight others on the so-called 'Lollard gallows' besides St Giles.

'JACK CADE THE CLOTHIER MEANS TO DRESS THE COMMONWEALTH'

In 1450 the counties of Kent, Sussex and Essex were once again the forcing ground for a rebellion which found its way to London, just as they had in 1381 and during the Lollard unrest. Jack Cade's revolt followed the pattern of the earlier risings in that it benefited from some elite support, in this case from the House of York – soon to be conducting the larger struggle of the Wars of the Roses. Indeed some of Cade's supporters claimed that he was a cousin of Richard, duke of York. In addition he had the support of some knights and squires, but it was nevertheless an overwhelmingly popular movement. However, the popular forces involved were no longer peasants as they had been in 1381: now they were composed of agricultural labourers, yeomen farmers, artisans, traders and merchants. They rose because Henry VI had extorted tax from them at home and engaged them in the Hundred Years War in France, from where raiding parties threatened the coast.

The rebellion began in Kent and Cade marched his supporters to Blackheath, just as Wat Tyler had done seventy years before. They numbered 46,000 according to the account of William Gregory, mayor of London in the year following the rebellion.[42] The demands they made in 'A Proclamation Made by Jack Cade, Captain of Ye Rebels in Kent' were more directly political than those of previous revolts: it observed the formality of recognizing the authority of the king and blaming 'certain persons' for daily informing him that 'good is evil and evil is good'. But the proclamation

---

41   'Lollard Petition to Parliament', in Hampton (ed.), *A Radical Reader*, pp. 74–5.
42   See Gregory's account in Hampton (ed.), *A Radical Reader*, p. 78.

immediately went on to refute those who 'say that our sovereign lord is above his laws to his pleasure and he may make it and break it as him list' by insisting that 'the contrary is true, and else he should not have sworn to keep it'. Moreover, the proclamation also contradicted those who 'say that the king should live upon his commons, and that their bodies and goods be the king's'. Again, for Cade's followers 'the contrary is true, for then needeth he never Parliament to sit to ask good of his commons . . .'. The proclamation also raised directly economic grievances about lordly extortion and the use of political power by the aristocracy to get and keep property.[43]

To start with, Henry raised an army to confront the rebels and they dispersed. But the cause was popular even among Henry's soldiers and fear at the dissolution of his own forces made the king quit the capital and retire to Kenilworth in Warwickshire. On the first day of July 1450 the rebellion moved its forces to Southwark, Cade setting up at the White Hart. The 'Proclamation' had won the approval of many in London already discontented with Henry's rule and Cade's forces, perhaps now numbering 25,000, crossed London Bridge and entered the City. There was some looting but the main work of the insurrection was the execution of the king's henchmen. William Crowemere, sheriff of Kent, was beheaded in a field at Aldgate, while the detested lord treasurer, Lord Saye and Sele, was 'beheaded in Cheap before the Standard', according to Gregory.

As the rebel occupation of London wore on, however, support from the elite drained away – especially when Cade proposed levying rich Londoners to sustain his supporters. The Common Council raised a force of Londoners to confront the rebels on the night of 5–6 July, and from 10pm to 8am there was fierce fighting on London Bridge. The drawbridge was set alight and the Marshalsea prison was broken open; 'many a man was slain and cast into the Thames', records Gregory. The rebellion was defeated and the price of 1,000 marks put on Cade's head. He was eventually killed by the sheriff of Kent while retreating through the Weald of Sussex. His naked body was brought to London where he was beheaded and quartered. His head was set on London Bridge where only days before those of the rebellion's enemies had been. There was widespread repression, especially in Kent, where beheadings were so numerous that 'men call it in Kent the harvest of the heads'.

Cade was immortalized by Shakespeare in *The Second Part of King Henry VI*, although the Bard mocks Cade's lowly origins, his supposed claims of noble origin and his promises of relieving the economic distress of the poor. Yet Shakespeare surely catches an authentic note when he has the rebel leader say: 'For our enemies shall fall before us, inspired with the spirit

---

43   Ibid., pp. 79–80.

of putting down kings and princes'. This levelling tone was submerged beneath the dynastic squabbles of the Wars of the Roses which followed five years after the end of the rebellion.

The division of the country in that conflict, with the South and East in support of the House of York and the West and North in support of Lancaster, prefigured the geographical division of the country in the English Civil War. As A. L. Morton observed, 'Supporting the Lancastrians were the wild nobles of the ... most backward and feudal elements surviving in the country. The Yorkists drew their support from the progressive South, from East Anglia and from London, even if this support was not usually very active.'[44] The victory of the House of York therefore was also the victory of the areas in which feudalism had been most eroded by emerging market relations, and for this reason it secured the support of the nascent market-oriented classes for the Tudor monarchy over the next century.

THE REFORMATION OF LONDON

One final revolution helped to complete London's transformation from a feudal to an early modern capital: the dissolution of the monasteries. The experience of the Lollards foreshadowed what now became English Protestantism, but Henry VIII's break with Rome and the final establishment of an English Protestant Church was also a moment of economic transformation as well as a political and ideological milestone in the establishment of the early modern nation state. It could scarcely be otherwise when the Church that Henry nationalized was a major economic force in its own right. Some churches like St Mary Spital and St Mary Clerkenwell owned property in sixty parishes. Over 100 English monasteries held property in London.[45] In all, twenty-three major religious houses in or near the City were taken over by the king between 1543 and 1547. In most cases they were immediately sold off to raise revenue for the Crown's wars in France and Scotland. This economic revolution broke the Church's grip on large numbers of shops and tenements that had been bequeathed to the monasteries over the centuries.

Aristocrats new and old were among the beneficiaries; the duke of Norfolk inherited a new mansion on the site of Holy Trinity Priory and called it, unimaginatively, Duke's Place. Lord Lumley's mansion was on the site of Crutched Friars. The lord treasurer, the soon-to-be marquess of Winchester, sold off the stones and lead that had once been Austin Friars and built himself a townhouse. The Charterhouse passed to three

44   Morton, *People's History of England*, p. 150.
45   Inwood, *History of London*, p. 154.

aristocratic owners before becoming, in 1614, a school and home for poor gentlemen. The 'inns' of abbots and priors that lined much of Holborn, the Strand and Fleet Street became hostels for travellers: those of the abbots of Glastonbury, Lewes, Malmesbury, Peterborough, and Cirencester were reborn as the Dolphin, Walnut Tree, Castle, Bell and Popinjay Inns. Others became residences for nobles and rich aldermen: the bishop of Worcester's inn became Somerset House, the bishop of Bath's inn became Arundel House, the bishop of Carlyles's inn became Bedford House. Norwich Place passed through several hands before it came into those of the duke of Buckingham in the 1620s. Its river gate, York Watergate, still runs down the side of Charing Cross Station. The king's new Palace of Whitehall, with its tiltyard for jousting, cockpit and tennis court, expanded on the archbishop of York's confiscated palace. All of it, save James I's Banqueting House, was destroyed by fire in 1698.

The emerging 'middling sort' also gained from the dissolution of monastery land. Housing for 'Noble men and others' was built on the land of Whitefriars, St Mary Spital and Holywell Priory. Tenements for 'brokers, tiplers, and such like' were built near St Bartholomew-the-Great. Two livery companies, the Mercers and the Leathersellers, gained new halls. St Mary Graces was demolished to make way for naval stores and a ships' biscuit factory. Ploughs, no doubt, were beaten into swords at St Clare's, conveniently near the Tower, when it became an armoury. A wine tavern opened at St Martin-le-Grand and there was glass-blowing (and a tennis court) at Crutched Friars. Belief in the Almighty was replaced by the willing suspension of disbelief as theatres rose on the sites of Blackfriars – soon home of the Queen's Revels and Blackfriars Playhouse – and Holywell Priory, later to house the Curtain and the Theatre. Due to a legal loophole, the grounds of former monasteries were still beyond City regulation, making these sites ideal for industry, theatres and crime. Some monasteries did, however, retain a religious function, becoming Protestant churches. Others were converted into institutions of pastoral care as schools or hospitals.[46] Broadly speaking, the anonymous poem 'Skipjack England' contained an estimate not too far from the truth:

> The Abbeys went down because of their pride
> And men the more covetous rich for a time;
> Their livings dispersed on every side,
> Where once was some prayer, now places for swine.[47]

---

46   Inwood, *History of London*, pp. 154–6.
47   'Skipjack England' in Hampton, *A Radical Reader*, p. 103.

THE BOUNDARIES OF LORDSHIP

Slowly, over the time in which the rebellions took place, feudal society faded and an incipiently modern world came into view. The revolts themselves, and the economic changes they reflected, were staging posts in the shift from a feudal economy – based on the militarily enforced labour service of the peasantry – to a commercial-capitalist economy, based on market-driven profits expropriated by a new trading class from labourers working for wages. The driving force of these changes was the people now becoming known as 'the middling sort' – yeomen farmers, traders, merchants and masters who could mobilize their apprentices. The power of the aristocratic nobility was being challenged, its old Church transformed. The new classes were reading their English Bibles, grabbing some monastery land and wondering aloud (at times) about the virtue of kings and the idleness of nobles.

Over many decades the boundaries of lordship were being driven back and the commercialization and monetization of all exchange and social relations proceeded to undermine the structure of feudal society. The challenge to the old Catholic Church, the shift to the individual's own Bible-led relationship with God at the expense of the prelate-dominated, hierarchically mediated relationship with God, was one ideological reflection of this change. The growth of Universities and Inns of Court, and the invention of the printing press, meant that Church was no longer the sole repository of knowledge. Printing, for instance, meant that one of the Church's key services to the monarchy, the handwritten reproduction of documents, was rendered an anachronism. The English state at first benefited from putting itself at the head of these changes, most obviously through the Reformation.

The Tudors, especially Elizabeth I, enjoyed the crystallization of these elements as a period of national, Protestant, reaffirmation. English nationalism, in the era of Drake and Raleigh, was reborn. The Stuarts faced the dissolution of this temporary stability. There was still another century before all these elements would fuse in the mighty Civil War against monarchy but by 1540 the seeds had been sown. And ideas that were first mummered by Lollards in the 1380s would be cried aloud by Levellers in the 1640s.[48]

---

48   See C. Hill, 'From Lollards to Levellers', in *Religion and Politics in Seventeenth-Century England* (Brighton, 1986), pp. 89–116.

3

'The Head and Fountain of Rebellion'

The only and sole legislative law making power is originally inherent in the people.
John Lilburne

LONDON'S REVOLUTIONARY REPUTATION

If 'posterity shall ask', said one Royalist, 'who would have pulled the crown from the king's head, taken the government off the hinges, dissolved Monarchy, enslaved the laws, and ruined the country; say, "twas the proud, unthankful, schismatical, rebellious, bloody City of London".'[1] Edward Hyde, earl of Clarendon and Charles I's advisor, was inclined to the same view. He saw London as 'the fomenter, supporter and indeed the life of the war'.[2] For the philosopher Thomas Hobbes it was obvious that 'but for the city the Parliament never could have made the war, nor the Rump ever have murdered the King'.[3] Sir Edward Walker described London as 'the head and fountain of this detested rebellion'.[4]

It is certainly true that King Charles I was driven from London at the start of the Civil War, eventually establishing his headquarters at Oxford. And it is also true that at the end of the civil wars London was the scene of his execution and the establishment of a Republic. But the radicalism of London was not inevitable nor was it uncontested. London was the site of a struggle between revolution and counterrevolution. At the outset of the conflict the City had to break its ties to the Crown, which were considerable. Later on, there were pro–peace demonstrations at various times during the war. In 1647 those moderates who wished to conclude a treaty which

---

1   Quoted in V. Pearl, *London and the Outbreak of the Puritan Revolution* (Oxford, 1961), p. 1.
2   K. Lindley, *Popular Politics and Religion in Civil War London* (Aldershot, 1997), p. 404.
3   S. Porter, 'Introduction' to S. Porter (ed.), *London and the Civil War* (London, 1996), p. 1.
4   B. Manning, *The English People and the English Revolution* (2nd edition, London, 1991), p. 281.

would 're-inthrone' Charles organized an effective counterrevolutionary petitioning campaign.[5] And if it is true that, in general, the forces of revolution were victorious, it is also true that they did not win alone. On two occasions, in 1647 and again in 1648, the New Model Army had to enter the capital in force to restore the fortunes of the revolution.

The London of the revolutionary 1640s was a fast-expanding city, but it was still composed of three distinct areas separated by open country. The old walled City remained the core of the metropolis, but it was spilling eastwards beyond its stone boundary in the Tower Hamlets and along the river, through the seafarers' town of Wapping, to Limehouse. Ribbon development was spreading towards the new buildings of the Strand, that were themselves the outgrowth of the second governmental centre of the city at Westminster. But this development was limited, with Covent Garden, where Leveller John Wildman's Nonsuch Tavern was located, as its newest centre completed in the 1630s. South of the river, Southwark stretched along the banks of the Thames and was expanding, but it was still only connected to the north bank of the river by London Bridge.[6]

In 1640 the population of the old City and its associated parishes was 135,000. But the population of the suburbs was already larger. The main trades were clothing, metal and leather working, and building. Manufacture engaged 40 per cent of the working population, retail another 36 per cent. In one parish, St Botolph Aldgate, the proportion of manufacturing workers increased from 48 per cent to 72 per cent between 1600 and 1640.

The City was already a great port. Shipbuilding yards stretched along the Thames at Blackwall, Wapping and Limehouse. South of the river food and drink businesses clustered in Boroughside, watermen congregated in Clink Liberty and Paris Garden, seamen in St Olave's, along with leather-makers, tanners, candlemakers and soap boilers. Dutch immigrants with new or specialized trades – brewing, felt and hat making, dyeing and glass making – settled in East Southwark.[7]

THE LONDON CROWD AND THE
OUTBREAK OF THE REVOLUTION

In November 1640 the Root and Branch Petition, calling for radical reformation of Church and state, was presented to Parliament by 1,000 Londoners

5   R. Ashton, *Counter-Revolution: The Second Civil War and its Origins* (New Haven and London, 1994), Ch.4.
6   P. Earle, *A City Full of People: Men and Women of London, 1650–1750* (London, 1994), pp. 7–9.
7   R. Weinstein, 'London at the Outbreak of the Civil War', in Porter (ed.), *London and the Civil War*, pp. 33–8.

and signed by 15,000 of their fellow citizens. It was of the pattern that was to become so familiar in the revolution: mass petitioning followed by mass demonstrations in support of the petition. Petitions had traditionally been a method of raising private grievances with MPs or the Crown, but the revolution made them into popular political tools. Hence Sir Edward Dering's shocked reaction to the printing of the Grand Remonstrance by the Long Parliament in November 1641:

> When I first heard of a Remonstrance, I presently imagined that like faithful Counsellors, we should hold up a Glass unto his Majesty: I thought to represent unto the King the wicked Counsels of pernicious Counsellors ... I did not dream that we should remonstrate downward, tell stories to the people, and talk of the King as of a third person.[8]

Dering was right to worry. Petitions were promoted by radical preachers in sermons, and signatures were collected after services; alehouses were another favourite petitioning site. House-to-house canvassing was also used. Masses of people far beyond the political elite were now being asked, at the very least, to express an opinion about the nation's affairs of state. Indeed when Lord Digby spoke against the Root and Branch, it was precisely the 'manner of delivery' that bothered him. 'No man of judgment', he said, 'will think it fit for a Parliament, under a Monarchy, to give countenance to irregular, and tumultuous assemblies of people. ... Sir, what can there be of greater presumption, than for petitioners, not only to prescribe to a Parliament, what and how it shall do; but for a multitude to teach a Parliament, what, and what is not, the government, according to God's word.' Digby added, unnecessarily, that he did not intend to 'flatter a multitude'.[9]

By May the following year, demonstrations were at once more numerous and featured more of the 'poorer sort' who were pressing that justice be done against Charles's advisor, the earl of Strafford. Parliamentary leader John Pym pressed the charge of treason. Crowds variously estimated at between 5,000 and 15,000 blockaded and barracked members of both Houses calling out for 'Justice and Execution'. Charles, who had intended to come to Parliament, thought better of it, and the Lords sent out a messenger to tell the crowd that they were going to accede to the petition to execute Strafford. John Lilburne had been one of the leaders of the crowd that day; he was arrested and brought before the Lords for the speech he had made to the protestors. Fortunately, the witnesses against

---

8   Quoted in T. C. Pease, *The Leveller Movement* (Gloucester, MA, 1965), p. 17.
9   Manning, *The English People and the English Revolution*, p. 55.

him differed in their evidence and he was discharged.[10] When the bill proposing Strafford's execution was debated in the Chamber, many of the earl's friends were absent – for fear of the mob, they claimed. And when Charles reluctantly signed his confidant's death warrant it was, explained Charles's nephew, because 'the people stood upon it with such violence, that he would have put himself and his, in great danger by denying the execution'.[11] But Strafford's death did not stop the protests.

In the closing days of December 1641 massive crowds of Londoners, often spilling down Ludgate and along Fleet Street and the Strand, came to Whitehall and Westminster. They were angered by Charles's appointment of a court loyalist as lieutenant of the Tower, seeing this as part of preparations to subdue the capital by force. In the face of demonstrations the appointment was reversed, but more radical demands followed. Now the crowd chanted 'No bishops! No bishops!' – the bishops being some of the most royalist members of Parliament. As they tried to take their seats, many were physically prevented from doing so. In response Royalists attacked the crowd with swords. The crowd fought back with bricks, tiles, and cobblestones. As news of the fighting spread, London as a whole mobilized. Some 10,000 armed apprentices surrounded Parliament. The London Trained Bands were called out, but refused to disperse them. On 30 December the Commons impeached twelve leading bishops, and the Lords dispatched them to prison. Church bells pealed across the City and bonfires blazed in the streets.

Less than a week later, on 4 January, the king entered the House of Commons with a sizeable armed guard, intent on arresting the five members of the Commons identified as the leaders of the revolt. Forewarned, the five men had fled to the City and it is likely that they found shelter in the house of one of the emblematic figures of the early phase of the revolution, Isaac Penington. Penington was a wealthy merchant, an alderman of the City and an MP. He was blamed by the Royalists for organizing one of the first political demonstrations aimed at forcing the Long Parliament to adopt the Root and Branch petition. His house was near one of the centres of revolutionary activity, St Stephen's Church in Colman Street, in the heart of the City. It is probable that it was here that the fugitives sought shelter.[12]

But if Isaac Penington sheltered them, it was the whole City that stood guard. 'Gates were shut, portcullises lowered, chains put across streets. For several days, thousands of men stood ready, armed with halberds, swords, staves, and whatever came to hand. Women brought stools and tubs from their homes to build barricades, and boiled water 'to throw on the

---

10   Ibid., pp. 61–4.
11   Ibid., p. 69.
12   I. Roy, '"This Proud Unthankful City": A Cavalier View of the City of London in the Civil War', in Porter (ed.), *London and the Civil War*, p. 154.

Cavaliers'. But the Cavaliers did not come. London, it was clear, had passed to the side of the revolution. It was not to be recovered with the forces to hand. On 10 January, the king fled the capital. The following day, the five MPs returned to Westminster through cheering crowds.[13]

REVOLUTION AND WAR

Popular mobilization was no less important when the Civil War did break out. 'In this summer the citizens listed themselves plentifully for soldiers ... The youth of the City of London made up the major part of [the] infantry.' In a single day, 26 July 1642, 5,000 enlisted at a muster in Moor Fields.[14] Lilburne was in action immediately. He led a heroic defensive action at the Battle of Brentford in November 1642, personally rallying retreating forces back to the front line and buying the time for the artillery train to escape Prince Rupert's grasp. He was captured and taken to Oxford as a prisoner, the first prominent Parliamentarian to be imprisoned.[15]

The following day the Royalists advanced to Turnham Green, threatening to invade London, but were halted by the mass mobilization of the London militia and the Trained Bands. They streamed out of London along the western road until 24,000 of them confronted the king's army of half that number. In a moment of indecision Charles drew back without giving battle, his dream of an early assault on the capital dashed. As S. R. Gardiner, the great Edwardian historian of the revolution, wrote: 'Turnham Green was the Valmy of the English Civil War. That which seemed to Charles's admirers to be his triumphant march from Shrewsbury had been stopped in the very outskirts of London.'[16]

But the Royalist threat to London had retreated for the winter, not disappeared. And, as it would again when the war went badly, the London crowd could also be mobilized in favour of a peace settlement with the king. In 1643 a crowd of women were at the doors of Westminster, shouting 'Give us those traitors that were against peace!' and 'Give us that dog Pym!' The militia sent to disperse them were seen off with rocks and brickbats, and a troop of horse had to be deployed against them. This demonstration, however, was modest compared to the main mobilization of Londoners that

---

13   N. Faulkner, '1640–1645: Revolution and War in England', Part 41 of *A Marxist History of the World*, available online at counterfire.org.

14   Manning, *The English People and the English Revolution*, p. 281.

15   P. Gregg, *Free-born John: A biography of John Lilburne* (London, 1961), pp. 100–101. Lilburne was later exchanged for Royalist prisoners.

16   S. R. Gardiner, *History of the Great Civil War*, vol. 1 (London, 1987), p. 60. Valmy was the first major victory of the army in the French Revolution.

year.[17] In early 1643 Londoners began to construct defence works against any renewed Royalist attempt to take the capital. These works were on a massive scale: some eighteen miles of forts, sentry posts, earthworks, trenches and lines of communications that ringed the entire metropolitan area.

Isaac Penington was again at the forefront of promoting the work. But the construction itself was the result of an unprecedented popular mobilization. No doubt some worked out of zeal for the Parliamentary cause, others because they feared what Royalist invasion could mean for them, their families and their property: Prince Rupert's sack of Brentford was still fresh in the memory.

But, whatever the motivation, the work was an impressive result of popular, collective effort. One contemporary recorded: 'The daily musters and shows of all sorts of Londoners here are wondrous commendable, in marching to the fields and out-works with great alacritie ... with roaring drummes, flying colours, and girded swords; most companies being also interlarded with ladies, women, and girls two and two, carrying baskets for to advance their labour ...' Obviously the guilds were involved in the mobilization: 'The greatest company which I observed to march out according to their tunes were the taylors, carrying fourtie-six colours, and seconded with eight thousand lusty men. The next in greatnesse of number were the watermen, amounting to seven thousand tuggers, carrying thirty-seven colours; the shoemakers were five thousand and oddes carrying twenty-nine colours.'[18]

At times more than 20,000 people were working without pay on the construction of the forts and earthworks. The lines of defence transformed the look of the city, and the diarist John Evelyn travelled to London to view them. Streets in the modern capital commemorate them – Mount Street in Whitechapel, for instance, where the giant Civil War earthwork wasn't demolished until the early nineteenth century. The efforts of Londoners were not in vain: the capital was never seriously threatened with invasion again. Indeed, the main threat to the revolution in its birthplace was from counterrevolution within, not military force from the outside.

REVOLUTION AND COUNTERREVOLUTION

The Parliamentary camp always contained some who saw the war as a militarized form of negotiation with the king, designed to get him to accept a compromise that he was unwilling to accede to in peaceful discussion.

17   A. Plowden, *In a Free Republic: Life in Cromwell's England* (Stroud, 2006), p. 78.
18   W. Lithgow, 'The Present Surveigh of London and England's State', quoted in D. Flintham, *London in the Civil War* (Leigh-on-Sea, 2008), p. 19.

Others reckoned that the king would have to suffer an outright military defeat before he could be brought to accept the ascendancy of Parliamentary rule. Others, still more radical, came to believe that the whole system of government needed to be refounded on the basis of popular sovereignty.

At different points during the revolution, this division expressed itself over different issues. In one critical phase it was fought out over the creation of the New Model Army, with Cromwell leading the 'win the war' party against the compromisers. Between the First and Second Civil War the division lay between Cromwell with his son-in-law Henry Ireton and the more moderate forces who were trying to negotiate with the king, on the one hand, and the Levellers on the other. After the Second Civil War it lay between the moderates who wished to return the king to his former powers and Cromwell, Ireton and the Levellers, now in alliance, who had concluded that the king could not be trusted.

THE LEVELLERS AND THE CITY

The political conflicts of the revolution could not help but be reflected in the City of London government. The revolution exploded the quasi-democratic but fundamentally oligarchic structure of livery companies and the Common Council, nominally the representative foundation of City government. The struggle focused on the rights of the commonalty to elect its own officers and leaders: Lilburne and fellow Leveller John Wildman were campaigning for the right of citizens to elect the mayor, sheriffs and burgesses. They also wanted an end to the veto that the mayor and aldermen claimed over decisions of the Common Council. In *England's Birth-right Justified* (October 1645) and in two pamphlets written while he was imprisoned in the Tower the following year – *London's Liberty in Chains* and *The Charters of London* – Lilburne demanded reform of the City government. This was not simply a democratic issue, since the same party of compromise that dominated Parliament was also in power in the City. The Common Council was controlled by a group of traders and merchants allied with their Parliamentary co-thinkers.[19]

Lilburne's approach was, as ever, both highly polemical and highly legalistic. His argument was that the rights granted by King John to the City of London were being usurped by the current oligarchy. The fundamentals of the Leveller approach are visible in these writings. In Lilburne's view, 'the Lord Mayor and Court of Aldermen, for anything I can perceive ... lay no claim to their pretended power of voting to make laws in the Common

---

19 Gregg, *Free-born John,* pp. 147–8; H. N. Brailsford, *The Levellers and the English Revolution* (Nottingham, 1961), pp. 607–8.

Councell but the authority of the Charter of Edward III which in such case is not worth a button.' For Lilburne,

> the only and sole legislative law making power is originally inherent in the people ... in which the poorest that lives hath as true a right to give vote, as well as the richest and greatest; and I say that the people by themselves, or their legal Commissions chosen by them for that end, may make a law or laws to govern themselves, and to rule, regulate and guide all their magistrates (whomsoever), officers, ministers, or servants.[20]

These views are strikingly similar, as we shall see, to those expressed the following year when the Leveller programme, the 'Agreement of the People', was presented at Putney Church. Lilburne's struggle against the Presbyterians in the City was part of a wider, tripartite struggle for power that had begun with the end of the First Civil War in 1645. Charles I was intent on regaining as much of his previous power as he could, mainly by playing upon divisions among his enemies. The moderates among the Parliamentarians were willing to restore Charles, as long as he would guarantee a Presbyterian form of national church. The Independents, who did not believe in a nationally enforced form of church worship, were strongest in the officer corps of the New Model Army. The Presbyterians understood that the New Model Army was the obstacle which stood between them and a deal with Charles. So they moved to disband the army, without payment of arrears, and to send some of its regiments to Ireland to suppress Catholic rebels.

The army revolted and the regiments began to elect 'agitators' (the then meaning of the term being the same as 'agent') to address their concerns. A series of increasingly political manifestos, drafted with the help of those soon to be known as Levellers, began to flow from the presses. In June 1647 the king was seized by a mere junior officer, Cornet George Joyce, who rode to Holmby House in Northamptonshire and took him into the army's custody.

The Presbyterian ascendancy in Parliament began to raise their own military force. Pro-Presbyterian apprentices rioted, and forced fifty-eight Independent MPs to flee to the army for safety. In response the New Model Army broke camp in August and occupied London. Colonel Thomas Rainsborough's regiment was the first to gain access to the City from Southwark. Lieutenant General Oliver Cromwell and Commissary General Henry Ireton began their own negotiations with the king, now held at Hampton Court and already being urged by some supporters to

---

20 J. Lilburne, *The Charters of London: or, the Second Part of London's Liberty in Chaines Discovered* (London, 1646), p. 4, E366 (12).

escape. Leveller Edward Sexby says that these negotiations with the king had left Cromwell's reputation 'much blasted'. The New Model Army was now divided between the Grandees, or the Silken Independents as Cromwell and his followers were known, and the agitators and their Leveller allies.

THE LEVELLERS AND LONDON

On 28 October 1647 these forces assembled in Putney Church, then west of London. And it is from this location that the debates held in the church, and on subsequent days in the nearby Quartermaster General's lodging, take their name. William Clarke, secretary to the New Model Army, took down the Putney debates in his own shorthand. The most remarkable presences are those of ordinary and elected soldiers, debating with the highest officers in the army. 'Buffcoat' is all the name Clarke gives one participant. The Levellers and agitators presented the 'Agreement of the People', their plan for a more far-reaching and democratic settlement of the nation than anything Cromwell and Ireton had in mind.

Thomas Rainsborough and Henry Ireton were the key protagonists, and it is their formulations which most fully express the opposed positions in debate. The content of the debate addressed the nature of the written constitution itself, but its significance for the participants bore upon what would happen to the revolution in the future. Would it stall? Who would benefit? The Levellers were seeking to detach the radical forces of the revolution from their affiliation with the Grandees, and get them to force through the radical vision of a new England.

One of the most famous exchanges in English political history took place between Rainsborough and Ireton as they discussed the right of the poor to vote for a government – or was this to be the preserve of property-owners? As soon as the 'Agreement of the People' was read to the meeting, Ireton objected that it seemed to argue that 'every man that is an inhabitant is to be equally considered'.[21] Rainsborough's reply is justly celebrated:

> For really I think that the poorest he that is in England hath a life to live, as the greatest he; and therefore truly, sir, I think it is clear, that every man that is to live under a government ought first by his own consent to put himself under that government; and I do think that the poorest man in England is not at all bound in a strict sense to that government that he hath not had a voice to put himself under . . .[22]

21   A. S. P. Wodehouse, *Puritanism and Liberty, Being the Army Debates (1647–49) from the Clarke Manuscripts* (London, 1938), p. 52.
22   Ibid., p. 53.

Ireton's argument for narrowing the franchise was straightforward: 'All the main thing I would speak for, is because I have an eye to property ... let everyman consider with himself that he do not go that way to take away all property.'[23]

Rainsborough's words are now carved into the stone balcony at Putney Church. But when they were uttered they were as much an urgent call for the revolution to continue as they were a timeless statement of constitutional rights. We should remember that, while they talked, Robert Lilburne's regiment (Robert was brother of John, then in the Tower) was refusing to march north as ordered by New Model commander Lord Fairfax. Agents from cavalry regiments addressed them, reading out a letter which urged them to stand up for 'England's freedom and soldiers' rights'. The debates were interrupted by messengers coming for instructions on how they should seek to quell the unrest.

Indeed, the conclusion of the Putney debates was that there should be a rendezvous of the army to consider the issues. The Independents manoeuvred to ensure that this was three separate meetings, not the single assembly the Levellers had imagined was decided. 'England's freedom, soldiers' rights' was the very slogan that Robert Lilburne's regiment brought, defying their generals, to the army rendezvous at Ware. The rebellious soldiers were forcibly suppressed by the New Model's senior officers, and one of their number was shot. The crushing of the Ware mutiny settled, for the time being, the questions that were raised at Putney. But Leveller organization in and around London continued to grow.

On 17 January 1648 John Lilburne and John Wildman addressed a Leveller meeting in Wapping, home of the Rainsborough family. Lilburne had been invited to the meeting 'by some friends' in order to answer the scruples and objections that 'some honest people, in or about Wappin' had concerning the Large Petition for which the Levellers were canvassing.[24] George Masterson, a Presbyterian minister from Shoreditch parish, attended the meeting to spy and the following day he denounced the meeting as a traitorous conspiracy to both the Lords and Commons.

On 19 January, Masterson, Lilburne and Wildman all gave evidence at the bar of the House of Commons. Lilburne was immediately committed once more to the Tower, and Wildman to the Fleet prison. Both were charged with treason. The next day Masterson gave evidence again, to the Committee of Both Houses sitting at Derby House. He published his evidence as a pamphlet on 10 February, and the same material was published by the government at about the same time.[25]

---

23   Ibid., p. 57.

24   J. Lilburne, *An Impeachment for High Treason against Oliver Cromwell and his son-in-law Henry Ireton Esquires* (London, 1649), E568 (20).

25   W. Haller and G. Davies, *The Leveller Tracts 1647–53* (New York, 1944),

Lilburne and Wildman hotly contested Masterson's charge of treason, but, as Norah Carlin has shown, the picture that emerges from Masterson's account of the Wapping meeting and Lilburne and Wildman's responses gives us our most detailed picture of how the Levellers and their supporters organized.[26] The purpose of the Wapping meeting was to promote the current Leveller petition and, once enough signatories had been gained, to organize a demonstration in its support. At the meeting Lilburne and Wildman fielded questions about the petition and explained the methods by which it was to be promoted. Masterson recorded part of Lilburne's speech as saying that the Levellers were appointing Commissioners to promote the petition in every town in the Kingdom if they could.[27] These Commissioners met in the Whalebone Inn and in Southwark, Wapping and towns in Kent.[28]

The Whalebone Inn was one of the regular meeting places of the Levellers, located in Lothbury near the Royal Exchange in the City. Lilburne's speech also revealed 'that 30,000 of the petitions were to come from the printing presses the following day'. To fund this work, Lilburne told the meeting, money needed to be raised and treasurers had been appointed for the purpose.[29] It is some indication of the scale on which the Levellers were operating at this time that 30,000 petitions were being printed: this would be a substantial number for a contemporary political campaign, designed to reach the modern population of the country. Lilburne, Wildman, John Davies and Richard Woodward also sent a letter to the 'well affected' of Kent encouraging them to support the petition.[30]

The picture of the Levellers that emerges from this episode is one of sustained, methodical, widespread political organization. No doubt the same methods that Lilburne describes the Levellers using in January were used in July to gain the 10,000 names for the petition to free Lilburne from the Tower, and, in August and September, to gain 40,000 signatories for the Large Petition and the turnout on the demonstration at Westminster which accompanied its presentation.[31]

---

pp. 88–9. See also N. Carlin, 'Leveller Organization in London', *Historical Journal* 27/ 4 (1984): 955–60.

26   Ibid., especially pp. 958–60.

27   'A Declaration and Some Proceedings', in Haller and Davies, *Leveller Tracts*, p. 98.

28   Ibid., p. 100.

29   Ibid., pp. 100–101.

30   Ibid., p. 103.

31   J. Frank, *The Levellers: A History of the Writings of Three Seventeenth-Century Social Democrats, John Lilburne, Richard Overton, William Walwyn* (Harvard, 1955), p. 167.

LONDON AND THE SECOND CIVIL WAR

London was a city on edge when hostilities broke out once more in 1648. The Second Civil War was composed of a series of local engagements against Royalist risings, plus the struggle against the invading Scottish army allied to the king. Cromwell was in command of the Parliamentary forces sent to crush the rebellion in Wales and then to oppose the Scots. Sir Thomas Fairfax was in command of the forces that dealt with the Royalist rising in Kent.

The Kent rebellion was led by the earl of Norwich who aimed at a rendezvous at Blackheath, thereby threatening London. Fairfax drove away the 1,000 who gathered at Blackheath on 30 May 1648, and decisively defeated the rest of the Royalists at Maidstone on 1 June. Norwich attempted to gain Blackheath again with his remaining 3,000-strong force, but was seen off by the City militia under the able command of Philip Skippon. Norwich crossed the Thames at Greenwich, the foot in boats and the horse swimming alongside. In Essex his numbers rose again as he was joined by Royalists from London, including Sir Charles Lucas and Sir George Lisle. The Royalists were pursued by Parliamentary forces under Colonel Whalley. They reached Chelmsford and then, on 10 June, they decided to enter Colchester, Lucas's home town. By 12 June Fairfax was two miles from Colchester, having brought his troops across the Thames at Gravesend. Norwich's Royalists had to make a stand.

The siege of Colchester, lasting for eleven weeks, was the most bloody and dramatic face-off in the Second Civil War.[32] But it is not the grisly course of the siege that is of interest here, but the events that attended its conclusion. The eventual surrender of the Royalists, after dismissing three offers of quarter from Fairfax, was a controversial affair. Rainsborough acted as one of the Commissioners who agreed the Articles of Surrender, and Fairfax's victorious troops entered Colchester on 28 August. Fairfax's Council of War, which included Commissary General Henry Ireton, Colonel Whalley and Rainsborough, decided that Lucas and Lisle should be executed. This was part of a harsher political climate in the Second Civil War, 'for during the *Second* Civil War the New Model's leaders' ascription of the term "Man of Blood" to Charles I, as guilty of a deliberate and almost sacrilegious action which, *after acceptance of clemency*, had cost the lives of others, was sometimes taken to apply to his commanders also.'[33]

---

32 Some accounts say that there was a threat to strip the women but it was not carried out. See for instance Gardiner, *History of the Great Civil War*, vol. 4, pp. 200–1.

33 W. R. D. Jones, *Thomas Rainborowe (c1610–1648) Civil War Seaman, Siegemaster and Radical* (Woodbridge, 2005), p. 112.

Whalley, Ireton and Rainsborough were charged with ensuring that the verdict of the Council of War be carried out, although it was Ireton who seems to have been most closely associated with the actual execution, involving himself in a lengthy argument with Lucas about the judicial basis of the sentence.[34] The Royalists instantly claimed Lucas and Lisle as martyrs, while Fairfax and Rainsborough were demonized for their part in the killings. Only a month after the execution the first attempt on the life of Rainsborough took place. At this time the New Model Army headquarters had moved to St Albans. Shortly before he went north with orders to take over the siege of Pontefract, Rainsborough was riding between London and St Albans, accompanied only by a captain, when he was attacked by Royalists. The report of the event given to the Commons records:

> Colonel Rainsborough, it was also informed, was likewise set upon by three of the King's Party between London and St. Albans, he having a Captain in his Company; the Cavaliers seeing their Gallantry and Resolution, put Spurs to their Horses and rode for it, and being extraordinary well mounted over rid them.[35]

On this occasion Rainsborough's bravery prevailed. Other Parliamentarians had also recently survived assassination attempts. On that same day the Commons heard that 'A Member of the House . . . and another Gentleman, coming yesterday out of the City, were affronted by three Gentlemen, who very well knew the said Member, calling him by his Name: Two of them drew their Swords, and sell [sic] on him, the Third had a Dagger to stab him, but by great Providence and Courage, he gave them a Repulse.' Others had not been so lucky, for the House was told that 'A Captain of the Army was likewise killed in London, and a Major the last week'. The final months of the Second Civil War were a dangerous time in London when the animosities generated by years of conflict were reaching a crescendo.

THOMAS RAINSBOROUGH'S FUNERAL

Rainsborough was a Leveller hero after Putney, the highest-ranking officer of the New Model Army to support their cause. He became detested by the Royalists for his role in the siege of Colchester, and was lucky to have survived the attempt on his life on the road outside St Albans. But in late

---

34   Gardiner, p. 203; B. Donagan, *War in England 1642–1649* (Oxford, 2008), pp. 364–6.
35   J. Rushworth, 'Proceedings in Parliament: September 1st – October 2nd 1648', *Historical Collections of Private Passages of State*, vol. 7: 1647–48 (1721), pp. 1248–80.

October 1648 he was not so lucky: a Royalist raiding party killed him at his lodgings in Doncaster where he was conducting the siege of the last Royalist stronghold, Pontefract Castle.

The funeral of Thomas Rainsborough was a calculated, political demonstration of the Leveller movement. It was an 'unofficial, revolutionary pageant' designed as 'a gesture of defiance against the established powers'.[36] The funeral took place at a politically critical juncture; many radicals feared that Parliament was about to conclude a treaty with the king that would mean an unacceptable restoration of the monarchy. Rainsborough's funeral was a symbolic moment of resistance to this course of action. The day before the funeral a single-side sheet, 'An Elegie Upon the Honourable Colonel Thomas Rainsborough', explicitly argued that Rainsborough's death should be understood as a providential warning against a treaty with the king:

> What if Heaven purpos'd Rainsborough's fall to be
> A prop for Englands dying Libertie?
> And did in Love thus suffer one to fall
> That Charles by Treaty might not ruine all?
> For who'l expect that Treaty should doe good
> Whose longer date commenc't in Rainsborough's blood?'[37]

The verse went on to tell 'noble Fairfax' and 'bold Cromwel' that if they were to 'Conclude a peace with Charles' they would end up riding in 'robes of Scarlet' dyed in 'your own dearest blood', because 'instead of Gold' Charles would 'pay you all with steel'.

It was in this atmosphere that the date and time of Rainsborough's funeral were announced in the Leveller press. *The Moderate*, the Leveller news-sheet, gave an account of Rainsborough's death, ending it with this call to arms: 'Can the soldiery of this Kingdom be silent, and not revenge the barbarous murder of their incomparable Commander ... The Lord stir up your hearts to be avenged of these bloody enemies.' And the *Moderate* made a public appeal to all the 'well-affected' (a term having much the same meaning as 'citizen' in the French Revolution) to join the funeral procession:

> The Corps of the never to be forgotten, English Champion, is to be brought to London on Tuesday next, the 14 instant, to be there interred. Major Rainsborow his brother, with other of his kindred goes

---

36   I. Gentles, 'Political Funerals during the English Revolution', in S. Porter, *London and the Civil War* (London, 1996), p. 207.

37   J. T., 'An Elegie Upon the Colonel Thomas Rainsborough, butchered at Doncaster Sunday the 29 Octob. 1648', 669 f.13 (48).

to Tatnam-High Cross to meet them; All the well-affected in London
and parts adjacent are desired to accompany them; the hour of ten in the
morning is desired to be the longest for their being in Tatnam.[38]

The scale of the procession must have exceeded the Levellers' expectations, although the most detailed accounts of the funeral itself come from
sources hostile to the Levellers. The Royalist newsbook *Mercurius Elencticus*
described Rainsborough's funeral as the event that 'crowned the day':

> [Rainsborough's] sacred corps conveyed from Doncaster, came this
> day to London, being met and attended on by a great number of the
> well affected of all Professions, Will the Weaver, Tom the Tapster, Kit
> the Cobler, Dick the Doore Sweeper, and many more Apron youths of
> the City, who trudg'd very devoutly both before and behind this glori-
> ous Saint, with about 100 she-votresses crowded up in Coaches, and
> some 500 more of the better sort of Brethren mounted on Hackney
> beasts . . .[39]

Apart from conveying the scale of the procession, this account is immediately striking in two ways. Firstly, an unmistakable note of snobbery
pervades the piece, giving us a glimpse of the force of class feeling engendered by the revolution but not so clearly visible on other occasions.
Secondly, the particular reference to 'she-votresses' exhibits hostility both
to the participation of women in politics and to democracy more generally.
The account in *Mercurius Elencticus* does however give us a detailed account
of the route of the funeral procession:

> The Body came in by way of Islington, and so through Smithfield,
> (where they should have burnt it) thence along Old Baily (in defiance
> of Newgate and the Sessions house) and under Ludgate, not through
> Pauls [for there the Organs stood, but on the backside of the church and
> so along Cheapside. Sure they were aware of the Ground whereon the
> crosse was founded] and through Cornwall, in great pompe, and with a
> variety of sad postures; at length they arrived at Wapping chappell, where
> they bestowed this precious peece of Mortality, as nigh as might be to the
> tombe of the Honourable and expert Skuller his father, where the Godly
> Party (with their hands in their pockets) lamented his untimely Grave.[40]

38 *The Moderate*, No. 17, Tuesday 31 October to Tuesday 7 November
(London, 1648), E470 (12).
39 *Mercurius Elencticus*, No. 52, Wednesday 15 November to Wednesday 22
November (London, 1648), E473 (9).
40 Ibid.

As a mark of official respect, the cannon at the Tower were fired as the funeral took place.[41] For the Levellers' supporters, the size of the procession was not the only remarkable element of the day. The inscription on Rainsborough's tombstone at the family church in Wapping tells its own story:

> He that made King, Lords, Commons, Judges shake,
> Cities, and Committees quake:
> He that fought nought but his dear Countreys good,
> And seal'd their right with his last blood.
> Rainsborow the just, the valiant, and the true,
> Here bids the noble Levellers adue.[42]

Another moment of symbolism from the day of funeral also became identified with the movement: the adoption of the sea-green colour as an identification of the Leveller movement. 'Azure and black' were Rainsborough's colours and as Ian Gentles records, 'from the time of his funeral his personal colours, green and black, were adopted as the badge of the Leveller movement.'[43] Certainly attacks on the Levellers that associated them with sea-green followed the funeral.

A satirical attack on the Levellers in the single sheet 'The Gallant Rights, Priviledges, Solemn Institutions of the Sea-Green Order' tells readers that the Levellers have chosen 'deep Sea Green … our Flag and Colours, and do hereby ordain and authorize it to be worn as the lively badge of Constancy, Sufferance and Valour in grain, the cognizance of Justice, and the mark of Freedom and Deliverance'; it calls on all who 'groan under the present Extortions, unequal taxes, unjust Levies, inevitable Monopolies, new Charters, plunders and avarice of Committees … to take up our Colours … and in so doing Sea green shall be their badge of warrant and protection'.[44] In what seems likely to be a direct reference to the practice at Rainsborough's funeral, this sheet continues: 'That every one so wearing our Colours in hatband, cuff, garment, bridle, mayn, or sail … shall hence forth, according to our Noble Order, be intitled the Free born Assistant of Justice …' The sheet was then reprinted, with minor alterations, as an eight-page pamphlet under the title *The Levellers Institutions for a Good People and Good Parliament*.[45]

---

41   Ibid.
42   *The Moderate,* No. 18, Tuesday 7 November to Tuesday 14 November, (London, 1648).
43   Gentles, 'Political Funerals', p. 217.
44   'The Gallant Rights, Christian Priviledges, Solemn Institutions of the Sea-Green Order', (1648), 669. f.13 (4).
45   *The Levellers Institutions for a Good People and Good Parliament* (London, 1648), E474 (4).

The practice of wearing sea green to denote association with the Leveller cause seems to have become widespread. As we shall see, it was worn again at the funeral of Leveller Robert Lockyer in April 1649. In May *Mercurius Militaris* was describing 'the brave Blades of the sea-green order honest Johns Lifeguard', and the 'bonny Besses, In the Sea-green dresses' who strike fear into 'Nol and his asses'.[46] And in July Leveller leader Richard Overton was himself writing to 'my Brethren of the Sea green Order'.[47] One might say that the adoption of the sea-green ribbon by the Levellers marks the invention of the party badge.

The show of force at Rainsborough's funeral was part of the great Leveller push in the second half of 1648 to stop the moderates coming to a treaty with the king. In order to achieve this end the alliance with the Independents, Cromwell and Ireton – broken at Putney and Ware – had to be re-established. It was this Independent–Leveller alliance that generated sufficient momentum to prevent a treaty, mount Pride's Purge to drive the moderates from Parliament, execute the king, and declare a republic.

Charles was executed on a scaffold outside the Banqueting House in Whitehall in January 1649. But at the moment of victory the differences between the Levellers and the Independents reasserted themselves. The Levellers saw Cromwell's regime as illegitimate, because it was not based on any expression of popular will. Having found the Levellers indispensable in the battle against those who wanted to 're-inthrone' Charles, Cromwell and the Independents now found them a danger to the new government. There were revolts brewing, including the mutiny in the army that ended in Burford. In London, a young Leveller named Robert Lockyer was at the heart of another.

A LONDON LEVELLER: ROBERT LOCKYER

Robert Lockyer was twenty-three years old or thereabout in 1649. At sixteen he had undergone adult baptism, a sign of radicalism, in Bishopsgate where he had been brought up. He served in Cromwell's Ironsides and followed them into Colonel Whalley's regiment of the New Model Army. Like Rainsborough and Sexby, he was a veteran of the Battle of Naseby. He had also been with Rainsborough at Ware when the mutiny was crushed by the Army Grandees. Whalley's was a radical regiment of which its chaplain, Richard Baxter, complained the troopers could be heard arguing 'some-times for state-democracy, sometimes for church-democracy'. It was one of

46   See Jones, *Thomas Rainborowe*, p. 136; *Mercurius Militaris*, 8 May 1649, E554 (13). 'Nol' was a nickname for Cromwell.
47   Richard Overton, *The Baiting of the Great Bull of Bashan*, quoted in A. L. Morton, *Freedom in Arms* (London, 1975), p. 287.

five regiments that, with John Lilburne's encouragement, re-elected more radical agitators in September 1647.[48]

On 24 April 1649 Lockyer was part of a mutiny in his regiment. The regiment was stationed around Bishopsgate when it was ordered out of London, but the soldiers were owed arrears of pay. Lockyer and about thirty other troopers went to the Four Swans Inn in Bishopsgate Street and seized the colours of the regiment and took them to the Bull Inn, also in Bishopsgate Street. When their captain arrived and asked them to account for their actions, they retorted that 'They were not his colours carriers' and 'That they, as well as he, had fought for them'.[49] The mutiny lasted into the following day, when some of the back pay was provided by the regiment's officers. Then a general rendezvous of the regiment was called in Mile End Green, with the intention of at last getting the troopers to march out of the city and find quarters in the surrounding country. But the mutineers stayed fast and 'put themselves into a posture of defence in Galleries of the Bull Inn, with their swords and pistols, standing upon their guard'.[50] There was another attempt to take the colours from Lockyer and his fellow troopers but, again, it was unsuccessful. Then loyal troopers and more senior officers of the regiment were brought down to the Bull to confront the mutineers, but this too proved unsuccessful. The mutineers held to the galleries of the Bull Inn, demanding two weeks' pay, and 'cryed out for the Liberties of the people'.[51] Finally the Lord General, Sir Thomas Fairfax, and the Lieutenant General, Oliver Cromwell, arrived on the scene just at the moment when Lockyer and fourteen others were being taken into custody. Some other mutineers were punished, but only Lockyer eventually faced the death penalty.[52]

Some accounts of the mutiny sympathetic to the Leveller cause claimed that Fairfax and Cromwell singled out Lockyer because he had participated in the Ware mutiny, demonstrating his support for the Leveller 'Agreement of the People'.[53] Certainly, in reply to demands for clemency, Fairfax said that he would not pardon Lockyer because of the volatile situation in the City and the Army.[54]

---

48   A. Southern, *Forlorn Hope: Soldier Radicals of the Seventeenth Century* (Lewes, 2001), pp. 73–7.
49   *A True Narrative of the late Mutiny made by several Troopers of Captain Savage's Troop* (London, 1649), E552 (18) p. 4.
50   Ibid., p. 6.
51   *The Impartiall Intelligencer*, No. 29, 25 April to 2 May (London, 1649), E529(29), p. 69.
52   *A True Narrative of the late Mutiny*, pp. 8–11.
53   *The Army's Martyr, or a more ful relation of the barbarous and illegall proceedings of the court martial at Whitehall on Mr Robert Lockier* (London, 1649), Wing A3414A 1221 (18), p. 5.
54   'To his Excellency Thomas Lord Fairfax Generall of the English Forces', in *The Army's Martyr*, p. 13.

Cromwell and Fairfax were facing more than Lockyer's mutiny during these days in late April. Three days of demonstrations by women supporters of the Levellers, the 'lusty lasses of the leveling party', were held at the doors of Westminster, petitioning for the release of the Leveller leaders from captivity in the Tower. MPs were mobbed by 500 angry women who were undeterred when the sergeant-at-arms was sent out to tell them to go home and 'look after their own business, and meddle with their huswifery'. In reply to a remark that it was strange to see women petitioning, they replied that 'it was strange too that you cut off the King's head, yet I suppose you will justify it'. On 25 April, just as events at the Bull Inn were in motion, twenty women of the 'sea-green order' were admitted to Parliament to present a petition said to bear 10,000 signatures. But they were rudely bundled out again by soldiers who cocked their pistols as if preparing to fire.[55]

John Lilburne and fellow Leveller leader Richard Overton petitioned Fairfax for mercy for Lockyer from their own imprisonment in the Tower, but his sentence was not repealed. He was taken to St Paul's Churchyard where he faced a firing squad of musketeers. After saying his farewells to friends and family he refused a blindfold, and addressed the soldiers. He said: 'Fellow soldiers, I am here brought to suffer in behalf of the People of England, and for your Privileges and Liberties, and such as in conscience you ought to own and stand to: But I perceive that you are appointed by your officers to murder me; and I did not think that you had such heathenish and barbarous principles in you ... when I stand up for nothing but what is for your good.' Colonel Okey, in charge of the detail, accused Lockyer of still trying to 'make the soldiers mutiny'. Lockyer asked the firing squad to shoot when he raised both his hands. And so they did.[56]

Lockyer's funeral was, if anything, even larger than Rainsborough's. And it served the same function of rallying Leveller support, though this time in a moment of retreat rather than advance. The procession began in Smithfield and went by way of the City to Moorfields where Lockyer was buried in the New Churchyard, now becoming a favoured resting place for dissenters. Seven trumpeters 'sounded before the Corpse'. Lockyer's horse, draped in black and led by a footman, followed the coffin which was covered in rosemary branches dipped in blood and had Lockyer's sword laid on it. This was an elevation of the ordinary trooper to the status of a 'chief commander'. Some 4,000 to 5,000 people joined the original procession, among them an estimated 300 soldiers and some discharged men. A company of women brought up the rear of the cortege. When the

55   Plowden, *In a Free Republic*, p. 49.
56   *The Army's Martyr*, p. 10.

procession reached its destination, the marchers were joined by more of the 'highest sort' who had stayed aloof from the controversial progress through the City. The funeral took place on the 27 April 1649. It was watched by 'many thousands of spectators'.[57] Black and green ribbons, now recognized as the Leveller colours, were widely worn among the mourners.[58] There were eulogies but no sermon in the New Churchyard. The speeches pointed up the Leveller programme and aimed criticism at the new government of Grandees.

FROM REPUBLIC TO RESTORATION

Cromwellian London was not the dour capital of a dour nation. The ravages of war, a war in which proportionally more people lost their lives than in any conflict before or since, were gradually overcome. Alehouses and taverns remained popular centres of life. Dancing, street music and fairs continued much as they had always done. The first coffee house opened near the Royal Exchange in 1652; many more followed, and by 1662 in the City alone there were eighty-two coffee rooms. Cromwell, unlike Charles II, did not try to close them.

Religious toleration was wide if not universal, and did not, of course, extend to Catholics. But it did extend to Jews, who in 1656 were 'readmitted' to England for the first time in 365 years. They built the first synagogue in Creechurch Lane in 1657.

The return of the Jews to England represented the kind of political compromise crossed with political principle which was the hallmark of Cromwell's rule. Some Jews fleeing the Spanish Inquisition were already in England, though they identified themselves as Spanish or Portuguese. While Cromwell was certainly a believer in religious toleration, he was unwilling to raise the issue directly in the case of the Jews; he was chiefly motivated by commercial considerations in seeking to attract Jewish merchants from Amsterdam so as to secure their trading relationships with Spain. He was sympathetic to the appeal from Amsterdam Rabbi Manasseh Ben Israel when he came to London in 1655, but referred the issue to the ruling Council of State. The plea for readmission ultimately came before a wider Conference involving lawyers, merchants and ministers, where the lawyers opined that there had never actually been any law forbidding Jews to reside in England.

That was enough for Cromwell, since it made the problem disappear. Just one sticking point remained: the 1650 Act which decriminalized

---

57 *Impartiall Intelligencer*, No. 29, p. 72.
58 Gentles, 'Political Funerals', pp. 219–21.

non-attendance at Church on the Sabbath did not apply to Jews. Cromwell met this difficulty by giving Jews a verbal assurance that no action would be taken against them, and indeed the synagogue at Creechurch Lane continued to function unhindered. When war broke out with Spain in 1656, Jews in England attested to their religion rather than have their property seized as Spanish nationals. Land was purchased for a Jewish cemetery in 1657, and a Jew became a broker at the Royal Exchange without having to swear the usual Christian oath. Prejudice there was, but de facto toleration was the norm.[59] As moneylenders, Jews were under the protection of the Crown and this alone caused much resentment particularly in times of economic hardship when they and other foreign nationals were liable to persecution. Their identification as Christ-killers, and the popularity of the Crusades from the late eleventh to the end of the thirteenth century, also exacerbated hostility towards Jews.

Radical puritans preached more freely than they ever had done, or ever would do until long after the Restoration. The diarist John Evelyn was horrified at the 'blasphemous and ignorant mechanics' that he found preaching in London pulpits, sometimes elected by the congregation. It was in fact Parliament, not Cromwell, who ruled against celebration at Christmas, the term 'Christ's Mass' smacking too much of Catholicism; Puritans preferred the term 'Christ-tide'.

Though theatres were closed, reputed as centres of delinquency, in 1656 the first English opera, 'The Siege of Rhodes', was performed and women sang on stage.[60] There were many musical clubs and taverns in London, and Cromwell's court promoted dancing and music. John Milton was Secretary of Foreign Tongues, assisted by Andrew Marvell as Latin Secretary, making Cromwell's government the only one in British history to contain such unrivalled poets, though neither was known as such at the time.

Evelyn managed to banish the spectre of 'mechanic' preachers by attending coach races in Hyde Park. Spring Gardens near Charing Cross was a rendezvous for 'the young company' of 'ladies and gallants' who could be found there 'till midnight', enjoying the fact that 'the thickets of the garden seemed to be contrived to all the advantages of gallantry'. In all these ways, says historian Stephen Inwood, 'the puritan decade was a time

---

59   S. R. Gardiner, *History of the Commonwealth and Protectorate*, vol. 4 (Aldestrop, 1989), pp.11–18.

60   Before the revolution some theatres had attracted significant lower-class 'groundling' audiences. And theatres were regarded as centres of sexual licence: brothels grew up around the Globe, for instance, and prostitutes came to the theatres to find clients. When they were reopened under the Restoration they were almost exclusively elite institutions and, therefore, sexual 'impropriety', on and off stage, could be tolerated.

of change, but change towards, rather than away from, greater individual freedom.'[61]

The Restoration of Charles II was a moment of political reaction, made possible by Cromwell's inability to weld the forces that had made the revolution into a stable basis for post-revolutionary administration. Critically, stabilizing the new order meant crushing the Levellers and radical left of the revolution without being able to re-unite with monarchist conservatives. And despite a brief resurgence of the radical old cause when Cromwell died in 1659, the establishment preferred the return of a Stuart monarch – or at least they did at first. Politically, the Restoration meant reaction. Some regicides were executed, others fled to Europe and to America. John Milton escaped with his life, partly due to the pleading of Andrew Marvell. They were both lucky since, with John Dryden, they had marched in Cromwell's funeral cortege.

There was political retreat, but the state machine was not restored to its condition under Charles I. The French ambassador to the court of Charles II observed, 'It has a monarchical appearance, and there is a king, but it is very far from being a monarchy.'[62] Socially and economically it was even harder to push the wheel of revolution back. On the land feudal tenures had been abolished in 1646, a mighty blow to medieval relations in the countryside, and as soon as Charles II was on the throne he confirmed that abolition.

The Royal Society and the Bank of England can stand as the two symbols of the longer-term deep impact of the revolution. The Royal Society, established in 1660, owed its origins to a group established at Gresham College in the heart of the City in 1645, dedicated to furthering scientific study for business purposes. Scientifically and philosophically cutting-edge ideas would never be subordinate to the Church again. The philosopher John Locke was not a Leveller, but without what they did and thought, his work was inconceivable. In the movement's wake, work like that of Locke, across the whole spectrum of science and philosophy, could no longer be suppressed. The Bank of England was not established until six years after the 'Glorious Revolution' of 1688 had put an end to absolutist ambitions once and for all, and effectively subordinated the monarchy to the wider governing classes. It made loan capital available on a greater scale, an essential feature of a capitalist economy. Guilds and monopolies were gone and the merchants and money men were now free of the Crown, even if the Crown was not free of them.

---

61   Inwood, *History of London*, pp. 236–7.
62   Quoted in C. Hill, *Reformation to Industrial Revolution* (London, 1967), p. 136.

The Great Fire of 1666 marked the physical extermination of the old City that had given birth to the revolution. And although it was not rebuilt on the grid-plan that Christopher Wren favoured, it was still a new city in many ways. The Restoration had meant a loss of power for democratic movements in the City as well as in national government. Small masters were driven to the margins in the City companies. But industrial struggles began to assume a more modern form. There were strikes, mutinies and combinations in pursuit of higher wages at the Royal Dockyards in the 1660s. And in the following decade, as London was rebuilt after the Great Fire, sawyers tried to form craft unions. Machine-breaking began: in 1675 a few hundred ribbon weavers, 'good commonwealth's men', broke into houses and destroyed the machines that were putting them out of a job. Cloth workers refused to work for less than twelve shillings a week. 'The trend of economic development', says Christopher Hill, 'was in the direction of sharper differentiation between classes; a landless working class dependent on wage labour increased, the yeomanry and the masters declined.'[63]

The apprentices, so central to the London crowd of the revolution, had been growing fewer even in the 1640s. The new bosses who emerged fortified by the revolution hastened that decline and a new class was formed, and formed itself, from the same human material. But it took a century in the making. And it formed itself out of long decades of struggle for the democracy that had seemed so tantalizingly close in the 1640s, but had been receding ever since.

The settlement of the Glorious Revolution of 1688 was the political expression of this new social reality. Absolutism and the Stuarts were gone for good. Constitutional monarchy, albeit a constitution in which the monarch retained real power, was its replacement. But within this new framework, even at the beginning, the new money men were more powerful than they had ever been. In the decades that followed they were set to become more powerful still.

---

63 C. Hill, *The Century of Revolution 1603–1714* (Wokingham, 1961), pp. 178–9.

4

Old Corruption and the
Mob That Can Read

And because I am happy and dance and sing
They think they have done me no injury
And are gone to praise God and his priest and king
Who make up a heaven of our misery.

William Blake

OLIGOPOLIS

By the eighteenth century, the elite that ruled Britain and its pre-eminent city, London, was one of the most unaccountable, unrepresentative and inhumane ever known. The wealth generated through trade and a developing empire, the political success of the Act of Union with Scotland and the lack of any democratic control from below all helped to produce an oligarchy whose main aim was the creation of fabulous wealth, regardless of the human or social consequences. Politics was run by a small elite of Whigs and Tories who presided over the networks of a unified, London-based, political, business and office-holding class. Conversely, the vast majority of the population had no say in who was elected: 'There were a few constituencies where perhaps 10 per cent of the male electorate could vote, but these were easily outnumbered by the "rotten boroughs", where the Member was effectively nominated by his patron, a lord or a landowner or both.'[1] The rotten boroughs and pocket boroughs ensured no wider democratic mandate, leading to a rampant corruption and of politics dominated by greed, self-interest, corruption and careerism.

London was the centre of this 'Old Corruption' and, housing more than a tenth of the whole population of England and Wales, dominated the rest of the country: 'London was then far more important commercially,

---

1   P. Foot, *The Vote: How It Was Won and How It Was Undermined* (London, 2005), p. 46.

industrially, and socially, in relation to the rest of the country than it has ever been since. . . . The only place it could be compared with was Paris, and people were fond of discussing which was the larger and which the more wicked.'[2]

A city which grew at such speed exhibited many of the features we now associate with cities in the developing world: precarious living, slum dwelling, and no support mechanisms for the poor; unbounded and ostentatious wealth for the rich. As a result of the appalling death rate the city relied on a population born and brought up elsewhere to increase its size. That changed around the middle of the century, when mortality began to fall. 'In towns deaths exceeded births, and yet the towns continued to grow. It was clear that they grew only at the expense of the healthier country districts; London, in particular, was regarded as a devouring monster.'[3]

The London of the eighteenth century was a city in transition. At its beginning, England had not long before reached the political settlement known as the Glorious Revolution which marked a compromise with its turbulent seventeenth-century past. The nation was establishing itself as the world's number one trading and imperial power, but industry was still based on small craft and artisan production, while politics was not clearly defined on a modern class or economic basis.

Nevertheless, the city was starting to become more defined: the enclosure of the docks changed the patterns of work on and around the river and launched a new era of trade. Streets and buildings encroached more onto traditional open space, creating new areas and suburbs. Between 1720 and 1745, five of the great London hospitals, including Guys, came into existence and by 1800 there was the beginning of serious attempts to regulate the city in terms of health and housing, as well as law and order.[4] In the last decades of the century, there were also improvements in London streets through paving, lighting and drainage: 'In the [1780s] the pavements, the street-lamps, the water supply, and the sewers of London were regarded as marvels. It is worth noting that foreign visitors were deeply impressed with the safety of pedestrians in London.'[5] This freedom was connected by some with the wider issues of liberty: 'their laws are not made and executed entirely by people who always ride in chariots.'[6]

Politically, this was a time of hiatus among working people: they had left behind the radicalism of the English Revolution, although it lingered

---

2   M. D. George, *England in Transition* (London, 1962), pp. 29–30.

3   Ibid., p. 68.

4   Porter, Roy 'Cleaning up the Great Wen: Public health in Eighteenth Century London' in *Medical History*, Supplement No. 11, 1991: 61–75.

5   George, *England in Transition*, pp. 71–2.

6   Ibid., p. 72.

on in many forms. Even at the end of the eighteenth century, poets like Blake defined themselves in terms of the radical impetuses of that revolution, and E. P. Thompson recalls how 'the wilder sectaries of the English revolution ... were never totally extinguished, with their literal interpretations of the Book of Revelation and their anticipations of a New Jerusalem descending from above. The Muggletonians (followers of the tailor-prophet Ludovic Muggleton) were still preaching in the fields and parks of London at the end of the eighteenth century.'[7] Many were influenced by a range of radical ideas, from Tom Paine's astonishing bestseller *The Rights of Man*, to the theories of the Enlightenment and the ideas of the French and American revolutions. At the same time, forms of working-class and collective organization were still embryonic.

The city was the scene of great extremes of affluence and poverty. Its fabric was held together by wealth made from slavery and empire. The rich spread out in this century from the traditional confines of the old City and Westminster to fill in many of the spaces in between, building fine houses in the Georgian squares of Bloomsbury and Marylebone. The upper and middle classes employed bevies of servants: one estimate puts the number at 200,000 in 1796, around a fifth of the city's population at the time.[8] The poor and the working people, on the other hand, lived in the growing suburbs which surrounded the city walls – Clerkenwell, Islington, Tower Hamlets, and Southwark, as well as in parts of the City and Westminster themselves. They were artisans, apprentices, small masters, servants, river workers, sailors, street vendors, criminals and prostitutes. The trades which Londoners carried out included carpentry, butchery and shoemaking, as well as silk weaving which was the specialty of French, Irish and other immigrants in Spitalfields.

THE SPITALFIELDS RIOTS

The silk weavers were among the most pugnacious sections of London society, strongly organized to protect their trade and repeatedly forced to defend themselves. In 1675 and 1697 they rioted against the introduction of new machines and production techniques. When in 1719 the weavers assembled again in Spitalfields and at the Mint (near the Tower of London) to protest against the import of calico which threatened the silk industry, they had the recently passed Riot Act read out to them.[9] As one of the key sections of the embryonic London working class, they helped

---

7   Thompson, *Making of the English Working Class*, p. 52.
8   B. Hill, *Eighteenth-Century Women: An Anthology* (London, 1987), p. 8.
9   Linebaugh, *The London Hanged*, pp. 19–20.

to define class consciousness in the city. Spitalfields was the centre of their home and work, wedged between the City and the East End, providing a densely packed area in which radical ideas could ferment. Many of the silk weavers were themselves refugees or descendants of refugees, Huguenots from France who fled Louis XIV's anti-Protestant pogroms in the 1680s. They were notorious for militancy in pursuit of their trade: any dispute with the masters would involve them not only stopping work but ripping the silk which had been already woven, rendering it worthless. They also smashed machinery and did as much damage to their masters' enterprises as they could, in this presaging some of the movements against industrialization and new machinery which took place outside of London. They were a formidable force that also played a major part in all the political and social upheavals of the time.

France began forced conversions to Catholicism in 1681, and in 1685 the Revocation of the Edict of Nantes outlawed Protestantism in France. Some 50,000 to 80,000 of these Protestants settled in England, about half of them in the London area, where they gravitated towards the two established French churches: in Threadneedle Street in the City, and at the Savoy in the West End. The Huguenot communities thus became based in Spitalfields and Soho. By 1700 there were nine French Protestant churches in the East End and twelve in the West End.

Protestant immigrants received a better welcome in London than others, partly as a result of virulent anti-Catholicism, partly because of propaganda that dwelt on the atrocities committed against Protestants in France. Despite the threat of anti-Huguenot riots in the East End in 1675, 1681 and 1683, there appears to have been little physical violence directed against the French refugees. After the Glorious Revolution in 1688 and the accession of William and Mary, Huguenots received a remarkable level of charitable support.

The Spitalfields silk workshops occupying the majority of the Huguenots made their owners extremely wealthy. One, Francis Goodchild, became lord mayor of London. Weaving only declined in the late 1700s, as silk was driven out of the market by new Indian and Chinese fabrics. The Spitalfields Acts passed between 1765 and 1801 aimed at controlling wages and working conditions, and to protect the domestic market from overseas competition. But the business continued to shrink. Weavers fought their masters to protect their livelihoods in violent clashes, particularly in 1768–69.

The Spitalfields Riots of those years were the result of heightened class conflict in the industry. This took place against a background of hardship and poverty among the working people of London and growing industrial unrest in a number of areas. The silk weavers wanted to control the prices in the industry. The conflict started as one between different groups of journeyman weavers, the single-hand or narrow weavers and those with engine looms. The masters had reduced the prices they paid for piece work, adding to the grievances. Angry weavers resorted to direct action, cutting the silk in the looms of those weavers who had 'broken the book' of fixed prices. In the summer of 1768, there were repeated 'cuttings' in Spitalfields. The weavers went armed, and in one raid shot a young man dead.

A new agreement in the wake of these events rapidly broke down. By now, the journeyman weavers had formed committees which collected a levy from any who owned looms to pay for organization and strike action. They called themselves the Bold Defiance. And they demanded money from the masters. One who refused to pay the levy was sent a threatening letter: 'Mr Obey, we give you an Egg Shell of Honey, but if you refuse to comply with the demands of yesterday, we'll give you a Gallon of Thorns to your final Life's End.'[10] The weavers met in various pubs in the area to collect money and to organize. In 1769 they set their own prices in the food markets.[11] Amid shortages of food and fuel, the weavers repeatedly resorted to destroying looms and cutting silk.

The looms of one journeyman weaver, Thomas Poor, were cut by a group led by John Doyle and John Valline. Valline also headed a crowd of 1,500 who attacked seventy-six looms belonging to master weaver Lewis Chauvet, because he wouldn't contribute to the committee funds. The authorities decided to intervene, and a meeting of silk weavers in the Dolphin pub in Bishopsgate was broken up by soldiers, with deaths on both sides. The big masters, led by Chauvet, now underwrote the costs of soldiers billeted in Spitalfields and effectively occupying the area; Doyle and Valline were tried and sentenced to death. In an attempt to cow the unruly and militant weavers, the authorities decided not to hang them at Tyburn as was usual, but in Bethnal Green at the heart of the weaving district.

Crowds lined the lengthy route from Newgate to the gallows, erected outside the Salmon and Ball pub which is still standing by Bethnal Green tube. The men expected to be rescued by the angry multitude which pelted the guards with rocks, but the execution went ahead. In anger and frustration, the gallows were torn down and reassembled outside Chauvet's house as thousands attacked the building, burning furniture and breaking windows.[12] The authorities never again dared to hang a weaver in Bethnal Green, and years later the weavers still bore a grudge against those who

---

10   G. Rudé, *The Crowd in History, 1730–1848* (London, 1981), p. 76.
11   Linebaugh, *The London Hanged*, p. 271.
12   Linebaugh, *The London Hanged,* pp. 280–1.

betrayed them. Eighteen months later, one of those who informed on them was cornered by an angry crowd and lynched.[13]

One lasting reminder of the Huguenot presence stands out. Just on the corner where Fournier Street, with its rows of Huguenot houses, meets Brick Lane in the East End of London stands the Jamme Masjid mosque. It started life in 1744 as a Huguenot church; fifty years later it became a Wesleyan chapel. From 1898 the building housed the Spitalfields Great Synagogue, serving the Eastern European Jewish community, until it was sold to the Bengali community in 1975. The building has been used for over two and a half centuries as a place of worship for the peoples of Spitalfields, yet the communities assembling within its walls have changed with successive waves of immigration to London. It stands today not only as the heart of the Bengali community but as a symbol of that movement and fluidity which is so characteristic of London's history.[14]

LOVE, MARRIAGE AND MOTHER'S RUIN

Marriages of the poor had often been common law agreements, but this changed with the Hardwicke Act of 1753, which tried to prevent clandestine marriages by decreeing that from 1754 all marriages had to be conducted in the Church of England (only Quakers and Jews were exempted). This was an attempt to staunch the tide of 'irregular marriages' in the early eighteenth century. In London there were dozens of 'Lawless churches', most famously the 'Fleet Prison Rules'. A business grew up around the Fleet prison to deal with clandestine marriages. The free market in marriages led to competition for custom, with people accosted in the streets 'Madam, you want a parson? . . . Sir, will you be pleased to walk in and be married?' Some 'marriers' would perform the service for two shillings and sixpence and sometimes even rented the ring to the couple. At another venue, the Savoy Chapel, it was estimated that almost 60 per cent of women marrying in the 1750s were pregnant.[15] Many women who became pregnant could not marry and found themselves in a desperate situation in the city. Newborn children were left abandoned or neglected by mothers who could not look after them. Thomas Coram set up his foundling hospital in 1741 in response to the number of such babies.

The paintings of Hogarth show perhaps some of the most familiar images of London, with scenes of dereliction and debauchery often as a result of drink. 'Gin Lane' was not an exaggeration: from around 1720 to 1750

13 Ibid., pp. 280–3.
14 See J. Price, 'History of Asylum in London', Researching Asylum in London, researchasylum.org.uk, accessed 6 July 2011.
15 J. R. Gillis, *For better, for Worse* (Oxford, 1985), pp. 90–8.

the excessive consumption of gin gave rise to major social and medical problems, and hence to a series of public outcries followed by attempts at social reform. In the early eighteenth century one in four houses in St Giles Rookery (the setting for Gin Lane) doubled as a gin-shop.[16] Distilling of gin was a major enterprise in London, encouraged by the government to deal with several years of over-production of corn. This highly alcoholic but popular drink no doubt served to dull the pain of existence for the poor and to endow them with a temporary sense of exhilaration. However, it destroyed the lives of many people, bringing to the slums an extra hazard and worsening standards of family life and health.

Various Acts of Parliament were passed to address this problem, but partial alleviation was actually a result of pricing it out of the reach of the poor. Reformers like Henry Fielding and Hogarth used their artistic talents to campaign against excessive drinking and its connection with poverty.[17] The cleaning up of Gin Lane by no means ended gin's influence in London; it remained a popular drink in London until well into the second half of the twentieth century, the Gordon's distillery prominent in pre-gentrified Clerkenwell until the 1970s and the name of 'mother's ruin' still in popular parlance as a reminder of its most notorious effects.

However, if the poor struggled they usually survived. While there was undeniable poverty and often, no doubt, hunger, those in power ensured that the basics were available. There were few bread riots in London since the civic authorities were careful to maintain affordable prices for bread and wheat. In addition there was less threat of riot from the countryside in lean years: 'England ... had virtually ceased to be a peasant country, and London was, at its most vulnerable point, cut off from the countryside by the protective shield of the near-urban county of Middlesex.'[18] The alternative to living in desperation was the workhouse, although it only achieved its full depths of notoriety a century later following the introduction of the Poor Law in 1834. While the workhouse was in theory a means of looking after the poorest in society, the hideous and punitive conditions which prevailed there ensured that it was viewed by many of the poor as an instrument of coercion.

LAW AND ORDER

How was the government to maintain control of this growing population in such a city, where little was planned and where everyone was left to fend

---

16   We are grateful to Neil Faulkner for this point.
17   George, *England in Transition*, pp. 68–9.
18   G. Rudé, *The Crowd in History* (London, 1981), p. 48.

for themselves? The favoured strategy of much of the city's rich and ruling elite was to clamp down on anyone who might challenge its supremacy, and to turn the very condition of being poor into a crime. There was also a very visible policy of deterrence. London in the eighteenth century was full of prisons: the most famous was Newgate, whose site was by the present Old Bailey, and which was the equivalent in London consciousness (and London memory) of the hated Paris Bastille. But there were also the Fleet, the Clink, the various Bridewells, and other lock-ups scattered across the working-class areas of Clerkenwell, St Giles or Southwark. The history of London in the eighteenth century is repeatedly interwoven with the history of these prisons. In a city as closely packed as London, with no police force until well into the nineteenth century, the prisons were a constant reminder to the poor of the weight of the law and how close they might be to retribution. And many of them were very close.

The number of hanging offences in English law expanded dramatically in the course of the eighteenth century, nearly all of them for crimes against property rather than the person. The Black Act passed in 1723 increased potentially capital offences to more than 200.[19] Theft in many cases was a capital offence, and many went to the gallows for stealing bread or a piece of meat. If the poor sometimes ended up as dangerous criminals, this legislation was also part of a process of criminalizing poverty itself. Those who stole from their masters, who left their apprenticeships early, or who were desperate to feed their families could all move very quickly from leading respectable working lives to seeing the inside of the prison walls.

Jack Sheppard was one of the poor who became a criminal. He was a legend in his own very short lifetime. When in 1724, at the age of twenty-two, he went to the gallows at Tyburn Tree he was a popular hero. In the public imagination his remarkable escapes from prison and the cat and mouse game he played with the authorities dwarfed his career as a robber; he remained a hero long after all his contemporaries were dead. He was the inspiration for the highwayman Macheath in John Gay's *The Beggar's Opera*, written four years later, and in which his nemesis Jonathan Wild was the jailer Peachum (to 'peach' meant to grass or inform). His story became an instant hit at fairs: *Harlequin Sheppard* was performed at the Bartholomew Fair in Smithfield, just round the corner from Newgate, only months later.[20] More than a century after his death in 1839, the novel *Jack Sheppard* written by Harrison Ainsworth proved a bestseller. It was also turned into a stage play, and frequently pirated.

---

19   R. Holmes, 'Introduction' in R. Holmes (ed.), *Defoe on Sheppard and Wild* (London, 2004), p. xiv; Thompson, *Making of the English Working Class*, pp. 64–6.
20   Holmes, *Defoe on Sheppard and Wild*, pp. xxvi–xxvii.

Such was the fear of Sheppard's example influencing the London poor that the Lord Chancellor responded by banning the licencing of any play with the name 'Jack Sheppard' in it for forty years.[21] His fame spread far outside London: Commissioner Horne, from the Children's Employment Commission, reported in 1841 that, of children in Wolverhampton, 'several had never heard the name of the Queen nor other names, such as Nelson, Wellington, Bonaparte; but it was noteworthy that those who had never heard even of St Paul, Moses, or Solomon, were very well instructed as to the life, deeds, and character of Dick Turpin, the street robber, and especially of Jack Sheppard, the thief and gaol-breaker.'[22]

Sheppard was not from a criminal family. Born in Spitalfields, the industrial silk-weaving area, in 1702, he was left in the Bishopsgate workhouse when his widowed mother went into service in the house of a draper. He was eventually apprenticed to a Covent Garden carpenter to follow the family trade. Indeed, Sheppard first fell foul of the law and was imprisoned for breaking his indentures, the terms of his apprenticeship as a carpenter, by leaving before his time was served. His path from apprentice in a respectable household to notorious criminal was not so distant from the lives of many young people in the city. His good looks, his romancing (his lover was Elizabeth Lyon, known as Edgworth Bess) and his daredevil behaviour all made him a hero in many eyes. Sheppard first escaped from the St Giles roundhouse in April, then from the new Bridewell prison in Clerkenwell in May, then from Newgate in August. Edgworth Bess helped him in a number of these escapes (as he had originally helped her), and his departure from Newgate was carried out by him dressing up as a woman. Recaptured the following month, Sheppard escaped from Newgate yet again, despite precautions including handcuffs, irons and chains within a locked room.

The amazement of the authorities and of London's population knew no bounds, although Jack himself was more modest in his 'true confessions': 'though people have made such an outcry about it, there is scarce a smith in London but what may easily do the same thing.'[23] Richard Holmes argues that while the escapes were daring, they were comprehensible in light of 'his outstanding skills as a carpenter and builder ... his great physical strength combined with a small gymnastic body [which] gave him a natural mastery of building materials and an instinctive understanding of the construction (and deconstruction) of every

21   R. Douglas-Fairhurst (ed.), 'Introduction' to H. Mayhew, *London Labour and the London Poor* (Oxford, 2010), note p. 443.
22   Quoted in F. Engels, *The Condition of the Working Class in England* (Moscow, 1973), p. 151.
23   Holmes, *Defoe on Sheppard and Wild*, p. 59.

kind of lock, wall, window, bar, spike, chimney-breast, floor, ceiling, roof or cellar.'[24]

In the period between his third and fourth escapes, when he was recaptured disguised as a butcher and again imprisoned in Newgate, Daniel Defoe described the mood in the city:

> His escape and his being so suddenly retaken made such a noise in the town, that it was thought all the common people would have gone mad about him, there not being a porter to be had for love nor money, nor getting into an alehouse, for butchers, shoemakers and barbers, all engaged in controversies and wagers about Sheppard … Tyburn Road [was] daily lined with women and children, and the gallows as carefully watched by night lest he should be hanged incog., for a report of that nature obtained much upon the rabble. In short, it was a week of the greatest noise and idleness among mechanics that has been known in London.[25]

The anticipation of Jack's fate at the gallows was more intense than usual, but of a piece with eighteenth-century attitudes to hanging. As E. P. Thompson put it, 'all the symbolism of "Tyburn Fair" was a ritual at the heart of London's popular culture.'[26] Executions attracted crowds with all the drama and paraphernalia of fairs and entertainments, despite their grim meaning. Tyburn was not the only place to fulfil the need for grisly spectacle. Across London, at Execution Dock in Wapping, hundreds of pirates were hanged between 1716 and 1726.[27] And in what is now part of south London, Surrey's convicts were hanged on Kennington Common.

DISSENT BEYOND THE LAW

The poor were not the only ones criminalized by the eighteenth-century state. Nearly any form of oppositional activity, or indeed radical thought, was made illegal. There was no democracy in Britain in the eighteenth century: the oligarchy which controlled the city and the country decreed that those who opposed its rule would be subject to the most severe repression. In the space of only eight years the Riot Act (1715), the Transportation Act (1719), the Combination Act (1721), the Workhouse Act (1723) and the Black Act (1723) all became law. Collectively they represented a determination to prevent collective forms of action among the emerging working

24   Ibid., p. xxi.
25   Ibid., p. 24.
26   Thompson, *Making of the English Working Class*, p. 66.
27   Linebaugh, *The London Hanged*, p. 19.

class and labouring poor either in the form of demonstrations or trade union organization.[28]

Thought crime was equally frowned upon. Those who, for whatever reason, rejected God and Priest and King were persecuted, banished, prosecuted and sometimes even executed for their beliefs. Even some who did believe in God were driven out: there was one established Church, headed by the king, and those who espoused alternative religions or ideas were not even allowed to live within the city walls. Dissenters from the Anglican Church of England were persecuted by five Acts of Parliament brought in at the Restoration and collectively known as the Clarendon Code, after Charles II's advisor Edward Hyde, Earl of Clarendon. The Five Mile Act (1665), the final act of the Code, ruled that Dissenting ministers were forbidden from coming within five miles of incorporated towns or the place of their former livings. They were also forbidden to teach in schools. This act was not rescinded until 1812.

While the Five Mile Act had the effect of physically removing fomenters of opposition to the establishment from the most populated parts of the city, it succeeded in establishing areas where dissenting ideas flourished. And while dissent from established ideas was effectively banned, the strength of non-conformist views of a non-religious nature also grew, gaining impetus in the second half of the century under the profound influence of first the American and then, more spectacularly, the French Revolution. This in turn had a big impact on London politics.

In the mid 1780s Mary Wollstonecraft first came into contact with radical ideas in Newington Green, outside the limits of the Act. Here she was to encounter new ways of thinking about society, women and education that were all important themes in her most famous book, *A Vindication of the Rights of Woman*. She arrived in Newington Green in her mid-twenties with her sisters Eliza and Everina, and her friend Fanny Blood took on responsibility for all of them – having encouraged Eliza, who was suffering from a breakdown, to leave her husband and baby. Mary had long hoped to live with Fanny and was to take care of the financial upkeep of Fanny's parents, with whom she had lived for some time previously near Fulham. The trio was joined by Everina who had left the home of her disapproving older brother.

As a solution to the vulnerable situation in which the women found themselves, Wollstonecraft decided they should set up a girls' school. The educational requirements of girls were considered to be so inferior to those of their brothers that it was quite usual for such schools to be set up by women with no educational training. However, Wollstonecraft

---

28   Linebaugh, *The London Hanged*, pp. 16–18. The story of eighteenth-century London is well illustrated by this book, on which we will draw for some analysis.

developed an interest in radical theories of education, including those of the Enlightenment thinker Jean-Jacques Rousseau whom she would later reproach (in *A Vindication*) for his advocacy of an inferior quality of education for girls – something she argued was inconsistent with Enlightenment ideas of reason. These ideas were promoted in her first book *Thoughts on the Education of Daughters*, written at Newington Green.

Although an Anglican, Wollstonecraft soon became acquainted with the radical circle of Dissenters that lived in and around the Green. She went to the Dissenter chapel – which remains on the Green today – to hear the sermons of Dr Richard Price. Price had supported parliamentary reform and the American independence movement, and was in contact with foreign radicals including Benjamin Franklin and Thomas Jefferson. Perhaps most importantly for Wollstonecraft, many Dissenters held groundbreaking ideas about women's rights and had, in their milieu, women who defied convention and established themselves as commentators and pamphleteers on subjects including education and politics. Hungry for ideas, she made friends with John Hewlett, a local schoolmaster who introduced her to Dr Johnson, then living in nearby Islington, and Joseph Johnson, another Dissenter, interested in radicalism and ideas around education. He was also a publisher, and was to bring out Wollstonecraft's *Thoughts on the Education of Daughters* and *A Vindication of the Rights of Woman*.[29]

William Blake, the poet and artist, was also from a Dissenting family (though they managed to live well within the five-mile exclusion zone). In fact Blake could not have lived more centrally. Born in 1757, his parents ran a haberdashers shop in Golden Square in Soho, and he spent his youth in the streets of central London and the fields that were still to be found off Tottenham Court Road. Blake was an artisan, a radical, a non-conformist, a republican, and egalitarian in his politics. After training as an engraver with James Basire in premises near Lincoln's Inn Fields, by 1779 he had entered the Royal Academy, then at Somerset House in the Aldwych. He was at the head of the crowd when Newgate prison was destroyed in the Gordon Riots of 1780. Some say his engraving 'Albion Rose', with its line 'Albion rose from where he labour'd at the mill with slaves', is Blake's reflection on the riots.[30] He supported the French Revolution in the 1790s and 'courageously donned the famous symbol of liberty and equality – the *bonnet rouge* – in open day'.[31] His poem 'The French Revolution' was contained in the only book he ever produced that was designed for mass reproduction. It was

---

29   For more on Mary Wollstonecraft see C. Tomalin, *The Life and Death of Mary Wollstonecraft* (London, 1992), esp. Chapter 4, 'Newington Green and the Dissenters'.
30   See J. Cox, *William Blake, The Scourge of Tyrants* (London, 2004), p. 31.
31   Ibid., p. 38.

given to Joseph Johnson to print but it never saw the light of day. Perhaps Johnson was too intimidated to proceed; he certainly pulled out of Tom Paine's *Rights Of Man* for that reason.[32]

WILKES AND 'A MOB THAT CAN READ'

John Wilkes was also a Londoner, born in Clerkenwell, the son of a distiller. Part-educated in the Dutch Republic, he was sympathetic to dissenters throughout his career. He came into an estate in Buckinghamshire by his marriage to Mary Meade, though the pairing lasted less than a decade. Indeed Wilkes had a reputation as a rake despite being famously ugly, and was associated with the Hellfire Club of the Earl of Sandwich and Sir Francis Dashwood.

In the 1760s Wilkes was the MP for Aylesbury, a supporter of both Pitt the Elder and the Seven Years War. When Pitt was replaced by John Stuart, Earl of Bute, Wilkes started a newspaper to attack him. The earl's own paper was called *The Briton* and, in mockery of his target's Scottish origins, Wilkes called his paper *The North Briton*. Wilkes was particularly affronted by what he took to be the overly generous terms offered to the French in the Treaty of Paris of 1763, which was endorsed in George III's King's Speech to the Opening of Parliament in April that year. The speech was written by Bute and pilloried by Wilkes in issue No. 45 of the *North Briton*. The Treaty was, wrote Wilkes, 'the most abandoned instance of ministerial affrontry ever attempted', and the peace was 'certainly the peace of God, for it passeth all understanding'.[33]

George III charged Wilkes with seditious libel and issued a general warrant for his arrest, along with forty-nine others said to have been involved in the publication of the libel. The general warrant was a despot's dream: it could be issued for the arrest of unnamed persons and for the seizure of unspecified papers. A general warrant made it legal for the state to 'force person's houses', break open their desks and take their papers. However, the government bungled the arrest as Wilkes outwitted those sent to detain him. His case was heard in front of a fellow Pitt supporter, Chief Justice Pratt, in the Court of Common Pleas, and in the second of two court appearances Wilkes made a brilliant speech in which he asserted that his case turned on 'a question of such importance as to determine at once whether English liberty shall be a reality or a shadow'.

---

32   For a detailed and interesting study of Blake and his ideas see E. P. Thompson, *Witness against the Beast* (Cambridge, 1993).

33   I. Gilmour, *Riot, Risings and Revolution* (London, 1992), p. 305.

Pratt released Wilkes, on the basis that he had acted under parliamentary privilege.

On his release the gathered crowd shouted 'Wilkes and Liberty!' for the first, but not the last, time. 'An immense mob', according to Boswell, 'saluted him with loud huzza while he stood bowing from his window' at his house in Great George Street.[34] This crowd contained people 'of far higher rank than the common Mob'. But later in the year when the government ordered the *North Briton* burnt outside the Royal Exchange it was some 500 of the 'lower orders' that pelted the sheriffs with mud and refused to let the hangman continue the burning.[35] Wilkes successfully sued the government over the general warrants case. It was a signal victory that left general warrants effectively dead, although the Commons did not make them illegal until 1766.

The victory encouraged Wilkes. He had a printing press set up in his own house, reprinting issue No. 45 of the *North Briton* and, for good measure, just a dozen copies of the obscene poem 'An Essay on Woman' with his own notes, as a satirical reply to Alexander Pope's 'Essay on Man'. The target was not Pope, but, as ever, Bute and the government. This he dedicated to his old Hellfire Club friends, the Earl of Sandwich and Francis Dashwood, now Lord Despencer. They didn't see the joke and immediately began a new action against Wilkes. The government actually printed more copies of 'An Essay on Woman' and Sandwich read it aloud to the House of Lords. When one peer called for the reading to stop, he was drowned out by cries of 'Go on!' It was, said Dashwood, the first time he had heard Satan preaching against sin. When Sandwich told Wilkes that 'you will die either on the gallows or of the pox', Wilkes is said to have replied, 'That must depend on whether I embrace your lordship's principles or your mistress.'[36]

But for all the laughable hypocrisy of the government, Wilkes was in trouble. At about the same time a premeditated trap was sprung to engage him in a duel, and he was badly wounded in the encounter. He also had to evade the attentions of a deranged Scot who attempted to break into his house and murder him. Despite being watched by government spies he managed to flee to Paris, where his beloved daughter Polly was living. The Commons immediately turned Wilkes out of his seat and, in a rigged trial, he was found guilty of libel and declared an outlaw. Wilkes did not return to London until 1768. His return occasioned an epic battle between the old order and the reform

---

34   Ibid., p. 307.
35   Rudé, *The Crowd in History*, p. 55.
36   J. Lynch, 'Wilkes, Liberty, and Number 45', *Colonial Williamsburg Journal* (Summer 2003), available online at history.org. (The quip is often wrongly attributed to Disraeli.)

movement, a battle in which, wrote one contemporary, 'a mob that can read and a Ministry that can not think are sadly matched'.[37]

THE OUTLAW MP FOR MIDDLESEX

Economic conditions had been worsening during Wilkes's years in France, 1763–68. The London weavers rioted in May 1765. Rioting and rick-burning were widespread in 1766, and the following year saw widespread industrial unrest in London during an exceptionally cold winter. Then, to add to government woes, Wilkes returned from France. He immediately attempted to become an MP for the City in March 1768. He failed, in a constituency still too conservative to respond to Wilkes's message. But the same month Wilkes stood as MP for Middlesex, a constituency which then included poorer urban areas surrounding the City and Westminster north of the Thames. Here, Wilkes's supporters among the tradesmen, craftsmen and 'forty-shilling freeholders' were in the majority.

Horace Walpole recorded the scene on election day:

> By five in the morning a very large body of Weavers etc, took posses-sion of Piccadilly, and the roads and turnpikes leading to Brentford, and would suffer nobody to pass without blue cockades and papers inscribed, 'No. 45, Wilkes and Liberty'. They tore to pieces the coaches of Sir W Beauchamp Procter, and Mr Cooke, the other candidates ... They stopped every carriage and spoilt several with writing all over them 'No. 45', pelted, threw dirt and stones and forced everyone to huzza for Wilkes ... At night they insisted, in several streets, on houses being illuminated [as a sign of support for Wilkes], and several Scotch refusing, had their windows broken. Another mob arose in the City ... and the Mansion House not being illuminated ... they broke every window, and tried to force their way into the House.

The Trained Bands were called out but they were insufficient, so Guards had to be brought from the Tower before the crowd could be dispersed. But at 1am the crowd gathered again and attacked the house of Wilkes's nemesis Lord Bute in Audley Street. 'They flung two large flints into Lady Bute's chamber, who was in bed, and broke every window in the house.'[38]

Wilkes was elected, making him both an MP and an outlaw on the run. He decided to give himself up, although he had to escape from his own

---

37   Gilmour, *Riot, Risings and Revolution*, p. 334.
38   H. Walpole, 'Wilkes and the Mob, March 1768' in J. E. Lewis (ed.), *London: The Autobiography* (London, 2008), pp. 218–19.

supporters in order to do so. He was incarcerated in the King's Bench prison and for two weeks the approaches to the jail were jammed with protesting, sometimes rioting, Wilkesite supporters. On 10 May 1768 a huge demonstration assembled outside the prison in St George's Fields, now the site of Waterloo station. Justice Gillan read the Riot Act, and was struck on the head by a stone for his pains. Soldiers chased the culprit but ended up bayoneting and shooting William Allen, a bystander not even involved in the demonstration. Unsurprisingly the crowd became 'more riotous and violent'. The Riot Act was read a second time, the order to shoot was given to the troops and eleven people, again including passers-by, were left dead. Many more were wounded. Weeks of rioting now shook the capital and the effect of the tumult was immediate. On 8 June even hard-line Judge Mansfield had to rule that Wilkes's outlaw condition should be undone.[39]

The Ministry that 'can not think' connived to deepen its own unpopularity. It ensured that no soldier involved in the killings at the massacre of St Georges Field was ever convicted. Then the Courts reversed the Mansfield ruling, fined Wilkes £1,000 and sent him to jail for twenty-two months. The electors of Middlesex responded by electing Serjeant Glynn, Wilkes's legal counsel in all his cases, as their second MP. Then, as the year 1769 opened, the electors of Farringdon Without in the City elected Wilkes as their alderman with 1,300 of the available 1,500 votes. On 3 February 1769 the government expelled Wilkes from the Commons, with the predictable result of more rioting. Middlesex re-elected Wilkes on 16 February, a triumph he could only enjoy from his cell. A day later the Commons declared the election void and expelled him again. Middlesex elected him once again on 16 March; the government expelled him yet again the next day. Wilkes stood yet again and won once more on 13 April, by which time even Parliament could see that this was not working. So, even though Wilkes had received 1,143 votes and his opponent, Colonel Henry Lawes Luttrell, 296, the House of Commons ruled that Luttrell 'ought to have been returned', and declared him the winner.[40]

Protest meetings flared into existence in all corners of London and beyond. Organized by the Wilkesite Society for the Protection of the Bill of Rights, some eighteen counties petitioned the king. Five days after his last exclusion, Wilkes had to leave prison to visit a judge in chambers. On his way back the crowd unhitched the horses from his coach to pull it themselves. For a second time Wilkes had to escape from his own

---

39   G. Rudé, *Wilkes and Liberty: A Social Study of 1763 to 1774* (Oxford, 1962), pp. 38–56.
40   Lynch, 'Wilkes, Liberty, and Number 45'.

supporters to return to captivity. When he was released in April 1770 he was greeted by the greatest crowds since the coronation. Unable to take his seat in Parliament, Wilkes used his position as city alderman to great effect in the battle between the City and the Commons over the right to report parliamentary debates in the public press.

The Commons had a tradition of regarding the reporting of its debates as a breach of privilege, and in 1771 it arrested a group of printers for so doing. Wilkes used the City's claim to jurisdiction within its own boundaries to create test cases where those attempting to stop printers reporting Parliament were found guilty, not the printers themselves. The Commons huffed and puffed, summoned Wilkes, and sent one of his fellow aldermen to the Tower. Huge crowds once again surrounded Westminster and 'some in very high office narrowly escaped with their lives', reported Charles Fox. The lord mayor was summoned to Westminster, drawn there in his carriage by his supporters and accompanied by another enormous mob. The Commons voted to send him to the Tower. But the government blinked, and refused to act on the vote. They ordered Wilkes to attend on 8 April, knowing he would not obey. So then they voted to adjourn the whole Commons until 9 April, a day after Wilkes would have been meant to attend. It was one way of having 'nothing more to do with that devil Wilkes', as George III had instructed his ministers. The printers were not prosecuted. It was another victory for Wilkes and the crowd.[41]

ATLANTIC CROSSINGS

It is impossible to view the events of the last quarter of the eighteenth century in London without setting them against an international background. In 1776, the English colonies in what is now the United States of America declared their independence from the English Crown, and so began a war which lasted for the best part of a decade but which eventually succeeded in establishing an independent country. In some ways the demands of the colonies echoed broader eigthteenth-century complaints about lack of representation, increased taxation and remote, autocratic government.

The years of Wilkes's popular ascendancy were also the years in which the crisis between the British state and its American colonies was reaching its revolutionary conclusion. In 1775 Wilkes, now restored to Parliament, spoke against the king's declaring Massachusetts to be in rebellion and wondered whether 'in a few years the independent

---

41   Gilmour, *Riot, Risings and Revolution*, pp. 322–5; Rudé, *The Crowd in History*, p. 57.

Americans may not celebrate the glorious era of the revolution of 1775 as we do that of 1688'.[42] He was only out by a year. Like Wilkes, the colonists resented the general warrants used against them, and they demanded the right to name their representatives. Wilkes was a supporter of the colonists and they, in the main, were supporters of Wilkes. Benjamin Franklin, then in London, may have dismissed Wilkes as 'an outlaw ... not worth a farthing', but James Otis, John Adams, Samuel Adams, and John Hancock all signed petitions in his favour. Wilkes-Barre, Pennsylvania, and Wilkesboro, North Carolina, took their names from the author of No. 45. In Boston the number 45 was inscribed on many windows and doors all over town. In South Carolina, workingmen 'consecrated' a pole with forty-five lights. In New York, a jailed writer comparing himself to Wilkes was, according to reports, visited by forty-five friends for a feast to consume forty-five pounds of beef, followed by forty-five toasts. Citizens of Virginia and Maryland resolved to send Wilkes forty-five hogsheads of tobacco, while forty-five women in Lexington, Massachusetts, joined together to spin American linen to protest British policies. When Wilkes was released from prison the Club Forty-Five in Charleston met at 7:45, drank forty-five toasts, and adjourned at 12:45. Some adulation was almost religious. *Britannia's Intercession for the Deliverance of John Wilkes, Esq., from Persecution and Banishment* included an imitation of the Apostle's Creed:

I believe in Wilkes, the firm patriot, maker of number 45. Who was born for our good. Suffered under arbitrary power. Was banished and imprisoned. He descended into purgatory, and returned some time after. He ascended here with honour and sitteth amidst the great assembly of the people, where he shall judge both the favourite and his creatures. I believe in the spirit of his abilities, that they will prove to the good of our country. In the resurrection of liberty, and the life of universal freedom forever. Amen.[43]

Wilkes had quoted Cromwell favourably in Parliament, and in 1776 the same parallel was occurring to colonial mothers in the backwoods who were naming their children Oliver in memory of Cromwell. The support for Wilkes in the Americas should remind us that radical traditions are international as much as national. And they are great migrators. They find a home abroad when domestic conditions are inhospitable, and they

---

42   Gilmour, *Riot, Risings and Revolution*, p. 327.
43   Lynch, 'Wilkes, Liberty, and Number 45'; B. Deming, 'Wilkes, American Colonists, and *The North Briton*: Why Was Colonial America So Fascinated with the Number 45?', online at suite101.com.

return home, enhanced by the experience of travel, when times improve. Importantly for London, the politics of the American revolutionaries and their religion was based on that of their predecessors, many of whom had fled England and crossed the Atlantic in order to be able to practise their Protestant religion and to adhere to democratic and republican beliefs. The links between the two countries were strong: with many having family ties on both sides of the ocean, ideological and religious beliefs were shared.[44]

LONDON AND THE SLAVE TRADE

London was as important to the slave trade as Liverpool or Bristol. By the end of the seventeenth century the Royal African Company had 500 ships involved in the 'triangular trade' of taking slaves to the West Indies plantations and bringing sugar back to Britain. By 1750, London merchants handled nearly 75 per cent of the sugar that Britain imported. The 'factorage' system, in which commission agents provided the long-term loans necessary for the slave trade, was run from the City.[45] Some of the most famous names in banking – Alexander and David Barclay, Francis Baring – made money from the slave trade. All through the eighteenth century the governors and directors of the Bank of England made fortunes by the same means. Such wealth was often used to buy seats in the House of Commons. In the mid-eighteenth century, contemporary observers reckoned that West India interests controlled forty seats in the Commons. When the abolition movement gained momentum in the last quarter of the century, it was this highly compacted bloc of economic and political power that it had to confront.[46]

Slaves were sold in the streets, coffee houses and taverns of London. In 1728 an advertisement asked buyers to 'Inquire at the Virginia Coffee-House in Threadneedle Street, behind the Royal-Exchange' if they wished to purchase 'a Negro boy, aged about Eleven years'. In 1769 another advertisement invited enquiries at the Bull and Gate Inn, Holborn, about the sale of a carriage, two horses and 'a well-made, good tempered Black Boy'. In the same year 'a Black Girl, the Property of John Bull, Eleven Years of Age' was offered for sale and described as 'extremely handy, works at her Needle tolerably, and speaks English

44   For a very good account of the politics and lead-up to the American Revolution, see E. Countryman, *The American Revolution* (London, 1985).
45   P. Fryer, *Staying Power: The History of Black People in Britain* (London, 1984), p. 44.
46   Ibid., pp. 47–50.

perfectly well; is of an excellent Temper, and Willing Disposition'. There were many other such bargains.[47]

London could also be a refuge for black people, and its local populations were sympathetic to escaped slaves. Most blacks originally lived in the relatively poor parishes of the East End, but by the eighteenth century black men and women were more widely dispersed across many of London's working-class communities. Some alehouses catered for a predominantly black clientele and social events were organized in black communities.[48] The aptly named racist Philip Thicknesse complained that 'London abounds with an incredible number of these black men, who have clubs to support those who are out of place'.[49] At the same time black people participated fully in the plebeian culture of the capital. In 1768 the magistrate Sir John Fielding, half-brother of the novelist Henry Fielding, bemoaned the fact that blacks in London were becoming 'intoxicated with Liberty'; worse, it was 'not only difficult but dangerous' to try and recapture escaped slaves, because they succeeded in getting 'the Mob on their Side'.

The year in which Fielding made this comment was the very year in which this 'mob' was pouring into the London streets and declaring for 'Wilkes and Liberty'. No wonder Fielding was perturbed that Blacks were having their minds 'enlarged' by 'the Sweets of Liberty and the Conversation with free Men and Christians'. This, he said, was making them 'restless' and liable to 'execute the blackest Conspiracies against their Governors and Masters'.[50]

1780: THE GORDON RIOTS

The fate of the American Revolution was the background to the Gordon Riots which broke out in the summer of 1780. The riots marked the most serious disturbances ever seen in London, lasted a week and saw the destruction of Newgate and serious attacks on the Bank of England. Hundreds of rioters were dead by the end, killed by troops who were sent in to disperse them. Here the London mob came into its own, kindling terror among the property-owning classes. Such was the memory of the events among Londoners that, decades later, Charles Dickens centred his novel *Barnaby Rudge* on the events.

The riots were identified with and named after Lord George Gordon, the highly eccentric Scotsman and militant Protestant who led a campaign

---

47 Ibid., pp. 60–1.
48 C. Emsley, T. Hitchcock and R. Shoemaker, 'Communities – Black Communities', Old Bailey Proceedings Online, oldbaileyonline.org, accessed 6 July 2011.
49 Fryer, *Staying Power*, p. 70.
50 Ibid., p.71.

for repeal of the Catholic Relief Act. This Act was aimed at ending some elements of the discrimination against Catholics which existed in Britain as a legacy of the previous 200 years of political and religious turmoil, especially in the aftermath of the Civil War and Revolution. The defence of this view was articulated by Gordon in the House of Commons shortly before the riots began, when he boasted to the Speaker: 'In a few days, Sir, I shall present you the Petition of the Protestant Association. It will extend, Sir, from your chair to a window at Whitehall that Kings should often think of.'[51]

Feelings ran high at the law being changed, not just because of the distrust which many Protestants felt for Catholics or because of the identification of Catholicism at home and abroad with reaction. The sense that Catholics would be recruited to the army to fight against their Protestant co-religionists in America led to a growing grievance, which Gordon articulated. 'Characteristic of Protestantism had been a fierce hatred of tyranny, by Pope or King. Yet here was a war, manifestly pursued by the Crown, which was using all the attributes of corruption and oppression to impose a tyranny on the descendants of those who had fought such evils.'[52]

Gordon's campaign against the Catholic Relief Act took the form of a mass petition which was to be delivered physically to Parliament by a huge demonstration going from St George's Fields, across the river. On a warm and summery 2 June, many thousands of men and women gathered, listening to speeches, cheering and eventually setting off, the petition held aloft on their shoulders – presumably resembling a huge rolled carpet, the document's different sections sewn together by a tailor.

The march followed two routes, one directly across Westminster Bridge, the other through the City until it too came to Parliament. Here the crowd attacked members of the House of Lords who were arriving at the House to debate. The manhandling of the lords outside the palace of Westminster showed the strength of feeling of the crowd. The lord chief justice, Lord Mansfield, had his wig torn from his head and his carriage windows broken; the archbishop of York was forced to repeat 'No popery'; Lord North had his hat snatched from his head while he sat in his carriage, while several MPs had their coaches demolished.[53] The march then turned into days of rioting across what is now central London; and yet the demonstration itself was highly organized and disciplined, although manifesting very high feelings. Even the rough treatment meted out to some lords and MPs followed

---

51   C. Hibbert, *King Mob* (Sutton, 2004), p. 40.
52   J. Nicholson, *The Great Liberty Riot of 1780* (London, 1985), p. 11.
53   Hibbert, *King Mob*, pp. 46–9.

a regular pattern which had occurred in various previous demonstrations and gatherings in Whitehall.[54]

The crowd which made its way from Whitehall, up through Covent Garden to what is now Kingsway, was rather different in its composition from the earlier demonstration. According to many accounts it contained more petty criminals, prostitutes and drunks, and less of the respectable hymn-singing Protestants who led the various divisions on the original march. In Holborn, the Catholic chapel of the Sardinian ambassador – a popular place of worship for rich English Catholics – was attacked and burnt.

Houses belonging to rich Catholics or their supporters, and especially to representatives of foreign Catholic powers, were attacked and burnt down. Anti-Irish demonstrations initially took place in Moorfields, one of the poorest suburbs just outside the City walls and home to large numbers of Irish Catholics.

Albany Wallis was walking past the Admiralty after dinner on 6 June when he met people hurrying in the opposite direction, and was informed they were going to burn Newgate. He returned to his dinner hosts to warn the party, which included the playwright Richard Brinsley Sheridan. 'They all laughed and no one would believe me. However, away I ran to Newgate ... Fortunately, while I was standing facing a door, an offer was made me, that upon paying sixpence I might place myself at the garret-window, which I readily accepted.'[55]

Newgate Prison was the hated symbol of an unjust law and a terrible oppression which hung over so many poor Londoners. It was also where a number of those arrested because of the riots had been taken. The aim was to free them and other prisoners, which duly happened as the flames from the destroyed prison lit up the night sky. The shock at the destruction of Newgate was palpable, not least because it was a clearly organized attack but because it was signalled in advance, implying that that the rioters had their own agenda, rather than being simply a spontaneous outburst.

A common view of the Gordon Riots is that expressed in Christopher Hibbert's popular history *King Mob* (and indeed in Dickens): that a cause was hijacked by an unruly and drunken horde of criminals, prostitutes and general riff-raff, who turned the demonstration into an orgy of destruction which, insofar as it had any aim, was a brutal and prejudiced expression of Protestant determination to keep Catholics down. Hibbert describes some of those tried and convicted for the riots thus: 'Among the pathetic motley of those condemned to death were two gypsies, a West Indian slave, a

---

54 Nicholson, *Great Liberty Riot*, pp. 31–2.
55 Quoted in Hibbert, *King Mob*, p. 83.

demented cross-eyed beggar, three abscess-covered climbing boys and a negro prostitute.'[56]

The idea of the riots as a series of mindless acts of crime and destruction does not do justice to the issues, or to the sensibilities and consciousness of the poor in eighteenth-century London. In fact, as much of the evidence in Hibbert's own book demonstrates, the character of the riots was much more complex than he allows. They were firstly the expression of the discontent felt by many of the poor and dispossessed in London. This discontent, not for the first or last time, expressed itself in part through militant adherence to the Protestant faith. However, the riots, whatever their anti-Catholic flavour – and consequences for the Irish in Moorfields, for example – quickly turned into riots against property, authority and reactionary foreign regimes. Indeed, 'the Catholics whose houses were attacked were not those living in the most densely populated Catholic districts' – that is, the more working-class areas such as the docks or St Giles – but rather in the better-off and more fashionable districts.[57]

This raises the question of how closely class and Catholicism were bound up together, and draws attention to the way class was beginning to over-take religion as a key division as the riots continued. That much was clear from the burning of the Sardinian ambassador's chapel, from the repeated attacks on the lord chief justice, including the burning down of his house, and from the destruction of Newgate prison and other prisons which were in part about, and resulted in, the freeing of prisoners – including those already imprisoned for the rioting. Indeed, even Hibbert makes the point that

> In alliance with these criminals and fanatics were the thousands upon thousands of ordinary, poor working men and women and children, flowing out of the slums of Shoreditch, Spitalfields and St Giles's and the unpaved, unlit, decaying warrens of streets and courtyards down by the river. Pale and forgotten people, ill, hollow-cheeked and hungry they poured from doss-houses, brothels, crowded cellars and workshops to watch the houses burning; to run forward to grab a leg of mutton from a larder, a bottle from a cellar, a scorched blanket from a bonfire.[58]

Nor were the targets random, or the product of mob sentiment. There was a very careful policy of the 'mob' to attack certain targets and people but

---

56 Ibid., p. 143.
57 Rudé, *The Crowd in History*, p. 24.
58 Hibbert, *King Mob*, p. 92.

not others. There was talk of the existence of lists of houses to be destroyed, which may or may not have been true, but which certainly was believed by many. As George Rudé's classic study points out:

> In the Gordon Riots, considerable care was taken to avoid damage to neighbouring property, and where the wrong targets suffered it was due to the wind rather than to the rioters' intentions. Violence was discriminating in another sense as well. It was limited to property and, of all the lives lost in 1780, it is remarkable that all were from the side of the rioters and not one from among their victims.[59]

In addition, the riots were attached to a political cause, however contradictory their cause was. They were campaigning against Catholicism, which they saw as a bastion of reaction, and they were given some licence and even help from certain sections of the political establishment, especially that of the City of London. 'The Common Council of the City of London ... which prided itself on its political independence ... opposed the policies of Westminster and St James's almost continuously ... between 1730 and 1780.'[60] In this way the political leaders of the City became 'the real political educator of London's "lower orders"'.[61]

While there is some evidence that the lord mayor initially turned a blind eye to the riots for these reasons, for example doing nothing to stop the attacks on Irish houses in Moorgate, it is also clear that the rioters went from expressing defence of the Protestant cause and resentment of Catholicism, to attacking targets which were, essentially, the symbols of law and order, repression and wealth. While the prisons were partly stormed for the immediate aims of freeing rioters and others, such actions were also a cry of rage against an extensive system of repression which must have cast a long shadow everywhere in that London of gaols, Bridewells, roundhouses, compters and lock-ups.

There were also attacks on industrialists, judges and aristocrats. The same night that the London crowd torched Newgate they went on to Bloomsbury Square, about a mile away, and destroyed the house of Lord Chief Justice Mansfield. This was no accidental act of marauding bands, but a deliberate attack on a hated judge who, as Peter Linebaugh notes, had 'adapted a legal system that had arisen in feudalism to the requirements of a ruling class aspiring to world conquest and indebted to merchants and capitalists'.[62] Sitting at the Old Bailey at least once a year, over the seventeen sessions

---

59   Rudé, *The Crowd in History*, p. 60.
60   Ibid., p. 51.
61   Ibid.
62   Linebaugh, *The London Hanged*, p. 358.

which he presided '29 people were branded, 448 were transported and 102 were hanged'.[63]

From court records it is also clear that the majority of the rioters were not the '200 house brakers with tools; 550 pickpockets; 6000 of alsorts; 50 men that … give them orders what to be done; they only come att night' that one anonymous informer suggested. Instead, repeatedly, workers and artisans were brought up for trial. As George Rudé says, 'we may be reasonably confident that the rioters were a fair cross-section of London's working population: two in every three of those tried were wage earners –journeymen, apprentices, waiters, domestic servants and labourers; a smaller number were petty employers, craftsmen or tradesmen.'[64]

So the Gordon riots were the doing of large numbers of working and poor Londoners, driven to these actions by a combination of identification of Catholicism with reactionary sections of the ruling class, class resentment, and hostility to changes in the way the city was organized, for example the tolls on the new Blackfriars Bridge; in sum, a rage against the criminalization of their lives which was such a part of politics and society at this time. And it was the class divisions and destruction of property, not the religious issues, which eventually led to a brutal crackdown on the rioters in which up to 500 died, having themselves caused no loss of life whatsoever.

The troops eventually sent out to crush the riots were initially sympathetic, as were some of the more privileged of London. There is some evidence that the riots were at first 'licensed' by sections of the establishment for their own interests. That changed when the rioters attacked the Bank of England, following on from their success at Newgate. They also tried to destroy the tollbooths on Blackfriars Bridge. This affront to property and the whole economic system in London was an attack too far. The popular Londoners' hero John Wilkes, who had been supported by the London mob through thick and thin, now led the yeomanry to fight the rioters and to restore order in the City. Hundreds of Londoners died in the riots, especially in the fighting round Blackfriars Bridge where many were pushed into the river.

THE LONDON CORRESPONDING SOCIETY, THOMAS PAINE AND THE REVIVAL OF RADICALISM

Thomas Paine was from a Quaker family in Thetford, Norfolk. He probably heard John Wilkes speak when he was a tax official in Lewes in Sussex, when he certainly already held radical views. But it was his migration to

---

63   Ibid., p. 360.
64   Rudé, *The Crowd in History*, pp. 60–1.

America and his participation in the War of Independence which made his name. He fought his fellow countrymen as a soldier in the revolutionary army, but it was with his pen that he became famous. *Common Sense* (1776), Paine's anonymously published, first mass seller, was a defence of the revolution. But even this achievement was overshadowed when he returned to Britain and wrote *The Rights of Man*, published in two parts in 1791 and 1792, although joint editions followed. The *Rights of Man* was a reply to Edmund Burke's *Reflections on the Revolution in France* – itself an attack on a sermon by Richard Price, the dissenting minister from Stoke Newington's Unitarian Chapel. Paine's direct and democratic prose style explains much of its success, but it is also true that the *Rights of Man* could not possibly have had the impact that it did without the organizational effort of the London Corresponding Society.

While many reform societies were shocked by the radically egalitarian message of the *Rights of Man*, the LCS was deliberately formed to disseminate that message among the poor. Thomas Hardy, a Piccadilly boot-maker employing half a dozen craftsmen, founded the LCS shortly after Paine published Part One of the *Rights of Man*. Hardy, and his associates Horne Tooke and John Frost, were determined that the message of the American Revolution should reach 'tradesmen, shopkeepers and mechanics'. The LCS, formed by nine 'well-meaning, sober and industrious men' in the Bell Tavern in Exeter Street, off the Strand, in January 1792, had by the end of the year the support of about a thousand artisans, tradesmen and workmen, each paying a penny a week.

Swiftly the LCS membership swelled to 5,000 and its meetings were held in pubs across the metropolis, especially in Spitalfields. The club was soon at the heart of a national network of corresponding societies and, from May 1792, was in touch with the Jacobin Club in Paris. Some of the leaders were well-off, like the lawyers Joseph Gerrald and Maurice Margarot, but in general the LCS was characterized by a more radical, popular and working-class hostility to the political and economic status quo than had previously been expressed in the movement for political reform.

Through the channels of the LCS network, letters and cheap copies of Paine found their way across the country. LCS leader John Thelwall's popular lectures and the publications of radical bookseller Thomas Spence of High Holborn were part of this expanding popular radicalism. As John Keane, Paine's modern biographer, records: 'Paine's name became identical with the agitation, at a depth and with an intensity unheard-of since the failed revolution of the 1640s, if ever, for the extension of democracy.' Opponents complained that Paine's supporters 'load their asses with their pernicious pamphlets and . . . get them dropped, not only in cottages, and in highways, but into mines and coal-pits'.

A sixpenny copy of the *Rights of Man* was found in the hands of croft-ers in Scotland, tin-miners in Cornwall, shepherds in Cumbria, shoemak-ers in Norwich as well as in 'almost every hand' of those in the Midlands Potteries and of 'every cutler' in Sheffield. North Wales was, complained a government informer, 'infested with Methodist preachers who descant on the *Rights of Man* and attack Kingly Government', and an equally hostile observer in Dundee asked: 'can you imagine that a single person has sold here more than 1,000 of T. Payne's pamphlet'. In the whole of Scotland, it was claimed, 10,000 copies a week were being sold 'at a very low price'.[65] In England, Scotland and Wales the *Rights of Man* are conservatively estimated to have sold 200,000 copies.[66]

By 1792 the British government, assailed on three fronts, was sufficiently alarmed to begin a sustained campaign of repression. Firstly, the radical-izing course of the French Revolution meant that the government could no longer argue that France's turmoil was more of an opportunity for the British state than a threat to it. Secondly, the likelihood of revolutionary contagion throughout Europe menaced the balance of power on the conti-nent and British interests themselves. Thirdly, the impact of the Revolution domestically was to embolden and encourage British radicals.

As a result Paine found himself specifically targeted. In April 1792 he was arrested outside the London Tavern, supposedly for an unpaid debt to a former colleague. The bookseller and printer Joseph Johnson, Mary Wollstonecraft's associate, stood bail. Then in May, on the same day that the government issued a proclamation against 'wicked and seditious writ-ings', it also issued a writ for seditious libel against Paine, who was forced to flee to France. But Paine was not the only target. John Frost was arrested for saying in a Marylebone coffee house that he was 'for equality' and 'no king'. He was put in the pillory and jailed for eighteen months. In 1794 Margarot and Gerrald were sentenced to fourteen years' transportation. Billstickers and booksellers were harassed and spied upon, arrested, fined and imprisoned. LCS meetings were broken up. Government-sponsored or inspired petitions and letters inveighed against Painite radicalism. The Association for Preserving Liberty and Property Against Republicans and Levellers waged a campaign against 'seditious and treasonable libels', and popular reactionary burnings of Paine effigies were officially condoned, not to say encouraged.[67]

In May 1794, after a great rally in Chalk Farm, twelve leaders of the LCS including Hardy, Thelwall and Tooke were arrested and charged with high

---

65 J. Keane, *Tom Paine, A Political Life* (London, 1996), p. 331.
66 Ibid., p. 333.
67 Ibid., pp. 336–7.

treason. But they were acquitted at trials in November and December the same year, their release the occasion of popular celebration throughout the capital. The crackdown shook the LCS and drove Hardy into temporary retirement. But the following year, as food prices continued to rise, the LCS organized more mass demonstrations. Some 100,000 people gathered at each of two rallies, the first at St George's Fields in June, the second at Copenhagen Fields, Islington, in October. The government responded by making it an offence to organize a meeting of over fifty people without a licence, or to bring the Crown or constitution into contempt.

The mutinies in the British navy linked issues of reform with sailors' grievances to present a serious challenge to the government. Following the example of their counterparts at Spithead near Portsmouth, sailors at Nore in the Thames estuary mutinied in May 1797, airing grievances over pay, food, discipline and lack of shore leave. In protest they sent the Admiral ashore and refused to accept concessions while their leader, Richard Parker, signed a manifesto which said 'The Age of Reason has at length revolved'. Red flags flying, they succeeded in blockading London for several days but were trapped when the buoys marking the estuary's shallows were removed and the lights put out. Eventually Parker was hanged, and further repressive legislation followed.[68]

In early 1798 another fifty LCS members were arrested and held without trial for over three years, and in 1799 the LCS as a whole was outlawed. This was a devastating blow, yet some LCS members tried to keep the underground organization alive. Others, like John Thelwall and the Charing Cross Road tailor Francis Place, retreated into educational work. Thomas Hardy reappeared in City politics where radicals managed to get the reform MP Harvey Combe elected as mayor in 1799. Sir Francis Burdett, of whom we will hear more, was elected in Middlesex by a single vote in 1802.

War with revolutionary France was declared in 1803 and lasted until 1815. Patriotic fervour combined with government persecution to disperse the forces of LCS and Painite radicalism. But Burdett was elected again, this time for Westminster, in 1807 with the help of old LCS members Horne Tooke and Francis Place. Burdett held his seat for thirty years and he, and the organization around him, were part of the link between the LCS and the reform agitation that culminated in the Great Reform Act.[69]

A critical element of the democratic struggle was supplied by the political interaction between blacks opposing slavery and the wider movement

---

68   G. D. H. Cole and R. Postgate, *The Common People, 1746–1946* (London, 1971), pp. 165–7.
69   Inwood, *History of London*, pp. 405–7.

for reform. Exemplary in this respect are the lives of Ottabah Cugoano and Olaudah Equiano. Cugoano was born in 1757 in what is now Ghana. He was sold into slavery at the age of thirteen and remained in the West Indies until he was brought to London in 1772, where he was set free. He entered service with the family of Richard Cosway in 1784 and here came in contact with, among others, William Blake. In 1786 Cugoano played a key role in rescuing a kidnapped comrade, Henry Demane. Cugoano contacted the abolitionist Granville Sharp who applied for a writ of habeas corpus, which arrived just in time to get Demane off the ship, already weighing anchor, that was to take him to the West Indies. In 1787 Cugoano wrote his *Thoughts and Sentiments on the Evil and Wicked Traffic of Slavery and the Commerce of the Human Species*, the first book by a black man to blast the slave trade and all who had any part in it. Cugoano wrote: 'History affords us many examples of severe retaliations, revolutions and dreadful overthrows; and of many crying under the heavy yoke of subjection and oppression, seeking for deliverance ... Yet, O Africa! Yet, poor slave! *The day of thy watchmen cometh, and thy visitation* draweth nigh ... *In that day thy walls of* deliverance *are to be built, in that day shall the decree of* slavery *be far removed.*'[70]

Cugoano may have been assisted in the writing of his book by fellow abolitionist Olaudah Equiano (also known as Gustavus Vassa, one of the slave names he was forced to adopt). Equiano was born in what is now eastern Nigeria around 1745. Aged eleven he was taken into captivity by a slave-owning African chieftain, before being sold on to European traders. He was taken first to Barbados and then to Virginia. Equiano had a succession of masters, one of whom sent him to his sister in England for schooling; it was only a brief interlude before he was once again sold, to a ship's master. His last owner, Robert King, a Quaker from Philadelphia trading in the Caribbean, said he would set him free if Equiano paid back the £40 for which he had been purchased. Equiano managed to save the money, partly because King allowed him to trade on his own account. King wanted Equiano to stay on as his business partner. But remaining in the Caribbean meant the risk of being kidnapped, and so Equiano made for London in 1767.

Equiano was increasingly drawn into abolitionist activity in Britain. He came to know Thomas Hardy, whom we have met as a founder of the London Corresponding Society and who went on to be a founder of Chartism. Equiano joined the LCS and passed on to Hardy the contacts he made during his frequent speaking tours. Hardy wrote to a Sheffield clergyman in 1792: 'Hearing from Gustavus Vassa [Equiano] that you are a zealous friend

---

70   See Fryer, *Staying Power*, p. 101.

for the Abolition of that accursed traffick denominated the Slave Trade I inferred from that that you was a friend to freedom on the broad basis of the Rights of Man for I am pretty perswaded that no Man who is an advocate from a principle for liberty for a Black Man but will strenuously promote and support the rights of a White Man and vice versa.'[71]

Equiano was staying at Hardy's Covent Garden house when he revised his autobiography, *The Interesting Narrative of the Life of Olaudah Equiano, or Gustavus Vassa, the African*. Originally published in 1789, shortly after Cugoano's book, it was also a devastating testimony to the cruelty of slavery. The book had a huge impact, and ran through eight editions in Britain, plus another six in the twenty-two years after its author's death. It propelled Equiano into prominence as a journalist and public speaker. In 1792, the year of his marriage to Fenlander Susan Cullen, he spoke in Scotland, Durham, Stockton and Hull. The following year he was in Bath and Devizes. With each engagement the subscription list for the next edition of the *Interesting Narrative* grew longer, bringing in revenues that eventually made him financially independent. Equiano died in 1797. His surviving daughter, Joanna, married a Congregationalist minister; they are both buried in Abney Park cemetery in Stoke Newington.

The link between abolitionism and radicalism remained strong. Both views were branded as supportive of the French Revolution by the government. John Thelwall of the LCS was echoing Hardy and Equiano when he argued that 'The seed, the root of oppression is here; and here the cure must begin ... If we would dispense justice to our colonies, we must begin by rooting out from our centre the corruption by which that cruelty and injustice is countenanced and defended.'[72] The movement was successful in banning the sale of slaves in the British Empire in 1807, but the keeping of slaves was not made illegal until 1833.

THE LONG ARC OF THE DEMOCRATIC STRUGGLE

The struggle for reform of the political system that commenced in the mid eighteenth century and lasted until the passing of the Great Reform Bill in 1832 was centred on London, though it had important bases of support throughout the country. The mass movements threw up three remarkable political leaders: John Wilkes, Tom Paine and Henry Hunt. The crowd that adopted them as their figureheads and that they helped to mobilize was a popular assembly that predated effective, organized or generalized labour movements.

---

71 See Fryer, *Staying Power*, p. 106.
72 See Fryer, *Staying Power*, p. 212.

Although these reform movements sometimes coincided with industrial action by wage-labourers, they were not primarily about the conditions of wage labour. Of course the crowds often mobilized the poor and those who worked for wages, but their social core was still, as it had been in the 1640s, made up of small business people, masters and their apprentices, though it was beginning to incorporate representatives of the emerging industrial middle classes who found themselves excluded from a political system still largely dominated by the aristocracy. But this was no parochial movement. It was bound up with the international patterns of war and revolution.

The Wilkesite movement was in part the result of discontent at the peace which concluded the Seven Years War – and the fact that the economic costs of the war were translated into increased taxation. This taxation was levied on Britain's American colonies as well as on the domestic population. And the period in which Wilkes was active coincided with the agitation in America which would eventually lead to the fundamental demand for 'no taxation without representation', and from there to revolution.

The second great figure of this reform movement, Tom Paine, was of course associated with both the American Revolution and Declaration of Independence of 1776, and the French Revolution of 1789. But the further development of the French Revolution and the Anglo–French war made any plan for reform in Britain modelled on French experience vulnerable to accusations of Jacobinism and treachery. Intensified government repression disrupted the reform movement, which only took on a more political character in the early decades of the nineteenth century. In the meantime the characteristic form of mass action was that of the crowd. In 1769 alone, Benjamin Franklin described England as experiencing 'riots about corn; riots about elections; riots about workhouses; riots of colliers; riots of weavers; riots of coalheavers; riots of sawyers; riots of sailors; riots of Wilkites, riots of chairman; riots of smugglers'.[73]

Not all of these riots were in London, but many were. London was the riot capital of the world.

---

73   J. Bronowski, *William Blake and the Age of Revolution* (London, 1972), p. 59.

5

Reformers and Revolutionaries

London is shabby by daylight and shabbier by gaslight.

Charles Dickens

REFORM AND THE CITY

In the first twenty-five years of the 1800s London's sheer scale stunned all who visited the city. With a population of 1 million at the turn of the century, London was already the largest city in Europe; just twenty years later the population had grown by more than a half to 1.6 million. In 1827 the German poet Heinrich Heine wrote, 'London has surpassed all my expectations in respect of its vastness; but I have lost myself.'[1] Blackened by coal smoke, the houses at the end of every street were barely visible in the winter months because of the all-pervasive fog.

One visitor to London recalled being told the story of a dinner party in Regent's Park, where twenty-two guests were invited to dine but only four arrived because the rest were afraid of losing their way. The US ambassador was 'tempted to ask, how the English became so great when they see so little daylight?'[2] A couple of decades later in *Bleak House* Dickens famously used the London fog as a metaphor for the legal system and the endless case of Jarndyce and Jarndyce, but it was also a literal account of the London environment for much of the year. And it could just as easily have been used as a metaphor for the political system in which all but a tiny elite were lost for influence on those that governed them.

By the beginning of the nineteenth century the electorate was more restricted than the one that elected the Long Parliament in 1640. The House of Commons contained MPs 'elected' by rotten boroughs such as Castle

---

1   Quoted in 'Introduction' to C. Fox (ed.), *London – World City 1800–1840* (New Haven and London, 1992), p. 12.
2   Ibid.

Rising (which had hardly any electors), New Romney (with eight electors), Old Sarum and Winchelsea (eleven electors each), Newport (twelve electors), Launceston (seventeen electors), Orford (twenty-two electors), Lostwithiel (twenty-four electors) and Heytesbury (twenty-six electors). Each of these constituencies returned two MPs each. There were another five MPs representing the universities of Oxford, Cambridge and Dublin. In contrast, there were no MPs at all for the cities of Leeds, Manchester, Birmingham and Sheffield.[3]

London, however, was different. The City of London was one of the largest constituencies in the country, returning four MPs to Parliament. Westminster and Southwark returned another two MPs each. Westminster was probably the most open constituency in the country, with 18,000 inhabitants entitled to vote in what were acknowledged to be the most turbulent parliamentary elections. And London electors also enjoyed some influence in elections in Middlesex and Surrey. The City of London, with its long history of struggles for self-governance stretching back to medieval times, was a long way short of full democracy, but it was still more democratic than practically anywhere else in the country. Some 8,000 livery men would meet in the Common Hall to elect the City's four MPs. In non-parliamentary elections some 15,000 resident freeman ratepayers chose the 236 members of the Common Council and the twenty-six aldermen, whose post was for life. Well beyond the enfranchised minority London also possessed a thriving political culture sustained by being the centre of the printing trade (London had the highest literacy rates in the country) and its dense undergrowth of taverns and coffee houses where all classes of society read about and discussed politics.

London radicals had, by the turn of the century, a long history of political activity on a wide range of fronts. Some had been involved in campaigns to abolish slavery, others to lift discrimination against Catholics and Dissenters embodied in the Test and Corporation Acts. In 1817 Robert Owen proposed in London that advancing capitalism should be replaced with self-managing communities of production and exchange. One such community was established at Spa Fields in 1821 and lasted for three years.[4] In the 1820s there were other 'labour exchanges', co-operative societies and oppositional magazines in London. But the cause that galvanized most radicals was the battle against 'old corruption' and in favour of parliamentary reform.

William Cobbett, the most prolific and widely-read journalist of the early 1800s, championed the cause in his *Political Register*. Jeremy Bentham's

---

3   J. T. Ward (ed.), 'Introduction', *Popular Movements c.1830–1850* (London, 1980), p. 2.
4   H. T. Dickenson, 'Radical Culture', in Fox (ed.), *World City*, p. 212.

utilitarianism was too stark a theory for truly popular use, but nonetheless it did influence radicals like James Mill, Francis Place and Francis Burdett and sometimes found reflection in the pages of W. T. Wooler's *Black Dwarf* and John Wade's *The Gorgon*. In 1807, frustrated by the timidity of the Whigs in Parliament, Francis Place and a score of other radicals formed the Westminster Committee with the aim of electing Francis Burdett as an independent candidate. The Westminster electorate was too large to be bribed or bought and the Committee, with the support of Cobbett's *Political Register*, mounted a vigorous campaign.

The Committee championed the smaller shopkeepers, tradesmen and producers against the old aristocratic elite, and there were plenty of these potentially supportive groups in London. There were some large producers in the capital, in shipbuilding, engineering and printing for instance, but there was also a mass of 30,000 businesses and 150 trades, most of which were on a smaller scale. About 15–20 per cent of male inhabitants were small businessmen or professionals, while of the 75 per cent of male inhabitants who worked for others, about one-third were skilled artisans and tradesmen (the remainder were unskilled or semi-skilled). This considerable section of society was neither part of the growing working class nor an accepted part of the ruling body of the nation. Political reform was an almost natural cry in circumstances marked by corruption, high taxes and exclusion from the franchise. A return to the 'historic rights of Englishmen' was the common theme of Cobbett, Burdett and the most effective orator of the day, the Wiltshire farmer Henry Hunt. Universal democratic demands based on natural rights of the kind popularized by Thomas Paine after the French Revolution were less common, though Richard Carlile's *The Republican* did support them.

The Westminster campaign was a roaring success. Burdett was voted top of the poll and another pro-reform figure, Lord Cochrane, won the constituency's second seat. The Westminster Committee remained in being and subsequently returned Burdett and other radicals. London radicals also worked through the Common Council in the City to demand parliamentary reform and promote petitions to the same end. These petitions were supported by speaking tours around the country to gain support. The radical John Cartwright was part of the campaign in 1817 that resulted in 700 petitions from 350 towns and cities, with over 1.5 million signatures being presented to Parliament. But petitions were only one method of reaching a public eager to hear the reform message.

The publication of newspapers and pamphlets was equally, if not more, important. In the first decades of the nineteenth century there was an explosion of popular print in London for which the only precursor was the outpouring of pamphlets during the English Revolution of the 1640s.

Between 1810 and 1832 annual newspaper sales almost doubled, from 16 to 30 million. The majority of these were produced in London and those outside London were heavily influenced by the newspapers of the metropolis. Pamphlets, magazines and satirical broadsheets added to the flood of paper hitting the streets.

Cobbett's *Political Register* began its attacks on the British *ancien régime* in 1806, but its relatively high price restricted readership to the middle classes. In 1816 he hit on the brilliant idea of taking his leading article and issuing it separately in a single folded sheet which would avoid the stamp duty on newspapers and sell for twopence. Cobbett's savage attacks on Old Corruption were popular, but he was also careful to establish an effective nationwide distribution system. The new paper instantly sold 44,000 copies a week, rising to 60–70,000 copies for the most popular issues. Where Cobbett led, others followed. The *Black Dwarf* began life in 1817, just as Cobbett was forced to flee to the US for fear of prosecution. More biting and satirical than the *Political Register*, it claimed sales of 12,000, even though at four pence it was double the price. The same year Carlile started the avowedly revolutionary *The Republican*, which claimed a circulation of 15,000 by 1819. That year these papers were joined by the *Medusa*, the *Cap of Liberty* and the *White Hat*.

Political clubs began to organize at least some of those that read the radical press. Government repression in the 1790s had closed many earlier political clubs, but these began to revive from 1811 on. In that year the Hampden Club – named after John Hampden, the hero of the Ship Money case in the reign of Charles I – was formed with a well-to-do membership and aiming at moderate parliamentary reform. John Cartwright didn't win the Club over to more radical views until 1814; in the meantime he set up the Union Society, although even its programme stopped short of calling for universal suffrage. And even though both Cobbett and Henry Hunt supported it, the membership fee of three guineas predestined it to a short life.

It was not until 1816, in the midst of widespread economic distress, that the Union Society and the Hampden Club were revived. The following year Cartwright was able to organize a meeting of seventy delegates from clubs around the country at the Crown and Anchor Tavern that, following Henry Hunt's agitation, called for universal suffrage. In addition to the Union and the Hampden, less formal clubs were springing up across the city: the British Forum, the Athenian Lyceum, the London Institute, the Polemic Club, the Socratic Society and the new Robin Hood Debating Society. In 1817 the mixed race Robert Wedderburn and Thomas Evans took out a licence to run a Dissenting Chapel in Archer Street. Wedderburn opened a second chapel in Hopkins Street in 1819 where the Bible was used as support for radical political change. The even more radical follow-ers of Thomas Spence, republican agrarian communitarians who believed that 'The Land is the People's Farm', set up a network of clubs in London taverns, like the George in East Harding Street and the Mulberry Tree in Moorfields.[5]

The clubs attracted activists but the truly mass events were processions, marches and open-air rallies. Henry Hunt was a master-orator and the main speaker at the huge Spa Fields meetings of November and December 1816 and February 1817. He was in action again at the Palace Yard rally of 1818 and the Smithfield rally of 1819. The November 1816 meeting in Spa Fields was in part organized by the Spenceans, including Arthur Thistlewood. Hunt addressed the crowd from the window of the Merlin's Cave tavern and one of Thistlewood's group, Jem Watson, made another speech from the back of a wagon, prompting the police commander to consider the speech as incitement. A tussle ensued as the order to arrest the leaders went out, but the police were unable to stop some of the crowd setting off for the Tower, breaking into gunsmiths and looting shops as they went.[6]

Henry Hunt went on to face down the yeomanry at the Peterloo Massacre in Manchester in 1819 and his return to London became a trium-phal procession. Hunt's goal was universal suffrage and his speeches were increasingly directed to 'the working class and no other'. He distained the old clandestine 'Jacobin' forms of organization, advocated mass pressure for change, but stopped short of calls for revolution. He was jailed for two years for his part in Peterloo.

Hunt's aversion to clandestine plots was more than justified by the fate of the 1820 Cato Street Conspiracy. A small group of Spencean plotters, including black activist William Davidson and Arthur Thistlewood, deter-mined on assassinating the prime minister, Lord Liverpool. Thistlewood was an arch-conspirator who had long been the object of government attention. A previous arrest had seen him taken to the Tower where he was picked out of a line-up with just one other person in it – and that was a Beefeater in full regalia.[7] He had also spent a year in prison for challenging the home secretary to a duel. The conspirators rented premises in Cato Street, near the Edgware Road, as their operational base. However, one of the group, George Edwards, was a spy and agent provocateur working for the Home Office. With the full knowledge of the government, he suggested an attack on a dinner which the prime minister was expected to attend, drawing the

---

5   Dickenson, 'Radical Culture', in Fox (ed.), *World City*, pp. 219–20.
6   C. Bloom, *Violent London: 2000 Years of Riots, Rebels and Revolts* (London, 2003), p. 189.
7   Ibid., p. 190.

group's attention to a newspaper announcement which the government itself had put in the press.

As the group assembled at Cato Street, London's first police force, the Bow Street Runners (originally formed by novelist Henry Fielding), were sent against them. The Runners burst in and, in the resulting fight, one of the officers was killed by Thistlewood. Edwards's involvement in the entrapment meant that his evidence was discredited, but two of the conspirators turned the others in to save their skins. Five of the Cato Street group, including Thistlewood and Davidson, were hanged at Newgate – a scene witnessed with revulsion by the young Charles Dickens.[8] Five more were transported for life.

Repression was general. The Cato Street Conspiracy was used to justify the Six Acts passed earlier in 1819 which made any meeting in favour of radical reform 'an overt act of treasonable conspiracy', and required that any meeting of over fifty people concerned with 'church and state' had the prior permission of a magistrate. Repression certainly took its toll on the radical movement in the 1820s, but there was one last outburst of popular energy. The unlikely cause of unrest was the scheme of the new king, George IV, to divorce his wife, Queen Caroline. Although they had lived apart for many years and the queen had been abroad since 1814, the king's treatment of his consort became a conduit for radical sentiment, rather as in the modern era popular sympathy devolved on Princess Diana as a reproach to the rest of the royal family. Popular opinion came to see the queen as wronged and injured in the same way in which the monarchy and aristocracy treated the common people of the nation.

So it was that radical London Alderman Matthew Wood caused a sensation by escorting the queen back to England in June 1820. Her arrival sparked months of popular agitation laced with bitter denunciation of the king and his Tory ministers. Cobbett and the radical press sided with the queen, although the *Black Dwarf* pointed out that the whole affair was a diversion from more important issues. Pamphlets and broadsheets ripped into the government, while some 800 petitions of support were delivered to the queen. Mass rallies and pageants, deputations and public meetings erupted across the capital in defiance of the Six Acts and the crackdown that followed the Cato Street trial.

The agitation checked the government campaign against the queen, although she was denied a place at her husband's coronation. When she died a year later, in 1821, the government was so fearful that her funeral would be the occasion of another radical demonstration that they attempted to route the cortege around the perimeter of London on its way to the

---

8   Ibid., p. 194.

Channel and the ship that would take the body on towards its final resting place in Brunswick. But the London crowd was not to be denied. Mass demonstrations, in which two lost their lives in clashes with troops, forced the cortege through the centre of London where thousands more lined the route.

The funerals of the two 'martyrs' brought some 80,000 onto the streets, the last such demonstration of the decade. The harassment and imprisonment of radical journalists and activists was part of the explanation. A relative improvement of economic conditions in the 1820s was another. And, in response, the opposition, never homogenous, became more disparate. But something specifically to do with London's place in the nation was changing as well.

London had been at the forefront of political mobilization for reform from the Wilkes and Liberty movement of the 1760s until the Queen Caroline demonstrations. But that was less true in the decades that followed, as the growing working class of the Midlands and North began to enter the lists. Mass industry was not absent from London, but it was a smaller part of the whole than it was in, say, Manchester or Leeds. Individual industries could never dominate a city like London in the way they did elsewhere; London was never going to be simply a 'coal town' or a 'cotton town'. London was growing as fast as any northern city but, in an age before fast urban transport, the expansion of the city was creating relatively self-contained urban villages without a pan-metropolitan sense of collectivity.

So when the Reform Bill crisis broke in 1830–32, London was far from the only or even the main site of the action.[9] In the election of 1830 the most dramatic aristocratic defeat was the return of Henry Brougham in Yorkshire, where the anti-slavery radicals of Leeds were in the van. It was the Birmingham Political Union that threatened, but only threatened, armed insurrection in support of parliamentary reform. In Manchester the middle-class coterie that would become the Anti-Corn Law League were at the heart of agitation. Above and beyond all domestic causes, the 1830 revolution in France spurred radicals to action and, once more, struck fear into the hearts of the reactionaries. A little of the atmosphere around this time can be felt in this description of a protest at Calthorpe Street, off the Gray's Inn Road, in 1833:

The procession, into which it was formed, consisted of about one hundred and fifty persons, and they carried among them eight banners. The most conspicuous of these was one which bore the motto 'Liberty or Death', with a skull and cross-bones on a black ground and a red

---

9   The story of the Reform Bill is told brilliantly in Foot, *The Vote*, Chapter 2.

border: others bore mottoes of 'Holy Alliance of the Working Classes', and 'Equal Rights and Equal Justice'. There were also to be seen a tri-coloured flag, the flag of the American republic, and a pole bearing at its head the Cap of Liberty.[10]

The event became famous because one of the thousands of police officers sent to break up the protest was killed. The subsequent repression made the government more unpopular. But this is not the aspect which concerns us here. What is of interest in this context is the mixture of working-class and democratic demands combined with the revolutionary fervour of the crowd and their slogans. These features of the movement were very clearly visible to the ruling elite. Indeed the whole division between Whigs and Tories at this time can be accurately summarized with respect to the threat of revolution. The Tories opposed reform because they believed that it would open the door to revolution. The Whigs supported reform because they thought it would not only appease the radicals in the short term but, by including 'the middle class' (the industrial ruling class) in the governing classes of the nation, also provide a bulwark against revolution in the long run.

Sure enough reform, when it came, achieved almost exactly what the Whigs had hoped: as soon as the industrial employing classes were brought into government, most agitation subsided, and all seemed set fair for stability. This outcome aroused a deep sense of betrayal and disorientation among the radical wing of the reform movement. And yet it was this disappointment with the lacklustre results of the period of agitation which would prove a rich seedbed for the next generation. The coming revolt was, however, much more than another edition of the same struggle. It marked the rise of a specifically working-class movement for change, and it was to set radical pulses racing faster than ever.

CHARTISM

Chartism is distinguished from previous movements for reform in a number of important ways. The Charter itself was a more coherent and widely understood summary of reform demands than had previously been available. Chartism was, though not without important local variation, a more truly national and structured movement than its predecessors. It was predominantly working-class, although individuals and organizations from the middle class also supported the Charter. Chartism was more concerned with social and economic issues than its precursors, although its primary

---

10   Available online at exclassics.com/newgate (accessed 6 November 2011).

demands were political. The avowedly revolutionary wing of Chartism was stronger than the revolutionary elements in previous movements for constitutional change. Finally, Chartism did better in the new industrial centres of the Midlands, the North, Wales and Scotland than had earlier movements for reform, although something of this pattern of support had already been discernible in the corresponding societies and the reform movement of the 1820s. All in all, important though London remained, it was far from being the centre of Chartism.

Nevertheless, the London Working Men's Association founded in 1836 by the publisher of the unstamped *Poor Man's Guardian*, Henry Hetherington, and trade unionist and Owenite socialist, William Lovett, was a cornerstone of Chartism.[11] The LWMA formulated the six points of the People's Charter, as concise a list of the reform movement's demands as could be wished for: the vote for every man aged twenty-one or over; the secret ballot in elections; an end to the property qualification for MPs; the payment of MPs; equalization of the number of voters in each constituency; annual parliaments.

The minute book of the LWMA recorded the founding meeting: 'At a meeting of a few friends assembled at 14 Tavistock St., Covent Garden, June 9, 1836. William Lovett brought forward a rough sketch of a prospectus for the Working Men's Association. It was ordered to be printed for further discussion.' Hetherington and Lovett drew a group of like-minded artisans, workers and small tradesmen around them, including George Julian Harney. They then approached a number of middle-class radicals, including the MPs Francis Place and Feargus O'Connor (though O'Connor had been unable to take his County Cork seat when elected for the second time in 1835 because he failed the property qualification). It was a difficult alliance to stabilize, with many of the MPs wary of trade-union involvement and at least as interested in free trade as in the aims of the Charter. Nevertheless, when the final version of the People's Charter was agreed at 'an influential meeting held at the British Coffee House, London, on the 7th June 1837', it had twelve signatories, of which six were MPs and six were from the original organizers of the Charter.

The LWMA never achieved a mass membership despite its pioneer role in establishing Chartism. If London Chartists helped establish Chartism throughout the country, in London itself the organization was fragmented. The LWMA was the dominant force from the capital in the Chartist Convention of May 1839, but did not represent the views of local Chartist

---

11   The 'stamp' was a tax on newspapers designed to make them unaffordable to the poor. In 1815, the Tory government of Lord Liverpool had increased the stamp duty to 4d but could not stop the increasing numbers of unstamped papers.

organizations in St Pancras, Marylebone, Bethnal Green, Hammersmith, and Lambeth. Harney had already formed the more radical East London Democratic Association in 1837,[12] and it was joined by a West London equivalent. Both favoured the persuasiveness of physical force as advocated by the Northern Chartists and Feargus O'Connor's Chartist paper the *Northern Star*, rather than the more timid gradualism of the LWMA.

Neither wing, alone or together, managed to mobilize on the scale of the northern cities in the first phase of action. While perhaps 250,000 attended Chartist meetings in Manchester and the West Riding of Yorkshire in 1839, there were far fewer, perhaps 10,000 or 12,000, at the largest London events. In London only 19,000 people signed the petition of March 1839, but in Birmingham a full half of the city's population, 94,000 people, put their names to the Charter. A Dundee delegate to the Chartist Convention in 1839 had a ready explanation for the Londoners' lack of zeal, suggesting that as long as they 'could procure beef and porter, and enjoy their comforts' they would not mobilize like their comrades in the North.[13]

The truth beneath the jibe was that London was not suffering the same economic depression as the North in the first phase of Chartist development. Consequently the radical London Chartists' call to 'Arm, Arm, Arm!' went unheeded in their own city. But the same message found an echo in the poorly coordinated series of risings in Birmingham, Glasgow, Sunderland, some Lancashire towns and, the last of them, in Newport, South Wales. They were all crushed, and the repression that followed broke up the original Chartist leadership through arrest and imprisonment. The first Charter had gained more than 1.2 million names, but was rejected by the authorities out of hand.

Chartism, however, recovered and became stronger as new leaders emerged and the old leaders were released from jail. In July 1840 the National Chartist Association was founded with national executive, dues-paying members and local branches. The NCA moved to organize with the trade unions and two years later it had 40,000 members. The right wing, discredited by the failure of first-wave Chartism, was weaker within it. Feargus O'Connor was released from prison in August 1842 and the *Northern Star* now had a circulation of 50,000. In London a new trade depression cut away the old conservatism as thousands of distressed stonemasons, tailors, printers, silk weavers, hatters, carpenters and other craftsmen turned to Chartism for succour.

In May 1842 some 100,000 Londoners marched to Parliament to present the second Charter. This time over half the adult population

---

12   Soon renamed the London Democratic Association.
13   Inwood, *History of London*, p. 619.

of Britain, 3,315,000 people, had put their names to the Charter, yet still Parliament threw it out. In mid-August 1842, as strikes and riots shook the Midlands and the North, London Chartists demonstrated in sympathy in a series of rallies on Clerkenwell Green, Islington Green and Stepney Green. At the same time, the political atmosphere swept all sectors of society into action: in October 1842 the *Caledonian Mercury* reported the formation of a Female Chartist Association at the National Charter Association Hall in Old Bailey. The motion to establish the Association was proposed by Susana Inge but contested by a Mr Cohen, who argued that a woman's 'proper character and station' was at the 'domestic hearth'. This caused 'a sensation among the ladies'. Despite being heckled Cohen kept digging, asking what would happen if a woman were elected to the Commons and 'a lover' tried to 'influence her vote by his sway over her affections'? This point was answered by Miss Mary Anne Walker, who was

> astonished by the question put by Mr Cohen and at the remarks made by that gentleman (Hear, hear). She repudiated with indignation the insinu-ation, that if a woman were in Parliament, any man, be he a husband, be he lover, would be so base as to try and sway her from her strict line of duty (Hear, hear; cries of 'Bravo' from the men, and much applause).

The meeting ended with unanimous approval of the Female Chartist Association and 'thanks ... unanimously and enthusiastically accorded to Miss Mary Anne Walker', who called on the 'ladies present to enrol their names in favour of the National Charter'.[14]

Chartism also produced black leaders. The best known is William Cuffay, the son of a Kentish woman and a slave from St Kitts. He moved to London in 1819 where he worked as a tailor. Cuffay cut a diminutive figure at only 4 feet 11 inches tall, but he played a towering role in the nascent working-class movement. Cuffay disapproved of Robert Owen's Grand National Consolidated Trades Union formed in 1834 on the initia-tive of the London tailors, but joined eventually and went on strike with his colleagues that same year, demanding a ten-hour day between April and July and an eight-hour day the rest of the year, with pay of 6s 5d per day. The strike collapsed and Cuffay was sacked and blacklisted. He joined the Chartist movement on its foundation and was one of its leading figures, taking part in the Convention that prepared the great Kennington Common demonstration in 1848.

---

14   The report is available in the British Library. See www.bl.uk (accessed 17 June 2011).

Finally this phase of intense agitation concluded with 40,000 gathered on Kennington Common. But the Metropolitan Police, formed thirteen years earlier, mounted on horses, dispersed the crowd with sabres and truncheons. The strikes too were violently put down and this, combined with a revival in the economy, brought the second phase of Chartism to an end.

The final phase of Chartist activity was different in character again, but London was once more the scene of the decisive confrontation. The trade depression of 1847–48 was a causal factor, but so too were the 1848 revolutions in Europe, beginning in February in France and spreading to Berlin, Vienna, Milan and other European cities. The mood at this time can be gauged by the report printed in the *Northern Star* of the 'large meeting' in London that adopted the final Charter. It reproduces Harney's address to the meeting:

'What is our entire political and social system,' he said, 'but a gigantic fraud, erected and maintained for the benefit of idlers and impostors?

'Behold the Church! The bishops and archbishops appropriate to themselves enormous salaries while leaving the hard-working clergy only a few pounds a year. Millions of pounds, in the shape of tithes, are taken annually from the people; these tithes were originally destined mainly for the upkeep of the churches and the support of the poor; now there are separate rates for that, and the Church "sacks" all the tithes. I ask, is not such a Church an organised imposture? (Cheers.)

'Behold our House of Commons, representing not the common people, but the aristocracy and the middle class, and dooming six-sevenths of the adult males of this country to political slavery by denying them the right to vote. Is not this house a legalised imposture? (Loud cheers.)

'Behold those venerable peers who, whilst the wail of distress is heard through the land, can sit, evening after evening, waiting for the Coercion Bill coming up from the Commons. Will any one be good enough to show me the utility of the Hospital of Incurables – will any one attempt to defend this hereditary imposture? (Cheers.)

'Of course, the respect I entertain for that blessed specimen of the wisdom of our ancestors – the monarchy – forbids me to speak in other than the most loyal terms of so interesting a sovereign as Queen Victoria, who regularly, once a year, is delivered of a royal speech and a royal baby. (Laughter.) We have just had the speech, and I see an announcement that in March next we are to have the baby. Her most gracious Majesty expresses great concern for her people's sufferings, admires their patience, and promises them another baby – and when it comes to babies, she has never yet promised in vain. (Bursts of laughter.) Then, there is

Prince Albert, a celebrated hat-maker, a capital breeder of pigs, and a distinguished Field Marshal and who, for all his services, is paid thirty thousand pounds a year. No, citizens, the monarchy is no imposture.' (Laughter and applause.)[15]

From March to June a procession of Chartist mass meetings took place across the capital, often ending in fights with the police. On 6 March some 10,000 protestors occupied Trafalgar Square and held off the police for two days. There was rioting in Whitehall, St James's, Fleet Street and Ludgate Hill. Windows, shop displays and street lights were broken.

The Chartist agitation culminated in the call for another mass rally on Kennington Common and a march on Parliament on 10 April. But the state was preparing for a showdown and on the day 4,000 police, 8,000 soldiers and 1,000 pensioned-off servicemen were mobilized against the Chartists. Another 80,000 special constables were enlisted, though most were deployed on local duties. The General Post Office, the Bank of England, Somerset House, the Guildhall and other buildings were sandbagged and those inside were issued with muskets and cutlasses.

The Chartist mobilization in the face of this armed response by the state was impressive – figures vary considerably, but numbers between 100,000 and 200,000 are reasonable estimates for those gathered on Kennington Common. But numbers alone were not the issue. The strategy of the state was to raise the stakes so that the only meaningful response by the Chartists would have been to begin an insurrectionary movement. After all, if such a panoply of government forces had been defeated the very structure of the state would have been under threat. In order to launch such a movement the Chartist leaders would have had to have borne such a possibility in mind, and prepared their supporters to take such action. But those willing to contemplate such a strategy, even in the long term, were not the majority in the leadership, nor had they won the majority of their followers to take immediate action for this goal. Feargus O'Connor might still have decided to march on Westminster. But he did not. He abandoned the march and the rally dispersed from where it stood on Kennington Common. The government's gamble had worked. Chartism never recovered from this defeat without a battle.

William Cuffay was fiercely critical of Feargus O'Connor's decision not to push against the police lines in a bid to present the petition to Parliament and London Chartists did not give up the fight easily. April and May continued to see weekly open-air meetings in Bethnal Green, Somers Town and

15   F. Engels, 'Chartist Agitation', report in *La Réforme*, 30 December 1847, in *Marx–Engels Collected Works* (London, 1976),vol. 6, p. 412.

Paddington. Fusing with an Irish nationalist crowd angered at the transportation of John Mitchel, editor of the *United Irishman*, a Chartist crowd of 60,000 marched from Stepney and Clerkenwell to Trafalgar Square. We can gauge the atmosphere in London in these days from the evidence given in a later trial of one of the Chartist leaders by one Frederick Town Fowler, who told the court that 'I am in the habit of reporting for the public press, and have been so employed for five or six years'.

The Times was one of the papers for which Fowler reported, and the account is of the Chartist march on 29 May. Fowler was at Clerkenwell Green where one part of the demonstration assembled. He described the 2,000 to 3,000 protestors as 'the lower orders I suppose; they were very dirty and very ragged'. They were addressed by speakers, one of whom said 'The Government is not worthy the support of any honest man; it is too contemptible to be recognized, and you must use your best endeavours to overthrow it. And now I wish to impress upon you that there is one safe way of getting rid of bad rulers, who forget their duty to their country: I openly avow that I mean private assassination. What made the Emperor of Austria fly from his country? Why, the fear of assassination . . .'

After they had completed a long, circuitous march to central London the protestors, whose numbers had risen considerably, ended up in Dean Street in Soho, where there was a Chartist Hall. Fowler told the Old Bailey that the march 'was increased by large numbers at every street – the party said, "Fall in," and the people did fall in, as they went along; in fact, there might be 50,000 or 60,000 – I could not speak positively – Dean-street was completely filled from one end to the other, and they turned into Oxford-street – it was about a quarter to ten, or half-past nine, when I left them in Dean-street.' Asked if he noticed 'what effect was produced upon the inhabitants residing in the line of march?' Fowler replied, 'A great deal of fear, and terror, and surprise, it appeared to me – a number of them shut up their shops and closed their doors.'[16]

In late May and early June there were battles with police in Clerkenwell and Bonner's Field, Bethnal Green. The final destruction of the Chartist leadership by repression came as a result of their decision to join Irish nationalists in preparation for an insurrection on 16 August. Government informers did their work and twenty-seven Chartists were arrested, most of them in the Orange Tree in Red Lion Square and the Angel in Southwark where the insurrection was being planned. Six of them were transported for life and another fifteen were imprisoned. Cuffay was a victim of this repression. He was a member of the committee tasked with promoting

16   Old Bailey Proceedings Online, July 1848, trial of Joseph Ireanaus John Fussell (t18480703-1677), oldbaileyonline.org, accessed 29 June 2011.

the Charter after its rejection by Parliament, until he was arrested for his part, probably a reluctant one, in the preparations for the London-wide armed uprising. He was convicted on the evidence of two police spies, one of whom had infiltrated the Chartists' Wat Tyler Brigade. Cuffay was sentenced to transportation to Tasmania for life. He was granted a pardon in 1856, but remained in Tasmania and continued to agitate in radical politics.

It was the effective end of Chartism, but the achievements of the protestors were historic. Friedrich Engels was right to say that the six points of the Charter were, in that time and place, essentially revolutionary, 'sufficient to overthrow the whole English Constitution, Queen and Lords included'. He was right too when he said that it was 'of an essentially social nature, a class movement'. This was not because workers were the only force involved in the Charter, but because 'the "Six Points" which for the Radical bourgeoisie are the end of the matter ... are for the proletariat a mere means to further ends'.

MARX IN LONDON

Exiled by the defeat of the German revolution of 1848, Karl Marx made his home in London for the thirty-five years until his death in 1883. He and his wife Jenny lived in mostly difficult circumstances, arriving poor and no doubt exhausted and discouraged following the triumph of reaction across Europe. They already had a small family, and although Jenny gave birth to several more children, only three of them survived. They lived in lodgings in Dean Street, Soho, where the expensive Quo Vadis restaurant now stands. Soho was a centre of émigrés, with whom Marx and other German arrivals spent long evenings drinking in Soho pubs like the Blue Posts in the Tottenham Court Road, and disputing over politics. They were joined eventually by Marx's closest friend and collaborator Friedrich Engels, when he too reached London after fighting in the revolutionary war in Baden in 1849. They raised the perennial questions about defeat following in the aftermath of revolution: what went wrong? Who was to blame? How could it have been different? There was, needless to say, little agreement.

The communist diaspora soon fractured politically, with Marx increasingly frustrated with this type of émigré politics and determined to turn his back on sectarian arguments. He therefore abandoned much overt political activity from the early 1850s onwards, embarking upon a serious analysis of what capitalism was in order to explain more effectively how to change it.

It took time for the dust to settle following 1848, as is usually the case when there has been a great upsurge of struggle and when those most involved still hope and believe that it has only been temporarily defeated. It was clear that the great movement of 1848 had not succeeded in sweeping away the old order, yet it was also clear that the democratic revolutions, although failures in their own terms, had left their mark and that there would not simply be a return to the status quo. In the next twenty years the Russian autocracy was forced to decree the emancipation of the serfs; the US was riven by a civil war which represented the unfinished business of the eighteenth-century American revolution; Poland rose in revolt over Russian autocracy; and Germany and Italy were unified 'from above' to become modern nation-states, rather than a patchwork of feudal kingdoms and principalities.

All of these events had a marked impact on the economic development of capitalism and on politics, including in Marx's country of exile. Here the defeat of Chartism in 1848 marked a turning point for the working class, not just politically but culturally and socially as well. Working-class organization became in some ways more sophisticated, with the development of stable trade unions, the co-operative movement and various political societies. This led to some separation between skilled, organized workers and other sections of the working class. In the words of Dorothy Thompson, 'They left behind the mass politics of the earlier part of the century. . . . In doing so, the skilled workers also left behind the unskilled workers and the women, whose way of life did not allow their participation in the more structured political forms.'[17] This development coincided with and was partly fuelled by the stabilization of the system both politically and economically which occurred in the years following 1848, symbolized by the Great Exhibition held in Hyde Park with its Crystal Palace in 1851, which showcased the wonders of capitalism.[18]

The changes in social conditions and in consciousness following the defeats of 1848 were a challenge to Marx and demanded a different political response. The man who had launched his and Engels's *Communist Manifesto* onto a Europe full of revolutionary expectation in 1848 now had to settle into a routine of research and limited political activity, during a long period of quietude and calm. Marx and Jenny themselves moved from Dean Street and émigré Soho, and from Marx's drinking haunts on the Tottenham Court Road, to the lower slopes of Hampstead. They took a house in the then recently built but now demolished Maitland Park estate, today the site of a council estate of the same name and part of the sprawling hinterland

---

17   D. Thompson, 'Women and Nineteenth-Century Radical Politics', in J. Mitchell and A. Oakley (eds), *The Rights and Wrongs of Women* (London, 1976), p. 137.
18   The palace was later moved to south London where the area now bears its name, and where it was burnt down many years later − perhaps a symbol of Britain's industrial decline.

of Camden and Kentish Towns which grew up around the railway lines to the north. There were walks on Hampstead Heath, trips to concerts and to the theatre and proper schooling for the children.

They lived in an almost constant state of genteel poverty, as Marx's regular begging letters to Engels demonstrate, as does the evidence of juggling bills owed to the local tradesmen. It was in these years that Marx settled into the reading room of the British Museum to write *Capital*. Engels, on the other hand, was forced to move to Manchester to work in the family cotton business as a means of keeping himself and, for much of the time, the whole Marx family. The letters between the two men reveal frequent and desperate requests for money to which Engels usually acceded, providing sustenance far beyond basic necessities to include champagne and hock for Christmas. A particular low point was Christmas 1859, when there was a County Court summons pending, clothes in the pawnshop, debt to tradesmen, when the family 'gathered round the imaginary *Weihnachtsbaum* [Christmas tree] to drink the champagne Engels had sent'.[19] Engels also helped with the schooling of the three surviving children, Jenny, Laura and Eleanor, all of whom grew into politically aware and talented women, active socialists and campaigners.

UNIONS AND INTERNATIONALISM

While there was little scope for mass socialist organization in this period, London was not particularly quiescent in the 1850s and 60s. There was a process of consolidation and structuring of the working-class movement: there were co-operative workshops for tailors and shoemakers, and 'Workers' clubs prospered sufficiently to move out of the public house and find their own premises. Many were radical and educational in tone.'[20] There were also plenty of causes and political campaigns to take up, and the London crowd or mob had not lost its sense of justice and outrage. When the Austrian General Heynau, accused of brutality particularly against women in the Hungarian and Italian revolutions of 1848, visited London in 1850, he was horsewhipped by outraged draymen at the Barclay and Perkins brewery on Bankside and had to be rescued. A series of popular songs were written commemorating the event.[21] Today a plaque near The George on Bankside commemorates the spot.

Repression continued from above. In 1855 Lord Robert Grosvenor tried to introduce a bill banning Sunday trading with the aim of closing

19   Y. Kapp, *Eleanor Marx*, vol. 1(London, 1972), p. 36.
20   J. White, *London in the Nineteenth Century* (London, 2008), p. 368.
21   H. Mayhew, *London Labour and the London Poor*, Douglas-Fairhurst (ed.), p. 22 and note p. 444.

shops to enforce the keeping of the Sabbath. This followed a bill to restrict pub opening times which caused great anger. Marx explained: 'The workers get their wages late on Saturday: it is for them alone that trade is carried on on Sundays. They are the only ones compelled to make their purchases, small as they are, on Sundays.'[22] The Chartists called a mass protest by means of a wall poster which declared: 'An open-air meeting of artisans, workers and "the lower orders" generally of the capital will take place in Hyde Park on Sunday afternoon to see how religiously the aristocracy is observing the Sabbath and how anxious it is not to employ its servants and horses on that day.'[23]

The dig about servants and horses referred to a speech by Grosvenor which claimed that the rich also observed the Sabbath. The scenes in Hyde Park showed otherwise, as a mass demonstration — Marx estimated up to 200,000 — lined up to jeer at the carriages and finery of the rich. The aristocracy was made to run the gauntlet of the crowd with its cries of, among ruder things, 'Go to church!' When police reinforcements arrived, they too were jeered: 'Where are gone the geese? Ask the police!' — referring to the recent theft of geese by a constable in Clerkenwell. Leafleters issued a call for a meeting on the reorganization of Chartism at the Scientific and Literary Institute in Doctors' Commons.[24] Another very large demonstration was called for the following Sunday.

This time they went to Grosvenor's house first, but he had left London. Huge crowds again filled the park, although the rich had failed to turn out for fear of attack. Instead, the crowd was brutally attacked by police: 'Instead of the swishing of fans [was] the whizzing of the constables' leather truncheons. Last Sunday the ruling classes had shown their fashionable physiognomy, now they showed their political physiognomy.'[25] There was turmoil in London, with meetings, skirmishes and protests while the police truncheoned stone-throwing crowds. A third demonstration was called for the following Sunday, on top of the planned protests at the gentlemen's clubs in Pall Mall. The Sunday demonstration ended in window-smashing in Belgravia.[26]

Grosvenor withdrew his bill the next day. In part the ruling elite were divided, with some critical of the bill and some reformers supporting the demonstrators. Marx wondered whether the prime minister, Lord

22   K. Marx, 'Anti-Church Movement', 25 June 1855, in *Marx–Engels Collected Works* (MECW), vol. 14 (Moscow, 1980), p. 303.
23   Ibid., p. 304.
24   Ibid., pp. 304–7.
25   K. Marx, 'Agitation over the tightening up of Sunday Observance', 2 July 1855, in MECW, vol. 14, p. 325.
26   White, *London in the Nineteenth Century*, p. 370.

Palmerston, was content to allow the events to continue to divert attention from the war with Russia in the Crimea.[27] Nonetheless, agitation continued, and 'it would be many weeks before Hyde Park returned to normality and ceased to be the cockpit of class war'.[28] The peace was, however, disturbed later that year in a series of bread riots.

It is a common misapprehension that the British working class has always been noted for its lack of internationalism and somewhat narrow outlook; yet much of the history of the working-class movement tells a different story. The popular support for revolutionary and democratic movements was quite remarkable through the 1850s and 60s, and it centred on London. A number of important initiatives round international solidarity took place in the 1860s, particularly under the influence of the London Trades Council. This body was created out of a bitter struggle in the building trades for the nine-hour day, spreading from a lockout of masons in Pimlico in 1859 to involve all the building trades, with high levels of solidarity from other unions. The builders' strike committee set up the London Trades Council at a conference in May 1860, replacing a more informal arrangement where delegates from different trades had met at the Bell Inn at Old Bailey to discuss issues of common interest.[29] The Trades Council concerned itself with a wide range of international issues.

There was strong support in London for the liberal nationalism in Italy which was leading to the country's unification out of a series of small states. This enthusiasm for the Italian Risorgimento in 1861 allowed exiled Italian revolutionary Mazzini to make strong links with working-class and lower-middle-class Londoners. The deep and fervent identification with this and other struggles can be seen by the welcome given to the other hero of the Italian movement for national unity and independence, Giuseppe Garibaldi, who had led an army to fight for unification and helped overthrow royal despotism.

Garibaldi's visit in 1864 drew huge crowds wherever he went in London. On 11 April he arrived in a special train at Nine Elms in Battersea, where he was transferred to a carriage and greeted by half a million people who waved red scarves and handkerchiefs (the symbol of his movement). 'From every part of the metropolis and its suburbs the children of toil had made holyday and come out to receive a man whom they considered their especial hero.' The workers of London, with their friendly-society and union banners, 'were determined to make his entrance into London their own

---

27   K. Marx, 'Clashes between the Police and the People – the Events in the Crimea', 6 July 1855 in MECW, vol. 14, p. 334.
28   White, *London in the Nineteenth Century*, p. 370.
29   H. Pelling, *A History of British Trade Unionism* (London, 1971), pp. 52–4.

demonstration'.[30] In 1861 the Peek Frean's biscuit factory had already begun manufacturing the biscuit named after him, a peculiar honour which immortalizes him to this day.

Garibaldi was lionized by the rich as well as the poor, reflecting at least in part the interests of the British ruling class in backing movements such as that for Italian unity which, they believed, would help clear away the last vestiges of feudalism in Europe. Society ladies clamoured to be with him and for a few days he was the talk of London. However, he had his visit curtailed by a British government that feared his popularity and effect on working men and women, and did not want him to tour Britain as had been originally planned. Marx, irritable not for the first or last time at the British working class's political instincts coinciding with those of their rulers, said that 'all fool's day . . . has been extended, at least in London, to the whole of April. Garibaldi and Palmerston FOR EVER on the walls of London.'[31]

More important in shaping politics in London was the impact of the American Civil War from 1861 onwards. The course of the war and its eventual outcome had a marked influence on Marx and Engels, but also had a major effect on the progress of democracy in Britain and on the beginning of a revival of the working-class movement. The British working class, continuing its long tradition of sympathy with victims of tyranny and oppression, tended to side with the Union and the struggle against slavery in the cotton plantations of the southern states. Even those Lancashire textile workers made jobless by the interruption of cotton imports due to the war supported the Union. In London, while the government was clearly sympathetic to a southern victory, much feeling ran in the opposite direction. The movement in support of the North was galvanized after Lincoln's emancipation proclamation in late 1862, where he declared the abolition of slavery and thus gained the political initiative in the war.

On 28 March 1863 the London Trades Council held a public meeting on the war and against British intervention on the side of the South, a step being seriously considered by many politicians including Palmerston. Speakers included leading lights of the Liberal Party such as John Bright and John Stuart Mill. The packed meeting at St James's Hall in Piccadilly, then the largest meeting hall in London with a capacity of 2,000, was strongly anti-war. Marx describes how he 'attended a TRADE UNIONS meeting chaired by Bright. He had very much the air of an INDEPENDENT and, whenever he said "IN THE UNITED STATES NO KINGS, NO BISHOPS", there was a BURST OF APPLAUSE. The working men

30   *The Times*, London, Tuesday 12 April 1864, p. 9.
31   Letter from Marx to Engels, 19 April 1864, MECW, vol. 41, p. 516.

themselves spoke *very well indeed*, without a trace of bourgeois rhetoric or the faintest attempt to conceal their opposition to the capitalists.'[32]

One speaker at the meeting, a London university professor called Edward Beesly, declared: 'We are met here tonight . . . not merely as friends of emancipation but as friends of reform.' He continued, 'This is the first time, I believe, that the trade unionists of London have met together to pronounce on a political question, but I am sure it will not be the last.'[33] Beesly was making a crucial connection here: events in the US, with victory for the North and the emancipation of slavery, would have a profound impact on the demand for democracy in Europe, and especially in Britain.[34] The identification of the Union struggle with the general movement for democracy was not misplaced; victory in 1865 had a profound effect on the fortunes of the old world, giving a further boost to republicanism over monarchy, strengthening liberal opinion and leading more compellingly to the idea of universal and equal human rights.[35] Beesly concluded in 1865 that 'a vast impetus has been given to Republican sentiments in England.'[36]

THE FIRST INTERNATIONAL AND THE STRUGGLE FOR THE VOTE

International issues helped the working-class movement to revive and fortify itself. There had been various contacts between English and French workers, in particular when the Proudhonist leaders travelled to London in 1863 to speak at a meeting in solidarity with Poland, again organized by the London Trades Council. In the following year, on 28 September 1864, the St Martin's Hall in Long Acre was the scene of a historic meeting when various English and French socialists and radicals, including Marx and Engels, came together with trade union leaders to form the International Working Men's Association, or as it came to be known, the First International.

It reflected a growing internationalism and politicization among working people. Marx felt an enthusiasm for this new organization which he had not felt for many years, when the left had had to concern itself with the experience of defeat and where large-scale organization seemed possible.

32 Letter from Marx to Engels, 9 April 1863, MECW, vol. 41, p. 468.
33 Foot, *The Vote*, p. 127.
34 For an excellent account of the meeting and its consequences see ibid., pp. 125–7.
35 The historian James Macpherson credits the Union victory with, among other things, the passing of the Second Reform Bill in Britain in 1867, which gave the suffrage to a much larger number of working-class men than previously, and which he believed would have been long delayed if the South had won. J. Macpherson, *Drawn with the Sword* (Oxford, 1996), pp. 224–7.
36 Quoted in Macpherson, *Drawn with the Sword*, p. 226.

Not since the days of 1848 had Marx played such a crucial and active role, and although he was still working on *Capital*, he became central to the Association, which would almost certainly not have survived as long without his tactical sense and political acumen. He had to manoeuvre around a very wide and disparate set of politics: the English trade-union leaders who formed the backbone of the Association were politically Liberals or radicals, not Marxists; the émigré politicians such as Mazzini tended to a rather conspiratorial view of organization; the Proudhonists were against having intellectuals in the movement. Marx remained centrally involved in the organization, whose headquarters were at 18 Greek Street in Soho.[37]

Marx was elected onto the subcommittee responsible for writing the Association's manifesto. He was soon delegated to write the draft, which became the Inaugural Address to the International Working Men's Association.[38] Marx's founding statement for the organization is very different from his Manifesto of 1848, reflecting the experience of defeat of the previous decade and a half, and also an understanding that any revival in working-class organization and politics would have to take into account that the movement was not in a revolutionary phase and that it required unity among quite disparate groups. He understood that this meant different tactics and different aims for the First International, rather than simply, for example, proclaiming the need for communism. The piece reflects his long years of study on *Capital*, and begins with a powerful polemic about the condition of the working class in Britain, the levels of poverty and inequality, at exactly the time when British capitalism was approaching its peak of power and where London was now the centre of a mighty industrial power and a growing empire.

However, he was less specific on what needed to be done to change this. He wrote to Engels that 'it will take time before the awakened movement allows the old boldness of speech.'[39] So in the Address Marx tends to talk only in general terms of the need 'to conquer political power' as the 'great duty of the working classes';[40] there is no discussion of how to win universal suffrage, let alone of more revolutionary forms of action.[41] The Address ends with practical remarks on solidarity and the need to organize on an international level. This related to concerns among trade unionists

---

37   Kapp, *Eleanor Marx*, vol. 1, p. 59n. Kapp tells us that The Establishment club, a satirical cabaret, opened in the same premises in 1961.
38   'Inaugural Address to the International Working Men's Association' in MECW, vol. 20, pp. 5–13.
39   Letter from Marx to Engels, 4 November 1864, in *Selected Correspondence* (Moscow, 1975), p. 140.
40   'Inaugural Address', p. 12.
41   For a view on this see Foot, *The Vote*, pp. 130–1.

about the increasing use of foreign blacklegs to break strikes, and reflected their aim of working to improve the conditions of working men throughout Europe. There is also recognition that it was working-class opposition to war with the North in the US which prevented the government from pursuing it – 'it was not the wisdom of the ruling classes, but the heroic resistance to their criminal folly by the working classes of England' that averted intervention.[42]

The formation of the IWMA marked the creation of real unity between revolutionaries and those like the British trade-union leaders who had a much more limited outlook politically. This took on a new dimension with the struggle for political reform and the extension of the franchise. The movement for reform had been on hold since the defeat of Chartism in 1848, but now it began to develop a momentum. Only a few months after the First International was founded, the Association became one of the prime movers over the question of parliamentary reform, with yet another major meeting, again in St Martin's Hall, on 23 February 1865, which established a Reform League to campaign for one man, one vote.

There had been a series of very limited parliamentary attempts to extend the franchise and growing calls for a new reform bill, aimed at giving the vote to at least a section of working-class men. (There was still no notion of extending the franchise to women from any in Parliament; it would be nearly another half century before that issue featured seriously on the parliamentary agenda.) The newly elected Liberal government introduced a second Reform Bill in 1866, with the aim of introducing limited electoral reforms on the basis of votes per household, which would also exclude a large number of working-class men. Even this reform divided the Liberals and outraged the Tories, who dreaded ordinary workers having any democracy at all. The bill passed its second reading but was finally snuffed out in June 1866. The government fell shortly afterwards.

One reason that the Tories were able to defeat the bill was that its feebleness meant that there was little positive enthusiasm for it outside Parliament, and little agitation for reform: 'People were not interested in Gladstone's Reform Bill because it enfranchised so few of them.'[43] But now things changed, and those who had argued for limited progress within the Reform League found that the movement was charging far ahead of them, calling for universal (manhood) suffrage and for a secret ballot (a key demand of reformers to end the time-honoured practices of bribery, corruption and drunkenness which accompanied 'open' elections).

---

42 'Inaugural Address', p. 13.
43 Foot, *The Vote*, p. 147.

Even before the bill was quashed, a huge demonstration in its support gathered on Primrose Hill on 21 May. But in the weeks following the vote there were almost daily protests and demonstrations. There were repeated issues over the right of assembly, and reform galvanized large numbers of working-class radicals. A demonstration in Trafalgar Square on 2 July deplored the return of the Tories, and the call came for a huge protest later that month in Hyde Park.

The authorities now decided that this was too horrific an event to contemplate and the chief of police banned the demonstration, on the grounds that the park should not be used for political purposes. The march was illegal and would be prevented from entering the park.[44] A huge demonstration assembled before the park, but the gates at Marble Arch were locked tight. The League had been divided over tactics, with the majority arguing that they should try to gain entry but then if refused should go to Trafalgar Square. Demonstrations converged from various starting places on Marble Arch, the numbers exceeding all expectations. But despite leaflets telling the crowd to go on to the square, The Times reported that 'the gates, it is true, were strongly fortified, but to throw down the railings seemed a feasible undertaking, and this was promptly attempted ... breach after breach was made, the stonework, together with the railings, yielding easily to the pressure of the crowd.'[45] The crowd broke through into the park at Park Lane, and despite a number of injuries, a presence of Grenadier and Life Guards, and more than fifty arrests, the park was teeming with people by 8pm. This demonstration marked the start of nearly a year of protest over reform, making many of the Reform League leaders even more timid but attracting growing numbers of workers and convincing Marx that this was more evidence of growing radicalization: 'The reform movement here, which was called into being by our Central Council (in which I played an important part), has now assumed enormous and irresistible dimensions.'[46]

The Conservative Prime Minister, Benjamin Disraeli, produced his own Reform Bill which he pushed through Parliament in the following year. The usual objections were heard from much of his party, and all sides in Parliament still rejected universal suffrage. The builders' union leader, George Potter from the London Working Men's Association, in a speech in March 1867 called for a week's general strike if the vote were denied.[47] The agitation pushed the government into making more concessions in the bill, but they were not enough to stop the movement, which again, in the spring

44 According to Kapp, the march was at least partly about the right to free assembly: Eleanor Marx, vol. 1, p. 73n.
45 The Times, Tuesday 24 July 1866, p. 9.
46 Letter from Marx, 9 October 1866, quoted in Foot, The Vote, p. 150.
47 Foot, The Vote, p. 150.

of 1867, called for a mass demonstration for reform in Hyde Park, this time on 6 May. The vote, however, was contentious: the League's executive only passed it by five votes to three. The government once again decided to ban the march and served notice on the militant atheist Charles Bradlaugh as he was about to speak at a May Day demonstration in Trafalgar Square. This notice was a proclamation pasted up around town from the Home Secretary Horace Walpole, which said that since the demonstration was for 'political discussion' and because 'the use of the Park for the purpose aforesaid is illegal, and interferes with the enjoyment of the Park by the people' that people were warned that 'they will attend any such meeting at their peril'.[48]

The government attempt to ban the demonstration in Hyde Park, just before the bill was due to be debated, was a terrible blunder. The protestors were determined to press ahead even if it meant breaking the law, forcing the authorities to climb down. Even the League's most prominent figures such as the cautious Edmund Beales saw that it had to go ahead, and despite the atmosphere created by the government, media and respectable opinion, the size of the demonstration – estimated by the organizers at 500,000 – and the militancy of the crowds meant that they simply overwhelmed the soldiers and police who had been conscripted into service against them, and took over the park. His daughter Jenny described the events in a letter to Karl Marx:

> Here the people are up and stirring. The heat, which is excessive ... has warmed the blood of Beales and Co. For the last fortnight there have been continual skirmishes between the Government and the Reformers, in which the former have been most disgracefully routed. The success of the League is due to Bradlaugh who has behaved throughout with great pluck: at the last sitting of the League, most of the Reformers ... had thought it wisest to give in. But Bradlaugh, in a warlike speech, declared that if no one else would lead the people to the park, he alone was ready to do so.[49]

The authorities backed down but not before dispatching 5,000 mounted police and 15,000 special constables to control the crowd, who were confounded because 'the mob was as orderly as could be, much to the chagrin of the *special constables* who with their newly made truncheons

---

48   Foot, *The Vote*, pp. 154–5.
49   Letter from Jenny Marx to Karl Marx, n.d., early May 1867, quoted in O. Meier and F. Evans (eds), *The Daughters of Karl Marx: Family Correspondence 1866–1898* (London, 1984), p. 25.

"marched up the Park and then marched back again".[50] *The Times* reported rather sourly that of those on the vast demonstration 'probably not much more than a tenth were what we may call the Reformers'. Its explanation was that 'As all sorts of proclamations and warnings had been addressed to spectators to keep away, there were, of course, an unusual number present.'[51]

The movement succeeded in forcing Disraeli to make further concessions, and the 1867 Reform Act, when it became law some weeks later, enfranchised far more working men than had originally been envisaged – but did not of course result in the revolutionary upheaval and unrest predicted by the MPs in the various debates. Nor did the great success of the League in mobilizing large numbers translate into wider political change or indeed representation at party level. Instead, the movement had little of the real radical components of Chartism and so its limited success in 1867 tended to strengthen Liberalism, rather than any form of independent working-class organization. That would have to wait longer and would only be achieved after another great upsurge of working-class struggle more than twenty years later.

Marx, who had now finished Volume I of *Capital,* continued with his work in the IWMA. The movement for reform had begun to make tenuous contacts with individuals involved in the Irish movement, known as the Fenians, and to talk about linking the movement for Irish home rule with the movement for democracy in England. The tactics of the Fenians led them towards armed struggle and this in turn led governments and police towards greater repression of the Irish in Britain. An attempted jailbreak of Fenian prisoners in Manchester, in which a policeman was shot, led to the hanging of three Fenians, the 'Manchester Martyrs'. It caused outrage among the very large Irish community in many working-class areas. The day after the executions every Catholic priest in Manchester denounced the murder of the martyrs; in Hyde Park large numbers of people came to kneel and pray. The IWMA general council sent a memo, written by Marx, to the secretary of state before the executions suggesting they might be 'political revenge'. A demonstration was held on Clerkenwell Green in their defence.[52] But just weeks after the execution, support for the Fenians evaporated following an attempt to rescue two more prisoners, this time from Clerkenwell jail, which stood where the Mount Pleasant postal sorting office now stands. The amount of dynamite used in the jailbreak killed

---

50   Letter from Laura Marx to Karl Marx, 8 May 1867, in Meier and Evans (eds), *Daughters of Karl Marx,* p. 28.
51   *The Times,* Tuesday 7 May 1867, p. 5.
52   Kapp, *Eleanor Marx,* vol. 1, pp. 83–86. See also K. Marx in D Fernbach (ed.), *The First International and After* (London, 1974), p. 159n.

and wounded many, destroyed houses and caused fury in the press. The backlash against the Fenians was predictable, and Marx criticized the way in which they had lost political support by carrying out such acts. At the same time he made clear that the Irish needed independence from Britain. In a letter to Engels he said what the Irish needed were:

1. Self-government and independence from England
2. Agrarian revolution
3. Protective tariffs against England[53]

THE PARIS COMMUNE

The real test for the movement came not from Ireland but from France, which in 1870 went to war with Prussia – a conflict which ended in the overthrow of the despot Napoleon III and the victory of the Prussian forces. The defeat led to the occupation of much of France and the siege of Paris. By early 1871 the newly elected National Assembly was attempting to make its peace with Prussia, which lifted the siege. Meanwhile the French government had to disarm their own forces in Paris, and their craven capitulations plus the presence of German troops angered the National Guard, effectively a people's militia in the city, which seized power and heralded the election of the Paris Commune. The Commune lasted a bare two months: it represented the first attempt anywhere in the world at workers' self-government and genuine democracy. Its eventual failure was a bloody affair, with around 20,000 killed, many fighting on barricades, others in murderous pogroms in its aftermath, while thousands more were exiled, imprisoned or transported.

The importance of the events for Londoners was twofold: the IWMA and other working-class bodies demonstrated solidarity with protests and support, and held repeated debates on the course of events over the ten months from the war to the defeat of the Commune. Marx was charged with writing a series of statements on the issue, his most famous being the final one, *The Civil War in France*, written at the time of the defeat of the Commune in which he defended the Communards.[54] The document is forceful, written with the passion that only a partisan, watching the events unfold on a daily basis, and with friends and family involved in the struggle, can have. Marx put into the writing all his analysis of class:

---

53 Letter from Marx to Engels, 30 November 1867, in D. Fernbach (ed.), *The First International and After: Karl Marx's Political Writings* (London, 1974), p. 161.
54 MECW, vol. 22, pp. 308–59.

It is a strange fact. In spite of all the tall talk ... about Emancipation of Labour, no sooner do the working men anywhere take the subject into their own hands with a will, than up rises at once all apologetic phraseology of the mouthpieces of present society with its two poles of Capital and Wage-slavery ... The Commune, they exclaim, intends to abolish property, the basis of all civilization! Yes, gentlemen, the Commune intended to abolish that class-property which makes the labour of the many the wealth of the few.[55]

The tone and sentiments of the writing had long-term consequences politically for Marx, consequences which he neither could nor would have dreamt of avoiding. The events of 1871 broke the unity of the International and led to a rupture between those on the left, including Marx, and the rest, especially the trade union leaders. In the context of a political backlash against the Commune, the document written by him and put out in the name of the general council of the IWMA was much too strong a defence of what they perceived as violence and illegality, so that Benjamin Lucraft and George Odger resigned, followed by Robert Applegarth. The Paris Commune raised in a concrete form the dilemma of reform or revolution. Because the demands of both solidarity and propaganda required the revolutionaries to defend the Communards, the split in the IWMA was probably unavoidable. While the IWMA continued to exist for a few years afterwards, it was riven by sectarian debate with the anarchists and eventually its centre moved from London to New York, which effectively killed the Association off.

There were also personal consequences. London became a refuge for many French émigrés, exiled Communards who settled in the city for some years. Marx's middle daughter, Laura, had already married a French socialist living in London, Paul Lafargue. The other two daughters were themselves caught up in the danger of the Commune when they went to visit her in Bordeaux, just before Paris fell. Lafargue was a wanted man; his house was searched, and the Marx sisters were interrogated and held in custody. Marx wrote to his daughters in June that 'the cousins from the country' (the exiled Communards) were 'thronging [London's] streets. You recognize them at once by their bewildered air.'[56]

The exiles were in London for some years and many of them remained politically active. They were attracted to Marx and his household because of his uncompromising analysis in *The Civil War in France*. Marx and Engels also organized solidarity and relief work, trying to obtain jobs and housing

---

55   Ibid., p. 335.
56   Quoted in Kapp, *Eleanor Marx*, p. 128.

for them. The Communards had a club room at 40 Rupert Street, again in Soho, where they were supported by the International. While there had been public support for the Commune back in April, the onslaught by the press against their actions meant they had little working-class support. When they tried to mark the first anniversary of the Commune, they were 'not *allowed* to meet in *any hall* in London'.[57] But support for the exiles on the left continued, and in 1872 the French refugees set up a co-operative kitchen in Newman Passage just off Oxford Street.[58]

The French exiles were also frequent visitors to the Marx house. In 1872 Jenny Marx became engaged to Charles Longuet, a leading member of the Commune and for a time the editor of its newspaper. Eleanor too became engaged, to Prosper-Olivier Lissagaray – one of the bravest fighters in the Commune and the author of a history of the movement. But though the engagement lasted nine years, from the time that Eleanor was seventeen, he was not 'favoured by the Marxes as a son-in-law'.[59]

By this time Engels was living back in London, having extricated himself from the Manchester family firm of Ermen and Engels in 1870. He took a house in Regent's Park Road, facing onto Primrose Hill and near enough to Marx to see him every day, and lived there with his partner Lizzie Burns until her death in 1878. However, these were years of decline for Marx, who was dogged by ill health, wrote very little, and lost both his wife and eldest daughter Jenny before he too died on 14 March 1883.

Marx's funeral in Highgate cemetery in north London was a very small affair of around a dozen people, in contrast to the many thousands who still make the trip to Highgate to see his grave today. The tomb contains the remains of Marx, his wife Jenny, his grandson Harry Longuet who died in the same year at the age of four, and Helena Demuth – the family servant and companion with whom Marx had a child, Freddy Demuth. Engels wrote to his old German comrade Friedrich Sorge: 'Mankind is shorter by a head and by the most remarkable head of our time.'[60] The family rejected the idea of a more formal memorial, wanting his work to stand as monument enough. The giant bust of Marx which now marks the grave was erected at the direction of the Communist Party in 1954 and survived an attempt to blow it up in 1970.

Marx's legacy in terms of his writing is well known and widely acknowledged. His political legacy in Britain, however, should not be forgotten. There was no mass Marxist party in Britain either during his lifetime or afterwards. But his achievement in helping to found and direct the First

---

57   Letter from Engels to F. Sorge, 17 March 1872, quoted in ibid., p. 134.
58   Exhibition in Museum of London.
59   Kapp, *Eleanor Marx*, vol. 1, p. 143.
60   Letter from Engels to Sorge, 15 March 1883, quoted in ibid., p. 246.

International should not be underestimated. It brought together disparate but important forces inside the British labour movement to campaign over international issues, and replicated this unity in the struggle for reform, which remained a major question in British politics for another fifty years. He was a socialist and internationalist who was not prepared to compromise his principles, even if it were at the expense of the International. Marx's theory developed out of his practical engagement in politics, and much of this – albeit not the most exciting part – was carried out in London.

It is ironic that around the time that Marx died, a new socialist movement was burgeoning in London. Among the many moves towards improvements in education, housing and health, the election of School Boards from 1870 – bodies open even to women – created a flurry of interest among the left. Benjamin Lucraft, the trade union leader, was elected to the Finsbury school board.[61] The left was small but its members were able to work inside the mass movements and political turmoil which so marked the 1880s in the city.

An early indication of how things were changing was the occasion of a demonstration in 1884, on the first anniversary of Marx's death and also called to mark the thirteenth anniversary of the start of the Commune. Eleanor Marx wrote to her sister Laura:

> I never – nor indeed did any of us, for a moment – believe that we should have more than a very small gathering – but when I tell you that between five and six thousand persons assembled you will see that it was really a splendid affair. The procession, with band and banners, started in Tottenham Street, and we marched – I going with them too – along Tottenham Court Road, Hampstead Rd., etc., to Highgate. The cemetery authorities had had the gates closed – and inside them were drawn up *five hundred policemen with six mounted police!* As we were refused admittance, and we asked if I and some ladies bearing crowns could go in alone, we adjourned to the top of the street just by the reservoir. It was a really grand sight.[62]

---

61   Cole and Postgate, *The Common People*, p. 395.
62   Letter from E. Marx to L. Lafargue, 17 March 1884, in Meier and Evans (eds), *Daughters of Karl Marx*, pp. 176.

6

Union City

Strange to say, the historians hardly notice the revolution we created.

Will Thorne

'FOR THE FIRST TIME SINCE 40 YEARS'

There can be few decades in the history of working-class London that were as momentous as the 1880s, when the working-class movement that had long lain dormant briefly revived. By the end of the decade, London had seen an explosion of strikes unprecedented in its history, the radicalisation of whole layers of working people and intellectuals over issues from Ireland to free speech to police brutality, and had set in train events which were to shape the labour movement for much of the next century. Friedrich Engels wrote to Laura Lafargue after the May Day demonstration in 1890, its huge numbers swelled because of these momentous events, 'I can assure you I looked a couple of inches taller when I got down from that old lumbering wagon that served as a platform – after having heard again, for the first time since 40 years, the unmistakeable voice of the English Proletariat.'[1]

What brought about these changes? In the 1850s British capitalism was at its high tide, unchallenged as a manufacturing power, in possession of the largest empire in the world, unchecked by a democratic political system at home or abroad. Social inequalities were huge. Henry Mayhew described them when writing about the London poor in the middle of the nineteenth century;[2] yet there was no mass upsurge of struggle then, nor any growth in socialist ideas.

By the 1870s that had begun to alter. Britain was now facing competition with a newly unified Germany and with a United States which had

---

1   Letter from Engels to Lafargue, quoted in Y. Kapp, *Eleanor Marx*, vol. 2, (London, 1976), p. 380.
2   H. Mayhew, *London Labour and the London Poor* (Robert Douglas-Fairhurst (ed.), Oxford, 2010).

recovered from the Civil War and was economically expanding. The depression which hit in the early 1870s continued, punctuated with a couple of fairly weak recoveries, right through into the 1880s. The extremes of wealth created by the empire had done nothing to benefit the mass of working people, who lived in often atrocious conditions. London had been particularly acutely affected by the decline of traditional shipbuilding industries which moved from the Thames in East London to the Tyne and the Clyde in the 1860s.

The 1880s were marked by growing social crisis and economic hardship in London. Living standards had fallen from the Great Depression of the 1870s and now there was the spectre of unemployment. When Engels wrote a new preface to his *Condition of the Working Class in England* in 1885, he warned: 'But as to the great mass of working people, the state of misery and insecurity in which they live now is as low as ever, if not lower. The East End of London is an ever-spreading pool of stagnant misery and desolation, of starvation when out of work, and degradation, physical and moral, when in work.'[3]

This phenomenon became a motive for agitation on the left, and conjured up terrifying scenarios for the middle classes. The word 'unemployed' only entered the Oxford English Dictionary in 1882, and 'unemployment' was first recorded there in 1888.[4] The workless were a new, permanent feature of London life, many of them casual labourers who worked only part of the year, concentrated in deprived areas of London and especially the East End. As the decade wore on they became increasingly discontented with their situation. It was in this period that a range of surveys looking at the desperation of the poor began to appear.

The existence of such levels of poverty in such a rich country troubled religious figures perhaps more than the politicians, since most of those affected by unemployment had no right to vote. General Booth, the founder of the Salvation Army, published *In Darkest London* in 1890, which as the title indicates made a direct comparison between 'darkest Africa' and the 'submerged tenth' in London. Booth originally set out to disprove the claims of the Social Democratic Federation that a quarter of Londoners lived in extreme poverty, but his studies showed that the situation was actually worse.[5] The Congregational minister Andrew Mearns wrote *The Bitter Cry of Outcast London* in 1883, eloquently detailing the misery of the poor:[6]

---

3   Engels, 'Preface', *Commonweal*, 1 March 1885, reprinted in Engels, *Condition of the Working Class in England* (Moscow, 1973), p. 35.
4   R. C. K. Ensor, *England 1870–1914* (Oxford, 1936), pp. 111–12.
5   G. Stedman Jones, *Outcast London* (Oxford, 1971), p. 306.
6   See Briggs, *Victorian Cities*, pp. 313–14.

November 1883 it issued its first Socialist pamphlet, *Socialism Made Plain*;[14] an increasingly overt identification with socialism led to it changing its name to the Social Democratic Federation (SDF) in 1884.

The revolutionary socialists were few in number but, while they never became mass organizations, the groups contained within them a remarkable mix of people: workers such as Tom Mann, Ben Tillett, Will Thorne, John Lincoln Mahon and Harry Quelch (the first three of whom became prominent in the new union battles), women campaigners such as Eleanor Marx, Annie Besant, Clementina Black, Amy Hicks and Beatrice Webb, and artists and writers such as William Morris and George Bernard Shaw. These talented individuals were all very active at a practical and intellectual level. They produced writings on a range of political and social issues, including on women, and Eleanor Marx and her partner Edward Aveling wrote the pamphlet *The Woman Question* in 1887.[15]

However, the SDF was hampered by shortcomings both political and personal. Its leader H. M. Hyndman had undeniable virtues: he was an effective popularizer of socialist ideas and a determined propagandist. But in many ways he could not shake off his Victorian middle-class persona, had a tendency to jingoism which betrayed his Tory past, and displayed an autocratic approach to leadership. Hyndman was a curious figure who seems almost incomprehensible now, with his conservative background, his dependence on the Radical Liberals but also his (unreciprocated) admiration for Marx, which led him towards scientific socialism – to the point of trying to incorporate a bowdlerized section of *Capital* into his party's programme.

The socialists rapidly fell out among themselves. In 1884 the SDF, not long after adopting its new name, split – with the Avelings, along with William Morris, forming the Socialist League. The Fabians – a small group of intellectuals committed to more gradual change, including Sidney and Beatrice Webb, George Bernard Shaw and Graham Wallas – started to articulate an explicitly anti-Marxist point of view in 1884.[16] They comprised the core of the group that only a few years later set up the London School of Economics. However, there was still much overlap between the groups, and it was only later, when events polarized politics, that the differences became clear. Thus Shaw attended Socialist League meetings right through the 1880s.[17]

---

14   The pamphlet may be consulted on archive.org. See also E. P. Thompson, *William Morris* (London, 1977), p. 296.

15   E. Aveling and E. Marx, *The Woman Question* (Joachim Muller and Edith Schotte eds, Leipzig 1887)

16   Thompson, *William Morris*, p. 332.

17   J. Charlton, *It Just Went Like Tinder* (London, 1999), p. 67.

Part of the reason for these splits can be put down to the sheer inexperience of the groups: there was little precedent for working together, and so real but containable differences tended to become the bases for splits rather than being resolved within one organization. Over and above the question of Hyndman's personal domination of the SDF, there was a division between those who saw themselves as involved in the struggle and agitating for change, and those whose approach to socialism was more propagandistic. E. P. Thompson has described the problem succinctly: 'Limited reforms were looked upon by most Socialists in 1884 with intense distrust.'[18]

They therefore all too often saw limited or single-issue campaigns as a waste of time, since they would not overthrow capitalism. They had learnt that capitalism could not be reformed, but had not learnt of the need to organize round issues which could take the movement forward and so increase the influence of socialists and thus open up the possibility of socialist change. As the 1880s went on this division became greater, so that during the mighty struggles at the end of the decade individual socialists could play leading and often pivotal roles without the socialist organizations gaining in size or influence. This proved an enduring problem.

The workers would have done much of what they did, in all probability, without the input of the socialists; but there is little doubt that socialist ideas made sense to those coming to protest and strike action for the first time, and the socialists as individuals were committed to building those working-class activities in ways which made them relevant to working people across the board.[19] While these radical ideas were gaining increasing sway among sections of the London intelligentsia, it could escape no one's attention that the misery of the poor in London was increasing. It was out of this misery and the conditions which developed there that the working-class movement arose.

BLOODY SUNDAY

The new workers' movement spent some years being born. One of the most popular activities for socialists from 1884 was to hold meetings in parks and streets, and sell papers and other literature. The SDF paper was called *Justice*, and that of the SL, *Commonweal*. One of their first campaigns was about their right to make propaganda, a right repeatedly denied. Time and again there were issues around free speech and agitation. William Morris campaigned in Walham Green and on Hammersmith Bridge where the SL had set up stands, often accompanied by Shaw who was a fine outdoor

---

18   Thompson, *William Morris*, p. 337.
19   For a readable assessment on this see Charlton, *Like Tinder*, Chapter 4, pp. 64–8.

speaker. But agitation flourished above all in the East End, exemplified by the major campaign which took place in 1885.

The East End Radicals had been used to speaking regularly in open-air meetings on Mile End Waste, but were driven off by police harassment and moved to Limehouse. On one occasion, when the speaker was an SDF member, the meeting was stopped by police for causing an obstruction. The socialists moved to a quiet street nearby to continue their meetings. Week after week they mounted their soapboxes in Dod St, Poplar. But from August the police moved in to stop them. So every week a speaker would be arrested by police, bound over and fined. SDF member Jack Williams refused to be bound over and was sent to prison for a month. Thus began a mass struggle for free speech. On 20 September a demonstration of 7,000 heard an array of orators defending the right to free speech. The meeting broke up in scuffles with the police. The next day, eight were in court on charges of resisting the police or obstruction, including Mahon and the Jewish socialist Lewis Lyons. Those who gave evidence for them such as the Avelings were upbraided by the magistrate, who imposed a sentence of two months' hard labour on Lyons. The court erupted, and the police attacked the protestors. When William Morris came to Eleanor's defence he was arrested.[20] The following week up to 60,000 demonstrated again in Dod Street. This time the police did not intervene.[21]

Socialist and radical culture in East London was open-air: meetings would be held by the various groups in Victoria Park, Mile End Waste, the Salmon and Ball pub in Bethnal Green and Dod St.[22] The agitation was subject to regular attempts to close it down. Victoria Park was also a hotbed of sedition where every Sunday all manner of soap-box orators of various religious and political hues would attract large crowds. In 1888 the police enforced a by-law prohibiting collections in the park – thus denying the socialists a major source of income. The Socialist League called a protest meeting on 10 June, addressed by among others Annie Besant who was to play a major role in the match workers' strike. The crowd of 2,000 listened to speakers for several hours. Besant then made a collection which resulted in the park keepers taking her name. This process continued for several weeks, but the campaign prevented prosecutions and eventually the police abandoned their attempts.[23]

These events in the East End had their counterparts in the West End. In 1886 police cracked down at another meeting site, in Bell Street off the Edgware Road. The same pattern of arrests and harassment followed, with

---

20 Thompson, *William Morris*, pp. 394–7.
21 Kapp, *Eleanor Marx,* vol. 2, pp. 69–71.
22 Fishman, *East End Jewish Radicals*, p. 334.
23 Ibid., pp. 333–4.

heavy fines. But the socialists were determined to continue, finding new pitches if necessary and garnering support from wider layers of society. It was becoming clear that there would be big battles ahead.

In February that year panic broke out in London after a demonstration of the unemployed led by the SDF left Trafalgar Square and proceeded to Hyde Park through some of the richest streets of the capital, headed up by John Burns carrying a red flag. The response to this sight from the gentlemen's clubs in Pall Mall was for the unemployed to be pelted with missiles such as shoe brushes by the club servants. They countered by smashing windows along the way from Pall Mall to Piccadilly and South Audley Street in Mayfair and then Oxford Street, where they smashed more windows, looted shops and robbed rich passers-by. Many of the rich feared the worst: 'Rumours flew that the East End was marching through the fog to the West.'[24] Yet the actions had a direct and immediate effect: 'The Mansion House Fund for the unemployed rocketed overnight.' And 'the authorities in Glasgow found work for 895 unemployed in *one day* when the news of the Trafalgar Square riots came through.'[25]

Unrest continued in the next years as the conditions in London remained appalling for those out of work or in poverty, and socialist agitation grew. The following year, as was usual in hot summers, the homeless and unemployed took to sleeping in Trafalgar Square, and found themselves repeatedly harassed by the police. Again the socialists began to organize among them, demanding work. They attracted some sympathy and even bread vans to help feed them.[26] By October the square was a centre of near daily activity by the unemployed and their supporters. On 17, 18 and 19 October the square was cleared by mounted police and baton charges. When in early November daily meetings resumed, it was cleared on 4 November and the red flag taken.[27] This public presence of the poor on West End streets led the police to crack down. Sir Charles Warren, head of the Metropolitan Police, banned protests in the square. In response, William Morris proposed setting up a Law and Liberty League.[28] Events moved dramatically shortly after this: on 13 November 1887 a mass demonstration assembled in the square in defiance of the ban. It had been called on the issue of Ireland to protest at the prison treatment of the Irish MP William O'Brien, but was now also about the right to free speech. The demonstration was to have very far-reaching consequences, and did much to change the politics of radical London in the coming years.

---

24 Thompson, *William Morris*, p. 406.
25 Ibid., p. 407.
26 White, *London in the Nineteenth Century*, pp. 375–7.
27 Thompson, *William Morris*, p. 488.
28 Ibid.

The demonstration unified the disparate groups and campaigns into one big united rally, made up of a series of marches converging on the square from all the poor areas of London. Before they could reach the square, however, they were systematically attacked by the police under Warren's direction. The Clerkenwell feeder march was intercepted at the top of St Martin's Lane; the South London marchers on Westminster Bridge:

> Borne by members of the procession were about 15 banners and for these the police made ... During the melee, the police freely used their weapons, and the people, who were armed with iron bars, pokers, gas pipes and short sticks, and even knives, resisted them in a most determined manner ... A similar scene was being enacted in the Strand at the corner of Wellington Street.[29]

Few of the demonstrations could get into the square, but those able to do so formed up in St Martin's Lane and Northumberland Avenue, to be met with repeated police charges. The police brutality was countered with resistance, and the street battles continued for many hours. The Riot Act was read and troops from the various Guards regiments turned up with bayonets and rifles. Police batoned and injured many: 200 people were taken to hospital, two people died as a result of their injuries and there were 300 arrests.[30] Those arrested included a number of the leaders of the marches, such as John Burns and Cunninghame Graham MP, who tried to defy the ban and enter the square. Eleanor Marx arrived at Engels's house that Sunday evening with her clothes ruined. Eleanor wrote to her sister, 'I daresay the General [Engels] will tell you in what a condition "tattered and torn" I reached Regent's Park on Sunday evening. You know it really is no joke to get knocked about, and knocked down by a brute of a policeman.'[31] Eleanor also wrote to the *Pall Mall Gazette*: 'I have never seen anything like the brutality of the police, and the Germans and Austrians who know what police brutality can be, have said the same to me. I need not tell you I was in the thick of the fight at Parliament Street and afterwards in Northumberland Avenue. I got pretty roughly used myself.'[32]

The shock of the police violence and the brutal treatment meted out to demonstrators meant the day was thereafter referred to as 'Bloody Sunday', and a demonstration held on its fifth anniversary attracted crowds of many thousands. It marked another stage in the development of the emerging

---

29 Report from *Reynolds's Newspaper*, 20 November 1887, quoted in E. J. Hobsbawm, *Labour's Turning Point* (Brighton, 1974), p. 27.
30 Kapp, *Eleanor Marx*, vol. 2, pp. 226–7.
31 Letter to Laura Lafargue, 16 November 1887, quoted in ibid., p. 229.
32 *Pall Mall Gazette*, 14 November 1887.

socialist and trade union movement, as large numbers were confronted with the power of the state prepared to defend property and power in ways which had not been seen for decades. It was not until fourteen Irish protestors in Derry were shot by the British army in 1972, nearly 100 years later, that the term came to apply widely to a different event.

Immediately after Bloody Sunday the Law and Liberty League was founded, its slogan echoing the Irish cause: 'Home Rule for London'.[33] The Friday afterwards over 500 people crammed into its launch meeting at the Memorial Hall in Farringdon.[34] There had been much argument within the movement over how to respond to the ban on protests in Trafalgar Square. The Radicals tended to favour assembling somewhere else, so tacitly accepted the ban, while the socialists wanted to defy it. Police let it be known that protestors would be allowed to assemble in Hyde Park, but on the following Sunday very large crowds defied the ban and returned to Trafalgar Square. The police repeatedly attacked the crowds. This time a worker, Alfred Linnell, who was apparently only watching the demonstration, was mown down by police and died later in hospital.

The police had created a martyr. The reaction to the killing of Linnell can be seen in the huge size of the crowds which turned out for his funeral, wending all through London to the West End. William Morris and Annie Besant were among the pall-bearers. Even now police repression hampered those who turned out to pay their respects to the dead man. The aim was to begin the cortege at the spot where he fell, on the south side of the square by Northumberland Avenue. The way to assemble here was blocked, and the funeral procession was denied entry into Trafalgar Square. But the funeral continued through the City where at every major meeting point such as St Paul's Cathedral, the march was joined by ever more people. So Linnell was accompanied by a mass demonstration through the City to the East End, where at Mile End the crowd swelled even larger, and where he was buried.

At Mile End the streets were packed with East Londoners. One estimate put the procession in East London at nearly 100,000, stretching back a mile and a half.[35] The cemetery gates were closed to demonstrators, who had to squeeze through a side entrance to get to the grave. The procession was estimated to be the biggest since the Chartists. The artist Walter Crane designed the cover of a pamphlet which contained William Morris's song commemorating Linnell, and which was sold to raise money for his orphaned children. This death song was sung at Linnell's grave after a short service in the pouring rain and dark of December, presided over by the

---

33   *Pall Mall Gazette*, 14 November 1887.
34   Ibid., 19 November 1887.
35   See *The National Reformer*, 25 December 1887, p. 405.

Christian socialist Reverend Stewart Headlam and addressed by, among others, Morris, Harry Quelch for the SDF, and the London organizer of the Irish National League. Morris's song contained the final verse:

> Here lies the sign that we shall break our prison;
> Amidst the storm he won a prisoner's rest;
> But in the cloudy dawn the sun arisen
> Brings us our day of work to win the best.
> Not one, not one, nor thousands must they slay,
> But one and all if they would dusk the day.[36]

Cunninghame Graham, Burns and other participants were imprisoned following the demonstration. There was much agitation round this, and their release from Pentonville Prison on 19 February 1888 was greeted with social events and mass meetings addressed by socialists, radicals and Irish nationalists.[37]

Bloody Sunday marked a turning point: Shaw concluded that reform was the way forward and moved away from any commitment to revolutionary politics, along with the rest of the Fabians.[38] To others it demonstrated that the state and police would not countenance even peaceful protest. Many of those involved in demonstrating and protesting, and those who marched at Linnell's funeral, were to very quickly find themselves in another and much more sustained fight.

THE MATCH GIRLS' STRIKE[39]

At the end of 1887 the London working class was approaching boiling point. In the next two years it surprised everyone by organizing a series of mass strikes which involved precisely the people who had seemed so hopelessly poor and difficult to organize in all the descriptions and surveys of the East End. The first group to go were the match girls at the Bryant and May factory in Fairfield Road, Bow. The work was hard, carried out largely by low-waged and often very young women:

> At Stratford and near Stratford Bridge, in an awfully evil-smelling place called Marsh Gate Lane, there are several Lucifer-match manufactories,

---

36 Kapp, *Eleanor Marx*, vol. 2, pp. 241–2.
37 Thompson, *William Morris*, pp. 496–7.
38 Ibid., pp. 498–503.
39 The newest book on their strike refers to them as the Matchwomen. While we agree with the sentiments underlying this change, we have kept the traditional terminology simply because it is so much more familiar. See L. Raw, *Striking a Light* (London, 2011).

at which the hands employed appear to be chiefly female ... From one Lucifer-match factory gate alone I saw at least a hundred young girls emerge ... a more draggletail, poverty-stricked crowd of poor little wretches I never set eyes upon.[40]

The conditions in the Bryant and May factory were such that there was widespread discontent among the mainly teenage girls who worked there. They were subject to fines and deductions, penalised for minor infringements, and worked in such a toxic atmosphere that they developed a form of cancer known as 'phossy jaw' owing to the phosphorus used in match making. The company erected a statue to the Liberal leader William Gladstone in the Bow Road in 1882, the cost of which they deducted from their workers' pay; they also granted them an unpaid half-day holiday for its unveiling. The women so resented this treatment that they went along with stones in their pockets to throw, and some even cut their arms and let their blood fall on the statue, to show that they regarded it as paid for with their blood.[41] Even today, the statue is regularly daubed with red paint. A council official told Louise Raw in 2006 that it isn't always cleaned after such an attack, for fear of it happening again, because 'it's very expensive to get it removed'.[42]

The young women were mainly Irish or of Irish descent. And it is probably fair to make the assumption that they would have been, along with their families, involved in or at least affected by the Irish agitation over Home Rule which reached its crescendo in the 1880s with numerous demonstrations and meetings, especially in the Irish areas.[43] It is also likely that some would have come across the socialists in Victoria Park and elsewhere in the East End in the course of the various campaigns, such as that over free speech.

The strike was closely linked to such agitation. The socialist Annie Besant, editor of a paper called *The Link*, was persuaded to investigate and to expose the conditions at Bryant and May's in the summer of 1888, following a Fabian Society meeting addressed by Clementina Black in which the low wages and high dividends paid to shareholders were discussed. A resolution moved by H. H. Champion and seconded by Herbert Burrows was carried at the meeting:

40　J. Greenwood, 'White Slavery', from *Toilers in London* (1883), cited in Lewis, *London: The Autobiography*, pp. 308–9.

41　See 'White slavery in London', *The Link*, Issue 2, Saturday 23 June 1888 (London).

42　See Raw, *Striking a Light*, pp. 150–1.

43　On this point see Charlton, *Like Tinder*, pp. 22–5.

That this meeting, being aware that the shareholders of Bryant and May are receiving a dividend of over 20 per cent, and at the same time are paying their workers only 2 1/4d per gross for making matchboxes, pledges itself not to use or purchase any matches made by this firm.[44]

Besant talked to some of the workers and duly wrote a searing exposé entitled 'White Slavery in London', published in the *Link* on 23 June and distributed as a leaflet outside the factory. The response of the owners of the company was to threaten to sue, which she resisted, and to demand that all their workers sign a statement refuting the allegations. When they refused, the company victimized three of the workers who were alleged to have talked to Besant. The whole workforce stood behind them. The strike began on 5 July with 1,500 women walking out.[45] One contemporary report noted the spontaneity and solidarity of the strike:

> At the time of the strike . . . a girl was asked why it had taken place. 'Well, it just went like tinder,' she said; 'one girl began, and the rest said "yes", so out we all went.'
> When the girls were being paid their week's wages at Charrington's Hall on Mile End Waste after the strike, it was curious to see the waves of feeling that rolled over their faces, how all seemed influenced at the same time, and in the same manner, by what was said and done for them. And few people could help being touched by the way in which the girls were determined to stand together at all costs.[46]

Support for the strike was widespread throughout London, and especially in the East End. Socialists came and campaigned for the women, including the feminist Clementina Black, the Rev. Stewart Headlam and Besant herself. On 8 July the strikers passed a resolution to form a union, and a few days later a large delegation marched to Besant's house in Bouverie Street in the City, where they went to tea, and a smaller group continued to Parliament to put their case.[47]

George Bernard Shaw spoke at meetings to raise support for them, which came from well beyond the capital. Despite some of the women returning to work and the hope of the company that it could induce mass scabbing, the

---

44   From 'White Slavery in London'.

45   For accounts of the strike see W. J. Fishman, *East End 1888* (Nottingham, 2008), pp. 350–5. See also Charlton, *Like Tinder*. For the most detailed and interesting account, putting the workers themselves rather than Besant at the centre of the strike, see Raw, *Striking a Light*.

46   From *Toilers in London*, quoted in Hobsbawm, *Labour's Turning Point*, p. 78.

47   Fishman, *East End 1888*, p. 352.

strikers' own determination and the wide levels of solidarity and public support forced Bryant and May to capitulate, the women winning most of their demands. A week later a committee met to draft the rules of the new Matchmakers' Union. As well as Besant this included Clementina Black, representatives of the London Trades Council and Herbert Burrows. On 27 July the proposals were put to the women at the Stepney Meeting House in Stepney Green. It was a real achievement, and marked a turning point for union organization.

Just after the strike ended many of the women joined a mass demonstration against sweating, prompted by the strike and the ongoing House of Lords Sweating Committee. It assembled in Canning Town, marched through the docks to Mile End Waste to meet contingents from Limehouse, Bethnal Green and Berners Street; then to Gardiners Corner where it met up with a Hackney contingent, and on through the City and West End to Hyde Park. The women carried a large matchbox, with the list of prices paid for their work painted on the side.[48]

THE DAM BURSTS

Strikes now began to erupt on all fronts, with other East End match workers now coming out. The women had begun a wave of industrial action which would continue for two years. The crowning glory came in the following year, however, with the eruption of fights in support of the eight-hour day. Two major developments in union organization stand out in the East End. The first was the gas workers' dispute in March 1889, the second the great dock strike for the 'dockers' tanner' (sixpence an hour) which took place in late summer that year. The gas workers succeeded in winning a union without having to go on strike.

The gas workers were based in Beckton, part of the Thameside marshland which was an industrial wasteland, and now at the eastern tip of the London borough of Newham served by one of the most far-flung stations on the Docklands Light Railway. The gas workers' leader was Will Thorne, already a committed socialist in the SDF who had been agitating around issues such as free speech, and had chaired some of the open-air meetings in Dod Street back in 1885. He began to organize a union in Beckton, where twelve hours was the normal day, and where before and after this shift many workers had to walk miles home to Poplar or Canning Town. After four months Thorne's union had 20,000 members.[49]

The key demand of the gasworkers was for the eight-hour day. Thorne described the inaugural meeting:

---

48   Fishman, *East End 1888*, pp. 334–6.
49   H. Pelling, *A History of Trade Unionism* (London, 1971), p. 97.

Sunday morning, March 31ˢᵗ, 1889 – a lovely sunny morning – was the birth-day of the National Union of Gasworkers and General Labourers of Great Britain and Ireland ... Eight hundred joined that morning. The entrance fee was one shilling, and we had to borrow several pails to hold the coppers and other coins that were paid in ... The news of the meeting spread like wild-fire; in the public houses, factories and works in Canning Town, Barking, East and West Ham, everyone was talking about the union ... Sunday after Sunday we would start off from 144 Barking Road, our headquarters, to encourage the men at other gas-works. As many as twenty brake-loads of workers would go out on these Sunday morning crusades. [50]

The Gas Light and Coke Company and other major employers conceded the demands of the union, especially the eight-hour day, the shift pattern being changed to allow a third shift. Thorne was elected general secretary of the union in June 1889; by July there were forty-four branches in London alone and another sixteen outside the City. A mass victory rally was held in Battersea on 17 July, followed by a concert where the 'Third Shift' workers from Beckton presented Thorne with a silver watch and chain. [51]

THE DOCKERS' TANNER

The dockers' strike of 1889 – the greatest and most memorable of all – broke out on 14 August, just weeks after the gas workers won their demands. There were not just geographical links between the two groups of workers: gas work was seasonal, and many of those who were laid off from February found work as dockers over the summer. The dockers had hitherto been regarded as nearly unorganizable, apart from small numbers of relatively skilled men. Descriptions of the life and work of dock labour-ers repeatedly portray a brutalized, uncertain and divided workforce. Ben Tillett compared them to rats in a cage when they fought for work. [52] The general manager of Millwall Docks said that 'There are men who come ... on without having a bit of food in their stomachs, perhaps since the previous day; they have worked for an hour and have earned 5d; their hunger will not allow them to continue; they take the 5d in order that they may get food, perhaps the first food they have had for twenty-four hours.' [53]

50   W. Thorne, *My Life's Battles*, pp. 69ff.
51   Kapp, *Eleanor Marx*, vol. 2, p. 321.
52   See D. Torr, *Tom Mann and His Times*, vol. 1 (1956), p. 281.
53   Evidence to the House of Lord Committee on Sweating in 1888 from H. L. Smith and V. Nash, *The Story of the Dockers' Strike 1889*, p. 47, quoted in Hobsbawm, *Labour's Turning Point*, p. 82.

Henry Mayhew's study of mid-century London described a system where the men had to sometimes fight physically for a day's work, and were dependent on the whims and fancies of the foremen who hired them: 'As the foreman calls from a book the names, some men jump upon the backs of the others, so as to lift themselves high above the rest, and attract the attention of him who hires them. All are shouting ... Indeed, it is a sight to sadden the most callous, to see *thousands* of men struggling for only one day's hire ... To look in the faces of that hungry crowd, is to see a sight that must ever be remembered.'[54]

This general background was compounded by forms of piecework known as 'plus' which were controlled by the employers, pittance wages which had not risen for twenty years, and a growing precariousness due to the casualized methods which allowed absolutely no job security. The successes in Bow and Beckton fresh in East End memories, and led by the veteran socialist and militant Ben Tillett – who had already organized a union for the tea workers in 1887, and who had been central in building solidarity for the match girls and the gas workers – the dockers struck following a dispute on one ship.

The strike began at the West India Dock and it spread over the next week throughout the port area, including the newly opened Tilbury Docks downriver in Essex, bringing out not just the unskilled workers but many of the skilled such as the stevedores, who refused to work with strike-breakers. The dockers who stopped in one dock would go to other docks to persuade workers to come out. Within a week the whole Port of London was idle. The most famous demand formulated by the dockers was for 6d an hour – the 'dockers' tanner' – but the strike was as much about security of work, with dockers demanding at least half-day periods of employment when they were taken on and the abolition of plus.

The strike was remarkable in many ways. First, the dockers developed the tactic, masterminded by John Burns, of marching through the City of London every day. On the first march there were 'forty-one banners, some no more than red rags on poles, but some stranger. There were stinking onions, old fish-heads, and indescribable pieces of meat stuck on spikes, to show the City magnates what the dockers had to live on. Each day the processions were repeated, growing larger and larger, and commonly ending in Hyde Park.'[55]

Two contemporary witnesses describe the procession as having 'the appearance of a great church parade or demonstration of foresters' actually

---

54   H. Mayhew, *The Morning Chronicle Survey of Labour and the Poor*, vol. 1, pp. 71–2, cited in White, *London in the Nineteenth Century*, p. 185.
55   Cole and Postgate, *The Common People*, p. 428.

made up of 'stevedores, lightermen, ship painters, sailors and firemen, riggers, scrapers, engineers, shipwrights ... [and] Doggett's prize winners, a stalwart battalion of watermen marching proudly in long scarlet coats, pink stockings and velvet caps, with huge pewter badges on their breasts'.[56]

Secondly, the leadership of the workers was a group of determined and experienced socialists who threw themselves into the battle in what was in many ways a precarious strike. They showed high levels of tactical and strategic skill; they also realized the nature of the enemy and the importance of defeating it. People like Tom Mann understood the need for picketing which was organized highly effectively to prevent the ever present danger of strike-breaking. The strike was centrally managed from Wroots Coffee House in Poplar, and also conducted through a daily meeting at Tower Hill.

The third remarkable feature of the strike was the level of support that it gained from other trade unionists and from the public. The then immense sum of £30,000 was raised from Australia alone, and another £11,000 from the British public. The sense of solidarity which this engendered helped the morale of the strikers as well as providing sustenance for them and their families. The strike deeply impressed the left, as the two opinions below testify. The Fabian Beatrice Webb wrote of it:

> The strike is intensely interesting to me personally, as proving or disprov-
> ing, in any case modifying, my generalization on 'Dock Life'. Certainly
> the solidarity of labour at the East End is a new thought to me – the dock
> labourers have not yet proved themselves capable of permanent organi-
> zation but they have shown the capacity for common action. And what is
> more important, an extraordinary manifestation of practical sympathy, of
> effectual help, has been evoked among all classes in east London, skilled
> artisans making common cause with casuals, publicans, pawnbrokers and
> tradesmen supporting them.[57]

Friedrich Engels wrote to the *Labour Elector*:

> It is the movement of the greatest promise we have had for years, and I
> am proud and glad to have lived to see it. If Marx had lived to witness
> this! If these poor down-trodden men, the dregs of the proletariat, these
> odds and ends of all trades, fighting every morning at the dock gates for
> an engagement, if *they* can combine, and terrify by their resolution the
> mighty Dock Companies, truly then we need not despair of any section

---

56 V. Nash and H. Llewellyn-Smith, cited in Hobsbawm, *Labour's Turning Point*, pp. 84–5.
57 B. Webb, *The Diary 1873–92*, cited in Lewis, *London: The Autobiography*, p. 347.

of the working class. This is the beginning of real life in the East End, and
if successful will transform the whole character of the East End.[58]

It was not just on the left that the strike garnered support; some of the
loftiest representatives of respectable opinion stepped in to try to negotiate
with the employers. Two main players were the Lord Mayor of London
and the Roman Catholic Cardinal Manning – large numbers of the dockers were Catholics of Irish descent. The employers conceded most of the
demands in mediation with Manning, leading Burns at one meeting near
the end of the strike to refer to it as the 'Lucknow of Labour' (a reference
to the siege of an army garrison in the Indian town of Lucknow, where
they looked for the silver gleam of the bayonets of troops coming to relieve
them.) He continued: 'I myself . . . can see a silver gleam – not of bayonets
to be imbrued in a brother's blood, but the gleam of the full round orb of
the Dockers' tanner.'[59]

SOCIALISTS, STRIKES AND THE NEW UNIONS

The victory of the strike after just over three weeks led to the formation of
the new union which was to become the Transport and General Workers
Union (now part of Unite). The dockers flooded into the union, as did
other transport workers, their recruitment followed by a wave of strikes in
the East End as well as other parts of working-class London. One assessment puts the number of strikes, in a triangle going from the City to King's
Cross and Blackwall, at the end of August and beginning of September
1889, at more than fifty, excluding the docks strike; there were at least
another sixteen in South and West London.[60] This also puts the number of
strikers on 1 September 1889 in the same triangle (including the 150,000
on strike around the docks) at 300,000 – a huge number for a population
of under 6 million in the whole city. Interestingly, of those strikes outside
this triangle most were near the river – several in Bermondsey and Millwall,
which were dock areas and some in Lambeth, Battersea and Pimlico, which
front the river further west.[61]

These figures suggest turmoil in the riverside areas and in wider working-
class London, where there was no letting up of strikes, demonstrations and
meetings for the rest of the year. The gas workers continued their unionization drive at the South Metropolitan Gas Company. There was a major strike
of Jewish tailors overlapping with that of the dockers, who received solidarity

---

58   MECW, vol. 26, p. 545.
59   Cole and Postgate, *The Common People*, p. 430.
60   Charlton, *Like Tinder*, p. 98.
61   Ibid., pp. 137–8n.

from non-Jewish trade unionists. The Jewish tailors' trade unions followed on from some smaller strikes in the area. On 26 August at a public meeting called under their name they elected a strike committee, and also passed a resolution for a general strike. The tailors' strike involved 6,000 workers and closed 120 workshops. Its strike headquarters was in a pub off the Commercial Road, the White Hart in Greenfield Street, and its two leaders were the left-wingers Woolf Wess and Lewis Lyons. Their daily marches to Victoria Park were addressed by dockers' leaders like Mann, Burns and Tillett, and they received practical solidarity from their non-Jewish comrades. On 26 September a member of the dock strike committee handed over £100 to the tailors' relief fund, and three days later a mass demonstration in their support took place in Hyde Park and was joined by leading socialists.[62]

One major recurring name at the time was that of Eleanor Marx Aveling, who played an increasingly important part in the struggle for the 'new unions'. She performed both an agitational role – speaking at meetings and helping to spread the strikes – and an administrative one. Will Thorne, who had started work at the age of six and was unable to read or write, was helped by Eleanor to develop these skills. As we have seen, she was one of the main figures in the socialist movement at the time, tirelessly active until her lamented suicide at the age of forty-three in 1898. Many years later Thorne wrote: 'But for this tragedy, I believe Eleanor would have still been living, and would have been a greater women's leader than the greatest of contemporary women.'[63]

There were few who could match her in energy and intellect, or who had her incisiveness and understanding of class society. She combined a strong intellectual and theoretical grasp of socialism with a refusal to preach politics from the sidelines. She rejected the tendency of some socialists to regard the real struggles of workers, their growing readiness to strike and their commitment to building unions, as somehow lesser struggles than putting the pure case for socialism. Throughout the 1880s she worked with William Morris, joining the Socialist League when it split from the SDF in 1884; later, when it came under greater anarchist influence, they withdrew from that too, and formed the Bloomsbury Socialist Society.

She knew and worked with the leading left-wing trade unionists of the time including Tom Mann, Ben Tillett and John Burns, as well as Thorne, their names repeatedly cropping up as speakers on demonstrations and meetings alongside her. She loved theatre and translated the Norwegian playwright Ibsen, as well as doing play readings with George Bernard Shaw, who modelled two of the characters in his play *The Doctor's Dilemma*

62   Fishman, *East End Jewish Radicals,* pp. 169–79.
63   W. Thorne, quoted in Kapp, *Eleanor Marx*, vol. 2, p. 702.

on Eleanor and her lover, Edward Aveling.[64] Friedrich Engels was like a second father to her. Her political consciousness was such that she wrote to Abraham Lincoln at the age of ten advising him on how best to win the American Civil War, and two years later declared herself a supporter of the Irish Fenians. She retained a lifelong commitment to the cause of the Paris Commune, speaking at anniversary meetings which took place among exiles and socialists every spring in London.

However, Eleanor's great achievement was the role she played in building the new unions. As well as militating with the gas workers she supported other strikes in the East End and across London. She was on the executive of the Gas Workers' Union in recognition of her invaluable contribution – a remarkable achievement for a woman. She also set up a women's branch of the union. Her major intervention was in a lengthy and bitter strike of 2,000 workers in the autumn of 1889, which was eventually unsuccessful. It took place a short distance away from where the gas workers had achieved their demands for an eight-hour day. This time, the strike at Silver's – a firm processing rubber and gutta-percha latex in wasteland near the Thames, after which Silvertown is named – required daily travel there from her home in central London. Eleanor took on this work tirelessly, despite her many other commitments including efforts to form a new (second) International of socialists. Despite huge levels of protest and agitation involving marches to the City of London, rallies in Hyde Park, Clerkenwell Green and Victoria Park in the East End, the workers were after three months forced back to work without a victory.[65] Part of the reason for their defeat was their failure to get out the skilled engineers, members of the ASE, in support of the unskilled. Engels wrote to an old comrade in the US at the end of 1889:

> Formally, the movement is first of all a trade union movement, but utterly different from that of the *old* Trade Unions of skilled labourers, the labour aristocracy. The people are making a much greater effort than before now, they are drawing far greater masses into the struggle, shaking up society far more profoundly, and putting forward much more far-reaching demands: the eight-hour day, a general federation of all organisations, and complete solidarity. Through Tussy [the Marx family's name for Eleanor], the Gas-Workers' and General Labourers' Union has got women's branches *for the first time*. Moreover, the people regard their immediate demands as only provisional, although they themselves do not yet know toward what final goal they are working. But this vague

---

64   See Thompson, *William Morris*, pp. 367–9.
65   Kapp, *Eleanor Marx*, vol. 2, pp. 336–58.

notion has a strong enough hold on them to make them elect as leaders *only* downright Socialists.[66]

The year ended with workers having scored notable victories and made great strides towards union organization open to all workers. This was a major development and one which changed working-class organization in Britain. While previously the unions had been the preserve of a minority of skilled workers, mostly men, now the mass of the unskilled had found a place for themselves. Women workers, previously regarded as impossible to organize, now became a major part of the organized working class where they achieved remarkable prominence, given the general position of women in society at that time. Immigrant workers from Ireland and Russia showed that they could organize themselves and win disputes.

The East End did not become the 'cradle of new unionism' by chance: it was the location of the worst and in many ways most exploitative trades. The sweating faced by many workers including the tailors and the match workers led to waves of discontent. The dirty industries such as Silver's, based around the imports that arrived at the docks, were ripe for organization. In addition the poverty and crowded conditions of the East End created a degree of solidarity amid the misery of many workers, and turned the area into an asset for those building the strikes.

It is impossible to conclude that these strikes happened in isolation. The family, friendship, religious and neighbourhood ties of the East Enders all helped to disseminate ideas and actions, and to open up a new era in working-class struggle. The examples of strikes spread across the area: for example, Keiller's jam factory workers from Silvertown turned up at the Silver's strike in October 1889 to ask for advice on forming a union.[67]

The profound effects of the strikes continued in 1890, spreading to other parts of London and particularly to food-processing factories. The onion skinners in Crosse and Blackwell's East Ham plant struck for higher wages and won in August 1890. Eleanor Marx was signatory to a letter urging support for them.[68] The growing number of shop assistants also started to organize, as when the Hammersmith branch of the Shop Assistants' Union called for a boycott of shops which would not reduce their workers' hours. Again, after support from the socialists and more agitation, the retailers all gave in.[69] In September women workers at Barratt's sweet factory walked

---

66 Letter from Engels to Sorge in Hoboken, 7 December 1889, in *Marx and Engels Selected Correspondence* (Moscow, 1982), pp. 385–6.
67 Kapp, *Eleanor Marx*, vol. 2, p. 349.
68 Letter in *People's Press*, 19 July 1890, cited in ibid., pp. 392–3.
69 Ibid., pp. 367–8.

out and were joined by hundreds in a march through South Tottenham. They too later joined the Gas Workers' union.[70]

There was also what turned into perhaps the greatest triumph of 1890: a mass May Day demonstration, to mark workers' day and workers' organization. Although the initiative to hold May Day demonstrations was an international one, proposed at the Paris International Congress in 1889, the London May Day was a spin-off from the great movement of the previous year and this was reflected in its composition. Despite extensive arguments in the run-up to the day about whether it should take place on the first or fourth day of the month (the fourth won out) it was a big success. Demonstrators assembled

> until the grass was swallowed up and the only prospect was people thick – thronged everywhere ... and all the time the procession was still coming in. There was the banner of the Postmen's Union ... A slight break and up came the dockers, an interminable array with multitudinous banners. ... Then came a large contingent of women – rope-makers, matchmakers and others. Looked at from above they advanced like a moving rainbow, for they all wore the huge feathers of many colours which the East End lass loves to sport when she is out for the day.[71]

But it was already clear that despite the strikes and union organization, the employers were fighting a very tough rearguard action, and soon felt in a position to go on the offensive. We have already seen that in 1889 some of the disputes were failing to prevail, and as the strike wave ebbed the employers took their opportunity to win back the advantage. The biggest defeat for workers took place not in London but in the Manningham mill in Bradford in 1890, and from then on this offensive continued, culminating in the lockout of the skilled engineers – first in London and then nationally – when they demanded a reduction in their daily hours from nine to eight.

The balance sheet of these years was however of a move forward for the working class. Membership of unions expanded vastly over the next few years. The figure for union membership before the union upsurge in 1888 was an estimated 750,000 in the whole of Britain. This rose to 1,576,000 by 1892 and despite a dip rose to more than 2 million by the turn of the century.[72] Transport workers in unions multiplied by more than ten times in the period from 1888 to the outbreak of the First World War.[73] There were less than

---

70   Ibid., p. 401.
71   From *The Star*, 5 May 1890, cited in Hobsbawm, *Labour's Turning Point*, p. 111. Hobsbawn puts estimated numbers at 500,000.
72   E. H. Hunt, *British Labour History 1815–1914* (London 1981), p. 295.
73   Ibid., p. 297.

50,000 women trade unionists when the match girls went out on strike, but this figure doubled over the next five years and quadrupled again by 1913.[74]

The new unions expanded and even the old craft groupings began to see the benefits of this, with big increases for shipbuilding, building, mining and railway unions.[75] The consolidation of the unions went hand in hand with a growing bureaucratization. Some of the most vibrant and militant leaders of 1889 became heads of large general unions, and as a result much more politically cautious. However, the gas workers' and dockers' agitation of those years helped to found new general unions which for the first time attempted to organize across the board, including sectors previously considered beyond reach such as women and immigrants. Through a process of amalgamations they eventually went on to become today's two main manual workers' unions: Unite and the GMB.

LONDON'S NEW POLITICS

There were political consequences from this movement in London. In the general election of 1892 John Burns, one of the strike leaders, was elected as SDF MP in Battersea, and the Scotsman Keir Hardie won a similar victory in West Ham. Both had played an important part in the new union battles. Burns had organized around the big gasworks at Vauxhall and took part in a number of other disputes; Battersea was a strongly working-class area whose population grew in fifty years from under 7,000 in 1841, when Lavender Hill was the site of lavender fields, to 150,000 by 1891. It established one of the first local trades councils in 1893.[76]

West Ham was at the very centre of the dockers', gas workers' and latex processor's disputes. Born in Scotland in 1856, Hardie came from a poor working-class background, and endured a grim childhood: out to work as a delivery boy at the age of eight to help support his family, he was sacked on New Year's Eve at the age of ten, and then had to go down the pit. His life experience led him to union work and politics, although at first these were Liberal politics; and only later, in the 1880s, did he experience a slow conversion to socialism.

Elected as a socialist MP for West Ham, he became one of the first independent labour representatives in Parliament. Hardie formed the Independent Labour Party in 1893, and was instrumental in forming the Labour Representation Committee in 1900 which became the Labour Party; he later led the Labour MPs in Parliament.

---

74   Ibid., pp. 299–300.
75   Cole and Postgate, *The Common People*, pp. 430–1.
76   See bwtuc.org.uk.

Hardie was strongly committed to bringing socialist ideas to working people, and he was initially admired by Engels and Eleanor Marx. The formation of the ILP was hailed by many including Engels as a great step towards a socialist party on the continental model, and had Aveling centrally involved at its inception. However, the ILP failed to live up to this expectation. Hardie's own politics had its roots in Liberalism, and he never totally broke from these ideas.

The direction of the British left was not at all as Engels had envisaged. The ILP did not herald a mass socialist party. Instead, with strike action in abeyance and employers on the offensive, the unions and their supporters looked to a party which would represent their interests in Parliament. There developed a separation of economics and politics which led to trade union struggle being totally divorced from Labour representation in Parliament.[77]

In fact, the great struggles of the late 1880s strengthened Labourism. They helped to deal a mortal blow to the Liberal Party as the representative of working people and paved the way for the formation of a new party of labour, backed by the increasingly powerful general unions. The conclusion that many socialists and trade unionists drew was to turn to political organization as a response to defeat. Thorne and Burns both eventually became Labour MPs, and Tom Mann emigrated to Australia (although he returned to play a very important role in the British labour movement some years later). Eleanor Marx's relationship with Edward Aveling deteriorated, ending with his secret marriage to someone else and her suicide. He died a few months later. William Morris died in 1896. The small socialist groups had not made a breakthrough, despite the attempt with the ILP.

The tragedy of British working-class politics was that these socialists were either unable to organize large numbers of workers, or they led movements which only had a loose commitment to socialist change, and so they were unable to break out of their isolation. Yet these were times of immense hope: there were mass protests against unemployment, the working class finally erupted at the end of the decade in the fight for the new unions, and socialists were able to put themselves at the head of the movement. The struggle for an eight-hour day, enthusiastically taken up by the likes of Eleanor Marx and Tom Mann, appeared to be the issue which could bridge the gap between the socialists and the mass of militant workers. While they failed in their ultimate goal, the socialists and trade unionists of the 1880s played perhaps the most important role of socialists in Britain at any time: they attempted to put into practice their theory of working-class emancipation.

---

77   For an excellent and scholarly account of Hardie see C. Benn, *Keir Hardie* (London, 1997).

7

Things Fall Apart

The period from 1900 to 1914 is like the first two acts of a play whose third act was never written.

G. D. H. Cole and Raymond Postgate

TWENTIETH-CENTURY LONDON

The first years of the new century were years of crisis, as Britain was facing increasing competition from its rivals overseas. Germany and the US were rapidly catching up with a once-dominant Britain. The century began with war against Dutch settlers (Boers) in South Africa – another war over who controlled the far-flung corners of the empire, in which Britain was once more challenged militarily. Meanwhile great fortunes were made by the new breed of capitalists who controlled bigger and bigger enterprises. As a result Edwardian society was no advance over Victorian Britain in the level of inequality.

Everything seemed poised for change as the mounting political challenges facing Edwardian society became more apparent. There were major constitutional and political issues, ranging from reform of the House of Lords to Irish Home Rule to votes for women. There was rising trade union organization and industrial militancy. The Labour Party, formed at the turn of the century, was growing while the Liberals were losing their traditional working-class base. But all political developments suddenly stopped short in August 1914. The Great War marked the end of the old world shaped by Victorian capitalism and empire.

By 1900 London, with a population of 6 million, was already of a comparable size to what it was a century later, and its geographical spread would be recognizable to us today. The infrastructure of railways was in place, and the new deep tube lines were in the process of being built alongside the original cut-and-cover lines. Many of the outlying areas had over the previous half century been built upon, now providing housing for some working-class people and for the lower middle classes. Working-class areas stretched to Walthamstow and Tottenham in the Northeast, Stratford and West and East Ham in the East, and Woolwich in the Southeast; moving south to Crystal Palace, Wandsworth and Tooting and round to Acton and Harlesden in the West.

In the inner city the housing situation was also changing. London had its own council, the London County Council, from 1889. That allowed London to catch up with various other cities around the country. The LCC was a radical body from the start, containing within it a number of people committed to changing the city and to reforming its worst excesses. John Burns was one of the first councillors to be elected in 1889, and the majority of councillors up until 1907 were known as 'progressives', as opposed to the more right-wing 'moderates'. The council gradually accrued more responsibilities, but its main ones were housing, transport and, from 1904, education. This progressive majority made a tremendous difference to the city. It expanded the tram network across London (later the whole transport system would be unified). It built new roads such as Kingsway (1905), which linked slum clearance to the ambition for the sorts of grand avenue so admired in Paris or Berlin (although in London this was never achieved). The LCC oversaw the building of two tunnels under the Thames in the docklands, at Rotherhithe and Blackwall. It attempted to provide an education system which would incorporate not just elementary education but forms of further education for working people. Most importantly, it set about creating new housing estates to replace the slums.

This began with planned estates on the outskirts of the inner city and sometimes further afield, trying to make standard housing clean and spacious, enjoying decent amenities and sometimes gardens. One of the early LCC policy's enduring legacies is the Boundary Estate in Shoreditch, built to replace the notorious Jago or Old Nichol slum. Begun in 1893, it represented a completely new concept: an environment planned for working-class life. Its Arts and Crafts design incorporated a school, communal laundry and bakery, as well as a still existing bandstand built on the rubble of the Old Nichol.[1] However, few of the slum tenants qualified for housing which was given to more respectable working-class families.

Throughout Edwardian London there was evidence of the fruits of the last twenty or thirty years in the culmination of social programmes: the 'settlements' organized by the universities and public schools, such as St Hilda's and Oxford House in the East End, the education complexes such

---

1   See S. Wise, *The Blackest Streets: The Life and Death of a Victorian Slum* (London, 2008), p. 267.

as the museum and Technical Institute in West Ham, and the libraries in Whitechapel and other parts of East London, funded by the philanthropist John Passmore Edwards,[2] alongside campaigning improvements in public health. In Kensal Rise the US author and socialist Mark Twain opened a beautiful new library in 1900 – the same which in 2011 was the subject of a mass campaign to prevent its closure under local government spending cuts pushed through by Brent Council.[3] Many of these advances were the result of dedicated work by a number of 'pioneers', a good number of them women, who established some of these improvements: Margaret McMillan, Mary Ward, Arnold Toynbee are all names we still see commemorated on public buildings in London.

THE 1908 OLYMPICS

London was one of the first hosts of the modern Olympic Games. Recently recreated from their ancient and long-forgotten origins in ancient Greece, their new setting was growing rivalry between the great powers. Originally planned for Rome, the 1908 Games were relocated to London following the eruption of Mount Vesuvius near Naples. As with the 2012 Olympics, they were closely connected with the promotion of business interests. The organizers of a trade fair being held by France and Britain in London agreed to build a new Olympic stadium, in return for the majority of the takings from the Games.

The site of the trade fair was in Wood Lane near Shepherd's Bush, on 'a bit of farm land lying half-forgotten at the very doorstep of London'.[4] The White City site saw the erection of dazzling palaces on drained marsh-land. Four thousand workers were on the site by day, while the night shift numbered 2,000. There were allegedly many injuries and some fatalities, but the complex went up rapidly, and emerged with lakes, a funfair and many pavilions highlighting not just British and French industry but the economic role of their colonies in India and Africa.[5] The athletics stadium and swimming pool were built there, and visitors arrived by Tube at Wood Lane station or Shepherd's Bush.

The Games themselves often descended into farce or open conflict. The Irish-American flag bearer for the US team refused to lower the stars and stripes when he passed King Edward VII at the opening ceremony. One of his colleagues reportedly declared 'this flag dips to no earthly king'. This

---

2 J. Lewis, *East Ham and West Ham Past* (London, 2004), pp. 87–9.
3 See brent-heritage.co.uk. For the recent campaign to save it, see savekensalriselibrary.org.
4 G. Kent, *Olympic Follies* (London, 2008), p. 38.
5 Ibid., pp. 40–1.

was only one in a string of conflicts between the US and British teams which ended in mutual recrimination. While the Games attracted massive crowds to London, they were less than successful as a sporting or political event.[6]

WORKING-CLASS LIFE

The gross divisions in the city were all too manifest despite these displays. While London was indisputably the hub of an empire where fabulous wealth was made, the poverty and misery of the city had not diminished. Jack London, the American socialist author who wrote his *People of the Abyss* after living as a slum dweller in the East End, was shocked by the physique and small stature of the people he met.[7] Inequality grew in the Edwardian years as real wages fell for most workers, while profits soared.[8] Taking retail food prices as 100 in 1900, though fairly constant till 1907, they then rapidly rose to reach 109.4 by 1910, 114.5 by 1912, and 116.8 by 1914.[9] This had a major impact on working-class families, which were able to afford very limited amounts and ranges of foods, and who spent large proportions of their incomes on food. These price rises meant that 'the purchasing power of 20s (£1) in the hands of a working-class housewife in 1895 went down to 18s 5d in 1900, to 17s 11d in 1905, to 16s 11d in 1910, and to 14s 7d in 1914'.[10]

The effects of slum living, inadequate nutrition and lack of health care caused a crisis at the time of the Boer War, when it was discovered that many of the army's potential recruits were unfit to fight. The welfare reforms introduced by Lloyd George in the People's Budget in 1908 added something to the social wage, but spending on welfare was overshadowed by the huge increase in army and navy spending up to the First World War. Naval spending went from under £20 million in 1895 to more than £50 million in 1914.[11]

Most working-class people still lived in overcrowded and substandard accommodation, either in outright slums or housing not much better. Many had no bathroom or toilet, or piped water: 'A woman with six children under thirteen gives them all a bath with two waters between them on a Saturday morning in the washing-tub. She generally has a bath herself

---

6   Graeme Kent's book gives a detailed account of the Games.
7   R. Barltrop, *Jack London: The man, the writer, the rebel* (London 1978), pp. 80–1.
8   Cole and Postgate, *The Common People*, pp. 496–8.
9   T. Rothstein, *From Chartism to Labourism* (London, 1983), p. 299.
10   Ibid., p. 300.
11   Cole and Postgate, *The Common People*, p. 502.

on Sunday evening when her husband is out. All the water has to be carried
upstairs, heated in her kettle, and carried down again when dirty.'[12] This
was a typical scene in Lambeth investigated by Maud Pember Reeves of the
Fabian Women's Group. Even for these conditions, nearly half of the 'round
about a pound a week' earned by the man went on rent. Pember Reeves
pointed out that these were by no means the poorest Londoners, but families of usually unskilled labourers in work. She asked despairingly: 'How
does a working man's wife bring up a family on 20s a week?'[13] The answer
was that variety in food was unaffordable: women and children lived on a
diet of bread, potatoes and suet pudding augmented with treacle, margarine
or jam and the occasional piece of fish or meat, although where affordable
this was often reserved for the man. 'Without doubt, the chief article of diet
in a 20s budget is bread. A long way after bread come potatoes, meat and
fish.'[14]

   In the early part of the twentieth century, much working-class life still
took place outside the home. While the consumption of beer and spirits fell
in the period up to the First World War, alcohol still played a major part
in London life and in working-class areas there were often pubs on every
corner, where people would drink beer or gin. Many of the buildings still
remain, even if they have now been in many cases converted into expensive private flats. London entertainment revolved for half a century round
the music hall, which reached its heyday in the late nineteenth century and
in the period before the First World War. It was a peculiarly London experience – only in Lancashire did music halls become as popular – which may
well have reflected some of the attitudes of the traditional London mob.

   The artists became household names and could command huge fees for
their performances. The venues were originally attached to pubs, and sold
food as well as drink. Entertainment was originally an add-on, but these
pubs evolved into variety theatres.[15] The acts were highly popular and in the
halls 'sentiments veered between Chartist dissent and hearty patriotism'.[16]
The term jingoism, describing extreme populist warmongering and flag-
waving, was coined from the Jingo Song of 1878, written as Russian and
British forces prepared for war in the Dardanelles.[17]

   Yet many songs spoke to the experience of ordinary Londoners, dealing
with evictions ('My old man said follow the van'), the workhouse ('My

---

12   M. Pember Reeves, *Round about a Pound a Week* (1913; London, 1994)
pp. 55–6.
13   Ibid., p. 21.
14   Ibid., p. 94.
15   P. Du Noyer, *In the City* (London, 2010) p. 23–27.
16   Ibid., p. 25.
17   Ibid., pp. 33–4.

old Dutch'), homelessness ('I live in Trafalgar Square') and overcrowding ('If it wasn't for the houses in between'). The queen of the halls was Marie Lloyd, from Hoxton and sufficiently connected to her roots to support a strike of music-hall artists.[18] Her most popular song, 'The boy I love is up in the gallery', can be heard in the 1967 film *The London Nobody Knows*, shot inside the ruins of the once popular Bedford Music Hall in Camden Town. Her sexually suggestive lyrics and feisty behaviour lost her friends in high places, but she maintained a huge popularity throughout her life. Her funeral in 1922 attracted 100,000 mourners.[19] When she was omitted from the Royal Command performance in 1908, 'Marie staged her own show at the London Pavilion. Loyal fans had returned their Command tickets and came to see Marie instead. She was billed as the "Queen of Comedy" and she introduced new songs. Outside the posters bore strips which announced: "Every performance by Marie Lloyd / Is a Command Performance / By order of the British Public".'[20]

Charlie Chaplin, the greatest silent screen star of all, was born in poverty in Lambeth and started his career in music hall. His main character, the Tramp, is based on that experience which struck a chord with millions of working-class cinema-goers. All his work is suffused with the anti-authoritarianism of a working-class kid. Chaplin was a left-winger and anti-fascist who was eventually kicked out of the US for his radicalism, an attitude nurtured in pre-First World War London.[21]

The music halls never recovered from the war, or from the coming of cinema which superseded them as working-class entertainment. However, the songs' popularity persisted and they were regularly performed in London pubs up to the 1960s and 70s. Some of the purpose-built halls still exist: the Hackney Empire, the Hippodrome in Leicester Square and Wilton's Music Hall in the East End. Even today, the Christmas pantomime at the refurbished Hackney Empire recreates some of the atmosphere which must have existed every week for thousands of Londoners.

SEXUAL POLITICS

By the Edwardian years, women were beginning to play a greater social and political role. The central role of women in building the socialist movement and the working-class campaigns among the previous generation now helped to create a more conscious and aware group of women in the new

18   Ibid., p. 30.
19   Ibid., p. 31.
20   M. Rosen and D. Widgery, *The Chatto Book of Dissent* (London, 1991), p. 357.
21   D. Robinson, *Chaplin: His Life and Art* (London, 1992), esp. pp. 1–100.

century. Women became involved in left-wing politics, reflecting growing changes in their social position. Even most middle- and upper-class women were still denied a proper education until late in the nineteenth century; their participation in higher education was resisted nearly everywhere, and only granted slowly and reluctantly when Cambridge created women's colleges and London University allowed women to sit degrees. A narrow layer of middle-class women wanted to embark on careers in the public sphere or venture into the new areas of clerical work, which expanded extensively in the late nineteenth century, above all in London. Eleanor Marx trained as a 'typewriter' and like many middle-class women had no option but to earn a living. At the same time the Civil Service grew and became a recruiter of female clerks, while other women trained as teachers, nurses and telephonists.

Ideas about 'free love', which had developed from the 1880s onwards, found a place in the new century, particularly amongst women from the relatively privileged layer of the middle class who were able to work and to live outside the family home. The Norwegian playwright Henrik Ibsen in plays like *A Doll's House* expressed new and controversial views about women's role and the stifling nature of the family: he was a great influence on Shaw who saw his own writing as a vehicle for social change, his lengthy prefaces spelling out his view on many political and philosophical topics. The 'new woman' was in turn influenced by the novels of Shaw, George Gissing and Olive Shreiner, as well as by Ibsen. *Ann Veronica* by H. G. Wells, in which the heroine comes to London to escape the constraints of her background, symbolized the lengths to which women could go to rebel against conventional society.

While it was a daunting place for many women to live, London also provided them with opportunities and freedoms that they did not have in smaller towns and cities. In London social spaces such as theatres, restaurants, parks and even the underground rail system allowed a degree not just of freedom of movement but of social interchange, with an anonymity previously denied to most women of the middle class. The opening up of social opportunities for women was very important in creating ideas which were relevant to the larger movements which soon developed.

The new generation of women around the turn of the century began to turn their attention to a number of political and social issues: they researched social problems, like Beatrice Webb; helped to organize working women, like Mary McArthur; organized politically like the range of women in the Independent Labour Party, or Dora Montefiore in the Social Democratic

Federation. They also began campaigning in the suffrage movement.[22]

In an era when many women were becoming prominent political figures, the fate of Oscar Wilde reminds us of just how stifling and hypocritical social conformity remained. Wilde was an Irish writer who became one of London's most popular playwrights in the early 1890s. Known for his biting wit, flamboyant dress, and glittering conversation, Wilde became one of the most well-known personalities of the day.

In 1895 Wilde was at the height of his fame and success and his masterpiece *The Importance of Being Earnest* was on stage in London. At this moment Wilde sued the Marquess of Queensberry – the father of his lover, Lord Alfred Douglas – for libel. On 18 February 1895 Queensberry left his calling card at Wilde's club, inscribed 'For Oscar Wilde, posing somdomite [*sic*]'. Against the advice of his friends Wilde initiated a private prosecution against Queensberry, who was arrested on a charge of criminal libel, as sodomy was then a crime. Queensberry's note amounted to a public accusation that Wilde had committed a felony, and he could avoid conviction for libel only by demonstrating that what he alleged was in fact true.

The libel trial became a cause célèbre as salacious details of Wilde's private life began to appear in the press. A team of private detectives had directed Queensberry's lawyers, led by Edward Carson QC, towards the murky Victorian underworld. Wilde's association with blackmailers and male prostitutes, cross-dressers and homosexual brothels was recorded, and various individuals involved were interviewed – some being coerced to appear as witnesses, since they too had committed the crimes of which Wilde was accused.

The trial opened on 3 April 1895 amid scenes of near hysteria both in the press and the public galleries. The extent of the evidence amassed against Wilde forced him to declare meekly, 'I am the prosecutor in this case'. Eventually, on the advice of his lawyers, Wilde dropped the prosecution. Queensberry was acquitted, and the court found that his accusation against Wilde was justified, 'true in substance and in fact'.

The following day, Wilde was himself arrested on charges of sodomy and gross indecency. His eventual conviction led to two years' hard labour. The judge described the sentence, the maximum allowed, as 'totally inadequate for a case such as this', 'the worst case I have ever tried'. Wilde's response 'And I? May I say nothing, my Lord?' was drowned out by cries of 'Shame' in the courtroom.

Wilde was imprisoned first in Pentonville and then Wandsworth prisons

---

22   For more on this see S. Rowbotham, *A Century of Women* (London, 1997), pp. 7–35; C. Collette, *For Labour and For Women* (Manchester, 1989); A. V. John (ed.), *Unequal Opportunities* (Oxford, 1986); A. Richardson (ed.), *Women Who Did* (London, 2002).

in London, before being sent to Reading. Upon his release he left immediately for France and never returned to Ireland or Britain. There he wrote his last work, 'The Ballad of Reading Gaol' (1898), a long poem commemorating the harsh rhythms of prison life. He died destitute in Paris at the age of forty-six.

THE RUSSIAN CONNECTION

London was a major centre for Russian émigrés escaping from Tsarist repression. Russia rapidly industrialized in the second half of the nineteenth century, creating a sizeable urban proletariat. Pockets of militant opposition to Tsarism involved individual attacks and assassination attempts as well as organization among the peasants, and later the workers. By the beginning of the twentieth century there was a small but committed revolutionary movement composed of Marxists, anarchists and populists of various descriptions. They risked severe punishment, most often by long exile in Siberia, and were often forced to live outside their country.

The series of pogroms which drove out large numbers of Russian Jews in the 1880s and 90s helped to transform the East End, and many of the immigrants contributed to increasing political awareness and radicalism in the city. They faced high levels of racism and persecution, exacerbated by the passing of the Aliens Act in 1905 and the creation of the British Brotherhood, a racist anti-immigrant organization. Nevertheless, the Jews created a remarkable and unique political culture and organization in East London which lasted decades. This large and highly political émigré community formed a constant basis for agitation around a range of issues and an opposition to Tsarism.[23] Three of the five congresses held by the Russian Social Democratic Party (RSDLP) between its foundation in 1898 and the Revolution of 1917, took place wholly or in part in London.

Vladimir Lenin and his wife Nadezhda Krupskaya came to London in 1902 because it was becoming impossible to print their paper in Germany. They commenced publishing *Iskra*, the newspaper of the RSDLP, in London where the SDF allowed them the use of their Twentieth Century Press. Lenin was given a small office in Clerkenwell Green, where *Iskra* was printed in what is now the Marx Memorial Library. They lived nearby and today there is a plaque to Lenin in Percy Circus, near the Pentonville Road. In the 1940s, the local Finsbury council, known for its left-wing politics, erected

---

23 A demonstration in Hyde Park over the Kishinev Pogrom in 1903 attracted 25,000 people. See W. Kendall, *The Revolutionary Movement in Britain 1900–21: The Origins of British Communism* (London, 1969), p. 78. See also Fishman, *East End Jewish Radicals*, pp. 249–53.

a monument to Lenin. This caused a furore and was eventually removed.[24] Krupskaya describes how they saw London in the first few months there:

> Ilyich studied living London. He liked taking long rides through the town on top of the bus. He liked the busy traffic of that vast commercial city, the quiet squares with their elegant houses wreathed in greenery, where only smart broughams drew up. There were other places too – mean little streets tenanted by London's work people, with clothes lines stretched across the road and anaemic children playing on the doorsteps. To these places we used to go on foot. Observing these startling contrasts between wealth and poverty, Ilyich would mutter in English through clenched teeth: 'Two nations!'

Lenin and Krupskaya noticed and remarked upon the divisions inside the working class between skilled and unskilled workers:

> He scanned the newspapers for notices of working-class meetings in some out-of-the-way district, where there were only rank-and-file workers from the bench – as we say now – without any pomp and leaders. These meetings were usually devoted to the discussion of some question or project, such as a garden-city scheme. Ilyich would listen attentively, and afterwards say joyfully: 'They are just bursting with socialism! If a speaker starts talking rot a worker gets up right away and takes the bull by the horns, shows up the very essence of capitalism.' It was the rank-and-file British worker, who had preserved his class instinct in face of everything, that Ilyich always relied upon. Visitors to Britain usually saw only the labour aristocracy, corrupted by the bourgeoisie and itself bourgeoisified.

At one point they attended a socialist church:

> There are such churches in England. The socialist in charge was droning through the Bible, and then delivered a sermon to the effect that the exodus of the Jews from Egypt symbolized the exodus of the workers from the kingdom of capitalism into the kingdom of socialism. Everyone stood up and sang from a socialist hymn-book: 'Lead us, O Lord, from the Kingdom of Capitalism into the Kingdom of Socialism.' We went to that church again afterwards – it was the Seven Sisters Church – to hear a talk for young people. A young man spoke about municipal socialism and tried to prove that no revolution was needed, while the socialist who had officiated as clergyman during our first visit declared that he

---

24   J. Glancey, *London: Bread and Circuses* (London, 2003), pp. 131–2.

had been a member of the party for twelve years and for twelve years he had been fighting opportunism – and that was what municipal socialism was – opportunism pure and simple.[25]

Leon Trotsky came to London following his escape from Siberia in 1902, arriving at Lenin and Krupskaya's door at dawn unannounced and personally unacquainted with them.[26] Trotsky went to live nearby with other Russian revolutionaries, including Martov and Zasulich, in a lodging house with a living room 'in which we drank coffee, smoked, and engaged in endless discussions. This room, thanks chiefly to Zasulich, but not without help from Martov, was always in a state of rank disorder,'[27] The émigrés did a great deal of work editing and writing, keeping in touch with their underground cells in Russia, reading in the library at the British Museum, and making contact with other Russians settled in Britain – but also with British socialists. Trotsky gave a public lecture in Whitechapel where he was challenged by the 'patriarch of the Russian émigrés, Tchaikovsky' and by the anarchist Tcherkezov. 'I was honestly amazed at the infantile arguments with which these worthy elders were trying to crush Marxism. I returned home, I remember, as if I were walking on air.'[28]

The sensation didn't last: the 1903 RSDLP congress, begun in Brussels but moved to London because of police harassment, was the scene of a historic split over seemingly invisible differences. The *Iskra* board divided over the definition of membership of the organization into two groups: the Bolsheviks (majority) and Mensheviks (minority), in conditions which may have been demoralizing for some participants but which defined the shape of Russian politics for the next two years. In 1904 Russia entered into war with the rapidly industrializing Japan, a war which Russia lost and led to revolution in its heartland. When this broke out in 1905, the impact on Britain was substantial.

The Labour Representation Committee (LRC, forerunner of the Labour Party) conference pledged its support for the Russian revolutionaries by sending £150 for the relief of widows and orphans of those killed in fighting against the Tsar's forces in St Petersburg, and by passing a resolution which congratulated 'the Russian Trade Unionists on their courage in demanding ... the elementary, political and social rights which have been so long and so shamefully withheld from them ... [and] urges the workers

---

25 Consulted online at marxists.org. See also N. K. Krupskaya, *Memories of Lenin* (London, 1970). This latter is a different translation.
26 L. Trotsky, *My Life* (London, 1975), p. 146.
27 Ibid., p. 148.
28 Ibid., p. 149.

to continue the struggle till they have gained the rights of citizenship, of combination and of personal liberty'.[29]

The 'Friends of Russian Freedom', which had been established back in that year of upheaval 1889 and contained a number of SDF members, now campaigned on behalf of the Russian revolutionaries. After the defeat of the 1905 revolution and the subsequent crackdown by the Tsar it helped those who had to flee the country. This included thirty-two members of the crew of the battleship *Potemkin* (immortalized by Eisenstein's eponymous film), who gained asylum in Britain and whose leader Matutchenko came to live in Dunstan House in Stepney.[30]

In the heart of the Jewish East End, there was a highly politicized layer of activists. The anarchists had more influence in the East End than the socialists, organizing a club in Berners Street and then from 1906 the Arbeter Fraint club in Jubilee Street, Stepney (named after the successful Yiddish newspaper which had a lot of support in the area). The anarchists, led by the gentile Rudolf Rocker, agitated among workers in the tailoring and baking industries, and were involved both in defending Jews in Russia and in dealing with the more immediate issues facing Jewish workers in London.[31]

British socialists were also drawn into helping the Russians. One, S. G. Hobson, helped to smuggle out 6,000 Browning revolvers packed into barrels of lard in East Ham for shipping.[32] Maxim Litvinov, who attended the 1903 congress, later settled in London, having organized gun running in central Europe.[33] In response the Russian and Jewish communities were singled out as 'extremists' and 'terrorists'. There was constant police surveillance, infiltration and attempts at entrapment.[34]

The Arbeter Fraint club was a big success: organized on co-operative and libertarian principles, it put on political, cultural, social and educational events. There was chess, tea and political discussion. As one participant said: 'discussion would go on far into the night between Bundists [Jewish socialists], Zionists, Anarchists and Social Democrats, who argued excitedly together. We Anarchists were very tolerant. All workers were our comrades.'[35] Lenin visited the club when in London for the 1907 conference: 'I occasionally saw a small, intense man who sat alone at a table in the corner. He had slant eyes, balding reddish hair, drank Russian tea and

---

29   Kendall, *Revolutionary Movement in Britain*, pp. 79 and 342n.
30   Ibid., p. 82 and Fishman, *East End Jewish Radicals*, p. 258.
31   Fishman, *East End Jewish Radicals*, p. 261.
32   Kendall, *Revolutionary Movement in Britain*, p. 80.
33   Ibid.
34   Fishman, *East End Jewish Radicals*, pp. 269–73.
35   Quoted in ibid., p. 267.

spoke little. He was Lenin.'[36] On one occasion Lenin recognized a police spy there and in the ensuing commotion Special Branch intervened, arresting Lenin and four others. It needed prominent émigrés such as Prince Kropotkin to get him released later that night.[37]

The Russian SDLP conference in 1907 attracted around 300 delegates to London for the three-week event, held at the socialist Brotherhood Church in Southgate Road, Islington. The proceedings revealed the renewed divisions between the Bolshevik and Menshevik wings of the movement, temporarily overcome during the 1905 revolution. *Justice*, the SDF paper, reported that 'If the "Majority" wing is saturated with Blanquist tendencies, the other wing cannot be said to be free of Opportunism.'[38] Some of the best-known figures in the Russian and Polish socialist movements were at the conference: Lenin, Trotsky, Stalin, the writer Maxim Gorky, Martov, Plekhanov and the Polish-German revolutionary Rosa Luxemburg. Luxemburg wrote to her lover Kostya Zetkin of her impressions of Whitechapel on the eve of the conference, illustrating both her view of London and the irritation and boredom which all too frequently accompany political conferences.

> I'm sitting in the middle of the famous Whitechapel district. I'm sitting alone in a restaurant and have been waiting for an hour (it's after 10pm). The actual business gets under way for the first time tomorrow. ... In a foul mood I travelled through the endless stations of the dark Underground and emerged both depressed and lost in a strange and wild part of the city. It's dark and dirty here ... Groups of drunken people stagger with wild noise and shouting down the middle of the street, newspaper boys are also shouting, flower girls on the street corners, looking frightfully ugly and even depraved ... are screeching and squalling. ... It is chaos and also wild and strange ... But suddenly inside me now some gipsy blood has been awakened. The shrill chords of night in the big city, with its demonic magic, have touched certain strings in the soul of the children of the great city.[39]

The Russians' mode of clandestine and illegal political organization took its financial toll. Despite receiving money from the German SPD, the conference ran out of money and it was only when the Jewish SDF member, Theodore Rothstein, along with H. N. Brailsford, approached a sympathetic

36 Millie Sabel, quoted in ibid., p. 264.
37 Kendall, *Revolutionary Movement in Britain*, p. 82.
38 *Justice*, 15 June 1907, quoted in ibid., p. 81.
39 Letter from Luxemburg to Zetkin, 13 May 1907, in G. Adler, P. Hudis and A. Laschitza (eds), *The Letters of Rosa Luxemburg* (London, 2011), pp. 239–40.

millionaire to bankroll the conference with a loan that it could continue. (After 1917, the Soviet government repaid the debt.) Harry Quelch from the SDF gave fraternal greetings to the conference. Will Thorne, now an MP, raised the question of police surveillance in the House of Commons. In addition on 24 May a reception was held for the delegates in the Holborn Hall. The esteem in which the Russian socialists were held by the left in Britain was clear. However, the gulf between Bolsheviks and Mensheviks grew wider, if anything, as a result of the conference.[40]

SIDNEY STREET

Russian political activity in London could not always rely on benevolent millionaires, however, and there was something of a tradition of attempted robberies to finance socialist and anarchist activity. On two occasions this option famously went wrong. In 1909 two Latvians carried out a payroll robbery in Tottenham and were pursued by police and the public across Tottenham Marshes to Walthamstow and Chingford. While the chase had elements of farce – they commandeered a milk cart at one point – the two robbers and one policeman lost their lives, while around twenty people were injured. The 'Tottenham Outrages' led to a wave of anti-'alien' articles in the press.[41]

The following year saw an incident which was to prove much more serious and damaging. On 17 December 1910, a bungled break-in at a jeweller's in Houndsditch, near Petticoat Lane, left three policemen dead. The gang leader, seriously wounded, was taken to a house off the Commercial Road where he died a few hours later. The hunt for the other robbers, especially one known as 'Peter the Painter', was stepped up. The alleged perpetrators were eventually discovered in January holed up at 100 Sidney Street, very close to the Arbeter Fraint Club in Jubilee Street.

The conduct of what became known as the Siege of Sidney Street was taken over by Winston Churchill, then home secretary in the Liberal government, who directed police and troops in an onslaught which ended with the building in flames and two dead bodies inside. Churchill revelled in such confrontations, and exploited the furore over the killing and the emerging popular press's witch-hunt of anarchists to stoke up his own reputation and justify repressive methods overall. In fact the dead men were not anarchists but Latvian social democrats, engaged in what was called an 'expropriation for the cause'. The third man, Peter the Painter (Peter Piatkov), escaped,

---

40   Kendall, *Revolutionary Movement in Britain*, pp. 80–1.
41   Bloom, *Violent London*, pp. 249–50; Fishman, *East End Jewish Radicals*, p. 272.

prompting much speculation and rumour. One account has it that he got back to Russia in time for the revolution and became a member of the Cheka, or secret police.[42]

The backlash against the left, the Jewish community and Russians was substantial following the robbery and siege. Attendance at the club fell, as did audiences for outdoor meetings, and there was a big increase in police surveillance. Popular hostility was common: 'Anyone who walked along in a Russian blouse was considered a suspicious character and sometimes assaulted', according to one contemporary anarchist.[43]

VOTES FOR WOMEN

The suffragette movement was born in Manchester, but the stage for its great performances was in London. Led by Emmeline Pankhurst, the widow of an eminent figure in the labour movement and women's suffragist, Dr Richard Pankhurst, and her daughter Christabel, the suffragettes helped to shape politics for the next decade.

The lack of women's suffrage was a growing outrage to increasing numbers of people. The Reform Acts of 1867 and 1884 had excluded women, denying them the vote or the opportunity to stand as candidates in most elections. This situation was increasingly anomalous, and by the beginning of the twentieth century a number of women and their organizations wanted to do something about it. The National Union of Women's Suffrage Societies formed in the north of England in 1897, and by 1903 a petition for women's suffrage was doing the rounds of the Lancashire cotton areas.[44]

The ILP, formed in 1893 and effectively the Labour left for the next forty years, contained within it a number of highly talented and resourceful women, many of whom were strongly committed to campaigning for women's suffrage. The foremost politician on Labour's left, Keir Hardie, was also a strong supporter of women's right to vote. He had helped to form the Labour Representation Committee in February 1900 at a conference in the Memorial Hall in Farringdon; this body was formed as a compromise between the trade unions who wanted labour representation in Parliament, and those socialists who wanted a much wider social transformation. It must

---

42   See Fishman, *East End Jewish Radicals*, p. 291 on this point and pp. 287–93 for details of the events around the siege.
43   Ibid., p. 292.
44   For the story of the NUWSS, mainly concerned with women in the textile industry in the north of England, see J. Liddington, *The Life and Times of a Respectable Rebel* (London, 1984) and J. Liddington and J. Norris, *One Hand Tied Behind Us* (London, 1978).

have seemed possible then that the struggles for workers' representation and for women's rights might dovetail over the next few years, but despite the best efforts of many – including Hardie and another of Emmeline's other daughters, Sylvia Pankhurst – this did not happen.

However, the demand for the vote swelled into a mass movement. The Women's Social and Political Union (the popular name 'suffragettes' was originally derogatory, until adopted by the women themselves) was formed in 1903. It attracted little attention until 1905 when Christabel and Annie Kenney, a Lancashire mill worker, were imprisoned for disrupting a meeting at Manchester Free Trade Hall addressed by the Liberal Sir Edward Grey. The movement really began to take off only after the great Liberal election victory of 1906, when the centre of gravity shifted to London. Offices were taken at Clement's Inn near the Law Courts, and the organization was run by the Pankhursts and a married couple introduced to them by Hardie, Emmeline and Frederick Pethick Lawrence. These were wealthy but committed socialists who played a major role in funding and organizing the WSPU for the next few years. It rapidly became clear that Christabel had no real interest in backing the emerging Labour Party in elections, and she and her mother resigned from the ILP soon after they came to London. This was the beginning of their gradual severing of links with the labour movement.

The authorities' response to petitions and delegations was at best indifferent. From 1907 onwards the suffragettes staged a number of spectacular demonstrations and protests. The campaign devised ever more inventive and daring activities to highlight their cause: members chained themselves to railings at Downing Street; they broke up public meetings of cabinet ministers with a campaign of heckling, and printed fake tickets when the meetings were ticket only; they went on hunger strike when imprisoned. When late in January the Royal Procession came to open Parliament, women from the Women's Freedom League rushed forward with a petition but were beaten back by soldiers. A Women's Parliament was called at Westminster's Caxton Hall in February, which sent a delegation to Prime Minister Herbert Asquith.

In the years 1908–09 the suffragettes held meetings attracting more than a thousand people in the Royal Albert Hall no less than thirteen times.[45] In June they organized a huge demonstration in Hyde Park on Midsummer Day. Thirty special trains brought supporters in from seventy towns; a quarter of a mile of park railings were taken up to ease the passage of the march (an improvement on those showdowns in the mid nineteenth century when the park gates were locked against demonstrators); there were hundreds

---

45   Foot, *The Vote*, p. 199.

of silk banners; the march was branded in the new suffragette colours of purple, green and gold. The whole affair cost £4,813, a phenomenal sum coughed up by some of the WSPU's very wealthy supporters.[46]

The preparations for the march led to shops and committee rooms being set up all over London. Sylvia was an organizer in Chelsea, Fulham and Wandsworth:

> London had probably never been flooded with such intensive propaganda for any cause. At each new open-air pitch our first meeting was a fight with noisy uproar, our second mainly sympathetic, our third a triumph of unanimity, ending in cheers. The manager of the Chelsea Palace called at our shop in the King's Road, and asked me to provide a Suffragette to speak for five minutes at each performance. The cinemas announced the demonstration, and gave scenes from the campaign. Leading London shops gave displays in the colours, an evidence of the popularity of the movement.[47]

When the demonstration was rebuffed by the prime minister the WSPU called a public meeting on Parliament Square, which was attacked by police. The war of attrition went on with the rushing of Parliament three months later. Suffragettes streamed out of Westminster Central Hall and attempted to charge into the House (it was possible then to get right to the doors of the building without meeting barriers or security checks). Mayhem broke out in the square as bands of women and their supporters repeatedly charged. Those watching included Lloyd George and his daughter Megan, and John Burns – now much more respectable than in his union days. Cordons of police stood five feet deep around the square. There were twenty-four women and twelve men imprisoned as a result, and ten people were hospitalized. In reference to celebrations during the lifting of a siege in the Boer war, the papers called it 'like Mafeking night without the disorder'.[48]

Christabel and Emmeline were summonsed and temporarily imprisoned. Christabel, in her finest hour, turned this into a high-profile case. She called Lloyd George and Herbert Gladstone as witnesses, and used her legal training to humiliate them in cross-examination.

The treatment of the women was typical of the relentless custodial punishment meted out to the suffragettes. Between spring 1907 and spring 1908, demonstrators were sent to prison for a total of 191 weeks; this rose

---

46   S. Pankhurst, *The Suffragette Movement* (London, 1977), pp. 276–84.
47   Ibid., p. 284.
48   Ibid., p. 289.

to 350 weeks over the following year.[49] It did not deter the campaigners. These were the golden years of the suffragettes, as they repeatedly mobilized huge numbers and won the backing of far more. But growing problems meant that while the support for the vote never wavered amongst most women and a growing number of men, mass active participation declined and the political divisions which had seemed relatively minor in the heyday of the movement soon came to the fore.

These divisions began in 1907, when the first major split occurred with the departure of Charlotte Despard and Teresa Billington Greig. The Pankhursts, backed by the Pethick Lawrences, were becoming more autocratic within the movement and reluctant to ensure democratic accountability. As a result Despard and Billington Greig set up the Women's Freedom League, campaigning along the same lines as the WSPU.[50] In 1906 Margaret Macdonald set up the Women's Labour League to work on women's issues in the Labour Party.[51] Part of the problem lay in the fact that there was effectively no democratic voice in the original organization, everything being decreed from a small command centre; another part lay in the politics of the leadership of the WSPU, now hopelessly detached from the labour movement.

Relations worsened as the sentiment inside Labour divided, with many taking the view that it could only support the demand for adult suffrage as a whole. The debate on women's suffrage vs adult suffrage – whether women should settle for the vote on the same limited basis as men, or whether they should fight for all women and men to be enfranchised – created real divisions inside the movement, with questions of class coming to the fore. Some, including Hardie, suspected that many of those arguing for adult suffrage within Labour did not really want to commit to women's rights; he described the Adult Suffrage League as a 'dog in the manger'. Yet it was hard to dismiss the fact that a very large proportion of working-class men was still unenfranchised, meaning that any progressive politics should be calling for universal suffrage.[52]

The women also faced increasing state repression. In response to their repeated arrests, many of them took the dramatic step of going on hunger strike. In 1909 Marion Wallace Dunlop went on hunger strike for the right to be treated as a political prisoner, a step up from the common criminal. She was released after several days refusing to eat, and other women soon followed her example. The government found itself in a quandary but

49   Foot, *The Vote*, p. 199.
50   Pankhurst, *The Suffragette Movement*, pp. 263–5.
51   For background see Colette, *For Labour and For Women*.
52   For a good and comprehensive account of this debate see Foot, *The Vote*, pp. 171–237.

refused to give in. It introduced forcible feeding, which was carried out in the most brutal conditions in prison.

One impassioned suffragette, Emily Wilding Davison (who famously died at Epsom trying to stop the king's horse on Derby Day), threw herself from the upper gallery in Holloway to protest at this treatment, but was saved from death by the netting below. In agony when she regained consciousness, she found that 'To my amazement, the doctors came to forcibly feed me that afternoon, in spite of the torture it caused me.'[53]

In 1913 one such case provoked a particular outrage. Lillian Lenton, on remand in Holloway charged with arson, went on hunger strike and was force-fed. She was soon released, being 'in imminent danger of death', according to the home secretary. Lenton had struggled with a doctor and seven wardresses as she was force-fed and food had entered her lung, leading to pleurisy. Even in Parliament there was uproar, although largely because the honourable gentlemen felt the punishment was too soft. 'Some members maintained that the women should be left to die; Lord Robert Cecil thought that deportation might answer; only Mr. Keir Hardie suggested, as a logical solution, that women should be given the vote.'[54] Logic didn't come into it with the Liberal government. Instead, within a week, it had introduced The Prisoners (Temporary Discharge for Ill Health) Bill, popularly known as the Cat and Mouse Act and widely vilified for its measures to allow hunger strikers to be released when their health deteriorated, only to be re-arrested when their health improved. Progressive circles were scandalized: George Bernard Shaw said at a public meeting in 1913, 'If you take a woman and torture her you torture me.'[55]

The bill received royal assent in April 1913, and was quickly followed by the banning of WSPU meetings. The Union offices were raided and attempts were made to silence its presses.[56] In response Shaw remarked: 'The Suffragettes have succeeded in driving the Cabinet half mad. Mr. McKenna [the home secretary] should be examined at once by two doctors. He apparently believes himself to be the Tsar of Russia, a very common form of delusion.'[57]

---

53   Davison, quoted in the *Daily Herald*, 4 July 1912, cited in J. Marlow (ed.), *Votes for Women: The Virago Book of Suffragettes* (London, 2000), pp. 168–9.
54   G. Dangerfield, *The Strange Death of Liberal England* (London, 1970), p. 185.
55   G. B. Shaw, Kingsway Hall, 18 March 1913, cited in Pankhurst, *The Suffragette Movement*, p. 451.
56   Dangerfield, *Death of Liberal England*, pp. 186–7.
57   Ibid., p. 187.

THE TWO SIDES OF THE SUFFRAGE MOVEMENT

Yet the tactics of the suffragettes were themselves causing problems in the movement. The stress was more and more on conspicuous acts of militancy carried out by a few dedicated activists, not on the action of the mass of women. And so the great demonstrations and popular agitation in working-class areas diminished. In their place was more emphasis on the smashing of windows in shops and public buildings throughout the West End, carried out with small hammers which the suffragettes kept in their handbags. Acts of arson and attacks on country houses, post boxes and other targets increased. These were directed by Christabel in secrecy from Paris, where she had moved to avoid arrest. In her militancy she became more contemptuous of the labour movement and of forms of mass action. She repeatedly made clear that she held no brief for the emerging Labour Party. She did not see a political role for working-class women, or indeed men, and did not seek their help in winning the vote. Emmeline Pankhurst worshipped Christabel and never challenged her in any way, inevitably leading to disagreements with Sylvia and eventually to a split in the movement. In the years between 1910 and 1913 support for the WSPU plummeted, with subscriptions falling.[58] Any who could not countenance Christabel's autocratic behaviour were also forced out. In 1912 the Pankhursts parted company with their oldest allies, the Pethick Lawrences.

Sylvia, however, the accomplished artist who came to London in 1904 as a student at the Royal College of Art, never lost the socialism learnt in her ILP family in Manchester. She became a close friend and later lover of Keir Hardie, and frequently travelled from her home in Park Walk, Chelsea, to visit him in his lodgings at Neville Court, Fetter Lane. She first spoke at an outdoor meeting in Ravenscourt Park in Hammersmith,[59] and her artistic and organizing talents were put to use by the WSPU in making posters and banners. On the 1908 demonstration her contingent from Chelsea alone comprised 7,000. Her special interest in working-class women drew her increasingly to the East End, where she set up a local group which was to become the East London Federation of Suffragettes. She organized women and men around the question of the vote, but also worked on child care and welfare. She was fully part of WSPU's campaigns and herself went on hunger and thirst strike, but she became increasingly disenchanted.

From 1912 there was growing discord between her and Christabel, especially over class questions. This was evidenced in the conflicts which emerged when George Lansbury resigned his seat in Bow and Bromley to force a

---

58   A. Rosen, *Rise Up, Women!* (London, 1974), p. 211.
59   Kendall, *Revolutionary Movement in Britain*, p. 201.

by-election on votes for women. Lansbury needed the backing of suffrage supporters outside the East End to win and while some work was done for him by the WSPU, when the rich suffrage supporters failed to produce their cars on the day to ferry voters to the polling booths, Lansbury lost the election. This failure deepened the rift between the different sides and increasingly, the WSPU effectively withdrew from work in the East End.[60]

Matters came to a head in 1913 at another mass meeting at the Albert Hall, this time in support of workers in Dublin who had been locked out by a vicious employer, William Martin Murphy. Sylvia went and spoke at the meeting in defence of Jim Larkin, the imprisoned Irish socialist and trade unionist. This was too much for her mother and sister. As George Dangerfield sums it up: 'Sylvia might have been allowed to pursue her way in peace, but for two perhaps inevitable drawbacks. She had the family flair for publicity, and she was a socialist. These grave offences Mrs Pankhurst and Christabel could not forgive her.'[61] She was pushed out of the organization and the breach was finalized the following year, when the two sides took very different positions on the outbreak of war. The suffragette movement was effectively over.

THE GREAT UNREST

The years before the First World War saw the longest and most sustained wave of strikes in British history. While they involved many groups of workers, such as miners, who were outside London, they were also played out in the city. The Great Unrest began in 1910 and its underlying cause was the fall in living standards of millions of workers.

The first movement of the Great Unrest in London was the formation of the Transport Workers' Federation over the summer of 1910. The movers were the various unions of the carters and the dockers, who wanted joint action to win their demands on wages and conditions. In 1911 the transport workers, having put forward a series of demands to the port employers, came out in August and stayed out for several weeks. The strike was much larger than that of 1889, and brought London to a halt: 'Delivery of foodstuffs and goods from the port and the railway stations was stopped; factories and works were forced to curtail production; the newspapers were forced either to cut down their circulation or to cease publication altogether, and only such institutions as hospitals, or public services like drainage and waterworks etc., obtained the necessary permits

60 Pankhurst, *The Suffragette Movement*, pp. 422–7.
61 Dangerfield, *Strange Death of Liberal England*, p. 190.

from the strike committee.'[62] The warm summer weather saw meat rotting on the docks, butter going rancid, the strikes spreading west to Brentford and east to Medway.

Churchill, fresh from his success in Sidney Street, wanted to bring in the troops to smash the strike. But the stand-off was settled through the good offices of John Burns – in 1889 a strike leader, now a Liberal cabinet minister.[63]

The Transport Workers' Federation had 200,000 members in 1911, having started with 14,290 less than a year before the strike.[64] The following year the Federation called another national strike, which was poorly supported and eventually defeated by the port employers, headed by Lord Devonport. Famously, at one of the strike meetings at Tower Hill, Ben Tillett cried: 'O God! Strike Lord Devonport dead!' While there was no divine intervention, the overall direction of the movement was upwards, despite these and other setbacks.[65]

Working-class London was again in ferment, as it had been in 1889. Women too began organizing, not just for the vote but for strikes as well. In Bermondsey, part of the docks area on the southern side of the river, women in a confectionery factory came out one hot August day. They then effectively picketed out other factories in the neighbourhood: 'As they went through the streets, shouting and singing, other women left their factories and workshops and came pouring out to join them.'[66] Strikers from factories making jam, pickles, biscuits, cocoa, downed tools side by side with distillery workers, rag pickers and tin box makers.

As the strikes spread, the women were organized through the National Federation of Women Workers. In 1906 the remarkable Mary Macarthur, an ILP member, had set up the NFWW along the model of the general workers' unions. It was aimed at those women who were excluded from male unions. By 1909 the Federation had 4,000 members and campaigned against the sweated trades, the worst paid and organized jobs so often carried out by women, sometimes in their homes. This led to the forma-tion of the Anti-Sweating League.[67] The Federation took a militant stance on strikes, understanding that women would only be able to achieve their demands by taking such action – although Macarthur was not above appeal-ing to royalty, and Princess Beatrice opened the exhibition on sweating in

---

62   Rothstein, *From Chartism to Labourism*, p. 310.
63   Dangerfield, *Strange Death of Liberal England*, pp. 233–5.
64   Rothstein, *From Chartism to Labourism*, p. 310.
65   See Pelling, *History of British Trade Unionism*, pp.136–9.
66   Dangerfield, *Strange Death of Liberal England*, p. 236.
67   S. Lewenhak, *Women and Trade Unions* (London, 1977), pp. 115–19.

1906.[68] When the box workers at the Corruganza factory in Tooting came out in 1908 against wage cuts, Macarthur rallied to their support, organizing a demonstration and advising on strike tactics.

The NFWW was the natural home for the confectionery women who came out on that August day in 1911. Mary Macarthur organized a strike headquarters at the Bermondsey Institute, and 'day by day enthusiasm increased. Processions passed through the streets with collecting boxes. Fifteen thousand women, seething with rage and excitement, cheered Ben Tillett in a meeting at Southwark Park.'[69] The women won a wage rise after three weeks, gaining union recognition and new branches of the federation.[70]

The strike wave not only succeeded in its own terms, however; it also created a sense of inspiration among those who saw the women organizing, wearing their Sunday best in recognition of the pride they felt in the strikes: 'Many of them, dressed in all their finery, defied the phenomenal temperature with feather boas and fur tippets, as though their strike was some holiday of the soul, long overdue.'[71]

The example of successful struggle was highly infectious. Other women's strikes took place: in Machonochie's jam factory in Millwall, fifty women struck in protest at being replaced by inexperienced girls at a lower rate of pay. The workforce of 1,200, both male and female, walked out and were unionized by the Federation (which enrolled 960 women) and the National Union of Gas Workers and General Labourers. There followed three packed meetings in Poplar Town Hall, and a mass demonstration in Trafalgar Square. The strike ended in victory, with a wage rise to boot.[72] Then came the struggle of the LCC charwomen (cleaners) who cleaned the elementary schools and formed a branch of the NFWW to press their demands. They rapidly won a minimum wage, full pay during holidays and direct employment.[73] There was also the strike at Murray's confectionery factory, where 300 women strikers held a meeting on Clerkenwell Green addressed by Mary Macarthur. The women wanted a wage rise, abolition of fines and a tea break. There was a concert on Clerkenwell Green to raise money for them, and on one occasion they managed to get hold of food being taken in for scabs. Their strike song said it all: 'Murray's White Mice,

---

68   Ibid., pp. 118–19.
69   Dangerfield, *Strange Death of Liberal England*, p. 237.
70   For accounts of the strike see S. Boston, *Women Workers and the Trade Union Movement* (London, 1980), pp. 68–71 and B. Drake, *Women in Trade Unions* (London, 1984), pp. 45–6.
71   Dangerfield, *Strange Death of Liberal England*, p. 237.
72   Drake, *Women in Trade Unions*, pp. 46–7.
73   Ibid., p. 47.

See how they fight/They collared the fish, the cheese and the bread/T'was meant for the blacklegs, they ate it instead/And the boss was so wild he stood on his head/Murray's White Mice.'[74]

Some strikes lost, as at the Idris bottling factory in St Pancras, where men scabbed on the women's strikes.[75] But overall, they won big advances for women: in the years 1910–14, union membership nearly doubled to 358,000,[76] and the strikes extended surprisingly far. School-student strikes spread across the country in 1911, the first one in Llanelli in South Wales, calling for the abolition of the cane and in some cases shorter school hours. In London they took place in East Ham, Stepney, Hackney, Hoxton, Bethnal Green, Deptford, Fulham, Islington and Enfield, some of the main working-class districts in London, and many of them already seeing sustained strike action.[77] The strikes involved demonstrations, picket lines and spreading of action, suggesting that 'working-class children learned strategies of collective bargaining and resistance from the parent culture and practised them at moments when they seemed most likely to succeed.'[78]

In 1912 the tailors came onto the scene. The West End tailors, a highly skilled group of workers, came out on strike in April demanding higher pay and improvements in their conditions. On 2 May *The Times* reported a strike meeting of 7–8,000. The test however was whether the other tailors would show solidarity, and some days later the East End tailors agreed not to handle their work and to support them. A mass meeting attracted thousands of East End Jewish tailors who were addressed by Rudolf Rocker in Yiddish, calling on them not to handle the work. A vote asking who was willing to take action brought the whole audience to its feet, and was echoed in the overflow meeting outside. Within two days 13,000 immigrant tailors were out and on 13 May there was a joint demonstration on Tower Hill of West End and East End tailors. Again, the strike was largely successful.[79]

The industrial militancy continued right up to 1914, when there was talk of a general strike in the autumn of that year. A Triple Alliance had been formed between railway, mining and transport workers to build solidarity across the working class. The strike movement was especially strong in the railways and the coal mines, and therefore its centre tended to be outside London. However, political paralysis continued: the Liberal

---

74   Quoted in Boston, *Women Workers and the Trade Union Movement*, p. 71.
75   Ibid., p. 70.
76   Drake, *Women in Trade Unions*, Table 1.
77   S. Humphries, *Hooligans or Rebels? An Oral History of Working-Class Childhood and Youth, 1889–1939* (Oxford, 1995), p. 95.
78   Ibid., p. 97.
79   Fishman, *East End Jewish Radicals*, pp. 294–301.

government's confrontation with the House of Lords succeeded eventually (after two elections in 1910) in permanently weakening the upper house of Parliament, but little else was resolved. Strikes, suffragettes and Irish home rule dominated domestic politics; beyond, there was the growing threat of war.

In 1911 the Agadir crisis brought Britain and Germany to the brink of war, but they pulled back. The drive to war was nonetheless inexorable as rivalry grew between the major powers, both economically and in terms of possessions abroad. The governments were arming themselves, not least in Britain where spending on the army and most notably the navy grew rapidly in the years up to 1914. And all the governments of Europe were facing some of the same issues, especially industrial unrest. Where there were few political solutions, there was a turn to military solutions. The pressures driving to war therefore increased.

The left and the unions were growing stronger. Union membership grew in response to cuts in living standards, and with it a militant syndicalism which attracted many of the new leaders. The left also thrived, the SDF joining with sections of the ILP to form the British Socialist Party in 1911. Even then, Labour, despite being a relatively new party, was very cautious and often failed to demarcate itself from the Liberals.

The Labour Party made no real progress in the 1910 election and was advancing on a cautious path, not helped by the restrictions on trade union funding and organization represented by the Taff Vale and Osborne judgments. One development was the creation of the *Daily Herald* newspaper. Started as a strike sheet by printers in 1911, it became a left-wing paper in 1912 and from 1913 was edited by George Lansbury for a decade. Its editors and contributors included the cartoonist Will Dyson and the US left-wing syndicalist Charles Lapworth, who was according to Sylvia Pankhurst 'out of sympathy with Parliamentarism of any sort'.[80] Its advice on strikes was: 'prepare your organization and then strike. Strike and strike hard.'[81] Militancy and political awareness were increasing; yet the left were about to be put to the test.

THE WAR

The outbreak of war in August 1914 was met with a wave of patriotic fervour. Its immediate cause, the assassination of an Austrian archduke by Serbian nationalists in Sarajevo, was obscure to most people but it triggered a series of treaties and alliances which brought Britain, France and Russia

---

80   Pankhurst, *The Suffragette Movement*, p. 422.
81   Cole and Postgate, *The Common People*, pp. 485–6.

into war with Germany and Austria. Over the previous decade there had been a number of occasions in which war was threatened as part of the growing rivalry between Britain and Germany.

Thus far, the left had on each occasion rejected the chest-thumping and called for peace. When it came to 1914 and actual war was declared, it was a very different story. The justification for war in Britain was to oppose German tyranny. Stories of German atrocities in Belgium soon circulated, most of them fabricated. Russian tyranny was conveniently forgotten, since Russia was now an ally. This was therefore a very hard time for those on the left. Sylvia Pankhurst returned from Ireland with the first batch of soldiers going off to fight: 'The quays around Dublin were teeming with people cheering and waving; the men on board were cheering and waving too. All through the voyage they sang and laughed and shouted. So this was war.'[82]

Gone was the political crisis, replaced by an acceptance that everything had to change because of the war. Far from a general strike against the conflict, as the Socialist International had proposed at its Stuttgart conference in 1907, now an industrial truce was called for by Labour and the Trade Union Congress, the body which collectively represented the trade union movement. The TUC called off its September conference, and endorsed the government army recruiting campaign.[83] Opposition to war was strong before it started, in the few days before Britain joined in: on 29 July a demonstration in Brussels addressed by international speakers including Hardie opposed the war. A mass rally in Trafalgar Square on 2 August saw Labour leaders Hardie and Arthur Henderson call for peace. Yet two days later, when war was declared, the Labour Party fell into line. Ramsay MacDonald resigned as leader, to be replaced by Henderson, and Labour eventually entered into coalition with the Liberal government. There was disquiet inside Labour, especially among those still influenced by the ILP, but it was outweighed by inability or unwillingness to challenge the logic of war in a clear-sighted and forthright manner.[84]

Those who raised their voices against the war were few and far between. Even those who saw the war as pointless or wrong, or not serving the interests of working people, did not for the most part actually oppose it, at least in its early stages. Thus the BSP, while saying that the war would not help the working class, initially supported it. When the jingoistic Hyndman spoke belligerently against Germany, there were those inside

---

82   Pankhurst, *The Suffragette Movement*, p. 590.
83   G. D. H. Cole, *A History of the Labour Party from 1914* (New York, 1969), p. 20.
84   For a general overview of the crisis internationally see E. J. Hobsbawm, *The Age of Empire* (London, 1989), pp. 309–27.

the BSP who were critical of this position – including many in London branches – and protested when the BSP leadership advised supporting the government recruitment drive into the army. Stepney, North West Ham, Bow and Bromley, Central Hackney all opposed this, as did the Pollokshaws branch in Glasgow where John Maclean was based. Nearly all the London branches held a city-wide conference to demand that the statement should be withdrawn.[85]

The BSP finally dropped Hyndman in 1916, and their anti-war views became more pronounced. Hyndman went on to form a jingoistic anti-German party.[86] The ILP too was divided, many of its rank and file opposing the war while nearly all its MPs were in the pro-war camp. The anarchists were split, with Kropotkin supporting the war and Rocker against it.[87] Hardie was increasingly broken by the war and the treatment he received when raising arguments against it.[88]

No organization of any significance remained untouched by this, and all those on the left were taken aback by the strength of pro-war feeling. It was left to a small number of socialists, pacifists and conscientious objectors to make the case against war. All found it hard to do so and suffered persecution: pacifists like Fenner Brockway, ILP member and editor of *Labour Leader*, were imprisoned for campaigning against war and conscription, in his case in both Pentonville and the Tower of London. Bertrand Russell was also tried and jailed. Offices of newspapers were raided, and there was state harassment on a massive scale.

The cracks in the suffrage movement now broke wide open. Emmeline and Christabel became some of the staunchest defenders of the war effort. They changed the name of their paper to *Britannia* and filled it with anti-German propaganda. In 1915 Emmeline organized a 'right to serve' demonstration, attended by many and funded by the government, where she stood alongside Lloyd George.[89] Sylvia and her East London Federation took a very different attitude. She opposed the war, and now extended her welfare activities in the East End; she took over a pub which became a crèche and organizing centre, renamed The Mother's Arms. As the war went on, she found increasing numbers of issues to campaign on.

Jingoistic attitudes to the Germans, who were part of long-standing and settled communities in London, especially in the East, now became widespread. Laws restricted the movement of Germans and a number were

---

85   Kendall, *The Revolutionary Movement in Britain*, p. 88.
86   K. Laybourn, *The Rise of Socialism in Britain* (London, 1997), pp. 82–3.
87   Fishman, *East End Jewish Radicals*, p. 306.
88   Benn, *Keir Hardie*, pp. 322–31.
89   S. R. Grayzel, *Women and the First World War* (Harlow, 2002), p. 27; see also Pankhurst, *The Suffragette Movement*.

interned, while many were sacked or their businesses destroyed. French and German anarchists set up a communal kitchen in the West End to feed unemployed workers, and Rudolf Rocker set one up in the East End.[90] But these were small if principled gestures: the tide was running the other way. As ordinary people were being killed by U-boats or Zeppelins, anti-German chauvinism only grew stronger and more bitter.

In London there were serious riots against the city's sizeable German population, especially in 1915 following the sinking of the *Lusitania*. Such riots took place in East Ham, Stratford, Manor Park, Woolwich, Canning Town, Leyton, Hackney and Tottenham where German butchers, bakers and tobacconists were attacked. These recurred when London was hit by Zeppelin raids and when Lord Kitchener was drowned later in the war.[91] In Stratford, the King of Prussia pub became the King Edward.

The war changed London dramatically. Almost immediately most working people suffered hardship, with rents and food prices going up, and many families found themselves at least initially without proper support because husbands and fathers were in the army. There were campaigns for separation allowances and proper incomes for families. There were repeated outbreaks of protest over rent and food profiteering, which grew as time went on and patriotic enthusiasm turned to despair at the length of the war and its staggering loss of life.

Pubs had their opening hours restricted in order to improve the efficiency of war work. Later in the war, the Defence of the Realm Act allowed the military authorities to expel prostitutes from certain areas, while women with venereal diseases were forbidden under regulation 40D from soliciting or having sex with soldiers; they could be imprisoned for at least a week, and subjected to forced medical examination.[92] The bishop of London launched a 'cleansing London' campaign in 1916 to 'purge the heart of the Empire before the boys come back.'[93]

There was also the first experience of aerial warfare in London, from 1915 when Germany sent over the huge Zeppelin air balloons. The first raid dropped incendiaries and bombs on Stoke Newington and Hackney, then Stepney, West Ham and Leytonstone.[94] The cumbersome airships were replaced with standard aeroplanes later in the war and these carried out day as well as night-time raids. In June 1917 they hit the infants' class of

90   Fishman, *East End Jewish Radicals*, p. 307.
91   Bloom, *Violent London*, pp. 288–97.
92   Grayzel, *Women and the First World War*, p. 71.
93   Ibid., pp. 70–1.
94   G. Weightman and S. Humphries, *The Making of Modern London* (London, 2007), p. 103.

North Street School in Poplar, killing sixteen and injuring thirty.[95] London suffered fifty-two air raids between January 1915 and August 1918.[96]

London became a major centre of arms production for the war. Munitions factories were hugely expanded at the Woolwich Arsenal and new ones were built, as in Park Royal in North West London, which after the war became the largest industrial estate in the country. Large numbers of women were conscripted to work. Women workers were particularly numerous at Woolwich Arsenal, which had used hardly any women before the war, but employed nearly 10,000 by 1916 and around 25,000 by the end of 1917. The factory complex was so large that it stretched three and a half miles wide by two and a half miles long.[97] The Well Hall estate nearby was built in garden-city style, specifically to house the workers.

The job was dangerous, what with the numerous explosions, and very unhealthy: workers sometimes turned yellow as a result of handling TNT. Munitions workers were, however, reasonably well paid. A number of strikes over the 'dilution' of the male workforce by the female – one of the earliest took place in Crayford on the edge of London – had had the effect of pushing up women's wages, at least for piece rates. Women also took over many other men's jobs in London, from tram and bus conductors, to carters, office workers and even butchers; and this made a marked differ-ence to their lives. Many of the women came from jobs in domestic service or on the land, and in general they greatly preferred the independence and increased income of the war work.

As the war progressed there was growing discontent on a number of fronts. One was the hideous human cost of the war itself, the wounded and men on leave a constant reminder of what was taking place not many miles across the Channel. A munitions worker described the sight of ambulances coming up to the Royal Free Hospital in King's Cross carrying the wounded. Casualties were so great that they stopped moving them by day, and only transported them at night: 'When we were on the night shift, during the break my friends and I used to go into the Gray's Inn Road and wait for the convoys to pass. They moved very slowly and a lot of the ambulances had open backs so we ran alongside them, chatting to the less seriously wounded and giving them the cigarettes and chocolates we'd bought.'[98]

The air raids and a new big gun which it was rumoured would allow the Germans to attack London from afar brought new and frequent fears, and Londoners began to take refuge in the Tube stations while food shortages,

---

95   Grayzel, *Women and the First World War*, p. 59.
96   G. Braybon and P. Summerfield, *Out of the Cage* (London, 1987), p. 97.
97   Ibid., p. 41.
98   Alice Connor (née Kedge), cited in J. Marlow, *Women and the Great War* (London, 1999), pp. 85–6.

price rises and profiteering continued. There were endless queues for food and other necessities.[99] Rationing was eventually introduced near the end of the war for foods such as sugar, meat, jam, bread, butter, margarine and lard – the staples of working-class life.[100] It was around this time that an experiment in communal food provision began, when a National Kitchen was opened in Westminster Bridge Road in 1917, aimed at women workers and their children.[101] Strikes and rent strikes proliferated. After the Russian Revolution in February 1917, discontent increased and there was widespread sympathy among working people. The second Russian Revolution in October 1917 concluded Russia's part in the war – one of its key demands – and marked the beginning of the end for everyone, although fighting dragged on for another bloody year.

Sylvia Pankhurst continued her work in the East End. Following her expulsion from the WSPU in early 1914, she set up the East London Federation of Suffragettes (ELFS), producing a paper called the *Women's Dreadnought* (after the popular name for the battleship). In 1916 she changed the name of the organization to the Workers' Suffrage Federation and then after the Russian Revolution again to the Workers' Socialist Federation, the paper now being called the *Workers' Dreadnought*. Sylvia campaigned on a range of issues: food shortages; housing; keeping open her food kitchen and toy-making workshop; campaigning against Queen Mary's workshops or 'sweatshops' as Sylvia called them; promoting proper allowances for those whose husbands were in the army; and the vote, where she rejected the limited women's suffrage which was on offer from the government. Her paper was highly regarded, with Shaw maintaining a subscription, and it had a rising circulation.[102]

The war ended in November 1918. By then, London had seen its first equal pay strike from women working on the buses and trams.[103] It also saw women munitions workers demonstrating outside Parliament to maintain their jobs in the face of lay-offs. There was little rejoicing for most people. Vera Brittain, on whom the war had such a formative effect, wrote: 'When the sound of victorious guns burst over London at 11 am on 11 November 1918, the men and women who looked incredulously into each other's faces did not cry jubilantly: "We've won the War!" They only said: "The War is over."'[104]

---

99   Ibid., pp. 268–9.
100   Braybon and Summerfield, *Out of the Cage*, p. 103.
101   Ibid.
102   S. Harrison, *Sylvia Pankhurst: A Maverick Life, 1882–1960* (London, 2004), p. 191.
103   *Workers' Dreadnought*, 24 August 1918.
104   V. Brittain, *Testament of Youth* (London, 1978), p. 460.

8

The Strike and the Slump

The whole of Europe is filled with the spirit of revolution.

David Lloyd George

'THE MOST SERIOUS CRISIS SINCE THE TIME OF THE CHARTISTS'

The First World War suppressed domestic discontent – for a time. Strike action was banned by agreement between the TUC and the government, and the Labour Party joined Prime Minister Lloyd George's coalition government in December 1916. But discontent was rising by the end of the conflict. The casualties and the privations of the first industrial war left their mark on Londoners as on others. As a result union membership had almost doubled, and revolution was a palpable reality in post-war Europe. First Russia, then Germany, then Hungary had already exploded in revolution. Britain was not an exception to revolutionary pressure. Historian Walter Kendall argues that 'the evidence shows that the crisis which British society faced between 1918 and 1920 was probably the most serious since the time of the Chartists'.[1] The official history of the TUC records:

1919 witnessed the broadest and most serious strike wave yet seen. Thirty-five million working days were lost in strike action – six times as many as in the previous year. This included strikes of the police and the armed forces. Miners, transport workers, printers joined those who had been taking action throughout the war. Their mood was influenced by the news of the workers' rising in Germany and Hungary and their strong support for the fledgling Soviet Russia. At the forefront was, once again, the Clyde Workers' Committee which organized a mass

---

1   Kendall, *The Revolutionary Movement in Britain*, p. 187.

strike in January 1919. In Belfast too a huge strike wave paralysed the city.[2]

The strikes were nationwide and their most advanced centres were not necessarily in London – the Clydeside general strike of 1919 probably has that distinction. But the crisis of the state machine, which was extreme, was concentrated in the capital. In the first instance this was a crisis in the armed forces of the state: the army and the police. Police wages had been eroded by inflation and a police union, the National Union of Police and Prison Officers, although clandestine, had built considerable support, especially in London, since its foundation in 1913. As London bus workers, Lancashire cotton workers, Welsh railway workers, and Yorkshire miners began the post-war strike wave the police were drawn towards the organized workers' movement – six NUPPO members served on the London Trades Council. When in August 1918 Constable Tommy Thiel of the Metropolitan Police was sacked for union activities, the vast majority of police in London downed truncheons, leaving the capital with no force capable of maintaining order. The strike was strongest in the city centre, and flying pickets, some 600 strong, enforced the strike. A large demonstration was held at Tower Hill.

The government was caught completely off guard, and Prime Minister Lloyd George surrendered in order to buy time. In November 1918 the police union grew from 10,000 members in August to 50,000, and more mass rallies were held in the Royal Albert Hall, Trafalgar Square and Hyde Park. Government forces reorganized, appointing a new Commissioner of the Metropolitan Police, Nevil Macready, a veteran of the suppression of the 1910 Tonypandy miners' strike. But it was only after the government provoked a second strike in London in May 1919, and then sacked all the 1,000 police who came out, that the situation was brought under control.[3]

The police strikes would have been serious enough in themselves, but they coincided with the most extensive series of mutinies in the army and navy that the British armed forces had ever experienced. Again these mutinies affected every corner of the country, but in London they brought the mutineers into direct confrontation with the government and the army high command. The first soldiers' mutiny was in Folkestone, January 1919, where 10,000 refused to embark boats taking them for another tour of duty abroad. They won speedy demobilization – which the government was resisting partly because it was planning military intervention against the

---

2   M. Davis, TUC History Online, 1918–1939, available at unionhistory.info, accessed 22 June 2011.
3   Kendall, *The Revolutionary Movement in Britain*, p. 192. Police struck in other areas too, such as Merseyside and Birmingham.

Russian Revolution. The London evening papers reported these events and this sparked further mutinies in and around the capital.

At Osterley Park west of London 3,000 men of the Army Service Corps were stationed, many of them former bus drivers with trade union experience. They demanded demobilization, but when they got no reply about 150 of them took three lorries and headed towards central London, planning a visit to Lloyd George. Other regiments joined them at Downing Street, where they obtained accelerated demobilization and the promise that none would be sent overseas. This last point was important as, on the day of the demonstration, the *Pall Mall Gazette* reported 'the excitement among the Army Service Corps at Osterley and elsewhere is attributed in many quarters to the oft-repeated rumours that plans are being prepared for sending a considerable force to Russia.'[4]

The movement spread. In Grove Park, south-east London, about 250 drivers marched to see their commanding officer at a barracks half a mile away from their camp, knocking over the sergeant major who tried to halt them at the gates. On 6 January in Uxbridge, West London, 400 men of the Armament School upset the mess tables in protest at the poor food, broke camp and marched down the High Street, singing 'Britons Never Shall Be Slaves' and 'Tell Me the Old, Old Story'. The following day they set up a Grievance Committee and sent a deputation to the War Office. At Kempton Park, South West London, thirteen lorries packed with troops drove to the War Office. The lorries were chalked with slogans among which were 'Kempton is on strike', 'No red tape', 'We are fed up' and 'No more sausage and rabbits'. They elected a delegation of eleven to negotiate with the War Office. Meanwhile, some 400 at Fairlop naval airfield near Ilford threatened to go to Whitehall if their demands were not met. There were more protests in White City and Upper Norwood.

On 7 January in Park Royal some 4,000 ASC troops demonstrated with a view to speedy demobilization, shorter working days, no draft for Russia, an elected committee, and no victimizations. They were promised most of their demands. The following day a big delegation arrived in Whitehall to present the demands to government. At Paddington and again on Horse Guards Parade the commander of the London district, General Fielding, tried to stop them with threats of police action. The strikers ignored him and marched to Downing Street where the former Chief of the Imperial General Staff, Sir William Robertson, came out to hear their demands. Discussion followed and a general was sent to Park Royal to investigate the complaints. Demobilization was speeded up as a result, and it was agreed

---

4   A. Rothstein, *The Soldiers' Strikes of 1919* (London, 1980), pp. 43–4.

that no one who had been overseas or who was over forty-one years old would be sent on draft, including to Russia.[5]

Soldiers were not alone in opposing Lloyd George's plan for a British expeditionary force to the Russian port of Archangel. A 'Hands Off Russia' committee forced the government to withdraw its forces, though it continued to support the White counterrevolutionaries with money and supplies. In April 1920 this indirect intervention reached its climax when Poland invaded Russia, with British and French backing. In May a renewed campaign against intervention was launched at London's East India Docks. A ship called the *Jolly George* was awaiting a cargo of arms destined for the Polish army, but the dockers refused to load the ship and prevented it from sailing. A week later they were publicly congratulated by their leader, Ernest Bevin. Following the dockers' lead, the railwaymen's executive called on its members to refuse to handle munitions destined for Poland. But in August, when the Poles were being driven back, Lloyd George threatened large-scale military action against the Soviet Union unless its army withdrew.

Anti-intervention demonstrations were held throughout Britain. A national conference summoned by the Labour Party and the TUC authorized the formation of the Council of Action, granting it powers to call a general strike in the event of an attack on Russia. Local councils of action formed spontaneously throughout the country, led by the trades councils and local Labour Parties. The government realized that the war against the Soviet Union was opposed by the vast majority and that persistence could lead to a much more revolutionary situation. Lloyd George abandoned his plans and advised the Poles to make peace.

Perhaps something of the atmosphere in working-class London at this time can be caught in black American writer Claude McKay's recollection of his first meeting with Sylvia Pankhurst:

> Sylvia Pankhurst ... wrote asking me to call at her printing office in Fleet Street. I found a plain little Queen-Victoria sized woman with plenty of long unruly bronze-like hair. There was no distinction about her clothes, and on the whole she was very undistinguished. But her eyes were fiery, even a little fanatic, with a glint of shrewdness. She said she wanted me to do some work for the *Workers' Dreadnought*. ...
>
> The association with Pankhurst put me in the nest of extreme radicalism in London ... Pankhurst herself had a personality as picturesque and passionate as any radical in London. She had left the suffragette legion for the working-class movement when she discovered that the leading ladies of the legion were not interested in the condition of working women.

---

5   Rothstein, *The Soldiers' Strikes*, pp. 44–7.

And in the labor movement she was always jabbing her hatpin into the hides of the smug and slack labor leaders. Her weekly might have been called the *Dread Wasp*. And wherever imperialism got drunk and went wild among native peoples, the Pankhurst paper would be on the job. She was one of the first leaders in England to stand up for Soviet Russia. And in 1918 she started the Russian Information Bureau, which remained for a long time the only source of authentic news from Russia.

Soon after I became associated with the *Workers' Dreadnought*, a sawmill strike broke out in London. Most of the sawmills were in the East End, where also the publishing office of the *Dreadnought* was located. One mill was directly opposite the *Dreadnought* office. I was assigned to do an article on the strike. A few of the sawmill workers were sympathetic to the *Dreadnought* organization, and one of the younger of them volunteered to take me round.

There were some sixty sawmills in London, one of the most important of which was either owned or partly controlled by George Lansbury, Labour Member of Parliament and managing editor of the *Daily Herald*. Some of the strikers informed me that the Lansbury mill had in its employ some workers who were not members of the sawmill union and who were not striking. Technically, such workers were scabs. The strikers thought it would make an excellent story for the militant *Dreadnought*. So did I.[6]

This developing revolutionary situation came to a head with the threat of strike action by the Triple Alliance of the miners, transport workers and rail unions. The scale of the threat and the incapacity of the existing leadership of the labour movement to play their strongest card were encapsulated in the exchange between the union leaders and Lloyd George. Robert Smillie recounted the scene as follows to Aneurin Bevan:

'Lloyd George sent for the Labour leaders . . . he said to us: "Gentlemen, you have fashioned, in the Triple Alliance of the unions represented by you, a most powerful instrument. I feel bound to tell you that in our opinion we are at your mercy. The Army is disaffected and cannot be relied upon . . . In these circumstances, if you carry out your threat and strike, then you will defeat us.

"But if you do so," went on Mr Lloyd George, "have you weighed the consequences? . . . For, if a force arises in the state which is stronger than the state itself, then it must be ready to take on the functions of the state,

---

6 From C. McKay, *A Long Way From Home* (London, 1985, originally published in 1937).

or withdraw and accept the authority of the state. Gentlemen," asked the Prime Minister quietly, "have you considered, and if you have, are you ready?" 'From that moment on,' said Robert Smillie, 'we were beaten and we knew we were.'[7]

This was the moment when the outcome of the General Strike of 1926 was foretold; the moment too, therefore, where the power of the left and the unions, on the rise since the 1880s, passed its zenith. Lloyd George understood that the Triple Alliance had created a potentially revolutionary situation, but the Alliance, and the workers' movement as a whole, lacked a revolutionary leadership capable of acting on that potential.

POPLAR COUNCILLORS AND LONDON LABOUR

Britain only became recognizably a democracy in 1918, with the passing of the Representation of the People Act. This legislation did more than the three preceding Reform Acts put together and enlarged the electorate from 7.5 million to over 20 million, although women aged between twenty-one and thirty would not be enfranchised until 1929. In addition, property ownership as a precondition for the vote was lifted. The municipal elections of 1919 were the first in which 'paupers' could vote.

Herbert Morrison had built the London Labour Party into an efficient electoral machine which won 39 per cent of the vote and control of half the twenty-eight borough councils in the capital. It also won 35 per cent of the vote in the London County Council elections, but this only gave it fifteen of 123 seats. In the East End, Labour was now in control of the town halls. In Poplar Labour won thirty-nine out of forty-two council positions, and George Lansbury became mayor. Lansbury had been a pacifist opponent of the war, and he was very clear that things must change in Poplar. His line was that 'Labour councillors must be different from those we have displaced, or why displace them?'

Perhaps no other local authority has ever started with so little and done so much. Infant mortality was cut, and a council-house building programme launched. Libraries were refurbished. Public works – road mending, house repairs – were set in train to alleviate unemployment. A four-shilling bonus had been paid to all council workers who joined a union. From 1920, after agreement with trade unions, Poplar council paid a minimum wage of £4 a week to its employees, who had previously received £1.50. Equal pay for

---

7   Quoted in R. Challinor, *The Origins of British Bolshevism* (London, 1977), pp. 203–4.

women was enacted, which gave them a wage rise of 70 per cent.[8] But the really big fight was over benefits for the unemployed.

Workers who could not claim unemployment benefit, or who were poor for reasons other than lack of a job, were still dependent on the provisions of the 1834 Poor Law for assistance. A government committee had recommended its abolition in 1917, but it was still there in the 1920s. Control over local councils and the Boards of Guardians placed socialists in a powerful position as unemployment began to rise in 1921. Workhouses were paid for by a common fund for all London boroughs. But rather than put people into the workhouse, Labour councillors preferred to pay them 'outdoor relief'. This was paid by the individual borough and the money was raised through the rates, a tax levied on property.

Poplar was a poor borough and property rents were low. But since tax was assessed on the basis of a 'rateable value' deriving from rents, Poplar had to set a much higher rate in order to produce the same amount produced by much lower rates in wealthy boroughs. In addition, Poplar ratepayers were charged a precept to pay for the London County Council, Metropolitan Police, Metropolitan Asylums Board and the Metropolitan Water Board. Poplar called for complete equalization of the rates so that the same rate brought in the same income both to Poplar and to wealthier West London boroughs, and refused to pay the charges for the LCC, police, Asylums Board and Water Board.

In July 1921 the Conservative government summoned thirty Poplar councillors to the High Court. At the head of 2,000 supporters they marched the five miles from Poplar against the backdrop of a banner that proclaimed: 'Poplar Borough Council, Marching to the High Court and Possibly to Prison, To Secure The Equalisation of Rates For Poor Boroughs'. The Poplar plan for equalization of the rates was declared illegal, while the Labour Party nationally refused to back Lansbury. J. H. Thomas, the right-wing trade union leader, called the Poplar councillors 'wastrels'.[9] In September the councillors were sent to Brixton and Holloway prisons, supporters singing the Red Flag outside the jails and a huge number of visitors continually harassing the prison authorities. The campaigning pressure forced the Home Office to allow all the councillors to hold Poplar council meetings in Brixton prison. One delegation emerged with this message from the councillors to their supporters: 'Comrades, stand fast! We will stand out to the bitter end. We believe that we are fighting the fight of the poor and heavy-laden not only in East London and Poplar but throughout the world.' The authorities were fearful of the popular mood and released

8   K. Flett, 'Poplar 1921: Guilty and Proud of It', *Socialist Review* (June 2005).
9   B. Pearce, 'What is Poplarism?' *The Newsletter* (3 May 1958).

the councillors within six weeks. Some 2,000 crowded into Bow Baths, with another 2,000 overflowing into the Roman Road, to greet them on their return to the East End. That weekend a 'monster demonstration' was held in Victoria Park.[10]

But the real fruit of victory was the new legislation which transferred most of the cost of outdoor relief to the Ministry of Health. Poplar's annual external funding rocketed from £50,000 to £300,000. From this the borough – and others in the East End including Clement Attlee's Stepney – paid outdoor relief at twice the level of unemployment benefit. The figures for claimants tell their own story: between 1888 and 1908 the numbers getting outdoor relief in the County of London and West Ham had hovered around the 60,000 mark. By 1923 that number was 276,000.

It was a great victory, but there had been a price to pay. Prison conditions had been dire and Lansbury reckoned they had damaged the health of a number of councillors. His own sister and fellow councillor, Minnie Lansbury, became ill immediately after her release and died at the age of thirty-two a few weeks later. Thousands of women assembled near her home and walked in procession to her funeral.[11] And there were limits to how far the system could be challenged by local councils. Herbert Morrison remained hostile, worried that the middle-class vote he was attempting to woo across the city would be alienated by the left policies in the East End. Eventually financial problems and lower wage levels in Poplar generally forced a reduction in benefits.

The Poplar councillors were not the only London politicians to conquer office on the back of the radicalized post-war mood of the first two decades of the century. Shapurji Saklatvala was only the third Indian-born member of the House of Commons; he was also one of the first Communist Party members elected as an MP, only two years after the party born out of protracted negotiations among Britain's socialist groups. Saklatvala's daughter Sehri recalls his deep immersion in the socialist culture of Britain at that time:

> Between his return to England in 1913 and his entry into the British Parliament as Member for North Battersea in 1922, his political aims were expressed in increasing activity in the Socialist Movement, the Independent Labour Party, (which he had joined in 1909 in Manchester), the Fabian Society, the Trade Union Movement, the Womens' Suffrage cause, in the Conscientious Objectors' Movement and, of course, above

10   N. Branson, *Poplarism 1919–1925: George Lansbury and the Councillors' Revolt* (London, 1979), p. 102.
11   Ibid., p. 113.

all, the urgent and compelling cry for India's freedom from foreign rule as imposed by the British Government; indeed, he worked to free all peoples from any form of imperialism, the peoples of Africa, China, Ireland, and all others ... He went further than that; he wanted working people all the world over who, after all, were the creators of any country's wealth, to own the means of production in which they worked ... believing that nothing less could liberate the working people of the world from exploitation, tyranny, illiteracy and want.[12]

In 1922 Saklatvala was officially backed by the Labour Party. And he was again in the general election of 1923, which he lost. But in his final successful campaign, in 1924, he ran on the Communist Party ticket without Labour support. It was a tough campaign dominated by the furore surrounding the Zinoviev Letter – a forgery designed to embarrass the CP by revealing that it received support from the Soviet Union – published in the *Daily Mail* just before the vote. Notwithstanding, Saklatvala was returned to the Commons for the last time with a majority of 554. He exercised a powerful anti-imperialist voice in the Commons, and later went on to form the League Against Imperialism.

One of Saklatvala's early supporters was the Liverpudlian John Archer, the son of a ship's steward from Barbados. Archer and his wife settled in Battersea in the 1890s and by 1900 he was fighting racism as a member of the Pan African Association. He was in Paris for the Pan African Congress of 1919, and chaired the Congress when it came to London two years later. In 1906 Archer was a Progressive Liberal local councillor, and in 1913 he became the first black mayor of a London borough. He counted socialists like John Burns and Tom Mann among his friends, and acted as election agent for Charlotte Despard, the Irish socialist and suffragette, in her bid for the North Battersea seat in 1918. He supported Saklatvala in 1922 and helped form the Battersea Labour Party in 1926. But after the final rupture between the Labour and Communist parties, Archer was the Labour Party agent in the campaign of 1929 in which Saklatvala was defeated.

THE GENERAL STRIKE OF 1926

The immediate causes of the General Strike are not hard to identify. The mines were in private hands and the owners, backed by the Conservative government, demanded wage cuts of between 10 and 25 per cent plus a longer working day. The miners' union fought under the banner of 'Not a

12 S. Saklatvala, *The Fifth Commandment: Biography of Shapurji Saklatvala* (Salford, 1991), Chapter 7.

penny off the pay, not a minute on the day' and the Trades Union Congress declared that the whole trade union movement would stand behind them.

London was not, of course, at the centre of the mining dispute but it was nevertheless important in the strike, for three reasons. Firstly, as soon as the General Strike began London's new and old industries were a key battle-ground. Secondly, the capital of the country and the seat of government was the nerve centre of the state's activities and of symbolic importance for both sides. Thirdly, the concentration of the rich and their supporters in London made it possible to organize them as strike-breakers more effec-tively than elsewhere.

The workers' response to the strike call on 3 May was immediate and overwhelming – some 1.75 million struck with an enthusiasm which took both the government and the TUC by surprise. The strike grew in strength and there were more people on strike on the last of its nine days than there were on the first. On the very evening of 3 May, London printers stopped all the later editions of the capital's evening papers in protest at their anti-union content.[13] London's transport workers, dockers, printers, power workers and workers in the chemical industry and metal trades all responded to the strike call.

Public transport was almost entirely shut down at the start of the strike. On the second day, all London taxicab drivers joined the action. In Canning Town and Poplar, police baton-charged strikers.[14] The following day police injured several people as they dispersed crowds in the Old Kent Road.[15] On the fourth day of the strike London's electricity power stations were out, though some, perhaps as many as half, were kept going by volun-teers and sailors with stockpiles of coal that the government had prepared. The London Strike Committee called out workers supplying electricity to the House of Commons.[16] By the fifth day of the strike a reported fifteen Councils of Action were functioning in London. These were often inspired by the Communist Party. In Bethnal Green the Council of Action occu-pied the Public Library. Most London Councils of Action issued their own typescript bulletins.[17]

The strike was strong in London, but so were the strike-breakers who had the proximity of government and the concentration of its police and armed forces to back them up. Twelve leaders of the Communist Party had been jailed in the run up to the strike. Over nine days, more strike supporters,

13   R. Page Arnot, *The General Strike, May 1926* (1926; Wakefield, 1975), p. 67.
14   Ibid., pp. 177–8.
15   Ibid., p. 185.
16   Ibid., p. 189.
17   Ibid., p. 192.

including Shapurji Saklatvala, Communist MP for Battersea North, were arrested and imprisoned.[18] The government seized the print works of the *Morning Post* and used it to produce its propaganda sheet the *British Gazette*, edited by Winston Churchill. The first copy of the *Gazette* only appeared, however, because Lord Beaverbrook sent over the night superintendent of the *Daily Express* who had to set the final columns of the sheet himself, after compositors struck and destroyed the already set type.[19]

The BBC news was vetted by government. The docks were put under the control of a Guards regiment and some 1,000 volunteers, including Cambridge students and Covent Garden porters, worked as strike-breakers in the Victoria docks. The government appeal to enrol special constables was met in London by nearly 52,000 volunteers. This was less than half the total number of strike-breakers who volunteered in London. On the fourth day of the strike, troops were granted immunity from prosecution for acts considered necessary to maintain order. On the fifth day a two-mile convoy of lorries, defended by sixteen armoured cars, cavalry, mounted police and guards in steel helmets, transported flour from the London docks to the government's depot sited in Hyde Park. The BBC reported that 'large crowds of people – many of them women – collected to cheer and welcome the flour on its way. The sight was as popular as the Lord Mayor's procession.'[20] The following day Churchill, at the heart of the government operation, deployed lorry-loads of soldiers all over central London. On the penultimate day of the General Strike the courts ruled the strike illegal, and the *Daily Mail* issued a leaflet and a leading article calling for the arrest of the TUC General Council.

The TUC leaders were terrified by two things: the power of the state, and the power of their own members. The TUC had been compelled into action by the scale of the attack on the trade union movement. But they had expected neither the enthusiastic action of their own members, nor the ferocity of the state's response. The decisive moment for the trade union leaders was when the courts lifted union immunity for damages on solidarity strikes. By this action the government directly threatened the financial basis of the unions, and hence the continued existence of the union bureaucracy.

The union leadership capitulated without even getting a promise of no victimizations from the government. London's dockers, print workers and transport workers remained out for a further six days in protest at the

---

18   Saklatvala had won the seat as a Labour candidate in 1922 but retained it in 1924 as a CP candidate; see pp. 190–1.
19   C. Farman, *The General Strike, May 1926: Britain's Aborted Revolution?* (St Albans, 1972), p. 163.
20   Page Arnot, *The General Strike*, pp. 192–4.

climbdown. The miners rejected the capitulation of the TUC and fought on until September, but without a hope of victory. It was a dark day that left working people in Britain disarmed in the face of the coming storm of the Great Depression.

HUNGER MARCHES AND UNEMPLOYED RIOTS

That storm broke in 1929, the year of the Wall Street Crash that brought the world economy down with it. As financial speculation turned to full-scale, economy-wide slump, unemployment figures reached new and terrifying heights. At the worst of the downturn, nearly a quarter of Britons were on the dole. It was higher in the US and higher still in Norway, at 31 per cent, and in Denmark at 32 per cent. Germany, already a victim of hyperinflation, now saw unemployment rates of 44 per cent. Even the so-called economic recovery after 1933 saw rates of unemployment of 16 to 17 per cent in Britain, reaching 20 per cent in the US and Austria.

In the wake of the defeat of the General Strike, central government undid the gains of Poplarism and provision for the unemployed became markedly worse. The 250,000 unemployed Londoners in 1930–33 could expect no aid from sympathetic Labour councils as they had done in the early 1920s. In 1931 Labour lost 31 out of 36 MPs, and 200 out of 459 borough councillors in the capital. This was the background as 2,000 hunger marchers arrived in London in October 1932, organized by the Communist Party-inspired National Unemployed Workers' Movement (NUWM). This was done without the help of the TUC or the Labour Party, hostile to the NUWM because of its CP leadership. The authorities regarded it as 'a red rabble which had to be put down or it would get out of hand', and 'the police habitually acted on these assumptions'.[21] There had already been fighting between the unemployed and the police outside London, in Birkenhead and Liverpool for instance in September 1932. The authorities were in belligerent mood, heightened by inaccurate reports from informers in the NUWM who claimed that the marchers planned to use trip wires, vitriol and iron bars in deliberate confrontations with the police.

On 18 October marchers and their supporters battled police outside County Hall at St George's Circus, the site of St George's Fields, where John Wilkes had once assembled the crowd. Ironically the police were intent on using the 1817 Seditious Meetings Act to prohibit meetings within a mile of Westminster. Nine days later there were, on the report of march organizer Wal Hannington, 100,000 in Hyde Park to greet the

---

21 N. Branson and M. Heinemann, *Britain in the Nineteen Thirties* (St Albans, 1973), p. 36.

march.[22] The 2,600 police mobilized to meet them were engaged in bitter struggles with protestors for most of the day. Untrained and panicky 'special constables' were responsible for much of the trouble.

Three days later, Sunday 30 October, an even bigger rally in Trafalgar Square was relatively peaceful. On 1 November Hannington tried to deliver a one-million-signature petition to the Commons. A huge crowd assembled, and was attacked by the police. Fighting spread out from Whitehall to Westminster Bridge, the Strand, Charing Cross Road, Trafalgar Square, Piccadilly, Victoria Street and the Embankment. As late as 11pm there was a crowd of 800 at Shepherd's Bush, and the central London fighting didn't end until 1.30am. Forty-two people were arrested as was, in a moment of high farce, the petition itself, taken into custody from Charing Cross Station's left luggage office where it had been placed for safe keeping at the height of the fighting. In the aftermath the leaders of the NUWM were rounded up, including a veteran of the 1889 dock strike, Tom Mann.[23]

The following year, in February 1933, the TUC were embarrassed enough to organize the single official demonstration over unemployment that ever took place during the 1930s. Scotland Yard and the official TUC marshals met and mutually assured each other that the NUWM would not be allowed to join the march. The chief constable informed the commissioner that the organizers had been very 'tame' and that they were 'anxious to consult the Commissioner as to his wishes re their demonstration'.[24] The demonstration mobilized 20,000. The NUWM did set up its own stage, but there was no trouble. Afterwards the head of the TUC, future baron Walter Citrine, thanked the police for their co-operation.

When the NUWM marchers again came to London in February 1934, the Metropolitan Police treated them with greater respect. No doubt they were influenced by the fact that the march organizers had invited H. G. Wells, Vera Brittain, Harold Laski, Julian Huxley and other London intellectuals, plus members of the newly formed National Council for Civil Liberties, to meet the demonstration in Hyde Park. This was part of a wider strategy adopted by the NUWM to end its isolation within the labour movement, and reach out to sympathetic Labour MPs and others. The strategy heralded a largely effective phase of mass agitation in the 1930s, although the most spectacular results were achieved outside London. In February 1935, for instance, the *Manchester Guardian* estimated that in South Wales alone there were 300,000 on the streets protesting at the reorganization of unemployment benefit.

---

22   The police estimate, then as now, was much lower at between 10,000 and 25,000. See J. Stevenson and C. Cook, *The Slump: Society and Politics During the Depression* (London, 1979), p. 176.
23   Ibid., pp. 178–9.
24   Ibid., p. 180.

The Jarrow Crusade of 1936, although the best known of the hunger marches, was probably the smallest, least militant and least effective. Organized by local Labour MP Ellen Wilkinson it steered clear of any involvement with the NUWM, described itself as 'non-political', and agreed to the police's strict conditions for presenting its petition to Parliament. As a result the Home Office ruled that the marchers should be allowed to take tea in the House of Commons: since 'the marchers show every sign of being orderly, it would be a good way of encouraging them'. Not that any of this saved Ellen Wilkinson from a rebuke at the Labour Party Conference for organizing hunger marches that might be associated with Communist tactics and result in disorder and disrepute. When the Jarrow marchers arrived in London, they refused an invitation to join a CP rally in Hyde Park in favour of their own event. The Special Branch reported that 'When H.M. the King passed through The Mall on the 3rd inst., the Jarrow contingent was placed at a vantage point opposite the Duke of York's steps, and showed their enthusiasm by cheering lustily.'[25]

THE BUSMAN'S PUNCH

One of the most effective union organizations of the 1930s was built on the London buses in the 1930s. It was a rank-and-file organization led by the Central Bus Committee (CBC) with its own lively paper, the *Busman's Punch*. It represented 20,000 highly organized workers with a strong sense of industrial democracy who worked in garages that allowed for close coordination. Uniquely the CBC had its own full-timer and direct access to the executive of their union, the Transport and General Workers Union (TGWU).

In 1932 the London Omnibus Company demanded wage reductions and 800 redundancies. Official union negotiations by the TGWU failed to get any concessions out of the company, and so CBC delegates began organizing mass meetings in the garages. Led by Bert Papworth, Bill Jones and Bill Payne, this rank-and-file organization won a four to one majority for strike action in an official union ballot. Papworth had led his first strikes during the First World War when he was only sixteen, and had been involved in disputes at the Woolwich Arsenal. He and Jones joined the Communist Party in the 1930s, although the press were denouncing the CBC as Communist-inspired long before the CP actually had members on it.[26]

---

25   Ibid., pp. 185–7.
26   A. Murray, *The T&G Story: A History of the Transport and General Workers Union, 1922–2007* (London, 2008), p. 64.

The CBC called for a strike. It is hard to know whether the company or TGWU boss Ernie Bevin was more startled by the militancy of the bus workers and their capacity for independent organization. At any rate the company withdrew their plans just as fast as Bevin could get new talks going. In the pit of the slump, it was a dramatic victory for rank-and-file organization. But the following year the company came back for more. New schedules imposing harder work were accepted by the union, but the reaction among the bus workers resulted in unofficial strikes that spread through thirty garages and also produced a threat of solidarity action by Tube workers. Bevin was furious at what he called 'an internal breakaway', but it took him another four years before he was able to undermine the CBC.

The economy began to revive in 1936–37 and the CBC felt it was time to launch a new campaign for better conditions: they put in a claim for a seven-and-a-half-hour working day. The new London Passenger Transport Board (LPTB) refused the claim, and on 30 April 1937 over 25,000 London bus workers walked out on strike. The strike was official, though Bevin had opposed it. The rank-and-file pamphlet, *London Busmen Demand the Right to Live a Little Longer*, made the strikers' case.

The walkout happened just as George VI was being crowned and it is hard to think of a more high-profile demonstration than the one which the bus workers held on May Day, marching in their white summer uniform behind a banner which read 'Twenty-five Thousand Busmen Can't Be Wrong'. The Ministry of Labour agreed that the busmen had a case for shorter hours, and the LPTB agreed to set up a joint inquiry with the union. The TGWU Executive recommended the strike be called off, but the CBC and the strikers overwhelmingly rejected this and called on the union to pull the tram and trolleybus workers out as well.

Bevin refused and, in the fourth week of the strike, repealed the powers of the CBC and ordered the busmen back to work. The Executive then declared the CBC a subversive organization with Communist connections, and made membership of it an expellable offence. Astonishingly the TGWU then kicked out the three leading militants, Papworth, Payne and Jones. Payne and the majority of the rank-and-file committee established a short-lived breakaway union, opposed by Papworth and Jones, who were CP members. Most members stayed with the TGWU and Papworth and Jones were later readmitted.[27]

---

27 Branson and Heinemann, *Britain in the Nineteen Thirties*, pp. 140–5.

THE 1930S AND FIGHTING THE FASCISTS

Britain's fascist movement was launched in 1932 just as Hitler was making his ascent to power. Called the British Union of Fascists (BUF) it was led by Sir Oswald Mosley, an establishment figure from an aristocratic background, who had served as an MP for both the Tory and Labour Parties. The BUF held its first rally in Trafalgar Square in October 1932 and within two years the Blackshirts had forty-two branches in London, the most successful in areas with a large Jewish population like Hackney and Stoke Newington. Mosley's new fascist party attracted a lot of support from the lower middle classes. Shopkeepers in the Hackney BUF, for instance, resented newly arrived Jewish businesses that were open for longer hours. But the BUF also gained support from figures higher up the social scale: Lord Rothermere, owner of the *Daily Mail*, was one such fellow-traveller. In January 1934 Rothermere signed a *Daily Mail* editorial headlined 'Hurrah for the Blackshirts'.

Mosley's BUF failed, however. Partly this was because the economic crisis of the 1930s, while serious, was not as catastrophic in Britain as it was in Germany. It was also because the NUWM already organized many of the unemployed, so that when the BUF attempted to get a foothold among them they found little political space in which to operate. And, crucially, the left united against the fascists in Britain – even though they sometimes had to ignore their leaders in order to do so.

In 1934 the Communist Party, tiny compared with its German sister organization, led 5,000 demonstrators to disrupt a fascist rally at London's Olympia, where the black-shirted stewards beat up the anti-fascist hecklers. The police refused to intervene, but the ruckus scared off some fascist supporters like Lord Rothermere. Later that year 100,000 anti-fascists protested at a counter-demonstration when Mosley tried to hold a rally in Hyde Park. Although the official leaders of the labour movement had told protestors to stay away, the demonstration was a great success, humiliating the mere 7,000 fascists who had to beg the police for protection.

Mosley tried to rebuild his support by dominating the streets of London's East End. Then as now the East End was a centre of immigration, a particular magnet for Jews arriving from Europe. Mosley's Blackshirts beat them in the streets, vandalized their businesses and marched through the area chanting 'The Yids, the Yids, we've got to get rid of the Yids'. They terrorized Jewish stallholders in Petticoat Lane market, attacked them outside the synagogue, painted the walls with anti-Semitic graffiti, and accused Jews of taking jobs from the locals. A BUF rally in Hackney's Victoria Park in June 1936 ended in fighting with anti-fascists. Yet neither the official leaders of the labour movement, nor the official leaders of the Jewish community, were prepared to support a militant mobilization against Mosley. George

Lansbury simply called for the Blackshirt march to be rerouted through 'less congested' areas, and suggested, in an early example of a now well-worn formula, that anti-fascists were giving the BUF publicity.[28] But the Communist Party, the Independent Labour Party and sections of the Jewish ex-servicemen's organization and the Jewish youth were prepared to resist.

In October 1936 a massive 100,000 protestors flocked to Cable Street in Stepney to stop Mosley marching. Bill Fishman was a member of the Labour Youth League, and he vividly remembers the day. For Fishman, as for others, the mobilization 'seemed like an act of solidarity because, on the same day, the Republicans in Spain were also preparing to defend Madrid against General Franco's nationalist forces'. Fishman recalls: 'I got off the 53 tram from Hackney just after noon, and there were already people marching and carrying banners proclaiming "No Pasaran" – the slogan we took from the Spanish Republicans meaning "They shall not pass". People were coming in from the side streets, marching towards Aldgate. There were so many that it took me about twenty-five minutes to get there along Whitechapel Road.' Fishman watched Mosley arrive from the Whitechapel Gallery, close to the BUF assembly point at the Tower of London:

I remember standing on the steps of the Whitechapel Art Gallery, watching Mosley arrive in a black open-top sports car. He was a playboy aristocrat and as glamorous as ever. By this time, it was about 3.30pm. You could see Mosley – wearing a black shirt himself – marching in front of 3,000 fascists and a sea of Union Jacks. It was as though he was the commander-in-chief of the Army, with the Blackshirts in columns and a mass of police to protect them. I had already seen him at a public meeting some months before. He had been standing on the back of a lorry parked outside the Salmon and Ball pub in Bethnal Green.

But Mosley's first approach was blocked:

The tension rose and we began chanting, 'One, two, three, four, five! We want Mosley dead or alive!' and 'They shall not pass!' Mosley encountered his first setback from a lone tram driver. About 50 yards away from me at Gardiner's Corner, I saw a tram pull up in the middle of the junction – barring the Blackshirts' route from Aldgate to Whitechapel. Then the driver got out and walked off. I found out later he was a member of the Communist Party. At that point the police charged the crowd to disperse us. They were waving their truncheons, but we were so packed together there was nowhere for us to go.

---

28   Vallance, *A Radical History of Britain*, p. 537.

The police made repeated baton charges to try and disperse the demo. 'I could see police horses going up in the air because some kids in front of me were throwing marbles under their hooves. That made the police more hostile and they spent the next hour charging into us.' The Metropolitan Police Commissioner, Sir Philip Game, told Mosley the fascists could go south through Royal Mint Street and Cable Street. The communists used loudspeakers and runners to redirect the crowd.

> I was young and afraid of what was basically a fight between the police and us, because we couldn't get near the Blackshirts. Cable Street then, as now, was narrow and there were three-storey and four-storey houses where Irish dockers lived. The dockers erected a barricade with an over-turned lorry piled with old mattresses and furniture.
>
> Women in the houses hurled rotten vegetables, muck from chamber pots and rubbish on to the police, who were struggling to dismantle some of the barricades. Things escalated again when the police sent snatch squads into the crowd to nab supposed ringleaders. Organised groups of dockers hit back with stones and sticks, while making several 'arrests' themselves! Indeed, there are some families in the East End who still have police helmets and batons as souvenirs!

This proved too much for the police:

> Finally, with the area in turmoil and the protesters at fever pitch, Sir Philip Game told Mosley that he would have to abandon the march, fearing too much bloodshed. He ordered Mosley to turn back and march through the deserted City. People went mad when the news filtered through. What had been a wild protest became a massive victory party, with thousands of people dancing in the streets.[29]

The BUF did continue to organize in the East End (there was violence at Mile End a few weeks later, for instance) but the defeat of Mosley at Cable Street was a turning point. The government passed the Public Order Act at the end of 1936 which banned uniforms and paramilitary organizations. The London County Council refused to let the BUF use its meeting halls. Still, the police and the authorities remained more sympathetic to the BUF

---

29   Bill Fishman's account can be found at edp24.co.uk, accessed 19 June 2011. Fishman estimates the numbers at Cable Street as no fewer than 250,000, though most historians use a lower figure of 100,000. There is no reason to suppose Fishman is wrong, but we have nevertheless used the conventional figure. For another first-hand account see J. Jacobs, *Out of the Ghetto* (London, 1978), pp. 235–58.

than to the anti-fascists. In 1939, a mere two months before the war broke out, Mosley held one of his largest rallies, with 20,000 in attendance, in London's Earls Court. Only in 1940 did the state move to break up the BUF and imprison its leaders.

LONDON, WORKERS AND THE SLUMP

The look of modern London largely reflects the way the city developed between the First and Second World Wars. During this period the centre of the city was significantly changed: the whole of Regent Street, from Oxford Circus to Piccadilly, was rebuilt in its modern form under strict building codes enforced by the Crown Estates (which is why the Liberty store boasts a mock-Tudor façade in Great Marlborough Street but not on the frontage on Regent Street itself). To the north the new quango, the BBC, moved in to its modernist HQ at Broadcasting House. To the west, Selfridges was finally completed. The new Piccadilly Circus underground station, on which few expenses were spared, opened in all its magnificence. Above ground the first ever traffic light blinked through its sequence in Piccadilly Circus in 1926. In the same year Hyde Park Corner, through which 51,000 motor vehicles and another 3,360 horse-drawn vehicles were passing every day, Piccadilly Circus and Trafalgar Square became the first one-way road systems. In Trafalgar Square Australia House and Canada House opened in 1935.

Modern Londoners think of the city as the area now enclosed by the motorway ring of the M25. Much of the urban character of the outer reaches of this area to the north, south, east and west is a result of suburban housing development begun in the 1920s and 1930s. The government feared that public disappointment over unfulfilled promises made in wartime might lead to unrest, and so began a public works programme aimed at building 500,000 new homes. But the money wasn't there, and in May 1920 Austen Chamberlain told the cabinet that 'the whole scheme of building houses must come to a standstill for lack of finance'. The housing programme largely ground to a halt in July 1921, when only 170,000 out of the 500,000 promised houses had been completed.

Some council housing did continue to be built – most famously the LCC's Becontree Estate of 26,000 houses, begun in 1921 and completed eleven years later. But it was only when interest rates fell and cheap money became available, a result of abandoning the Gold Standard in 1931, that private construction of working-class housing took off. There was little regulation to prevent this private house-building bonanza: 'The wide-ranging onslaught of the private builder across outer London in the later part of the 1920s and throughout the 1930s was little affected by the pitifully inadequate planning measures in place at the time. In the same way that there were few planning controls there were few statutory restrictions on the activities of the building societies', which were lending workers the money to buy houses.[30]

As war approached at the end of the 1930s wages rose in those areas of southern England where many new factories were situated, and it was in the areas around these factories that the new, speculatively built estates of 'Metroland' were erected. As Alan Crisp points out, without the growth of the economy that resulted from rearmament after 1936 the property boom of the 1930s may well have collapsed. But banks provided capital to the developers and fuelled stock-market support for construction companies: Wimpey, Taylor Woodrow, Costain and New Ideal Homesteads all went public during the 1930s.

The growth of these builders was rapid. Taylor Woodrow started building houses in 1930, using borrowed money, and by 1935 they were floated on the stock market with annual profits of £75,000.[31] The Metropolitan was both an underground rail company and a house builder. The company built ten 'garden villages' along its lines to Amersham and Uxbridge, Neasden, Wembley Park, Harrow, Pinner, Ruislip and Rickmansworth between 1920 and 1932. The expansion of the suburbs between 1921 and 1939 was immense: to the east, 116 per cent growth in Barking, 163 per cent in Romford, and 1,076 per cent in Dagenham. To the west there was 348 per cent growth in Ruislip-Northwood, 386 per cent in Hayes and Harlington, and 552 per cent in Wembley. In the south, two boroughs quadrupled their population: Merton and Morden, and Carshalton.[32]

By the late 1930s John Laing and Son of Mill Hill had built nine estates in North London and had a permanent 'new home exhibition' in Oxford Street, plus a full-size show home outside King's Cross Station. The houses were essentially identical but raided the back catalogue of English design, both architecturally and in the supply of interior decoration and furniture. Arts-and-Crafts-inspired features sat side by side with English Georgian and Jacobean accents. In the 1930s Modernism was added to the mix. One observer commented, 'Each house contains the same lounge hall, the same Jacobean dining suite, the same (to all appearances) dear little wife.'[33] But condescension is misplaced. For the working-class families that moved into these houses they had a number of advantages over their previous homes:

30   A. Crisp, 'Introduction', *The Working-Class Owner-Occupied House of the 1930s* (M.Litt Oxford Thesis, 1998), accessed online at pre-war-housing.org.uk, 23 June 2011.
31   Ibid., Chapter 1, 'Building Homes Fit for Heroes in the 1930s'.
32   Inwood, *History of London*, pp. 716–17.
33   See Ross and Clark, *London, The Illustrated History*, p. 255.

plumbing and indoor toilets, electricity, separate kitchens and individual gardens.

Despite these innovations, there were still desperate conditions in the city and many reasons for housing protests. The tenants' struggles in the East End were at the heart of many of these protests. In London overall, about 2 million of such private tenants were in 'controlled' accommodation, where they were legally entitled to withhold 40 per cent of the rent if the local sanitary inspector found that repairs had not been completed. This right was, however, hard for the resident to enforce. Michael Shapiro, Communist Party member and University of London lecturer specializing in land and town planning, began organizing the tenants in Stepney where he lived. The Stepney Tenants' Defence League estimated that half of those in controlled accommodation in London were being overcharged by landlords.

One of the first campaigns was in a block of 346 rundown flats in Quinn Square, Bethnal Green, where residents were struggling to cope with shared toilets and water taps, damp, collapsing ceilings, and broken hand-rails on the stairs. The property company tried to evict one tenant, and when local CP members looked into the case and found that she was being overcharged, a rent strike began. Only ninety of the tenants were control-led, and so able to legally withhold rent. But the other 250 residents joined the strike as well. Mass demonstrations followed, and every attempt by rent collectors to visit the estate ended with them being booed out of the area by crowds of women and children.

The company caved in within a fortnight, lowering rents and promis-ing repairs. The example spread throughout the East End. Most victories were equally swift – although the strike in 320 flats in Langdale Mansions and Brady Mansions lasted twenty-one weeks, and involved the residents erecting barbed-wire barricades against eviction and convoking frequent demonstrations. But here too the company eventually capitulated.[34]

The new estates in the outer suburbs were not immune to protest, either. Elsy and Jim Borders were CP members who had moved into a new house on an estate in West Wickham, Kent. They and others who joined their Coneyhall District Residents Association had taken advantage of a 95 per cent building-society mortgage, agreed with the house builders, to buy the property. But when they moved in they found the house was damp, the roof leaked, the woodwork was infested and the electrical wiring was faulty.

When Elsy didn't pay the mortgage for three months in 1937, the Bradford Third Equitable Building Society tried to repossess the house.

34 N. Branson, *History of the Communist Party of Great Britain, 1927–1941* (London, 1985), pp. 196–200.

Elsy counter-claimed, arguing for the return of her money on the basis the Bradford had lent it to her on insufficient security and had 'wilfully and fraudulently' misled her about the condition of the house. The case went to court in 1938, and Elsy hit the headlines for conducting her own case that lasted for months; the judgment was indecisive. So then, in February 1939, over 3,000 owner-occupiers in outer London went on mortgage strike. Some were quickly victorious, even though the government brought in legislation to protect the building societies. The Borders case dragged on into the first years of the Second World War, but by this time Elsy was a leading light in Michael Shapiro's now national Federation of Tenants and Residents Associations.[35]

Housing development was also made possible by the development of public transport, especially the bus and tube network. The first Underground line was the Metropolitan, which opened in 1863, then the District. These were joined up to form the Circle in 1884. The system continued to grow through the pre-war period, with important extensions after the war and through the 1920s and 1930s. Henry Beck's synthetic map of the Underground, still in all essentials in use today, was adopted in 1932. Beck, an electrical draughtsman, based his design on an electrical circuit board. Unlike previous maps it did not represent the tube system accurately in terms of distance or geography, making the central London area larger for clarity and 'shrinking' the distances to the outer London stations, but it was a great deal more comprehensible.[36]

But this was still a world in which the motorbus was king, replacing pre-war horse-drawn buses and, more slowly because they enjoyed an LCC subsidy, trams. Londoners took buses to the underground or rail station, which added to their part in overall transport usage figures. Partly buses became more popular because the pneumatic tyres permitted by the police from 1926 and the development of the covered double-decker improved the travelling experience. A new bus design nearly doubled passenger capacity and increased speed from 12 mph to 30 mph. Indeed these changed conditions, plus the new traffic lights and Belisha beacon crossings, were the basis for the busmen's demand for shorter hours in the 1937 strike discussed earlier in this chapter.[37] New roads were also being developed: the Great West Road, Eastern Avenue, the Great Cambridge Road and the North Circular. Many new industries developed along these arteries.

In 1900, much London industry was to be found in a rectangle whose corners were Camden, Stratford, Vauxhall and Greenwich. But the new roads

35   Branson, *History of the Communist Party of Great Britain*, pp. 200–1.
36   Black, *London: A History*, p. 317
37   N. Branson and M. Heinemann, *Britain in the Nineteen Thirties*, p. 142.

described very different industrial locations. The art deco Hoover Building on the A40 still stands as an emblem of the era. Firestone tyres, Studebaker and Packard concessions representing the US auto industry were on the Great West Road, so too were Trico windscreen wipers, Curry's electrical goods warehouse, Smith's Crisps, Maclean's Toothpaste, Gillette razors, Simmonds Aeroaccessories, Sperry's compasses and gyroscopes and others. Many of the magnificent art deco buildings in the 'Golden Mile' west of Chiswick remain, though the Firestone factory was demolished in 1980 just ahead of a preservation order being served. To the novelist J. B. Priestley, the Great West Road 'did not even look English. We might suddenly have rolled into California.'[38] No doubt continuing the journey as far as Slough would correct the impression.

Park Royal in north-west London started life in 1903 as the Royal Agricultural Society's showground. In 1915, it was taken over by the army, dislodging Queen's Park Rangers from their home ground. But in the 1920s it developed as a huge base of engineering and became home to, among others, GKN and Park Royal Vehicles where, after the war, the Routemaster bus was built. But Park Royal was also home to Heinz from 1925 and in the mid 1930s Guinness built the first new brewery in London for thirty years at Park Royal. At the end of the 1930s, Park Royal was home to 256 firms. In the east, Ford's giant Dagenham plant opened in 1931 on reclaimed marshland. It had its own docks and power plant, and it grew to eventually employ 40,000 workers. And at Silvertown the giant sugar refinery of the newly merged enterprises of Henry Tate and Abram Lyle was opened on Thameside where it still stands, opposite the new City Airport.[39]

London workers suffered in the slump, but not as much as those in other parts of the country. Only 1 percent of London's manual workers were employed in the five most hard hit industries – coal, shipbuilding, cotton, wool and iron and steel. The national average was 23 percent. The Ministry of Labour identified 23 industries with above average growth in the years 1923–37. A third of the national workforce in those industries was in London. Of the 3,635 new factories that opened in Britain between 1932 and 1937 nearly half were located in Greater London. These workplaces accounted for 40 percent of the new manufacturing jobs created in Britain in this period.[40]

---

38   See C. Ross and J. Clark, *London: The Illustrated History*, p. 260.
39   C. Ross and J. Clark, *London: The Illustrated History*, p. 258.
40   C. Ross and J. Clark, *London: The Illustrated History*, p. 258.

AID SPAIN

In the late 1930s a degree of economic recovery might be alleviating the misery of the slump for Londoners, but it was international affairs which would determine their future. Nothing foreshadowed this darkening prospect so much as the Spanish Civil War. General Franco's war against the Spanish Republic began in 1936, and there was an almost instantaneous public recognition that this battle might be the last that could halt the rise of fascism in Europe. There were those in Britain that supported Franco: some in the Tory party, the *Daily Mail*, the *Daily Sketch* and the *Observer* all pleaded the fascist cause. But in the wider society these voices were a tiny minority. Opinion polls show that the Francoists never got more than 14 per cent support, while support for Republican Spain ranged between 57 and 72 per cent.[41]

A huge solidarity movement with Republican Spain grew up, taking a variety of organizational forms. At the moderate end of the spectrum was the National Joint Committee for Spanish Relief, chaired by the Conservative Duchess of Athol, and including Labour, Independent and Liberal MPs. It coordinated aid with the Save the Children Fund, the Salvation Army and the Quakers. Closer to the left and the labour movement were the Aid Spain committees which appeared in practically every town and city. The response, especially but not only in working-class areas, was astonishing. Twenty-nine food ships were sent to Spain, stocked by local people and firms in places like Liverpool, Hull, Tyneside and Glasgow. Medical supplies were raised separately. The first British ambulance unit left for Spain in August 1936, paid for by local funding; it was the first of many.

The International Brigades took volunteers to fight in Spain. The British Brigade was half composed of Communist Party members, half of ILP supporters, Labour Party members and those of no party affiliation. Bert Papworth, one of the busmen's leaders, visited Spain and moved the resolution at TGWU conference in support of the Republic. Bill Jones, another of the leaders of the busmen's strikes, remembers fellow Dalston bus-branch member Bill Brisky joining the International Brigade. Brisky left behind one of his most treasured possessions with Jones: 'Should the Nazis take him prisoner they will not find Bill Brisky's trade union card; we have that, keeping our promise ... to keep it clear.' But Bill Brisky never did return for his card, dying in the defence of Madrid.[42] After 1937 it was made illegal to volunteer, to recruit volunteers, or to arrange the transit of volunteers to Spain.

---

41   Branson and Heinemann, *Britain in the Nineteen Thirties*, p. 338.
42   Murray, *The T&G Story*, p. 75.

In 1937 nearly 4,000 children, accompanied by teachers and priests, were admitted to Britain as refugees after the bombing of Basque towns by German aircraft. The condition of their admittance to the country was that they would not be paid for out of public funds. Voluntary donations flooded in. When the children landed at Southampton they were housed in a transit camp constructed at short notice by Southampton Trades Council, with tents it had borrowed from the army. The children were then settled in ninety-four 'colonies' across the UK, including homes in Clapton, Barnes, Barnet, Brixton and Hammersmith in London. To raise funds for the Basque children a huge rally was organized in June 1937 at the Albert Hall. Paul Robeson sang and spoke. Picasso provided the sketch for the front of the programme, and the original was auctioned on the night.

More London rallies followed. In January 1939 some 9,000 people came to Empress Hall, Earls Court to hear Harry Pollitt of the CP speak and welcome returning members of the International Brigade. The last 'Save Spain' meeting, held as the Republic was staring at final defeat, was in the Queen's Hall on 25 January 1939 with the presence, among others, of Aneurin Bevan, the cartoonist David Low, Lady Violet Bonham Carter and Stafford Cripps. This was the height of the CP's Popular Front campaign to unite all the anti-appeasement forces, including dissident Tories, against Neville Chamberlain. Cripps and Bevan were expelled from the Labour Party for supporting the call. When J. B. Priestley spoke he said he felt that he was moving in the middle act of a great tragedy. In the following year the final act of the tragedy began.[43]

---

43 Branson and Heinemann, *Britain in the Nineteen Thirties*, pp. 342–3.

9

London's Burning

He just couldn't stand Munich. Somewhere at the back of his mind it was weigh-ing on him: it had become part of his general feeling of disgrace, of the shame in which he in particular, and the world generally, was steeped. He still couldn't get over the feeling that there was something indecent about it – Adolf, and Musso and Neville all grinning together, and all that aeroplane-taking and cheering on balconies.

Patrick Hamilton, *Hangover Square*

TOTAL WAR

Neville Chamberlain's 'peace in our time' settlement with Hitler at Munich in the autumn of 1938 was greeted by cheering crowds in the streets of London. But within a year Britain was at war with Germany, following Hitler's invasion of Poland. London was under threat as never before. Experience of modern warfare, especially in Spain but also in China and Abyssinia, showed that it would be a war of aerial bombardment and that civilians would not be able to escape direct danger. In the course of the next six years until war ended in May 1945 there were 1,224 bomb alerts, with 354 raids by piloted aircraft and nearly 3,000 by pilotless bombs. A total of 29,890 people were killed and another 50,000 badly injured. Half of all the dead in the Blitz were in London. In Greater London 116,000 houses were destroyed, another 288,000 needed major repairs and a further million needed some repair.[1]

Lives were disrupted throughout the war. Men and women were conscripted into work and the armed forces. Food was rationed, as were clothes, and many goods simply were not available. Institutions and individuals were evacuated from London, and the population dropped sharply. Of those who remained, large numbers were homeless or living

---

1   Inwood, *History of London*, p. 809.

in overcrowded conditions with friends or relatives, having been bombed out. Many London schools were closed. Whole streets were blocked with rubble and bomb damage. Any journey could be subject to curtailment or lengthy diversion. Water and gas mains burst, beer from bombed breweries flowed in the gutters. Gin burnt in the distilleries. Fires raged following the bomb attacks. Even the river caught aflame. There were trenches in parks, bomb shelters and sandbags across the city while, above, barrage balloons filled the skies.

The common view of this wartime London is that it was a place where everyone 'did their bit', where all pulled together and maintained a solid defiance of Hitler. In reality, this was only part of the picture. The story of London's war records great heroism on the part of many ordinary citizens and emergency workers, but it is also one of fear and sometimes crime. Looting of damaged houses was quite common, with people returning home to find their possessions gone. A black market flourished in clothing coupons and food.

London had entered the war unprepared for what it would face: central and some local government failed to foresee the extent of the bombing. In addition, not all Londoners experienced the war in the same way. There were class divisions between the mass of Londoners and the wealthy who could escape danger and privation. These fissures emerged over a range of issues including provision of food and shelter, evacuation, conscription into work or the services, and housing. On a number of fronts, it was left to ordinary people to wrest some order from the chaos of war, to help protect and care for other Londoners and develop strategies for the more co-operative and egalitarian ways of living which they would try to put into practice after the war. This led to a consciousness and awareness which dreamt of a New Jerusalem once the war was over.

EVACUATION AND THE PHONY WAR

When war was declared on 3 September 1939, a mass evacuation of London children was already under way. On 1 September the long-planned exercise began with the departure of tens of thousands of children by rail, bus and even occasionally boat. Although it was not compulsory, evacuation was strongly advised, and was organized by the LCC through the schools. Mothers of under-fives were to be evacuated along with their children. In the end, around half of London's schoolchildren went – 393,700 – with 50,000 teachers and over a quarter of a million mothers and young children.[2] This was far fewer than expected, since many familes preferred their

---

2   Inwood, *History of London*, p. 780.

children to stay in London, despite the likely dangers. The scenes at schools and railway stations were upsetting for all concerned. Twelve-year-old Bernard Kops from Stepney, who was evacuated with his younger sister Rose, recalled:

> 'I want to stop with you. I want to get killed with you,' Rose screamed as we assembled in the playground with our gas masks and labels tied to our coats. And then we all moved away, all the children and all the parents crying. ... I knew that for my mother the separation from us was even worse than the thought of war. We marched away in crocodile fashion and I looked back at Stepney Green. The leaves so green in the September sunlight. This was the place where we were born, where we grew up, where we played and sang, laughed and cried. And now all the grey faces as we passed were weeping.[3]

Evacuation was painful, the journeys often long and scary. Even when the children arrived, there was often reluctance to take them in, despite households being paid to do so. Class or cultural differences frequently made things difficult for the evacuees. One young girl who abandoned evacuation explained in a letter, once back at her sister's in Greenford:

> I couldn't stick it any longer. We were treated like bits of dirt by the locals as though it wasn't bad enough going through what we did to get there. We started at 11 o'clock and did not get to Dunstable until 5 – after five changes by train and bus and standing on the curb in Luton for an hour and twenty minutes. We arrived at a skating rink and then were picked out so you can guess what some poor devils were like who had four or five children. They were still there on the Sunday and then eight families were put in an empty house and different people gave them bits of furniture.[4]

Despite strong government encouragement – even producing posters urging mothers to keep their children out of London – by the beginning of 1940 more than a third of the school-age evacuees returned to the capital, as well as nearly 90 per cent of the mothers and young children.[5] The lack of bombing during the 'phony war' period of the first nine months encouraged many families to believe it was safe enough to bring the children back. As a result, evacuation did not really succeed. A fresh attempt later in 1940

---

3   B. Kops, *The World is a Wedding* (Nottingham, 2008), pp. 48–9.
4   Letter from Agnes in D. Sheridan (ed.), *Wartime Women: A Mass Observation Anthology* (London, 2000), p. 64.
5   Inwood, *History of London*, p. 782.

was no more effective and although the government considered compulsory evacuation, they were never able to carry it out. Thus in September 1940, when air raids began, there were 520,000 schoolchildren living in the target area.

Elsewhere in the city, preparations were uneven. Chamberlain's government dithered over shelters, rationing, creating war industry and getting people into work. By 1940 there were stories of women who, when they volunteered for war work, discovered that there were no city-wide projects. The government was out of joint with Londoners, as the historian A. J. P. Taylor observed: 'The government was incapable of enlisting popular support. What was more, they did not want it. A war, based on popular enthusiasm, seemed to raise the ghost of the Left-wing Popular Front. It would be the Spanish civil war all over again.'[6]

Prime Minister Chamberlain was unpopular on all sides. When he opened a debate in the House of Commons on the disastrous campaign in Norway on 7 May, he was attacked most vociferously by the Conservatives on his own side. The Labour Party eventually decided to force a division, which amounted to a no confidence vote and Chamberlain's majority was slashed. The result was the formation of a coalition government with Labour. Winston Churchill took over as prime minister (against the wishes of, among others, a number of Tory MPs and the king, who preferred the appeaser Lord Halifax).

Churchill's record as a belligerent ruling-class apologist went back decades. In 1940, however, he found himself at the head of a five-man war cabinet with two Labour ministers in it, which worked closely with the trade unions to ensure war production. Ernest Bevin, the head of the Transport and General Workers Union, became Minister of Labour.[7]

From spring 1940, with Churchill in charge, the nature of the war changed. Across the Channel, British and French armies were being overwhelmed by Hitler's blitzkrieg as it swept through Belgium and into France. The fall of France in June meant that Hitler was now just across the Channel. The evacuation of the British army from Dunkirk by a flotilla of small boats was widely regarded as an act of heroism on the part of the thousands who risked death or injury to rescue the troops. It also demonstrated the gap between the courage of ordinary people and the failure of those in power to successfully conduct the war.

Dunkirk was a demoralizing and humiliating experience, bringing home to Londoners how close war was, a view that was reflected in reports from the Ministry of Information showing the growing unease of the city. A

6   A. J. P. Taylor, *English History 1914–1945* (Oxford, 1992), p. 458.
7   Murray, *The T&G Story*, pp. 78–80.

minister's admission that the government could not 'absolutely guarantee' evacuated children's safety led to a situation where 'women ran about housing estates crying and wanting to get children back'.[8] As the Germans approached Paris, one report noted: 'Public anxiously awaiting news from France. They watch the number of miles the Germans are reported to be from Paris and translate it into terms of London. The working classes appear to expect the fall of Paris but think the Germans will then over-reach themselves and come to a standstill.'[9]

The growing reality of war and the failure of the politicians to stop Hitler led to more radical consciousness. The best-selling political book of the summer was *The Guilty Men*, written under the pseudonym 'Cato'; the real authors were three journalists including Michael Foot, who would go on to become an MP for Plymouth in the Labour landslide of 1945, and eventually leader of the Labour Party. Written in the aftermath of Dunkirk, the book attacked appeasers such as Chamberlain and Halifax – the 'men of Munich'. Although banned by the major distributors, it sold 200,000 copies.[10]

Elsewhere a political battle was also being fought on the airwaves. J. B. Priestley was a nationally known novelist, columnist and playwright. At the time of Dunkirk, the BBC offered him a Sunday evening radio programme, *Postscripts*, in which he developed the vision of a People's War, championing not only the military conflict against Hitler and the Nazis, but also the struggle to build a society where the 'festering sores on the body of a diseased world' would not recur. At the programme's peak, about 40 per cent of the population tuned in to hear Priestley's sermons. The message was not welcomed by Churchill, however, who argued that Priestley's message was a diversion from the need to focus on the military effort. Other leading Tories were angered by such 'socialist ideas'. The chief whip was sent to complain about the 'leftish' talks and put pressure on the BBC, which took Priestley off the slot after only six months.[11] A second series, in early 1941, lasted for just eight broadcasts.

THE BATTLE OF BRITAIN AND THE BLITZ

By July 1940 Hitler was set to invade Britain, and there was very little to stop him. After the British Army had been all but destroyed at Dunkirk, he had the capacity to get an army across the Channel. But there was one thing that Hitler's invasion needed and which he did not yet have:

---

8   P. Addison and J. Crang (eds), *Listening to Britain* (London, 2010), p. 119.
9   Ibid., p. 111.
10   J. Gardiner, *Wartime* (London, 2004), p. 183.
11   C. Ponting, *1940: Myth and Reality* (London, 1990), p. 155.

command of the airspace above the Channel. In the summer of 1940 the air battle across the skies of southern England would decide the fate of the nation.

As the German bomber formations, protected by the Messerschmitt 109E, headed towards London and the ports, the RAF Spitfires and Hurricanes attempted to break them up. The fighters were almost exactly equal in speed, manoeuvrability and armament. The battle was a very close-run thing until 15 September 1940 when two massive waves of German attacks were decisively repulsed by the RAF. The total casualties on this day were sixty German and twenty-six RAF aircraft shot down. The German defeat caused Hitler to order, two days later, the postponement of preparations for the invasion of Britain. In the end the daylight raids by the Germans could not be sustained, and the RAF had done enough damage to halt the threat of imminent invasion. The effect on morale was as important as the military victory. The seemingly invincible Nazi war machine had been beaten for the first time.

The Battle of Britain may have been won, but the night-time bombing of British cities was about to begin in earnest. On 7 September 1940 'the Blitz' began, heralding fifty-seven consecutive nights of raids on London. Hour after hour of bombing induced near panic and destroyed much of the city centre. The bombing continued on an almost nightly basis right through to the following spring, and by the time the Blitz ended on 10 May 1941 some 43,000 civilians had been killed, half of them in London. The distinctive bend in the river in the dockland area of east London made it an easy target and the East End, along with the riverside areas of south-east London, received the worst pounding.

Londoners had been anticipating and making preparations all summer for this onslaught, but were still taken aback by its scale and ferocity. One evening early on, young Bernard Kops, now back from evacuation, was sheltering in his aunt's flat on the ground floor of their tenement in Stepney and went to look at the fires over the docks – bombed in daylight to provide a beacon for the night bombers: 'the whole world was red'.[12] Hundreds were dead, many buildings were damaged and an air of panic set in. Subsequent nights brought more terrible experiences. A school in West Ham was packed full with homeless people displaced by the bombing; despite the authorities being warned that it was a target, the people were not evacuated and on the third night it was bombed, with many fatalities. There was mass flight from the city. Deptford families made for the Kent hop fields.[13]

12   Kops, *Wedding*, p. 61.
13   Addison and Crang (eds), *Listening to Britain*, p. 402.

Home Intelligence reports on Tuesday 10 September stated flatly: 'Exodus from East End growing rapidly. Taxi drivers report taking party after party to Euston and Paddington with belongings. Hundreds leaving Deptford for Kent. Increased tension everywhere and when siren goes people run madly for shelter with white faces.' They also reported 'great shock' in West Ham at the school bombing, and 'grumbling and dissatisfaction openly voiced'. There was 'class feeling' because of working-class areas being badly hit, an increasing anti-Semitism, and 'dismay and wonder at apparent inadequacy of London defences'.[14] Homelessness was a much greater problem than predicted, partly because a higher proportion of deaths had been expected. Homeless shelters were both unprotected from bombing and inadequate, further contributing to the misery.

One of the major campaigning issues of this stage of the war concerned the provision of adequate air-raid shelters. It was obvious from the beginning that such provision did not exist, and attempts to rectify this situation were met with petty regulations and threats to those acting 'illegally' in trying to find shelter. The second night of the Blitz, the teenage Kops and his family headed to Liverpool Street Station on the Central Line, deep underground, along with thousands of others seeking shelter. The way was barred by soldiers who refused them entry even though the bombing was starting again. Despite the crush of thousands, the soldiers would not give way, but 'The people would not give up and would not disperse, would not take no for an answer. A great yell went up and the gates were opened.' A man near him said, 'It's a great victory for the working class. One of our big victories.'[15]

This was not what the government wanted: pre-war planning was based on fears that a 'shelter mentality' would develop if people were provided with central deep shelters in London. A plan for deep shelters in the London Borough of Finsbury designed by the left-wing architect Berthold Lubetkin that could accommodate the borough's whole population was rejected by government, because it would concentrate too many people in one place.[16] Instead the government's big ideas were to issue gas masks (already distributed during the Munich crisis and designed to combat one of the weapons of the previous war), and encourage people to construct flimsy, shallow 'Anderson shelters' in their back gardens.

The Anderson shelters were much cheaper than deep shelters, and were not even an option for those without gardens, especially in the inner cities. They were also small, damp and cramped and did not always provide

---

14   Ibid., pp. 410–11.
15   Kops, *Wedding*, pp. 63–4.
16   Gardiner, *Wartime*, p. 323.

adequate protection. Others relied on cellars, basements or even ground-floor cupboards to shield them. In addition, public brick shelters were built and trenches dug in parks, but these tended to be neither numerous nor strong enough to meet the need. Public buildings were designated shelters, and some department stores opened their basements to customers in an air raid. Within days it was clear that in the heavily bombed areas of London, shelter provision simply could not cope: 'The trench shelters in the little Stepney parks were a foot deep in water. ... It was quite impossible to use them, and certainly impossible to stay in them night after night. Now the street surface shelters were being put to the test. Many of them were destroyed.'[17]

As a result ordinary people started taking matters into their own hands. In the East End they occupied some of the huge warehouses near the docks. They tried to get down into the tube stations. They created shelters wherever they could. Many of the shelters were not properly equipped with basic sanitation or other facilities, and the authorities at least initially refused to install such facilities because they did not believe some of the buildings were suitable for this use. Conditions were sometimes appalling, most notoriously at the Tilbury shelter in Stepney on the Commercial Road. This margarine warehouse was home to up to 16,000 'shelterers' during the raids, and every description of it highlights the crowds, the squalor and the smell; a Mass Observation report described how bedding was just thrown over the manure left by horses who occupied the building by day: 'Over everything is sprawled a vast mass of human beings and their bedding. The dirt and stench is indescribable.'[18]

Others made the trek out to Epping Forest, or to the caves in Chislehurst, Kent, where special trains were soon taking 12–15,000 people from South and East London every night. The caves eventually had beds, canteens, a medical centre and a dance hall with a piano, and were designated as an official shelter by the local authority in November 1940. Still others travelled to the West End every night to stay in the superior shelters there, returning eastwards in the early morning to home or work, and to the sight of more devastation.

From the outset the Communist Party organized campaigns in the shelters. The London district issued 100,000 leaflets and 5,000 posters calling for immediate construction of bomb-proof shelters; opening of the tubes at night and proper equipping of them as shelters; the opening up of private shelters to the public; and the requisitioning of empty flats and houses for the

---

17   P. Piratin, *Our Flag Stays Red* (London, 1978), p. 72.
18   Gardiner, *Wartime*, p. 321.

homeless.[19] Despite police harassment and seizure of the publicity material, the campaign was highly successful. There was a picket in St Pancras
of the Carreras cigarette factory which had a shelter for 3,000, demanding
it should be opened to the public.[20] Shelter Committees were also formed
that began to create decent facilities and provide for feeding and sanitation.
They even brought entertainment to the shelters: the communist-domi-
nated Unity Theatre put on sketches and performed songs. The authorities
reluctantly took over many of these provisions, but none of them was initiated by officialdom.

In some places those taking refuge published their own magazines, such
as the *Hampstead Shelterers' Bulletin*, and in time a network of contacts
throughout London grew. In November 1940, a conference was held where
a total of seventy-nine delegates from fifty shelters decided to form the
London Underground Station and Shelterers' Committee. They elected
two implacable socialists, Harry Ratner and Alfie Bass (later to become a
well-known television comedian), as secretary.

The rich faced none of the problems encountered by London's poor.
While only a very small number of poorer children were evacuated abroad,
many of the rich sent their children to the US and Canada. The diarist
Chips Channon, who sent his son Paul to the US, described the scene at
Euston station in June 1940 waiting for the boat train to Liverpool: 'There
was a queue of Rolls-Royces and liveried servants and mountains of trunks.
It seemed that everyone we knew was there.'[21] Those with second homes
left London altogether in many cases in the autumn of 1940, while the
king and queen went to Windsor every night, and their daughters were
there permanently. Churchill often left for Chequers, or Ditchley Park near
Blenheim.[22] One American journalist, on a visit to the Dorchester Hotel in
Park Lane, discovered that the management had converted the cellars into
expensive luxury shelters, where nine peers slept each night, including Lord
Halifax, the foreign secretary. Throughout the night he stayed well-supplied
by a waiter with his favourite brand of whisky.

The Communist Party decided to organize a stunt at the Savoy, another
expensive London hotel, when seventy people from Stepney, women and
children among them, broke into the shelters there. Phil Piratin was one
of the raiding party: 'There were three sections. In each section there were
cubicles. Each section was decorated in a different colour, pink, blue and
green. All the linen, all the bedding, was, of course, the same uniform

---

19 Branson, *History of the Communist Party*, p. 303.
20 Ibid., p. 304.
21 Cited in Ponting, *1940*, p.148.
22 Ibid., p. 167.

colour. Armchairs and deckchairs were strewn around.'[23] Police arrived but couldn't evict the protestors, despite urgings from management, as the Blitz had already started outside. Once left in peace, the demonstrators called for tea and bread and butter, which they were informed wasn't served at the Savoy and in any case would cost a minimum 2s 6d. They argued they would pay prices equivalent to those at Lyons restaurants (cheap and popular eating houses), 2d for tea and 2d for bread and butter. The waiters huddled, went off and 'within a few minutes along came the trollies and the silver trays laden with pots of tea and bread and butter. The waiters were having the time of their lives.'[24]

The action raised morale and forced the government to begin improvements at the Tilbury shelter and other East End shelters. The Communists now led the fight for the Underground to be officially opened up, while Home Secretary Herbert Morrison resisted this on the grounds that children might be killed falling on the lines. Tube stations were again broken into, despite the police and staff moving protestors on: 'Various implements such as crowbars happened to be available, and while the police stood on duty guarding the gates, they were very quickly swept aside by the crowds, the crowbars brought into action, and the people went down. That night tens of thousands sprawled on the tube platforms.'[25] The next day Morrison finally announced that he was opening up the Tube, conceding a major victory for direct action and for the Communist Party. From now on the shelters began to be equipped with basic amenities, bunk beds and even entertainment. In the end, the authorities in London did make use of about eighty Underground stations to shelter up to 177,000 people.

Some stations received direct hits: there were many casualties at Balham and Bank. In Stoke Newington on 13 and 14 October, a bomb falling on a tenement at 157–161 Stoke Newington Road blocked all the exits from the basement shelter and burst a water main; the resulting horror saw 173 dead. On 29 December 1940 the 'second fire of London' brought devastation to the financial area of the City. It was a Sunday and many buildings were locked up, and the City population being small there were relatively few casualties, but many buildings had no firewatchers and so the fires spread quickly. As the Thames was at low ebb it was difficult to obtain enough water to fight them.[26] The famous picture of St Paul's Cathedral surrounded by flames from burning buildings comes from that night.

The final night of the Blitz in London was also its worst: on 10 May 1941 there was a 'bomber's moon', as they came to be called, and the river

23   Piratin, *Our Flag Stays Red*, p. 73.
24   Ibid., p. 74.
25   Ibid., p. 75.
26   A. Calder, *People's War* (London, 1992), pp. 206–7.

was again at low tide. There were over 2,000 fires, from Hammersmith in the west to Romford in the east, and many major buildings including Parliament, Westminster Abbey, the Law Courts and the Tower were hit; 1,436 people were killed. 'Next morning, a drifting cloud of brown smoke blotted out the sun. Charred paper danced in the woods thirty miles from the City. Churchill wept over the ruins of the House of Commons. A third of the streets of Greater London were impassable; 155,000 families were without gas, water or electricity. Every main railway station but one was blocked for weeks.'[27]

This marked the devastating end of eight months of hell. Hitler now abandoned his air war against London and turned his attention to the Soviet Union, which he attacked the following month. Londoners had not seen the end of attacks, however, which were to return with even deadlier weapons in the last years of the war.

The end of the Blitz was a victory for the mass of Londoners. The Nazi aim was to do on a much greater scale what German bombers did in Guernica during the Spanish Civil War: destroy the city, wrecking its infrastructure and industry and terrorizing its people, so that there would be mass pressure on the government to give up the war. The Battle of London – which is what it was – was a popular victory achieved by mass mobilization: a people's war.[28]

WORKING IN WARTIME

London remained a city in a permanent state of emergency, and there were large numbers employed in civil defence of various sorts. Every area had a system of air-raid precautions with wardens, most of them unpaid volunteers, whose jobs included checking the blackout – that there was no light showing from blacked-out windows – and registering the inhabitants of each house in their area. Throughout the Blitz they dealt every night with emergencies large and small. They had to get the local population to the shelters once the sirens had gone off, investigate any unexploded bombs or incendiaries that dropped, and patrol the shelters. Most of the volunteers were men, but the Women's Voluntary Service set up effectively as an adjunct to the ARP, providing services such as refreshments. In addition there were firewatchers (something which was made compulsory after the 29 December raids), stretcher parties, ambulance drivers, operators of anti-aircraft guns and barrage balloons, bomb

---

27   Calder, *People's War*, p. 214.
28   See N. Faulkner, '1940, The Battle of London: a new kind of war', *Military Times* 2, November 2010, pp. 26–31.

disposal units, searchlight operators, shelter staff, doctors, nurses and hospital workers.

Everyone was expected to contribute in some way, whether in paid employment, in the armed or emergency services, or as volunteers. Many were killed and injured in these conditions of extreme danger. One bomb disposal unit had to remove an unexploded bomb threatening St Paul's Cathedral. They put it on a lorry and drove it to Hackney Marshes (a distance of four or five miles) where they detonated it. The pond formed out of the bomb crater is still there today.[29]

The volunteer army the Home Guard created in May 1940 had as its original title the Local Defence Volunteers. The aim was to attract men between the ages of seventeen and sixty-five who would be given a uniform, training and weapons. Many volunteered across Britain, and there were Home Guard units attached to factories and other workplaces. Its birth was not accompanied by any great blessing from the government; the role of cheerleader was taken by Tom Wintringham, a former member of the Communist Party who had been the *Daily Worker* correspondent in Spain and had also fought there. He envisaged a new militia in the LDV, based on the revolutionary POUM militia in Spain, and with the help of the editor of *Picture Post*, for which he now worked, he secured the loan of a stately home, Osterley House in West London, which effectively became a private training school for the Home Guard despite official disapproval. The school taught stalking, hand-to-hand combat and tank ambush in its two-day courses; three Spanish anarchist miners demonstrated how to lob explosives at tanks. The London Home Guard ordered its members not to attend, but numbers still went up and the school was rapidly oversubscribed. During the summer of 1940 around 5,000 Home Guards went through training at Osterley.

The authorities were always uncomfortable with the possibility of a left-wing citizens' army being formed: Wintringham was vetted by MI5, and Communists were barred from membership from the end of May. The Home Guard was poorly armed, at least in part because of fears about where the arms would end up. By October 1940 Osterley had been taken over by the government as War Office No 1 School for the Home Guard. One of the Home Guard's most famous members was George Orwell, who had fought in Spain with the POUM and who now became a member of the 5th London LDV battalion, centred on St John's Wood. Fellow members included his publisher, a piano manufacturer, a van driver, a factory worker, a plumber and an unemployed ex-soldier.[30]

---

29   Calder, *People's War*, p. 165.
30   On the Home Guard see Gardiner, *Wartime*, pp. 193–214 and Calder, *People's War*, pp. 121–8.

A city at war had to continue working. Industry in London was turned over to war production to a very large extent, including munitions, arms, aircraft and components. There was also the production of essential clothing (including uniforms), utility furniture and other household goods – some carried out in the traditional furniture and woodworking districts of Shoreditch and Bethnal Green. Berger's Paints manufactured anti-gas paints at their factory in Dalston until it was bombed; the London India Rubber works in Hackney Wick made dressings and surgical rubber appliances for hospitals on the war's foreign battlefields.[31] The great factories of Park Royal, the North Circular and the Great West Road in the western suburbs became hives of war production.

Everyone who could be was ushered into work, the armed services or essential services. Conscription was introduced for all men between the ages of eighteen and forty-one on the day war broke out, although those in certain occupations could be exempted or 'reserved' from the armed services. There was also provision for conscientious objectors, on grounds of pacifism or for political reasons. Those wanting to take this path had to go before tribunals where they could be either unconditionally exempted or exempted on condition they took up specified work which could release others to join the forces.[32] While attitudes had progressed since the First World War, it was still difficult to be a CO, and the tribunals often treated applicants with harsh contempt.[33]

The major difference in this war, however, was the conscription of women. In a series of measures in 1941 and 1942, women were brought into some form of compulsory war work whether they wished it or not. Women in jobs such as retail were released for more essential work, and women could not change jobs without permission. Women aged between twenty and forty (and later, fifty) could find work only through employment exchanges. By 1943 nearly half of all women were working or in the services.[34]

This development meant big changes in London women's lives. It opened up horizons for many, gave them an income usually higher than they had had before, and infused many with a sense of purpose. They entered jobs that they had never thought of doing. But the trials of wartime were substantial: separation and fear of death of loved ones, regular experience of disruption, bombing and rocket attacks, shortages of food and other goods, rationing and long queues for food, long hours at work, tiredness and stress – all had their effect. This was particularly true of women

31   J. Golden, *Hackney at War* (Stroud, 2009), pp. 76–9.
32   Calder, *People's War*, pp. 51–2.
33   V. Brittain, *England's Hour* (London, 2005), pp. 63–70.
34   N. Soldon, *Women in British Trade Unions* (London, 1978), p. 151.

with families, since many London schools closed for much of the war and children often went months without proper schooling. In London women who wanted to work found there was little provision to cope with some of these difficulties. By 1941, there was a campaign over nurseries for working mothers, backed by the TUC Women's Advisory Conference and the Labour Party Women's Sections. A demonstration in Hampstead demanded 'Nurseries for kids – War work for mothers'.[35]

The provision of cheap meals was also important in mobilizing women workers. Factory canteens were now widespread, and the government introduced affordable restaurants. The precursor of these was the Londoners' Meal Service[36] and the LCC created about 250 such restaurants, including ones in the Victoria and Albert Museum, and one about every half mile in the East End. The WVS organized further restaurants[37] that filled a need for reasonable cheap food at a time when most working-class Londoners were not accustomed to eating out.

There was still much resentment at the way those with money could circumvent rationing and shortages. The Chamberlain government had not rationed restaurant meals in 1940 for fear of upsetting the middle classes, and all sorts of luxury foods such as lobster, chicken and fresh fruit were not rationed, so could be served in restaurants or bought at extortionate prices. Foods in short supply would be held 'under the counter' for favoured customers. The government allowed this to happen, but the growing criticisms of the rich not sharing in hardship led to restrictions such as a maximum price of five shillings for a restaurant meal (still a large amount, and easily evaded).[38]

This contrast was especially strong in London. Near the end of the war, a wealthy American living there commented on the 'look upon people's faces shadowed by a diet unhealthily heavy in starch, frighteningly short on fats, sugar and meat, almost completely lacking in vital fruit juices and with only a ½ pint of milk every other day!'[39] The bitterness caused by class divisions over food contributed to the wider class resentments which began to appear.

WAR, WELFARE AND BEVERIDGE

There were no elections during the war, and strikes were illegal, although they grew in number as the war went on, and a growing level of political

---

35 Braybon and Summerfield, *Out of the Cage*, p. 238.
36 Calder, *People's War*, p. 386.
37 Gardiner, *Wartime*, pp. 153–4.
38 Gardiner, *Wartime*, p. 153.
39 Quoted in ibid., p. 151.

consciousness was apparent. There was perhaps more opposition to the war in its early stages than might have been expected, given the record of the left in opposition to fascism in Europe and appeasement at home. Indeed, many on the left saw it as in some way a necessary fight against fascism – a continuation of the struggles of the 1930s, especially in the Spanish Civil War. However, on the left, the Communist Party at first supported it, then rapidly did a U-turn when Hitler and Stalin made a pact, denouncing it as an imperialist war. This began to change in 1940 when the seriousness of the situation forced the CP to express its concern at Hitler's advances. The party had considerable presence in London, with 150 workplace groups at the outset of war. It was especially strong in the aircraft industry and its factories like Hawker in Kingston and De Havilland at Edgware, and produced a rank-and-file paper called the *New Propeller*.[40]

The party hosted a sizeable conference in June 1940 which raised a series of class demands about the conduct of the war, and in January 1941 held the People's Convention in London to campaign for a 'people's peace'. Shortly afterwards the government banned the party's paper, the *Daily Worker*. Finally, still in 1941, war between Russia and Germany made Russia a major ally, and the CP swung behind the war effort. Eventually the *Daily Worker* was allowed to come out again.

The Second World War was a very different affair from its predecessor. This was total war, involving the mobilization of the civilian population, which meant that it could not simply be conducted by military means. The involvement of millions in active combat gave a broader dimension to social and political demands. From the beginning of the hostilities, the argument against appeasement was connected with the argument for a better world, free from the threat of unemployment and fascism which had so marked the 1930s. Unemployment and its accompanying privations were now looking like a thing of the past. By 1941 the jobless rate was very low, and instead there were labour shortages: women and men were now working very long hours to meet the needs of war production. Many people began to give more thought to how society could be run, how this full employment could be maintained and how those in need could be cared for.

The answer for many came in the shape of a government-commissioned report written by the Liberal William Beveridge, chair of the Committee on Social Insurance set up in 1941. In December 1942, Londoners queued round the block in Holborn to buy the newly published Beveridge Report outlining a future welfare state. It became a best-seller, with 100,000 copies purchased in a month, and it was widely read among the troops (although a

---

40   Branson, *History of the Communist Party*, pp. 281–3.

special edition for the armed forces was later cancelled by the War Office). In total it sold 630,000 and became the blueprint for the changes expected after the war. Beveridge identified five giants standing in the way of reconstruction: Want, Ignorance, Squalor, Idleness and Disease. He projected a health service and family allowances for after the war, and proposed a straight flat-rate contribution from all in work, in return for which state benefits would protect the population 'from the cradle to the grave'.[41]

At the same time, the fortunes of the war were turning against Hitler. By the end of 1942, victory had been declared at El Alamein in North Africa, and the Battle of Stalingrad was being fought – heralding a German defeat and the beginning of the Russian advance towards Berlin. The Americans had entered the war and were arriving in Britain as the base for a future invasion of occupied Europe. People became impatient for change and felt that it might be within their grasp to make some of these changes, and to continue with reforms such as free milk and orange juice, and school meals, which were already on offer during the war.

There were few visible political outlets for discontent during the war. There was an electoral truce between the main parties, who had decided that if a by-election arose during wartime, the seat would be contested only by the party which already held it. This pact allowed no electoral opposition to government policies, but the consensus began to crack as the war went on. In 1943 Independent Labour and candidates of the new Common Wealth party stood and did remarkably well, winning some by-elections and prefiguring the Labour landslide in 1945 – although few in the main parties seemed to notice.

LONDON LIFE GOES ON

Throughout the war London was full of troops doing essential work during the Blitz, passing through to other destinations, or stopping for a short time on leave. Dance halls, cinemas, skating rinks, restaurants, pubs and clubs became busy venues for the armed forces and attracted young Londoners who now often had money to spend, and a determination to enjoy their leisure time. The danger and uncertainties of war led to a sense that one might not be long for the world, and certainly might not be long in London. Many of the servicemen were foreign: exiles from occupied countries, especially Poland, and troops from the 'dominions' such as Canada or Australia. After the US entered the war there were also large numbers of American soldiers known as GIs (general infantrymen).

---

41   See J. Stevenson, *British Society 1914–45* (London, 1984), pp. 453–7; Taylor, *English History*, pp. 567–8; Gardiner, *Wartime*, pp. 499–503.

The dance halls such as the Streatham Locarno and Hammersmith Palais were full of soldiers and their partners, enjoying new crazes like the jitterbug and listening to the big swing bands. One woman described her trips to the Hammersmith Palais: 'I travelled twenty-nine stations on the Underground to get there and twenty-nine to get home again. The girls always managed to look colourful and attractive, and the servicemen of all nationalities appeared suave and handsome in their varied uniforms. We danced the night away jiving, jitter-bugging, waltzing, with a rhumba and a tango thrown in.'[42]

Sexual and social attitudes changed dramatically in Britain, and especially in London, in those years. The chance of sexual encounters and relationships was much higher, since women now often lived away from their family homes. They also had the independence that came from earning a wage. Work or being in the armed forces gave women more opportunity to meet men. Married women, often separated from their husbands for years on end, might begin new relationships. There was a spate of wartime marriages, many of which were to end in divorce shortly after the war ended. The proportion of children born outside marriage doubled during the war.[43] There was a rapid increase in venereal and other sexually transmitted diseases.[44]

Women's new freedoms began to alter social attitudes as well: for example, Mass Observation featured a survey in West London on whether women should go into pubs on their own.[45] One man said, 'before the war I was a bit old-fashioned about such things, but war broadens one's outlook somewhat.'[46] Another complained however about female drunkenness, with even mature women 'reeling about the tube stations, dancing Mother Brown on the escalators'. He felt that 'the quite young and the very elderly have lost all sense of proportion in this war.'[47] Women wore trousers and make-up, and growing numbers wanted more equality, not least in wages. Towards the end of the war the government set up a Royal Commission on Equal Pay.[48] Even some older people found their lifestyles changed as a result of the war: with many middle-aged women working at least part-time, there was more eating out, more cinema-going and more reading.

---

42   Du Noyer, *In the City*, p. 59.
43   S. Humphries, *A Secret World of Sex* (London, 1991), p. 65.
44   Braybon and Summerfield, *Out of the Cage*, p. 210.
45   Sheridan, *Wartime Women*, pp. 195–205.
46   Ibid., p. 198.
47   Ibid., p. 202–3.
48   *Royal Commission on Equal Pay*, Cmnd 6564 (1946).

THE LAST STRETCH: FROM DOODLEBUG
SUMMER TO VE DAY

By 1944 Hitler was on the retreat in the east, and it was widely acknowledged that an invasion of France was to take place that spring or summer. Two giant artificial ports called Mulberry Harbours were built in the London docks and floated downriver and round to the south coast in sections. More and more US troops massed in Britain. In Europe the partisans and resistance fighters were harrying the occupiers in Italy, France, Yugoslavia and elsewhere. There was a campaign to set up a second front against Hitler. The Russians had become wildly popular since entering the war, especially following the success of Stalingrad, and Anglo-Soviet Alliances sprang up in factories and communities.[49] But London had not seen the end of the fighting.

In 1943 a school in Catford was bombed, and thirty-eight children and six teachers died.[50] Two months later one of the war's worst disasters happened at Bethnal Green tube station, where people rushing to shelter after the sirens went off heard loud bangs coming from the direction of Victoria Park. Fearing a new weapon (in fact the sound was anti-aircraft guns being tested), people panicked on the stairs, where there was no handrail and just one light bulb. A woman slipped. More and more people piled on top of her. It happened incredibly quickly, but the final death toll was 173, a third of all wartime deaths in Bethnal Green.[51] Bernard Kops was one of those hurrying to the tube that night and feared that his mother and sister, who had gone ahead, were among the victims. They were safe, but he recalls people shouting to open the door down there: there was no door.[52] The government kept the incident quiet for fear of damaging morale, and there was little acknowledgement of the tragedy for decades afterwards. Kops now helps campaign for a permanent memorial to the dead.[53]

In the early months of 1944, the 'Baby Blitz' once again hammered London with nightly raids. Hopes were raised at the thought of an invasion that would open up the second front. D-Day was set for 6 June, when hundreds of boats and planes set out for Normandy. At around the same time London was hit with a new weapon: the V-1 rocket, commonly known as the 'doodlebug', a form of flying bomb which could not easily be shot down. The first hit a railway bridge in Bow, after which 100 to 150 projectiles a day were launched at London. The south and east and parts of

---

49   Golden, *Hackney at War*, pp. 99–100; Calder, *People's War*, pp. 348–51.
50   Gardiner, *Wartime*, p. 525.
51   Ibid., p. 526.
52   Kops, *Wedding* , pp. 101–2.
53   The campaign can be followed at stairwaytoheavenmemorial.org.

Kent were all very badly affected. In one Croydon factory, workers kept a tally on the night of 22–23 June: they endured twenty-five bombs and eighteen alerts, forcing them to go up and down into the shelters almost constantly.[54] The unpredictability and destructiveness of the flying bombs was coupled with their eerie whine and the fear felt when they 'cut out' shortly before crashing to earth.

The doodlebugs revived the terrors of the Blitz and people streamed out of London, causing chaos at the mainline railway stations and on the trains. By the end of the summer even more deadly weapons were launched, the V-2 rockets coming out of a blue sky without even the warning sounds of the V-1. The government pretended for as long as possible that the daily explosions being heard in and around London were due to gas mains. The V-2s were capable of terrifying hits, landing on hospitals, the Woolworth's in New Cross and the street market in Farringdon as late as March 1945. London was having to fight to the bitter end.

Victory in Europe Day, 8 May 1945, was the start of a two-day holiday that turned into the biggest London street celebration ever. There was no need for coupons to get flags and bunting, with queues for it in Barker's department store and Selfridges claiming the best selection.[55] One woman reported that 'all through the East End the battered little streets are gay with bunting – recent V-2 damage barely cleared up.'[56] Hundreds of thousands thronged the whole of central London, dancing, kissing, climbing up lamp posts and onto lorries, splashing in the fountains of Trafalgar Square, cheering the royal family on the balcony of Buckingham Palace and hollering their approval of Churchill.

London's pubs were drunk dry of beer. One window cleaner described how he had saved up to get plastered when the great day came: 'I've been putting a bit by each week so that on V-day I can get really blind drunk, what with getting bombed out in Balham ... I want to forget it all for a bit.'[57] Each neighbourhood celebrated with street parties, bonfires, dances and entertainments lasting two days. In Hackney, the largest party was given by a warden from Cazenove Road and his colleagues who treated 1,500 children to tea, Punch and Judy, and a magician. The mayor of Hackney attended seventeen victory parties over the Whitsun weekend that May.[58] Joy was mixed with sorrow at the cost of the war, and many people felt they had little to celebrate. But now the war was over, there would be an election, and the chance to bring about the changes talked about for so long.

---

54   Gardiner, *Wartime*, p. 550.
55   Ibid., pp. 566–7.
56   Ibid., p. 569.
57   Quoted in ibid., p. 567.
58   Golden, *Hackney at War*, pp. 109–10.

THE PEOPLE'S PEACE

The July 1945 general election took place with a depleted electoral register and with many troops still overseas. The Tories led by Churchill expected to cash in on their war record, yet when the results were announced Labour had a landslide. This was nowhere clearer than in London, which had suffered so much for the previous six years that it was even more determined never to return to the deprivation and inequalities of the pre-war years. The landslide should not have been a surprise: the experience of popular mobilization round the war had involved terrible suffering but also raised a sense of entitlement and confidence among working people. There was a huge ideological shift reflected in and influenced by the work of Beveridge and Keynes, while the old ruling-class politicians who had appeased Hitler were thoroughly discredited.

Compared with the last peacetime election, Labour gained twenty-nine more seats in Greater London and twenty-six in London County. It polled extremely well in the suburbs, especially in Middlesex and Kent, where many of the new housing estates and ribbon developments were located. For the first time, the working class and those 'black-coated workers' who often thought of themselves as more middle-class turned to Labour en masse, winning seats in Wimbledon, Barnet, Epping, Uxbridge and North Wembley with small majorities, and larger majorities in Dagenham, Dartford, Edmonton, Southall, West Willesden, West Ealing, North Tottenham and Barking. In London County it won a total of forty-eight seats to the Tories' twelve, and in Greater London forty-one to the Tories' seventeen.[59] The Communist Phil Piratin also won a seat in Mile End, and the left-winger D. N. Pritt stood successfully as a Labour Independent in Hammersmith North. There were similar results a few months later in the local elections.

The journalist Paul Foot was seven when the election results came out, and he well remembered the gloom at his grandfather's house at the news. In this well-known Liberal family, none of the parliamentary candidates prevailed except for his uncle Michael, who won Plymouth Devonport for Labour against all expectations. In mourning, his grandfather shut himself in his room for five days: 'The people had voted in the most decisive manner to dispense with the old political order.'[60] Labour's victory surprised even its own leaders, who had feared an early election would benefit Churchill.

Labour now knuckled down to a reforming programme which included nationalization of the utilities, railways and mines; the creation of the

---

59   Cole, *History of the Labour Party*, pp. 431–41.
60   Foot, *The Vote*, pp. 318–19.

National Health Service; the development of the education system, and the implementation of many of the Beveridge reforms. London's already existing health centres, such as those in Finsbury, Bermondsey and Pimlico, and the various hospitals were brought into the NHS in 1948. Children were given free milk and cheap or free school dinners. Family allowances and pensions meant higher and more secure incomes.

Housing was the biggest issue by far in London, and local councils and national government embarked on a house-building and infrastructure programme. Homelessness was still a big problem after 1945, and a squatters' movement swiftly emerged in mansion blocks and other empty flats and houses, encouraged by Communist activists. The best known was the squat in Duchess of Bedford House off Kensington High Street, where homeless or badly housed families moved in. Though they were evicted, a number were rehoused. In response to such actions, empty blocks of flats in areas such as Westminster were expropriated by local authorities to provide cheap housing.[61]

Another (supposedly temporary) solution to the housing crisis were 'prefabs', small bungalows prefabricated and in at least one case erected by German and Italian prisoners of war. Although they were supposed to last for five years after the war, there are still a few dotted around London and they remained surprisingly popular for many years after the war.

The Blitz cleared away much of the old housing, and even as the war raged on the planners were designing a new London. The 1941 Abercrombie plan saw the need to build new towns in Hertfordshire, Essex and elsewhere to cope with London's overspill. Vast sections of the city had to be rebuilt, much of it by local and national government.

Council housing plans were a product of conflicting forces. There was an acute housing shortage, to be sure, bomb-damaged slums had to be replaced and the war's end had generated radical expectations amongst the working class. As part of the mood for change a generation of progressives was pouring out of British architectural schools, inspired by European modernist radicals like Le Corbusier and Mies van der Rohe. And yet the ambitious building programme was also shaped by the failures of many interwar projects. There was a move away from suburban sprawl, towards integrated new towns on the one hand and keep-them-local inner-city policies on the other. There was also an increasingly cosy relationship between government departments, the LCC and the booming construction business.

The results were necessarily mixed. Sometimes the progressives were given their head, as when a group of young architects at the LCC created a

---

61   D. Kynaston, *A World to Build* (London, 2008), p. 122.

visionary estate at Alton West in Roehampton (1958), directly influenced by Le Corbusier's ideas of a planned community, and carefully designed to harmonize with its superb natural setting. Tenants were reportedly over-joyed with the level of facilities when they moved in and though the estate suffered from its isolated position it has remained relatively popular.[62] The great works of Hungarian radical Erno Goldfinger, like the monumen-tal Trellick Tower in Ladbroke Grove, used the best materials available, included state-of-the-art services, and showed a real concern for the needs and even the desires of its tenants; Goldfinger himself lived in the block while it was being fitted out. Today the Trellick Tower is the last word in inner-city chic.

The gap between the aspirations of the architects and tenants and the realities of post-war life meant that such high-quality council estates were few and far between. The appetite for such radical and often expensive experiments did not long outlast the immediate post-war years.

The London Olympics of 1948 were the Austerity Olympics of a bombed-out city; the Festival of Britain held in 1951 was a major achieve-ment in commitment to public space and to arts and popular culture. Both events were hailed as great steps forward in rebuilding London as a fully functioning, vibrant city. The centre of the Festival was a huge site on the south bank of the Thames which had been bombed and left derelict during the war; here were built many pavilions and structures celebrating the revived nation, including the Festival Hall – still a beautiful and popu-lar venue for Londoners – and the pleasure gardens further up the river in Battersea Park, based on the old pleasure gardens, with a funfair, tree walk and other entertainments which lasted until the 1970s. The commitment of the finest talents and materials to making the public Festival a reality was in great contrast to today's domination of London's built environ-ment by private speculation. This public ethos was one reason why, when Churchill got back into office in 1951, most of the Festival buildings were torn down.[63]

AUSTERITY

Many Londoners could have been forgiven for thinking that things could only get better after 1945. In the sense of being out of immediate danger and of a semblance of normal life returning, that was true. However, the post-war years were marked by austerity and hardship for many people. Conditions were difficult: housing was damaged and overcrowded. In 1946

---

62   View it at roehamptonview.co.uk.
63   J. Glancey, *London: Bread and Circuses* (London, 2003), pp. 131–3.

a survey of housing in Willesden found that 61 per cent were dissatisfied with their present homes, especially on grounds of overcrowding and lack of privacy.[64] Although 750,000 units had been built by 1948, this was still well below what was needed.

Food was still rationed, now including bread, which had always been available during the war. Bomb sites were everywhere. The winter of 1946–47 was exceptionally cold. Heating in houses and workplaces was often inadequate, relying most commonly on coal fires. Britain had been loaned vast sums of money by the US, but now the country was bankrupt. While Labour introduced nationalization and welfare policies, it was also forced to impose austerity measures and wage controls.

Strikes were restricted under wartime regulations until 1951. Within weeks of coming to office in 1945, the new Labour government used troops to break a strike in the London docks. London lorry drivers struck for longer holidays and shorter hours in 1947, but were not backed by their union leaders; this happened again with unofficial strikes by bus and tram workers in 1949 and 1950, when the general secretary of the TGWU, Arthur Deakin, told them he would 'not move one finger' to help them.[65] There were repeated attacks on the dockers who again came into conflict with the government in 1948 and '49, as a militant unofficial leadership emerged in frequent dispute with the official leadership. The government again used troops against the strike, and union leaders branded strike leaders as communists.[66] Other actions at the time involved the North Thames gas workers, ten of whose members were sent to prison in 1950 after an illegal strike.[67] In the same year Labour sent troops once again against Smithfield meat porters and power workers in London.[68] The hideous spectre of fascism had not vanished: Mosley returned to East London in 1948, speaking at rallies in Ridley Road market in Dalston, home to many Jewish people. Mass counter-demonstrations of Jewish and non-Jewish locals successfully drove support away, and Mosley never managed to secure a base.

No wonder that the dominant tone as the 1940s came to a close was one of disappointment. Figures from 1952 about the match between planned and actual provision of amenities on 100 post-war estates showed that out of forty-six planned libraries, only eleven had been built; of forty-six nursery schools, only one; of infant play spaces, only two of the projected

64   Kynaston, *A World to Build,* p. 156.
65   Murray, *The T&G Story,* p. 100.
66   Ibid., pp. 103–5.
67   K. O. Morgan, *The People's Peace,* (Oxford, 1992), pp. 98–9.
68   Cabinet minutes, 5 July 1950, cited in T. Cliff and D. Gluckstein, *The Labour Party: A Marxist History* (London, 1988), pp. 233–4.

twenty-two had materialized; and of thirty-three health centres, none had been built at all.[69] Phil Piratin's 1948 epilogue to his book is surprisingly bitter: 'The Stepney borough council planned to build 1,300 houses and flats in two years after the war. One-tenth of that number have been built in three years.' He denounced the lack of new schools and existence of a single health centre in the whole LCC area, while money was no object when it came to redecorating Clarence House for the future queen, or maintaining troops in Palestine.[70]

Money was soon found for other wars, notably in Korea in alliance with the US. Britain's former allies in Russia were now regarded as bitter foes by the Labour government, and their supporters in the Communist Party as 'the enemy within': this background would shape London politics in the decade ahead. By 1950 the hopes in the Labour government were dashed or declining. Even so its vote in the 1951 election was its highest ever, and higher than the Tories. But Churchill was back in government.

---

69 Cited in S. Fielding, P. Thompson and N. Tiratsoo, *England Arise* (Manchester, 1995), p. 106.
70 Piratin, *Our Flag Stays Red*, pp. 89–90.

Migrant City

London is the place for me.

Reggae artist Lord Kitchener

I can remember the top of Trinity Road, whitewashed on the wall was 'Go home Welshers', on the very spot where I was later to see 'Go home Blacks'. The very spot.

Syd Bidwell, Labour MP for Southall

WHO IS A LONDONER?

London is not, and never has been, a city of native Londoners. For nearly all of its history it has been fed by migration. This has taken two forms. Migration from the English countryside has been a repeated pattern. For as long as London has existed, but particularly from the eighteenth century onwards, country boys and girls have – like Dickens' David Copperfield and Oliver Twist – travelled to London when they could no longer make a living on the land, or simply in hopes of bettering their lives. It is often assumed that those who came to London from the country did so because urban living standards were so much higher. But just as often they were driven to the city by the hardships of rural life. Particularly as a result of the great changes in industry and agriculture from the mid eighteenth century through to the mid nineteenth century, work which permitted a decent level of subsistence was often no longer available in the countryside. That, coupled with a rising population, meant large numbers of especially young people had little choice but to come to London.

They were the ones often prey to the darker side of London portrayed in the writings of Fielding or the drawings of Hogarth. They might eventually turn to prostitution or crime as the only means of survival, thus sundering their links with their home villages even more. Hogarth might have been inspired by Richard Steele's description of an old woman hiring a young innocent girl that she meets at a coaching inn as her maid: 'Who should I see there but the most artful procuress in town, examining a most beautiful country girl.'[1]

The expansion of London and the often wretched existence on the land exerted both a push and a pull on successive generations. Many went to the city to become servants (country servants were regarded as 'green', and therefore more pliable in a low-paid and authoritarian domestic service). According to a contemporary magistrate, there were around 200,000 servants in London in 1796 – if correct, that meant nearly a fifth of Londoners were in service of one kind or another.[2] Others came to be apprenticed to the many trades available. By the early twentieth century, young people were also coming to work in the shops and offices which were playing an increasingly important part in the economy of the city. The women who often made up this new workforce were at first housed in hostels and dormitories attached to the big firms and department stores, as a way of bridging the gap between employers' hunger for cheap labour and the women's need for affordable but 'respectable' accommodation.[3]

The second form migration has taken is the influx from overseas. Foreign migration was influenced in the nineteenth century – specifically between 1826 and 1905 – by the fact that Britain's borders were open. The industrial revolution sucked in labour, and migrants helped sustain the prosperity of the Victorian period. An editorial in *The Times* on 19 January 1858 declared that 'every civilised people on the face of the earth must be fully aware that this country is the asylum of nations, and that it would defend the asylum to the last drop of its blood. There is no point on which we are prouder or more resolute ...We are a nation of refugees' – a language scarcely imaginable in the modern era. These attitudes began to change in the last quarter of the nineteenth century, as Jewish refugees from Russia and Eastern Europe began to arrive in large numbers.[4]

London was a great seaport until well after the Second World War. This waterside city became the centre of an empire which stretched around the world. Much of that wealth of empire was based initially on slavery and its crops, especially sugar, which is still refined by Tate and Lyle on the banks of the Thames in East London: a solitary reminder of the more than 100 sugar refineries which once operated in the city.[5]

---

1 R. Steele, *The Spectator*, 4 January 1712, quoted in Hill, *Eighteenth-Century Women*, p. 232.
2 Ibid., quoting magistrate Patrick Colquhoun, p. 8.
3 For some idea of this life by a contemporary source see G. Gissing, *The Odd Women* (Oxford, 2008), pp. 31–45.
4 See Price, 'History of Asylum in London'.
5 J. Walvin, *Fruits of Empire* (London, 1997), p. 120.

By the nineteenth century London was importing coals from Newcastle, canned and refrigerated food from Australasia, precious gems from Africa, tea from India.

Many who came to London would, in the language of today's political discourse, be called 'economic migrants'. But London has also long been a refuge for political exiles. In the nineteenth century the exiles benefiting from its liberal tolerance included the Latin American revolutionary Simón Bolívar, as well as less successful subversives – those who were forced from their countries for their part in the failed revolutions across Europe in 1848, or who fled the defeat of the Paris Commune in 1871. The most famous of the Europeans were Karl Marx and Friedrich Engels, active participants in the revolutionary movement in Cologne. The political descendants of Marx and Engels also found themselves in exile in London. As we have seen, a generation of Russians escaping Tsarist persecution settled here: Lenin, Krupskaya, Trotsky, Julius Martov and Vera Zasulich all lived in London. The Russian revolutionaries were based in the East End, off the Commercial Road, home by this time to thousands of Jewish refugees from Russian pogroms. Anarchists and socialists were an important part of this community, with their papers, meetings and bookshops, and represented a red line from Russia to some of the great struggles of the twentieth century in London, most notably the Battle of Cable Street against the fascist Oswald Mosley in 1936.

Exiles from Franco's Spain and from fascist Germany (and later from much of occupied Europe) settled in London, including eminent intellectuals such as Sigmund Freud. London's status as the hub of empire meant that many leaders of liberation movements found themselves gravitating to the city. Young students and intellectuals formed organizations, wrote articles and developed their ideas in London. Mahatma Gandhi from India and Kwame Nkrumah from Ghana both lived here. In the 1960s and 70s thousands of anti-apartheid South Africans, including exiles from the Soweto uprising in 1976, made London into one of their main bases, commencing a successful boycott and protest campaign.

After the brutal coup against Salvador Allende in 1973, many Chileans were forced into exile. Those who settled in London were among the most prominent and noisy demonstrators outside the exclusive Harley Street clinic where in 1998 the coup's architect, General Pinochet, was a patient under threat of arrest for crimes connected to the coup. Today, Palestinians, Iraqis, Iranians, Turks and Kurds all form part of this continuous history of political refuge from repressive regimes, actively creating and reaffirming the radical credentials of London.

MIGRANTS WHO BUILT THE CITY

The city had attracted people from around the world for hundreds of years – Jews first in the Middle Ages, then merchants from Italy, Germany and Holland. Persecuted French Protestant Huguenots came to work as silk weavers in Spitalfields in the seventeenth century. Black people from Africa and the Caribbean were already living in London in the early 1500s; by the end of the century their numbers had grown sufficiently for Elizabeth I to instruct the mayor and aldermen of the City to expel them. Her reason was that the presence of black people created 'great annoyance to her own liege people' who 'want the relief, which those people consume'.[6] The expulsions failed. The slave trade, which as we have seen played a major part in London's growth, increased the black population. There is much evidence of black Londoners in the eighteenth century, freedmen who increasingly joined in the political life of the city.[7]

We have discussed some of this history in other chapters, but it was in the nineteenth century that mass migration from abroad really began. And it was this 'industrialized' migration that has played the greatest part in building London. The city, its trade and its industry expanded on an unprecedented scale, and as it did so it drew in reserves of labour from across the world. A sizeable Italian migration settled around Clerkenwell. Vast numbers of Jews escaped the pogroms of Russia and Poland in the late nineteenth and early twentieth centuries to settle in the slums of the East End. But the biggest single source of migration to Britain has been Ireland: waves of Irish migrants over centuries helped to make London's character. By the nineteenth century, Irish people and Irish politics were impacting on working-class life and organization in the capital, and they have done so ever since.

THE IRISH, RADICALISM AND REPUBLICANISM

The Irish came to Britain to work in the docks and to build the canals in the 1780s, then the railways as 'navigators', or 'navvies' for short. They continued coming in successive waves, settling in East London and the other working-class areas and making their mark on the civil and religious politics of the city. Irish nationalism and republicanism had its reflection in the London Irish, whether the Fenians of the nineteenth century, the supporters of the locked-out Dublin workers in 1913, or the Anti-Internment League in 1971. The post-1945 wave of Irish migrants, settling

6   Fryer, *Staying Power*, p. 12.
7   Ibid., pp. 67–72.

in West and North London especially in Kilburn and Cricklewood, but also in Acton and Hammersmith, made a major contribution to politics and to the labour movement. By the twenty-first century many of the descendants of those immigrants continue to live in London, alongside over 157,000 Irish Londoners born in the Republic of Ireland and another 37,574 born in Northern Ireland.[8]

It was the era of the agricultural depressions following the Napoleonic Wars, the Industrial Revolution and the Great Famine in Ireland (1846–49) that produced the greatest surge of Irish immigration. The Irish had already been part of London life for two centuries, however. Early migration patterns were dictated by seasonal employment at harvest time, although during the eighteenth and early nineteenth centuries vagrancy and settlement legislation meant that seasonal workers were forcibly repatriated by local authorities. And there was another source of early Irish migration: 'as a result of the military adventurism of the eighteenth-century state, large numbers of Irish soldiers found themselves discharged onto the frequently unwelcoming streets of London at the conclusions of Britain's innumerable wars.'[9] Through all these fluctuations, the proportion of Irish-born Londoners reached its peak in the middle of the nineteenth century at approximately 4.5 per cent. From this high-point of 109,000 individuals, the Irish-born population of the capital fell steadily – to 107,000 in 1861, 91,000 in 1871, and 60,000 in 1901.

The Irish communities of London were frequently engaged in hawking, costermongering (selling wares from a barrow), and other informal street jobs. In the early 1850s Henry Mayhew estimated that there were 10,000 Irish men and women employed in these quasi-beggarly occupations.[10] Many of London's building labourers, chairmen, and porters were also Irish, as were the owners of the hostels and taverns, where the Irish slept and ate. Discrimination was a fact of life. It resulted in the almost complete exclusion of the first generation Irish from the better-paid jobs in London, condemning Irish communities to persistent poverty. This problem was exacerbated in the mid nineteenth century, when large numbers of very poor rural Irish men and women came to London to escape the Great Famine. Here, the living conditions were appalling too, poverty endemic and mortality rates astronomical.

Irish Republicans had been present in the eighteenth-century reform

---

8   E. Howes, Greater London Authority Data Management and Analysis Group, '2001 Census Key Statistics: Ethnicity, religion and country of birth', p. 42.
9   C. Emsley, T. Hitchcock and R. Shoemaker, 'Communities – Irish London', Old Bailey Proceedings Online, oldbaileyonline.org, accessed 5 July 2011.
10   Ibid.

movement and, still more visibly, in the figures of Bronterre O'Brien and Feargus O'Connor, in the leading ranks of Chartism (O'Connor's brother Francis became a general in Simón Bolívar's army of liberation in South America). The Irish Republican Brotherhood made its first London appeal in 1861, and by the middle of that decade there were secret Fenian societies in Soho and Finsbury. The first substantial outcome of this agitation was the 'Clerkenwell Outrage' of 1867, which, in a bungled attempt to release two Fenians from the Clerkenwell House of Correction, resulted in the deaths of twelve people in the adjoining Corporation Lane. Michael Barrett, along with five others, was eventually tried at the Old Bailey for these deaths, though only Barrett was found guilty. He was the last person to be publicly executed in England.[11]

In the 1880s, and associated with the agitation for Home Rule, two unsuccessful attempts were made to blow up the Mansion House, and in March 1883, to destroy the offices of *The Times*. More successful attacks were made against government offices in Parliament Street and against passengers at Paddington Station – injuring seventy-four people. In February 1884, a bomb exploded in the left-luggage department at Victoria Station, while three further devices were discovered and defused at other London stations in the same year. Attempts were also made to blow up Nelson's Column, Scotland Yard, the Junior Carlton Club, London Bridge, the Tower of London, Westminster Hall, the Admiralty, and the House of Commons. This wave of bombings in London subsided towards the end of the century, though the catalogue of attacks were far greater than the events of the current 'war on terror' in Britain.

The Irish played an active role in domestic politics, as we have seen; the emerging working-class movement which erupted in the strikes of 1888–89 had a big Irish component and coincided demonstrations for Home Rule. Again, in the early part of the twentieth century, the continued demand of the Irish to govern themselves was part of the wider London agitation of strikes and suffrage demonstrations in the years before the First World War.

LITTLE ITALY

There had been Italian traders in London ever since the Middle Ages, but the immigration of the nineteenth century was on a different scale. From the early 1800s Italians began settling in the area bounded by Gray's Inn Road in the west, Farringdon Road in the east, Mount Pleasant to the north and Holborn to the south. This became Little Italy. The first Italians were craftsmen from northern Italy specializing in precision instruments,

---

11   Ibid.

thermometers and barometers. One second-generation celebrity was Joseph Grimaldi (born 1778), the father of modern clowns, who often performed at Sadler's Wells theatre just outside Little Italy. Today he is remembered every year at the annual Clowns' Service at St Mark's Church in Dalston, and by the park named after him on the Pentonville Road. After the Napoleonic Wars poorer Italians came from Emilia-Romagna, Tuscany, and the Alto Adige in the north; some came from the even poorer south. By the 1870s 'the Rookery' tenement in Little Italy housed some of the most impoverished Londoners in the city's most overcrowded conditions. Occupations had changed too. By 1871 half the inhabitants of Little Italy were street musicians, playing barrel organs and hurdy-gurdies. Ice-cream sellers were soon to overtake street musicians as the favoured occupation of Little Italy's inhabitants. The Hokey-Pokey men (from the street cry 'ecco un poco' or 'here is a little piece') could been seen heading out with their highly decorated carts from early in the day.[12]

Little Italy, however, was far from picturesque. It was not only poor but a centre of crime and trafficking in children. Field Lane in Little Italy was the location Charles Dickens chose for Fagin's den in *Oliver Twist*. Children were sent out to beg by their 'padroni', who sometimes brought them over from Italy for the purpose, so lucrative was this scam. Many campaigned against the trade in children including Giuseppe Mazzini, the revolutionary Italian nationalist, then in exile from Italy with a death sentence hanging over him. Mazzini was one of the founders of the Free School for Workers which opened in 1841 at 5 Hatton Garden in Little Italy, where a plaque to Mazzini marks the site today. The school was for the children of Italian workers and the child workers of the area. Mazzini was one of the teachers, together with Joseph Toynbee and Gabriel Rossetti, father of the poets Dante Gabriel and Christina. Charles Dickens supported the school financially. On weekday evenings pupils were taught the three 'Rs' and on Sunday afternoons they had drawing and Italian history. Historian Thomas Carlyle called the school 'a nest of young conspirators'.

In 1864 that other hero of Italian unification, Giuseppe Garibaldi, made a triumphal visit to London. Shortly after the Society for the Progress of the Italian Working Classes was founded, later known as the Mazzini-Garibaldi Club. It was a mutual assistance club and became the heart of social life in Little Italy. Mazzini oversaw its first constitution and became its first president. It was closed during the Second World War when the British government requisitioned the premises as enemy property. Many Italian nationals were interned as 'enemy aliens', even though some were active anti-fascists.

---

12 T. Allen, *Little Italy: The Story of London's Italian Quarter* (London, 2008), pp. 6–19.

The club reopened in 1951. There was renewed Italian influx after the war, spurred by poverty at home. Many of the London cafés of the 1950s, 60s and 70s were run by these Italians. Some still survive but many have fallen prey to redevelopment, high rents and chain coffee shops. Little Italy went into decline in the post-war years and the Mazzini-Garibaldi club finally shut its doors in 2008.[13] The Italian church in Clerkenwell and an annual Italian festival, plus a few Italian shops and businesses, are what remains of the area today.

FROM THE RISE OF THE JEWISH EAST END TO THE ALIENS ACT

The last twenty years of the nineteenth century saw a major influx of Jews from Eastern Europe. Most came from Russia, but some also hailed from Poland and other countries within the Tsarist Empire. The anti-Jewish policies of Tsars Alexander III and Nicholas II led to pogroms in which thousands died; between 1881 and 1914, around 2.5 million Jews moved westwards from the Russian Empire. By the beginning of the twentieth century, the Jewish population in London had risen to 120,000. Many got straight off the boats at London's docks and settled down in the East End, especially in Whitechapel and Spitalfields, which became known as 'Little Jerusalem'. The number of Jews in London in 1881 was about 46,000, almost double the figure for 1815. By 1905 it was around 140,000. Some in the established, relatively integrated and prosperous Jewish community attempted to aid these needy co-religionists. The Poor Jews Temporary Shelter was established in Whitechapel in 1885 to house those just off the boats, and the Jews' Free School, established in the East End in 1817, had over 3,000 pupils by 1900.[14] Yiddish music halls and theatres were established, among flourishing kosher restaurants and bakeries.

The rapid transformation of parts of the inner East End into a predominately Jewish area provoked a racist backlash. Rumours that the Jack the Ripper murders of the late 1880s was the work of a Jew caused minor anti-Jewish disturbances, while a possible full-scale riot was avoided by a policeman who rubbed out the chalked message 'Jewes' at the site of the fifth murder. But it was mainstream anti-immigration campaigners like Arnold White – who inflated the number of Jewish immigrants to over a million and blamed them for all the East End's economic and social problems – that were a more enduring threat. Conservative politicians jumped on the bandwagon, and anti-Semitism certainly helped them hang on to seats in

---

13   Ibid., pp. 38–41.
14   Price, 'History of Asylum in London'.

the East End after 1890 – particularly in the 'Khaki' election of 1900, held in the wake of British imperial victories in the Boer War. The following year an East London Tory MP, Major Evans-Gordon, gave his support to the racist British Brothers League which held large rallies in Stepney and Bethnal Green, campaigning under the slogan 'England for the English'. It claimed to have 45,000 members and attempted, but failed, to build a paramilitary organization. In the wake of this pressure, the Jewish Board of Guardians, fearful that the new arrivals were creating hostility towards their more established co-religionists, arranged for the repatriation of 31,000 East European Jews between 1881 and 1906.[15]

The conservative sections of the Jewish community were not the only ones to make concessions to anti-Semitic forces. Arthur Balfour's Conservative government did so enthusiastically, setting up a Royal Commission on Alien Immigration which acted as an echo chamber for anti-Jewish prejudice. Its 1903 report gave the Tories some populist arguments to deploy in the next election. In 1905 the government proposed the Aliens Act which restricted immigration for the first time in eighty years. It gave immigration officers the power to search ships and exclude any 'aliens' who seemed criminal, diseased, insane or destitute, unless they were genuine refugees. The home secretary was also given the power to deport aliens who were paupers or living in 'unsanitary conditions' – of which there were great numbers in the East End. The Tories were all but wiped out in the East End in the 1906 election, but the Liberal government enforced the Act anyway, excluding some 4,000 migrants up to 1910. Jewish migrants coming to Britain fell by two-thirds in the same period.

THE COMMONWEALTH AND IMMIGRATION

The modern history of immigration into London begins in earnest after the Second World War. At its imperial zenith Britain ruled over more than 400 million people in an Empire that covered nearly a quarter of the globe. In the immediate post-war period the British Empire began to fall apart. India and Pakistan became independent in 1948, and the various islands of the Caribbean, many African countries and a host of other colonies followed suit. In order to maintain political and economic links with the former colonies, Britain encouraged them to remain part of the British Commonwealth.

These 'New Commonwealth' countries had had their economic development distorted by decade after decade of colonial rule. Some West Indians, Indians, Pakistanis and other citizens of these countries wished to

---

15   Inwood, *History of London*, p. 414.

exercise their right as British passport holders to travel to Britain, in search of work and a higher standard of living. The *Empire Windrush* arrived at Tilbury docks in London on 22 June 1948, carrying 492 Jamaican passengers determined on a better life in Britain. They faced no immigration controls, since at that time any citizen of the British Empire could travel freely to any other part of the Empire. Jamaica was only to attain full independence in 1962. The arrival of the *Windrush* was reported by the press but did not excite much wider interest. A few Labour MPs asked sympathetic questions about whether the immigrants would be assisted in finding jobs and houses. In Cabinet, however, there were already reservations, and some MPs sent a letter to Prime Minister Attlee warning of the danger of 'coloured people' arriving in numbers which would 'impair the harmony, strength and cohesion of our public and social life'.[16] The arrivals were provisionally housed in Clapham deep shelter, near the Coldharbour Lane employment office in Brixton where many looked for work. They were invited to the local church for tea, and to a Clapham Communist Party social where they sang calypso.[17]

It was a common enough story for immigrants from all over the Commonwealth in the 1940s and 1950s. British industry was short of labour as the post-war economic upswing took hold. British employers advertised for workers in the former colonies, and the British government was happy to see this vital resource tapped for the benefit of the economy. A committee reporting to the Cabinet in 1951 considered that any question of immigration controls would be dependent on 'an apparent or concealed colour test', and therefore 'so invidious as to make it impossible of adoption': 'any powers taken to restrict the free entry of British subjects to this country would ... be more or less confined to coloured persons.'[18]

Those who came to live and work in Britain did not find it easy. Most could only find accommodation in some of the meanest housing in inner-city areas such as Brixton and Notting Hill, and were prey to slum landlords, high rents and overcrowding. In a time of acute housing shortage, racist conflicts were exacerbated by deliberate policies which denied immigrants access to better housing. Local councils often collaborated in a form of 'colour bar' on council housing. In the 1960s two Labour councillors in Southall were expelled for voting with the Tories to impose a fifteen-year qualification before immigrant families could go on the council waiting list. Across London in Newham, a residential rule of five years in Greater

---

16 Kynaston, *A World to Build*, pp. 274–5.
17 Ibid., p. 276.
18 R. Miles and A. Phizacklea, *White Man's Country: Racism in British Politics* (London, 1984), p. 26.

London and one in Newham before qualifying for council housing was introduced.[19]

Even when immigrants tried to buy houses, they were sometimes prevented, as in Southall in 1963 when the residents' association petitioned the council to buy a house in Palgrave Avenue to stop it from being owned by an Asian family.[20] The new immigrants tended to take some of the worst-paid and most unpleasant jobs. Even then they encountered discrimination and frequent job segregation. Racism, personal abuse and even physical attacks were common.

From early on in the 1950s, voices were raised against immigration. It was possible to see the direction in which events were moving when Conservative MP Cyril Osborne asked this question of the prime minister in January 1957:

'What is Her Majesty's government's policy regarding the ... increase in immigration into this country of coloured people without tests of either health, technical skill or criminal record; in view of the recent increase in unemployment, what action [does] the government [propose] to take ...?'[21]

In just a few words, Osborne had managed to compress many of the prejudices that were to haunt the 'immigration debate' in the coming years. Firstly, Osborne refers only to coloured immigrants. Secondly, he suggests that these migrants are carriers of disease. Thirdly, that they are likely to be unskilled. Fourthly, that they are likely to be criminals. And fifthly, that they are responsible for unemployment. As a final flourish, Osborne implies that the government must restrict immigration to deal with this problem. And yet at the time Osborne spoke there were very few black or Asian people in Britain, and unemployment was at a historically low level.

This line of argument began to have an impact on the political mainstream. In 1955 the cabinet discussed immigration controls. Prime Minister Harold Macmillan's Cabinet contained the man he had replaced as Tory leader, Winston Churchill. Even Churchill was unhappy at the thought of introducing immigration controls, and Macmillan recorded in his memoirs: 'I remember that Churchill rather maliciously observed that perhaps the cry of "Keep Britain White" might be a good slogan for the election ...' In the event, there was no further cabinet discussion of immigration controls before 1958 – and by that time something else had happened.

---

19   Recollections of former Southall MP Syd Bidwell in D. Weinbren, *Generating Socialism* (Stroud, 1997), pp. 124–5; Newham Monitoring Project/ CARF, *Newham: The forging of a black community* (Nottingham, 1991), p. 5.
20   Weinbren, *Generating Socialism*, p. 124.
21   See Miles and Phizacklea, *White Man's Country*, p. 26.

THE NOTTING HILL RIOTS OF 1958

In August and September 1958 riots broke out, first in Nottingham and then on a larger scale in Notting Hill, West London. In the area around North Kensington and Notting Hill, between 23 August and 2 September, mobs chanting 'Down with the niggers' carried out a series of attacks on West Indian people and property. These were an escalation of the relatively commonplace attacks on black and Asian people by white gangs of teddy boys and others subcultures, egged on by fascist propaganda. By the end of August there were daily attacks, and after one open-air fascist meeting hundreds of white youths went on the rampage to the cry of 'Let's get the niggers'. Police did little to protect those under attack. Yet some black people did organize to fight back, attacking the building where the fascists were based. Eventually some 177 people were arrested, a majority of whom were British-born.

While the Notting Hill riots were over by the middle of September, levels of physical attack and racial abuse remained high. In 1959, Oswald Mosley, sensing the opportunity, returned from abroad to stand in the general election in North Kensington as a fascist Union Movement candidate. While he came bottom of the poll, he still received 8 per cent of the votes.[22] Also in 1959 a West Indian, Kelso Cochrane, was fatally stabbed in the street in North Kensington. His killer was never found.[23] A Union Movement member later claimed that one of their group had been responsible.

It might have been expected that the press and politicians would have unanimously condemned the racism manifested by these events. Far from it: *The Times* was the first to respond, on 27 August, under the headline 'Nottingham MPs Urge Curb on Immigration'. The following day's headline read: 'Renewed Call for Changes in Immigration Law'. The press and politicians were moving to redefine the problem. The issue became not racism directed against immigrants, but the immigrants themselves. In this framework the victims became the authors of their own misfortune. The clamour against immigrants continued to grow and in 1962 the Tory government qualified the right of Commonwealth citizens to enter the UK. Under the Commonwealth Immigration Act it was now only possible to enter the country by getting a Ministry of Labour employment voucher, or if you were a dependent of such a person already resident in Britain, or a student. It was said that the Act would only be temporary, but in reality it marked the start of ever more restrictive immigration legislation.

---

22   Morgan, *People's Peace*, p. 203.
23   See Fryer, *Staying Power*, pp. 376–81.

It was also said that the Act was not directed specifically at black and Asian people. Yet it did not cover citizens of the Irish Republic, 60,000 to 70,000 of whom were coming into the country every year, as the home secretary admitted in the Commons. The Act turned out to be counter-productive even in its own discriminatory terms. Migrants who came for the work, intending to return home after a period of time, were now faced with the choice of staying for good or being unable to return to Britain once they left. Many decided to settle and bring their families to live with them, so that the number of dependents coming to Britain soon exceeded the number of new immigrants. And, of course, once there were immigration controls there were also people who would try to evade them. So 'illegal immigration' now became part of the argument. This led to further racist and anti-immigration campaigns.

When the Act came up for renewal in 1964, a Labour government was in power which promptly renewed the Tory legislation. In order to mitigate the effects of the racist atmosphere generated by the immigration debate, Labour also introduced the 1965 Race Relations Act. Well-meant by some in the Labour Party, opportunistically supported by others, the Act by no means signalled a shift away from the party's new commitment to immigration controls. Local Labour politicians in those years all too often accepted the racist arguments: when they said, for instance, that no more immigrants should be allowed into areas such as Southall or Newham, the obvious message was that there were too many there already.

1968: ENOCH POWELL AND 'RIVERS OF BLOOD'

The Tory shadow minister Enoch Powell had been carving out a name for himself as an anti-immigration rabble-rouser before 1968. But in that year he made a speech in Birmingham that raised the rhetoric of the anti-migrant and racist right to a wholly new level. Powell painted a picture of mass immigration destroying the foundations of British society. He attacked the Race Relations Act for giving 'the stranger, the disgruntled and the agent provocateur the power to pillory' the indigenous population 'for their private actions'. The classically educated Powell declaimed: 'As I look ahead, I am filled with foreboding. Like the Roman, I seem to see "the River Tiber foaming with much blood"' unless immigration was halted.[24] Powell's speech called not just for an end to immigration but for the repatriation of those already settled in Britain:

I turn to re-emigration. If all immigration ended tomorrow, the rate of growth of the immigrant and immigrant-descended population would

24 Miles and Phizacklea, *White Man's Country*, pp. 64–7.

be substantially reduced, but the prospective size of this element in the population would still leave the basic character of the national danger unaffected ... Hence the urgency of implementing now the second element of the Conservative Party's policy: the encouragement of re-emigration.[25]

Powell was sacked from the Tory front bench, but the racist tide unleashed by his speech was overwhelming. Opinion polls claimed 74 per cent approval of such sentiments. London dockers struck in Powell's support, and 1,000 of them marched to Westminster from the East End on the day Labour's Race Relations Bill was being debated. More dockers, Smithfield meat porters and some local factories also struck in the days that followed. There was a counter-protest of 1,500 who marched to Downing Street under the banner 'Arrest Enoch Powell', but overall it was a shameful episode in working-class history. A socialist docker, Micky Fenn, recalled ruefully: 'It was the only time I felt really ashamed to be a docker and when I watched it on TV I felt really sick ... It was disgraceful.'[26] Terry Barrett, who argued against the march, recalled later that he didn't think it was spontaneous at all, so much as influenced by a small group of fascists within the docks who were exploiting real concerns about jobs. According to him, their pay wasn't stopped for striking and they were, unusually, allowed to take their banners right up to Parliament.[27] Students and protestors around *Black Dwarf* and the International Socialists, who staged the counter-protest, received rough treatment from some of the dockers. The Labour government erected further barriers to migrants by passing the Immigration Appeals Bill a year later.

1970s AND 1980s: FIGHTING BACK

London had two faces in the 1970s and 1980s. One London was a city of immigrants united with the working-class communities of which they were a part, and continually drawn into economic and political struggles alongside them; the other was a city of racism and violence against minorities. These two aspects of city life existed in tension, with poverty, market-derived competition and racism pulling in one direction and the decency of ordinary Londoners and the demands of solidarity pulling in the opposite direction. Black and Asian Londoners faced racism on many different levels.

25   The full text of Powell's speech is available at telegraph.co.uk (accessed 12 July 2011).
26   Quoted in NMP/CARF, *Newham*, p. 15.
27   Quoted in D. Widgery, *The Left in Britain, 1956–68* (London, 1976), pp. 410–11.

While by the 1970s, changes in the law and in social attitudes had ended some of the restrictions on jobs and housing, there was still discrimination, both overt and covert. There were also constant conflicts between blacks and Asians and the police. From the early 1970s a rise in far-right racism and fascism presented a new challenge. The battles over these issues defined black and Asian politics throughout the 1970s, and their outcomes changed the life of London and helped create the multicultural city we know today.

Police racism and harassment grew in the early 1970s. The campaigner Frank Crichlow, owner of the Mangrove restaurant in Notting Hill which became a political and cultural hub for radicals of every background, had his premises raided twelve times between 1969 and 1970. There were repeated and violent drugs searches, and police assaults right up to the late 1980s. The trial of the Mangrove 9, which ended in 1971 with their acquittal, was regarded by many as a turning point in black politics in Britain, but did not by any means mark the end of police harassment. The Notting Hill Carnival, based on the traditional Trinidadian parades, was first held indoors in 1959, but in 1966 it sashayed out into the streets. It was meant to celebrate Caribbean culture and music, but also to create a much greater community spirit across all races. One of its organizers was Claudia Jones, a Trinidadian deported from the US for her communist politics in the 1950s. The event grew in popularity and was attended by blacks and whites from across London. By 1975 the Carnival was attracting huge crowds, especially for the reggae music, with up to half a million attending.

Yet in 1976 the local council tried to have the Carnival banned (a repeated problem which the organizers face to this day). It suggested moving the event to Wormwood Scrubs or Chelsea football ground – both well away from the streets where it had originated. The police insisted on heavy security if it went ahead, and designated twenty-five policemen to surround each band that was playing. Hundreds of police swarmed the streets on the first day, raiding, harassing and arresting stallholders. On the second day a total of 1,600 police claimed to be arresting criminals and pickpockets, but used the pretext to harass black youth who then fought back. They threw bricks, cans and bottles, injuring 300 officers and showing – in what were the largest street disturbances since the war – their determination to resist the routine harassment they experienced. Police Commissioner Robert Mark later compared the Carnival crowds with those who had watched the executions in Tyburn.[28]

By the mid 1970s the battle lines involving police, fascists, and blacks and Asians had been drawn. The background was a growing racism. After

---

28   See C. Gutzmore, 'The Notting Hill Carnival', *Marxism Today* (August 1982), 31–3.

the Tories won the 1970 election, one of their early tasks was to address what Margaret Thatcher was to describe in a 1978 speech as the 'legitimate fears' about the country being 'swamped' by 'coloured immigrants'. The government replaced all previous legislation with the Immigration Act of 1971. The new law did away with any special status for Commonwealth citizens, and gave the home secretary and immigration officers wide discretionary powers to deport from and refuse entry to Britain. This legislation set the pattern for all that was to follow. The nine years between the Commonwealth Immigration Act of 1962 and the Immigration Act of 1971 had fixed the terms of debate about immigration into a fundamentally discriminatory pattern. It was a pattern from which the political right, in both Tory and fascist forms, would benefit.

The rise of the National Front came as the long post-war boom ended. By 1977 they were gaining 100,000 votes in the GLC elections, thanks to high racist votes in many of the old working-class areas of London. In Newham in 1974, the NF polled a quarter of the votes in each of two wards in the south of the borough, and in the October general election of that year got 5,000 votes across the borough – the highest NF vote in the country.[29] The NF's main form of organization was not, however, electoral. They relied more on a street presence reminiscent of the European fascist organizations of the 1930s. They tried to hold demonstrations and public meetings to build a popular following on the streets and intimidate their opponents. This tactic led to counter-mobilizations by the left, side by side with many black and Asian communities through whose areas the NF often deliberately chose to march.

The confrontations multiplied across London. In 1974 a twenty-year-old Warwick University student, Kevin Gately, was killed, probably by a blow from a police truncheon, in Red Lion Square at a protest against an NF meeting taking place in the Conway Hall. An important turning point came in Lewisham, South London, in the summer of 1977. Most of the left, local trade union organizations and the Communist Party held a rally in opposition to an NF march; the majority planned to march at some distance from the NF's proposed route. But those who thought the NF should be physically confronted – mainly the Socialist Workers Party and black youth from the local community – went on to gather at a point on the NF's route where they thought the march could be blocked. Despite a heavy police presence the anti-fascists did indeed break through the police cordon and disrupt the NF march. Mounted police charged the protestors, and riot shields were used for the first time in mainland Britain. Fighting with the police lasted long after the NF had gone home. The establishment's

---

29 NMP/CARF, *Newham*, p. 28.

disapproval was shrill, and even the left-wing Labour leader, Michael Foot, described those who had broken up the NF march as 'red fascists'. It was a watershed which led to the formation of the Anti-Nazi League (ANL).

The ANL was an attempt to build a broad and active anti-fascist movement to undercut white levels of support for racism. East London was a particular challenge, as the NF and other fascist groupings were very popular in areas such as South Hackney, Hoxton, Shoreditch and parts of Tower Hamlets. In the late 1970s, these remained largely white areas where blacks and Asians (and anti-fascist whites) often came under attack. In April 1978 the ANL organized a march from Trafalgar Square to the 100,000 strong Rock Against Racism Carnival in Victoria Park, where the Clash topped a memorable bill. It marked a turning point in the area, as thousands of local people of all races turned out to show their opposition to fascism.

The racist atmosphere in London remained dangerous, however. As in the 1950s, and as we would see again in the 1990s, a string of mostly young black and Asian people were murdered because of the colour of their skin. Whether or not the crimes could be directly attributed to fascists, they were certainly encouraged by such ideology. In June 1976, Gurdip Singh Chaggar was killed in Southall: the fascist Kingsley Read said of it a week later, 'One down, one million to go.' Although charged with incitement to racial hatred he was never convicted. But it was becoming clear, at least to the younger members of the black and Asian communities, that they would have to fight back.

On 4 May 1978, Altab Ali, a twenty-five-year-old Bangladeshi clothing worker, was murdered by three teenage boys as he walked home from work. Ten days later 7,000 people, many of them local Bangladeshis, marched behind his coffin to Hyde Park. Many young Bangladeshis were drawn into political activity in the aftermath of the murder. Altab Ali Park at the southern end of Brick Lane now commemorates the event. Later the same year an even larger ANL carnival was held in Brockwell Park, South London, though hundreds of those attending crossed London to defend Brick Lane when the NF used the opportunity to attack the area.

The increase in lethal attacks was met with demonstrations and protests, as was the continuing racism of the police. Young blacks and Asians were subjected to stop-and-search and general harassment. When involved in any sort of dispute with whites, they were all too often blamed and arrested when they were totally innocent parties. The Virk brothers were one such case: attacked by white racists while mending their car outside their house in East Ham on St George's Day, 1977, they defended themselves and were arrested, charged with grievous bodily harm and jailed. The death of Akhtar Ali Baig in East Ham in 1979 by a skinhead gang led to a march of

5,000, the downing of tools by black workers at Ford's and the shutting of local shops.[30]

Breaking the NF and defending communities against racist attacks was not, however, the same as stemming the tide of state-inspired racism, as the cases of Blair Peach and of the Deptford Fire were to prove. The police used the experience of the Notting Hill Carnival to demand more equipment – the following year they took riot shields to Notting Hill. They also appeared more sympathetic to the fascists in the increasingly bitter confrontations which marked the latter years of the 1970s. When the NF demanded the right to march in Southall in April 1979, the police allowed a small group of racists to intimidate the local population. Many counter-demonstrators were attacked by police, and some were seriously injured. A teacher, anti-racist activist and SWP member named Blair Peach was knocked unconscious by police and died the next day in hospital from head injuries. Fourteen witnesses said they had seen members of the Metropolitan Police Special Patrol Group (SPG) strike Peach. No one was ever charged.

The Deptford Fire was a devastating house fire which killed thirteen young black people during a birthday party in New Cross in South East London in January 1981. Police indifference and the racial tensions fanned by both the NF and the new Tory government made many suspect arson. Some 20,000 marched from the area to Hyde Park under the slogan '13 Dead, Nothing Said'. The coroner at the inquest steered the jury to return an open verdict. A subsequent High Court action agreed that the coroner's summing up had been inaccurate. The *Guardian*, while criticizing the local action committee for calling the fire a 'massacre', nevertheless concluded:

> Rarely can a jury have been faced with a more dismaying task: deciding the cause of a racially sensitive incident on the basis of hopelessly conflicting evidence and under the direction of a coroner whose conduct of the proceedings was openly criticised by a High Court judge. In such circumstances, an open verdict was the only realistic conclusion the jury could have reached – in other words, that they just did not know what to make of it all.

The article continued:

> Upon this sensitive and festering sore the Metropolitan Police then trod with all the delicacy at its command by appointing Commander Graham

---

30   NMP/CARF, *Newham*, pp. 35–43.

Stockwell to head the inquiry into the blaze. Mr Stockwell's history has not been an entirely happy one. As a police inspector in 1972, he took down the confessions of three young men who were then imprisoned for ... murder ... In 1980, they were cleared of any involvement in the crime after their confessions were found to be false. It was almost inevitable that the appointment of such a controversial policeman to such a sensitive inquiry as the Deptford fire would exacerbate the situation. Despite the involvement of 50 detectives who spent more than 40,000 man hours and £320,000 on their investigation, the inquiry provoked such bitterness among the black community that the inquest degenerated into a conflict between witnesses and the police.[31]

A second inquest in 2004 also returned an open verdict; some now accept that arson was not involved, while others insist that the investigations have not been conclusive. Nobody has ever been charged in relation to the fire. Both the murder of Blair Peach and the Deptford Fire indicated the depth of institutional racism in Britain, particularly in the police. The same issue would be conspicuously spotlighted by the death of Stephen Lawrence, also in South East London, in 1993.

Under Margaret Thatcher the British Nationalities Act was passed in 1981. Previously, any person born in Britain (with limited exceptions such as children of diplomats and enemy aliens) was entitled to British citizenship. After this Act came into force it was no longer sufficient to be born here, it was necessary for at least one parent of a United Kingdom-born child to be a British citizen or to have been granted permanent resident status. That same year Britain – and especially London – erupted in riots in many inner-city areas. The Brixton area exploded twice, as we shall see below; and the issue always came back to police treatment of young second- and third-generation blacks and Asians, who refused to take racism and harassment lying down.

The riots and their aftermath changed attitudes among blacks and whites. The National Front were effectively broken by the anti-fascist movement of the late 1970s, and in 1982 the British National Party split away from the parent organization. During the 1980s expressions of popular racism were easy enough to find in the rhetoric of Thatcherite Conservatives. But by the early 1990s, neo-Nazis in Britain had begun to regain some momentum.

The British National Party stood Derek Beackon in a council by-election in one of its old East London stamping grounds, the Isle of Dogs, in 1993. Beackon won with 1,480 votes (33.9 per cent), beating Labour by seven votes, on a turnout of 44 per cent. A mass demonstration was called

---

31   'Deptford: back to the beginning', *Guardian*, 14 May 1981, guardian.co.uk.

later in the same year against the BNP headquarters in Welling, South East London. In the three years since that office had opened, two young black men and one Asian had been murdered locally: in 1991, fifteen-year-old Rolan Adams was murdered on the local Thamesmead Estate; in 1992, Rohit Doggul was stabbed to death by a group of whites, and Stephen Lawrence was killed while waiting at a bus stop in April 1993.

In all three cases, institutional racism – eventually dragged into the light by the 1999 Macpherson Report into the death of Stephen Lawrence – led to denials of any racist element in the killings. But to a wider public the racism was obvious, and so was the link with the local BNP offices. The huge demonstration, which was savagely attacked by the police when it attempted to take a route past the BNP building, was the beginning of the end for the centre of race hate. The BNP were gone from Welling less than twenty-four months later; Beackon was kicked out of his Isle of Dogs council seat in 1994, a year after the Welling demonstration. It would be the next decade before the BNP mounted an effective electoral challenge again.

Winning justice for the long list of those who have died at the hands of racists or of the police has proved more elusive. The guilty verdict in 2012 against two of the killers of Stephen Lawrence took over eighteen years to achieve, and the majority of the gang thought responsible are still free. Repeated deaths in police custody or in the process of raids or arrests have brought black and white Londoners out onto the streets over and over again. From Joy Gardner to Smiley Culture, these cases have highlighted the abuse of black people and the continuing deep levels of racism in the city.

MULTICULTURALISM?

London today is a very different city from the one which greeted (or not) the passengers on the *Windrush*. In inner London at least, there is recognition of the role of black communities, their history and their culture. There is a plaque saluting the murdered Kelso Cochrane in Golborne Road, and another for Stephen Lawrence in Eltham; there are statues to Nelson Mandela, a library named after the Trinidadian Marxist CLR James in Dalston (despite attempts by the developers to erase that sign of black history), and even a Windrush Square, in Brixton. In 1987 Diane Abbott, Paul Boateng and Bernie Grant were all elected as Labour MPs for London constituencies with large black populations. There are now black and Asian MPs and councillors across London. The city celebrates Diwali and Eid in its schools and welcomes mosques, temples and gurdwaras alongside its synagogues, churches and chapels. The advances which have been made are a tribute to the many thousands who have fought discrimination, often in very bitter conflict and sometimes at great cost.

London remains a magnet for young workers from other parts of Britain, especially the depressed, post-industrial northern and western regions where jobs are far scarcer. They follow in the footsteps of generations who came to London to escape unemployment, especially in the 1920s and 30s; West London especially had a major influx of former miners and steelworkers from Wales. Even after the long boom ended in the 1970s, and forms of production altered, this mass migration has continued.

Globalization has brought many rich migrants from Europe, the US and the Far East to work in banking and finance, as well as the Russian oligarchs whose speculation helps keep up the high end of the housing market, and the Qatari royal family who will make one of their many homes in the newly built Shard skyscraper at London Bridge. But it has also brought some of the poorest, fleeing both hunger and political persecution, from all parts of Africa and Latin America, along with Turks, Algerians, Somalis, Poles and Russians. These groups now have their own communities bound together by language, religion and culture, with their own shops, restaurants, places of worship and community centres. A recent Greater London Authority report states that 'According to the most recent estimates, 32 per cent of London's residents and nearly 36 per cent of its workforce were born outside the UK. At the last census in 2001, 27 per cent of Londoners were born abroad.'[32] Most of these immigrants also move within the wider society: their children go to the same schools as other Londoners; they do the same jobs and join the same unions as other Londoners.

The great protests of the twenty-first century have been noted for their diversity: the anti-war protests, the student demonstrations and the trade union marches all reflect a working class totally transformed by the multiculturalism of the world city which London has become. It is one of the features of London most commented on by visitors, and most celebrated by Londoners. But, while many of the battles against racism and prejudice have been won, it is clear from the history of the past sixty years that there has been nothing automatic about that progress.

---

32   See: london.gov.uk/refugees-and-migrants.

II

Welcome to the Modern World

It isn't so much that hard times are coming; the change observed is mostly soft times going.

Groucho Marx

THE BOOM YEARS

In the less than thirty years covering the period of the post-war boom, London went from being a substantial manufacturing centre to an economy based on services. It began the era with rationing and ended it as a society gripped by consumerism. In the 1950s London had emerged slowly from bomb damage and austerity, but social change was clearly on the way. One of the biggest hits for Lionel Bart, a popular songwriter from the Jewish East End, contained the line: 'They've turned our local Palais/Into a bowling alley/And fings ain't what they used to be' (only in London could Palais rhyme with alley). Changes in music, lifestyles, housing, work, education and transport were all rapid.

Ideologically, however, the 1950s were by and large a conservative time – Conservative with a large C in government, but conservative culturally and socially as well. There was a left-wing culture but it was a minority interest. A handful of refugees from the McCarthyite witch-hunt in the US made their homes in London, such as the actor and film director Sam Wanamaker. And when the popular black Communist singer Paul Robeson was denied a passport to travel to London, his supporters filled St Pancras Town Hall to hear him singing over the phone. But, despite 'bohemian' enclaves in areas such as Hampstead or Soho, the dominant culture and values were narrow.

Ruth Ellis was the last woman to be hanged in Britain, after shooting her lover at the Magdala pub in North London. Her fate was partly to do with the Tory policy of maintaining a level of capital punishment despite growing opposition to the practice; but it also signified disapproval of a woman whose sexual behaviour did not conform to the dominant prejudices of society. Crowds clamoured to see the death notice outside Holloway prison, and the indignity of the case fuelled calls against the death penalty, which was abolished less than a decade later.[1]

The early 1950s also saw repeated right-wing scares about both homosexuality and prostitution, leading to a government inquiry in the form of the Wolfenden Committee (1957). 'The idea that the streets of London were a disgrace to an imperial capital was strongly expressed both at the time of the Festival of Britain in 1951 and in Coronation Year, 1953.'[2] Implementation of Wolfenden's main proposal on prostitution effectively privatized it. The Street Offences Act (1959) threatened punishment for streetwalking, leading to the setting up of agencies and more controlled rackets.[3] Male homosexuality was still illegal and subject to repressive policing.

Despite the very big changes in women's lives during the war, 1950s practices reverted to more traditional values, at least temporarily, reflected in an elevation of home and stability following the years of disruption and danger. The baby boom, improvements in housing and overall prosperity all helped to encourage this. There was full employment, a National Health Service and a welfare state, real increases in living standards for working people and a growing ability to afford consumer goods – washing machines, cars, televisions – which were beyond reach in the 1930s and 40s. The new 'consumer society' also created rebellion: South London's Teddy Boys rioted after seeing the Hollywood film *Rock around the Clock* in 1956, with over 3,000 of them overturning cars and breaking windows.[4] The rather more middle-class beatniks set up an alternative culture in Soho, revolving around jazz clubs and coffee bars.[5]

These small stirrings in the 1950s turned out to represent the beginnings of much wider changes in the 1960s, as higher living standards, the spread of education and a liberalization of various laws occurred. In the course of the 1960s hanging was abolished, abortion legalized, homosexuality decriminalized, divorce made easier and censorship in theatre ended. In London in particular, the 1960s opened up a counterculture of radical ideas expressed through a range of outlets, from Arnold Wesker's Centre 42 at the Roundhouse in Chalk Farm, which became a hub of protest, art, drama and agitprop,[6] to radical theatre groups. Newspapers and magazines ranged from

---

1 S. Rowbotham, *A Century of Women* (London, 1997), p. 305.
2 J. Weeks, *Sex, Politics and Society* (Harlow, 1981), p. 240.
3 Ibid., p. 244.
4 C. Booker, *The Neophiliacs* (London, 1992), p. 37.
5 C. Ross and J. Clark, *London: The Illustrated History* (London, 2011), pp. 284–5.
6 Wesker's Centre was called 42 after the number of a resolution passed by the

Private Eye, the vehicle for wicked satires on establishment corruption and complacency, to *Socialist Worker* with its more militant, campaigning style of politics. One link between the two was the left-wing journalist Paul Foot, already making a name for himself with books on immigration and a fine critique of the Labour Prime Minister Harold Wilson.[7]

During the course of these changes the thirteen years of Tory rule ended in the mire of the Profumo sex and politics scandal, to be succeeded by a Labour government headed by Wilson which ruled for eleven out of the next fifteen years. Radicalization over issues of war, empire, industrial struggle, students and sexuality meant that Britain and especially London was to trigger unrest, a growth of left-wing ideas and some of the most political strikes in generations.

HOUSING AND THE PROPERTY DEVELOPERS

London was physically changing in the 1950s and old communities were being broken up. The classic study of post-war working-class life, *Family and Kinship in East London*, depicted a transition in which the close-knit families and social networks of areas like Bethnal Green were beginning to unravel: the book also compared the changing life there with that in one of the new estates at the end of the Tube line in Essex, where many Bethnal Green families had decamped.[8] Housing remained one of the key issues in London. The London County Council, covering the inner London boroughs, played a huge role in housing following the devastations of the war, using its powers to build path-breaking estates such as Churchill Gardens in Pimlico, the Alton estate in Roehampton and the Lansbury estate in Poplar. When the LCC was replaced by the enlarged GLC in 1964, its housing work continued, often transferring inner-city Londoners to greener, more spacious environments.

Council housing was also provided by the thirty-two local London boroughs created as part of government reorganization. The standards aimed for in the idealistic post-war period were gradually eroded, however, under the constant pressure to build more houses – not just to deal with the post-war crisis but increasingly as part of slum clearance programmes. As the rate of construction accelerated, the quality deteriorated: of the 384 tower blocks built in London between 1964 and 1974, the vast majority

---

TUC in 1958, which demanded greater access to the arts and sought to find a popular audience for them. The huge circular train shed was a revolutionary space and a popular venue.

7   P. Foot, *The Politics of Harold Wilson* (London, 1968).

8   M. Young and P. Wilmott, *Family and Kinship in East London* (London, 1957).

were system-built to minimum standards.[9] They were boxes to sleep and eat in rather than Le Corbusier's more interesting idea of 'machines for living'.

Radical vision had given way to the priorities of the bureaucrats and the building companies. The tower blocks built in the London boroughs were overwhelmingly concentrated in the poorest areas: Tower Hamlets and Newham built over a hundred each, followed by Wandsworth with ninety-five, compared with forty in Camden and twenty-four in Hammersmith.[10] The tower-block boom only ended with the collapse of the just-opened Ronan Point in Newham in 1968, when a tenant turned on her gas stove to make a cup of tea and caused an explosion which demolished one whole corner of the block.

Sleazy collusions evolved between councillors and developers. The former Labour leader of Wandsworth council, Sidney Sporle, was jailed for six years in 1971 for taking money from T. Dan Smith, the corrupt Newcastle politician, to approve a particular development of tower blocks on Battersea's Doddington Road estate to replace rows of working-class terraces.

Throughout the 1960s and 70s there was a battle over what working-class housing could and should be. Radical architects like Alison and Peter Smithson continued to champion large, integrated schemes that were designed to cater for all aspects of working-class living and leisure.[11] Some of these projects, like Robin Hood Gardens in Limehouse or the Thamesmead Estate in Greenwich, have become bywords for urban anomie and inner-city failure and are used as examples of the folly of planned, modernist housing schemes. But it is worth comparing their histories with that of the Barbican, a residential estate on the edge of the City built in the same period – but for the rich – in a similarly Corbusian spirit, in the proudly modernist, concrete-faced style aptly named brutalism. Thamesmead was designed around a series of grand artificial lakes and included cinemas, an ice rink, a repertory theatre and a tube station – except that none of these were actually built; the very similar-looking tower blocks of the Barbican, also clustering round a landscaped lake, boast a world-class concert hall, three cinemas, an exhibition space, restaurants, a dedicated tube and its own miniature botanical garden.[12]

Even the best-designed housing could not overcome the problems of poverty and inequality that continued to plague London. But post-war housing conditions were a massive improvement on slum living. In the

---

9   P. Hall, *Cities of Tomorrow* (London, 2002), p. 225.
10   Ross and Clark, *The Illustrated History*, p. 295.
11   O. Hatherley, *Militant Modernism* (Winchester, 2008), p. 32.
12   Ibid., p. 31.

words of the Anglo-Soviet architect Bertholt Lubetkin, who built a series of popular London estates in the 1930s: 'These buildings cry out for a world that has never come into being.'[13]

Yet life on the new estates was by no means easy. At times tenants had to fight very hard for their rights, most famously in the St Pancras rent strike of 1959–60.

On 4 January 1960 over 2,000 council tenants in the borough of St Pancras were on partial rent strike. Their campaign was against the differential rent scheme introduced by the Conservative council. The numbers of tenants who were actually withholding the rent were to fluctuate during the nine or ten months that the struggle was at its height, and although two tenants were forcibly evicted and many others intimidated, the council was left at the end of the year with rent arrears totalling over £20,000.[14]

The previous Labour council had maintained low rents for some time, flying the red flag over the Town Hall on May Day. Yet this changed in 1958 when leader John Lawrence, along with thirteen fellow councillors, was expelled from the Labour group for Communist sympathies. Months later the Labour group forced through higher rents, despite opposition from the Independent Labour group formed by Lawrence and the others. The rents once again dramatically increased when the council went Tory in the 1959 elections. A mass tenants' movement was formed, which carried out demonstrations and other actions to back up their rent strike. At its climax, 'when Don Cook and Arthur Rowe were evicted from their council flats by a force of 400 policemen and twenty-eight bailiffs, a rocket signal brought railmen off the stations, had Irish building workers marching across London, brought the women of St Pancras onto the streets brandishing frying pans and ended in a pitched street battle between tenants and police and a Government ban on demonstration throughout the area.'[15]

In 1968 tenants across the GLC once more went on strike, in protest at the rent hikes brought in by the new Tory administration. Thousands refused to pay the increases, and got organized through the GLC Tenants' Action Committee. They were particularly incensed at being asked for more money while their wages were being held down by the current incomes policy. The slogan 'We won't pay a penny extra' was displayed on posters in windows of flats and houses, and the tenants won support

---

13   J. Allan, *Bertholt Lubetkin and the Tradition of Progress* (London, 1992), p. 366.
14   D. Burn, *Rent Strike: St Pancras, 1960* (London, 1972).
15   Widgery, *The Left in Britain*, p. 169.

from various trade union bodies.[16] In 1969 the Labour government passed legislation to limit rent rises. In the early 1970s there were again rent strikes across the country in protest at the Tory government increases, unfairly labelled 'fair rents'. These rent strikes helped highlight the need for cheap rents and were part of the battle to ensure that there was decent low-cost housing for Londoners.

These tenants' struggles took place against a wider background of rising rents and property prices, meaning that London's housing problems remained as intractable as ever. The 1950s and 60s were a time of major redevelopment, with new office blocks and commercial buildings often many stories high redrawing the London skyline, largely as a result of the Tory government's deregulation of building and rent. In 1957 the Rent Act removed statutory rent controls for privately let accommodation, allowing landlords to make fortunes from the old crumbling houses in inner London. Most notorious was Peter Rachman, a landlord later made famous in the Profumo scandal, who crammed vulnerable tenants, especially new immigrants from Trinidad, into insalubrious houses. Based in Notting Hill and North Kensington, he forced legal sitting tenants out through rackets and intimidation – a process known as 'winkling', which was also practised in other boroughs. The Milner Holland report, published in 1964 following the scandals over Rachmanism, painted a grim picture of London housing: Islington was the worst case, with the largest number of overcrowded houses in London and most of its households having to share running water, baths and toilets.[17]

However, the beautiful, decaying terraces in areas such as Islington were also becoming 'gentrified'. Sometimes this process was carried out by individuals who saw the potential to create splendid homes in areas close to where they worked, rather than moving out to the suburbs or new towns. But increasingly the gentrifiers were estate agents and landlords who saw a new property boom coming, and profits to be made. Winkling became common here too, and continued through the 1960s and 70s, with tenants intimidated out of their homes and sometimes their homes redeveloped around them.

Eileen Murphy came home from work one day to find her house in Stonefield Street, Barnsbury, being demolished. 'There was scaffolding up and they'd pulled all the wall down. There were these great big men standing there with pickaxes. . . . I was really frightened because the house was all open at the front and anyone could get in. I didn't want to be pushed out, you see. I'd been there twenty-one years, and I didn't think I was of an

---

16   Socialist Worker, 28 September 1968.
17   Weightman and Humphries, Making of Modern London, p. 467.

age to be moved around.' With help from lawyers, the tenants' association and the local MP, the tenants won a legal case against the estate agents and developers, Prebbles, and Islington Council took over the houses. But many other tenants gave in to the pressure and left.[18]

The freeing up of controls led to yet another of the building booms which have so marked London's history. By the early 1960s property shares were expanding rapidly: in 1962 they were valued at £800 million, compared with £100 million only four years earlier. During this period built or planned developments included the Hyde Park underpass, the Shell building on the South Bank which was momentarily the highest office block in Europe, and the Elephant and Castle shopping centre.[19]

London's size and rapid growth has always led to pressure for redevelopment. There were frequent campaigns opposing the demolition of cherished buildings or the gentrification of affordable areas. The most famous and one of the most successful was the opposition to the plan to redevelop the area east of Piccadilly Circus, including the old fruit and vegetable market which was being moved out to a new site at Nine Elms, near Battersea. As a result Covent Garden, now one of London's major shopping and entertainment areas, has retained most of its original buildings. This was not the plan of the developers, who wanted to bulldoze the lot and replace them with office blocks, but the Covent Garden Community Association campaigned to win the right to protect the infrastructure, also ensuring that a community centre and some council housing remained. On 1 April 1973 a demonstration with the slogan 'London belongs to us' assembled at St Paul's church in Covent Garden and rallied in Trafalgar Square. The poster, which can be seen in the Museum of London, was designed by the artist Ralph Steadman and produced by the occupying workers at Briant Colour Print.[20]

One particular scandal concerned Centre Point, at Tottenham Court Road tube station – an office block constructed by property developer Harry Hyams only to be left empty, because it was more profitable to do so in times of rising property prices and rents than to pay taxes on it. Centre Point, never an especially aesthetically pleasing structure, became the eye of the storm over housing. This was already a major political issue, especially since the 1966 television play by Ken Loach, *Cathy Come Home*, which highlighted the extent of homelessness and led to the setting up of the housing organization Shelter. An agitprop group demonstrating outside in 1968 produced a leaflet headed 'Cathy Come to Centre Point: It's Empty'

---

18   Ibid., p. 473.
19   Booker, *Neophiliacs*, pp. 133, 178, 204–5.
20   Ross and Clark, *The Illustrated History*, p. 293.

and declared: 'This building is a public scandal! ... There are 8,000,000 square feet of empty office space in Greater London alone – enough to house *all* of Britain's 10,000 homeless families in one go.'[21]

The 1960s marked the return of the squatters' movement. People moved in to take over empty council blocks and houses in boroughs such as Tower Hamlets which alone had 9,000 families on the council waiting list.[22] The years of apathy, neglect, and lack of action on the part of the London councils was now much criticized and sometimes successfully challenged. The 1970s squat in Tolmers Square, with its centre a disused bank building (helpfully known as the Bank), near Euston station, was a highly organized and long-lived squat which eventually succeeded in getting new council housing built alongside the glass office blocks which were rising all around. In 1977 the Coin Street Action Group was set up to oppose hotel and office development on the derelict South Bank, and embarked on seven years of campaigning. The high-class, centrally located co-operative housing and other facilities in Coin Street and the Oxo Tower on London's South Bank were finally won, in the teeth of opposition by developers, and after protracted court cases.[23]

There was also a series of protests over road building, most successfully when the motorway 'box' – part of a plan to provide concentric motorway rings around the city – was stopped after only one section, the Westway, had been constructed: the plan involved the demolition of 30,000 homes across London and was passionately opposed. In protest, eighty-five prospective councillors stood as 'homes before roads' candidates in the 1970 GLC election, and 28,000 objections were received by the public inquiry.[24] As a consequence of these protests, London has relatively few inner-city motorways compared with other major cities, and many of the older inner-city street patterns were preserved.

SUEZ, CND AND VIETNAM

London had a history of solidarity with progressive struggles – it had sided with the North in the American Civil War, with Garibaldi, with the Spanish Republicans. It also had a record of opposition to wars, although there were no mass anti-war movements before the 1950s. Such movements arose as a result of the experiences of modern industrial war, especially that of 1939–45, and in response to the murderousness of modern means of destruction. Experience of, and revulsion against, war meshed

21   Widgery, *The Left in Britain*, pp. 373–5.
22   T. Mahoney, 'The Arbour House squat' in ibid., pp. 428–36.
23   See coinstreet.org.
24   Ross and Clark, *The Illustrated History*, p. 293.

with anti-imperialist solidarity to produce peace movements on an unprecedented scale.

By the 1950s London was the capital city of a disintegrating empire: in the twenty years after the Second World War, the majority of the former colonies in Africa and Asia gained their independence. It was often a long and bitter fight, and relied on supporters and sometimes exiled leaders in London to help carry it out. There were however a number of countries where decolonization did not go smoothly. Southern Rhodesia was ruled by a white minority who declared their own independence rather than countenance black majority rule, and had to be ousted by liberation movements to form what is today Zimbabwe. South Africa, governed under a system of apartheid which segregated whites, blacks and 'coloureds', was a viciously racist and repressive state that was condemned as a pariah from the early 1960s, following the Sharpeville massacre and the country's exit from the Commonwealth. At the same time the Anti-Apartheid Movement was formed, and London became home to many exiles of all racial backgrounds politically active in Communist Parties, national liberation fronts and eventually in the Anti-Apartheid Movement itself.

The Suez crisis broke out in 1956. Britain and France had long regarded Egypt as a quasi-colony, and had many economic interests there when the pro-Western king was overthrown by a group of young officers led by Gamal Abdul Nasser in 1952. Nasser's independence and Arab-nationalist demands set him on a collision course with the old colonial powers; in 1956 British troops withdrew from the Suez Canal Zone, and soon afterwards the British and US governments announced they would no longer be funding Nasser's Aswan Dam project. Nasser produced his bombshell in July: the Suez Canal Company would be taken into Egyptian control.

The nationalization of the canal aroused hysteria, with the Tory Prime Minister Antony Eden calling Nasser a 'little Egyptian upstart' and even the Labour leader Hugh Gaitskell comparing him to Hitler and Mussolini.[25] By October, there were secret deals with the Israelis who invaded Egypt on the 29th. British and French war planes began bombing Egyptian airfields, and a force of Anglo-French troops embarked for Port Said. The pathetic assertion of imperial power came with the invasion on 5 November, just as Russian tanks were entering Hungary to crush the revolution there.

British opinion was split: opposition to the Suez adventure was shown by mass demonstrations, such as on Sunday 4 November when an estimated 30,000 gathered in London, 'by far the biggest political demonstration in Britain since the war',[26] and marched to Downing Street where they were

---

25   Booker, *Neophiliacs*, p. 115.
26   Ibid., p. 117.

charged by mounted police.[27] The campaign against Suez was backed by the Labour leadership who also spoke at the demonstration. It quickly became clear that internationally there was no support for the invasion. There was a run on the pound, threats from Moscow and a refusal by the US to back the British and French. The invasion collapsed and Eden retired, discredited and ill.

Suez marked a decisive turning point in the post-war consensus. It demonstrated that the old colonial powers could not prevent national independence, and that they would have to find different ways of asserting their interests in the Middle East and Africa. At the same time it showed that Britain could no longer act independently of the US, the world's latest superpower. Britain now moved to cement its 'special relationship' with the US – a relationship which meant total co-operation with US interests, the development of nuclear weapons, and the role of junior partner in whatever policies the US cared to pursue.

Suez also showed how fragile was the post-war peace. In the next few years London, and Trafalgar Square in particular, was to become the centre of protest over an issue which came to unite an older generation of political campaigners with a new generation of young people and students. This generation had grown up with memories of the Second World War still raw, overshadowed by the threat of nuclear annihilation following Hiroshima and Nagasaki in 1945. By 1950 Britain had its own bomb, and by the late 1950s the US and the Soviet Union, the two superpowers, were capable of inflicting nuclear damage on the other and its allies. After Suez, the Conservative government's new defence policy came to rely on an extension of nuclear weapons. Even the Labour Party, traditionally much less militaristic, backed the H-bomb at its 1957 conference with the help of the key figure of the left, Shadow Foreign Secretary Nye Bevan, and union bloc votes wielded by their leaders.[28]

Despite this there was growing disquiet over the possession of these weapons, and on Easter weekend 1958 the first Aldermaston march assembled in Trafalgar Square to walk the fifty miles to the Berkshire nuclear weapons research station. The march was backed by the newly formed Campaign for Nuclear Disarmament, which came out of a meeting in January at the St Paul's house of Canon Collins attended by Bertrand Russell, J. B. Priestley and the *Evening Standard* cartoonist Vicky. This select gathering was followed up with a mass meeting in the Methodist Central Hall in Westminster. The main hall was packed, as were four overflow rooms, totalling around 5,000 people.[29]

---

27 Dot Gibson, personal recollection of Lindsey German.
28 Booker, *Neophiliacs*, p. 127.
29 K. Hudson, *CND, Now More Than Ever* (London, 2005), pp. 44–5.

One of the speakers was Alex Comfort (later more famous for writing about the joy of sex), who urged everyone to take a stand, saying: 'I would remind you that once already in the last two years we have seen public opinion assert itself on a moral issue through the sheer force of unorganized indignation.' This reference to Suez showed how much it had inspired this new movement, and how determined many were to reject war. He went on: 'The people must take over – you must take over. The leaders of all the parties are waiting, as they always wait on any issue of principle, to follow public opinion. We can coerce them.'[30]

The Easter Trafalgar Square demonstration and march was inspired by the Suez rally,[31] and saw the first appearance of the CND symbol designed by the artist Gerald Holtom.[32] The following Easter 50,000 people were once more in Trafalgar Square, having marched this time from Aldermaston; the CND badge was 'becoming a teenage craze', according to one not particularly sympathetic observer.[33] By 1960 the Easter rally drew 100,000 to Trafalgar Square and was gathering the support of trade union leaders, especially Frank Cousins of the TGWU who forced through a CND-inspired motion at that year's Labour Party conference; it was bitterly resisted by the Labour leadership, however, and eventually reversed.[34]

In turn this development inspired an organization which grew out of CND but which led to a breach between Collins and the respected eighty-nine-year-old philosopher Bertrand Russell. The latter now helped found the Committee of 100, whose members included John Osborne (his play *The Entertainer* was inspired by Suez with its central character of a washed-up music-hall comedian representing a declining British Empire), Vanessa Redgrave, the playwright Shelagh Delaney and the film director Lindsay Anderson, all of whom committed themselves to more militant protest and direct action.[35] This 'committee of arty bigwigs camouflaged some very determined politicos',[36] as David Widgery put it. In February 1961 it organized 4,000 people to sit down outside the Ministry of Defence.[37] In September of that year it organized its biggest demonstration yet, but was refused permission to use Trafalgar Square. On 7 September, before the demonstration, Russell along with some supporters was arrested for

---

30 A. Comfort, 'The Duty to Rebel', from a speech to the founding meeting of CND in Central Hall, Westminster, 17 February 1955, published in Widgery, *The Left in Britain*, pp. 115–16.
31 Booker, *Neophiliacs*, p. 129.
32 Hudson, *CND*, p. 56.
33 Booker, *Neophiliacs*, p. 144.
34 Hudson, *CND*, pp. 61–6 ; Murray, *The T&G Story*, pp. 121–3.
35 Booker, *Neophiliacs*, pp. 151–2.
36 Widgery, *The Left in Britain*, p. 110.
37 Booker, *Neophiliacs*, p. 156.

incitement to civil disobedience. He spent a week in Brixton Prison, where he had been jailed as a conscientious objector during the First World War.[38] Here he wrote: 'Macmillan, Kennedy and Khrushchev are the wickedest people in the history of man.'[39] The demonstration (in Trafalgar Square despite the prohibition) saw thousands assemble, to be met with a police attack near midnight which led to the 'largest mass arrest in British history' when 1,314 people were arrested, including Osborne and Redgrave.[40]

Anti-war feeling was strengthened by the Cuban missile crisis in 1962 which brought the world to the brink of nuclear war, and CND's activities continued.[41] They spilled over into the state visit by the king and queen of Greece in 1963, when some demonstrators protesting at the murder of left-wing MP George Lambrakis booed the queen. There were ninety-four arrests and one demonstrator was planted with a brick by a corrupt police sergeant at Savile Row station.[42]

From 1964 there was a Labour government under Harold Wilson, re-elected with a much larger majority in 1966, and the two foreign policy issues which dominated his time in office were Rhodesia and Vietnam. The white prime minister of Rhodesia, Ian Smith, was determined to deny political rights to the black majority, antagonizing both the British government – still nominally the colonial power – and the United Nations. Wilson's indecision and delay over the question and his fear of standing up to Smith, who was backed by right-wing Tories in Britain, frustrated many on the left. In 1965 students at the London School of Economics held their first political demonstration over Rhodesia, and were met with police brutality.[43] They also campaigned against the appointment of a director, Walter Adams, who had been a college principal in Rhodesia.

Even more inflammatory was the situation in Vietnam, where the war now escalated dramatically with heavy bombing and more and more troops being sent in. Wilson prevaricated, as many Labour supporters opposed the idea of sending British troops to aid US government forces, and there was growing pressure on him to condemn the war in Vietnam. Wilson refused to do so: the deal he did with US president Johnson was to refrain from any criticism of the war, while not sending troops.

The Vietnam Solidarity Campaign, formed under the leadership of the former Oxford student Tariq Ali, organized some of the most militant

38   Hudson, *CND*, p. 74.
39   Cited in Booker, *Neophiliacs,* p. 165.
40   Ibid., p. 169.
41   Hudson, *CND*, pp. 82–6.
42   Booker, *Neophiliacs*, p. 206; Hudson, *CND*, pp. 93–4.
43   C. Harman, *The Fire Last Time* (London, 1998), pp. 143, 145–6.

demonstrations in the post-war period. In the autumn of 1967 one conflict involved fighting with the police in Grosvenor Square, site of the US embassy. In 1968 the protestors assembled in Trafalgar Square on 17 March and went on to the US embassy. Larger than the previous one, the march chanted 'Ho, Ho, Ho Chi Minh (after the leader of the North Vietnamese) and 'Victory to the NLF' (National Front for the Liberation of South Vietnam). Marchers carried NLF flags and fought to break through police lines.[44]

The second VSC demonstration on 27 October achieved mass press notoriety before it had even happened. Tariq Ali, revolutionary politics, threats of violence – it was too much for some of the media. In the event the 100,000-strong crowd poured into Hyde Park, since the organizers felt that the police presence in Grosvenor Square would make the march there impossible. The gathering was peaceful but militant: 'Last Sunday the marchers took command of the streets. There was no confrontation with the police because the numerical and political strength of the demonstration forced the state to retreat and allow the marchers to dictate their terms.'[45] There were criticisms from the Maoists, however, who took 1,000 people to Grosvenor Square and found their way barred by the police.[46]

STUDENTS OCCUPY

The student movement which erupted in the 1960s was fed by many different elements. Perhaps most fundamental was that for the first time in history there were significant numbers of young people in higher education. Universities had expanded in the post-war boom, and by the early 1960s 'new' universities and polytechnics were also being created. Groups of socialists existed in some London colleges from 1965 or '66, having been politicized through the Labour Party Young Socialists or CND, and they got involved in campaigns on war, imperialism and racism, as well as issues directly affecting students and their conditions. But the socialists were hardly representative; the founding meeting of the LSE Socialist Society in 1965 attracted only twelve people. These, according to David Widgery, included 'two IS [International Socialist] postgraduates, two air force apprentices who had been court-martialled for their sympathies with CND and had found their way to LSE, a *New Left Review* editor, and someone from Solidarity'. The society published

---

44   Ibid., pp. 146–7.
45   *Socialist Worker*, 2 November 1968.
46   For accounts of the march and related arguments see Widgery, *The Left in Britain*, pp. 382–8; Harman, *Fire Last Time*, pp.154–5.

its own magazine, held political meetings and 'conducted semi-permanent seminars theoretically combating bourgeois sociology in a large unpleasant circle in the bar'.[47]

Nevertheless the very first student occupation took place at LSE, in March 1967, and was organized against the appointment of Walter Adams as director, who was, as we have seen, hot from his post in white racist Rhodesia. It was moved by the Tory president but the Socialist Society played an increasingly important and radicalizing role. The students began to work with GLC tenants and to support the strikers at the Barbican site only a mile away.[48] Chris Harman, one of the IS postgraduates, estimated that as a result of the occupation IS grew from six members to around thirty in just over a year.[49]

The movement which erupted in Britain in 1968 was one of the smaller of those appearing around the world; in Germany, the US and especially in France, mass student movements rocked society. In London only two colleges were occupied, the LSE and Hornsey School of Art, but under pressure of events in France a conference at the LSE founded the Revolutionary Socialist Students' Federation. Every sort of left-wing idea now found expression in the LSE and despite some of the more ridiculous flights of fantasy, new vistas opened up, as David Widgery records: 'The appalling conformity and petty competitiveness which is the reality of undergraduate life had been momentarily shattered.'[50]

The LSE was occupied to provide accommodation for the huge Vietnam march in October 1968. The authorities responded by installing gates within the building, and introduced a new disciplinary code. The students removed the gates, using the 'tools which had been sitting all week in a van in Houghton Street', and the authorities then closed the school down altogether. An LSE in exile opened briefly at the University of London Union in Malet Street, but petered out when the left minority was cut off from the wider student body. The manoeuvre was completed when two sympathetic lecturers were sacked, and the IS found itself caught between the retreating students' union and the gesture politics of some of the left.[51] But while the momentum of the student movement at LSE was broken, other student struggles developed elsewhere in the following years when many young people became radicalized. A Hornsey student wrote: 'In the six weeks of the Hornsey Revolution I had more education than I had ever previously

47   Widgery, *The Left in Britain*, p. 310.
48   Ibid., pp. 310–11.
49   Harman, *Fire Last Time*, p. 144.
50   Widgery, *The Left in Britain*, p. 315.
51   Ibid., p. 316–17.

experienced. A new sort of freedom emerged, a freedom to work, learn and develop.'[52]

The radicalization provided a new readership for magazines which summed up the spirit of the times. *Black Dwarf*, edited by Tariq Ali from its foundation in 1968, was named after the radical paper produced in 1817. It had views similar to those of *New Left Review*, featured a very wide range of contributors on different topics, and was particularly focused on the student movement. It had a healthy circulation of 30,000. Alongside this were other, radicalized but not so political, 'hippie' publications. The 'alternative' listings guide *Time Out* – a far cry from its current glossy consumerist incarnation – appeared in the late 1960s. The 'alternative' or 'underground' press included *Oz* magazine, an Australian import published by Richard Neville. *International Times* was set up in 1966 by a group of Americans 'bored with Marxism'.[53] Both espoused radical politics, but were more concerned with lifestyles. Their attitudes to sex and drugs guaranteed problems for them, however, and in 1969 the police carried out a series of raids on the publications and their printers, including *Black Dwarf*.[54]

There was much right-wing opposition to the new culture, which reached its most vindictive in 1971 when Neville and his associates were prosecuted and imprisoned for the *Oz* Schoolkid's issue which was deemed obscene.[55] None of the magazines lasted many years, but they represented a break with the past and a sign that there was now a substantial left-wing audience for ideas.

The upheavals of 1968 changed the thinking of a generation. The new generation created a new left, based on movements against oppression and imperialism and usually critical of the traditional left represented by the Labour and Communist Parties.[56] The Communist Party in Britain had never been a mass workers' party like its counterparts in Italy or France, but it numbered its members in tens of thousands in the 1960s. Already suffering a long-term decline, most dramatically highlighted in 1956 when up to 10,000 of its members quit over the Soviet invasion of Hungary, it still retained a serious industrial working-class base. The events of '68 marked the rise of new left activist organizations which came from the student movement. Both the IS and the International Marxist Group grew over the next few years and played an important part in the struggles of the 1970s.

---

52 From the Hornsey students' duplicated paper Revelations, cited in ibid., pp. 332–3.
53 Ibid., p. 488.
54 R. Neville, *Hippie Hippie Shake* (London, 1996), p. 153.
55 Ibid., Chapters 17–21.
56 The story of the New Left can be found in C. Lin, *The British New Left* (Edinburgh, 1993). See also Widgery, *The Left in Britain*.

THE RISING OF THE WOMEN

The strike of the Ford Dagenham women machinists in 1968 is now famous as the equal pay strike which heralded the British women's movement. It didn't start like that, but as the organized expression of women's indignation at being treated as unskilled workers as they sewed the seat covers for the company's cars. They machined the awkward shapes needed for the covers with what used to be described as 'dexterity' by those who sought to separate 'women's skills' (nimble fingers) from the more highly paid 'men's skills' on the production line. Their demand was to be given parity with similarly skilled men, and ranked in the C grade. As with many women's strikes, once the women decided they had a grievance, they didn't hold back. They voted unanimously for an overtime ban and one-day strike, kept the picket line going all day, and walked out on an all-out strike when they received an arrogant letter from the company. The union officials were relatively supportive of the women, especially their convenor Bernie Passingham.

Labour Cabinet minister Barbara Castle intervened in the dispute to try to find a compromise. Passingham told the Ford industrial relations manager at a meeting in Castle's office that 'equal pay' was what was needed. In the end the women won 92 per cent of C grade, but the strike became famous as the first for equal pay.[57] It would be followed in the early 1970s by many local equal pay strikes – for example at Trico in Brentford – as employers in engineering in particular tried to regrade women so as to avoid Castle's Equal Pay Act.

The strike was popular among the new activists, especially the women who now began to gravitate towards ideas of women's liberation. Influenced by the women's movement in the US and radicalized by the student, civil rights and anti-Vietnam war movements, some trade union women started a National Joint Action Committee for Women's Equal Rights (NJACWER) which campaigned on equal pay. It organized an equal pay demonstration in May 1969. Other strikes followed: in December 1969, 200 women at Lucas's in Acton struck for equal pay. Bus conductresses campaigned for the right to become drivers and for equal benefits with men.[58] In 1970 a campaign began to organize women employed by contracting companies to clean the offices of major businesses such as Shell. As they still do forty years later, they toiled at night for low wages and in poor conditions. Spearheaded by May Hobbs, a cleaner from Hoxton, the organizing involved the cleaners themselves, the unions, socialist and

---

57   Murray, *T&G*, pp. 146–7.
58   Rowbotham, *Century of Women*, p. 350.

feminist women and men. Pickets at one workplace included 'cleaners, IS and Camden Women's Action Group. . . . as a result of these actions a representative of the TGWU negotiated with the cleaning company and it was agreed the two shop stewards were to be reinstated.'[59]

The women's movement developed from 1970, holding a London demonstration on International Women's Day 1971 which attracted several thousand, and a picket of the Miss World contest at the Royal Albert Hall. Women established consciousness-raising groups in areas like the Arsenal and Tufnell Park. Organized through the London Women's Liberation Workshop, the activists remained small in number, and usually with left backgrounds.[60] They were influential in a number of campaigns and with women from the left groups formed the backbone of the campaign against restrictions on abortion from 1975 onwards.

Similarly influenced by the much bigger movements in the US, the Gay Liberation Front was founded in London in October 1970 following the Stonewall riots in New York, and stressed gay pride and coming out. Although the GLF had collapsed by 1972, it helped establish a gay consciousness and culture in London which has only grown in the intervening years.[61] Like the women's movement, the gay movement was closely connected to and identified with working-class struggles, and gay activists campaigned within their unions for gay and lesbian rights.[62]

UNION CITY REVISITED

London in the 1950s and 60s was still a major manufacturing city and seaport. It accounted for 20 per cent of Britain's engineering jobs and, by the end of the 1950s, 45 per cent of ladies' tailoring, while one in three of all Londoners were employed in factories.[63] This changed over the next twenty years, as de-industrialization and recession hit London. By the end of the 1970s, the London docks had all closed and moved downriver to Tilbury while between 1959 and 1974 a full 38 per cent of London's manufacturing jobs were lost. Plants producing London buses, Fairey helicopters and motor parts all closed. The booming West London areas of the post-war years went bust. By the 1970s, office development and the expansion of the financial sector in the City were becoming the face of modern London.[64]

---

59   See report in *Shrew* 3/1 (1971).
60   See survey in *Shrew* 4/1 (1972).
61   Weeks, *Sex, Politics and Society*, pp. 285–6.
62   N. Field, *Over the Rainbow* (London, 1995), pp. 159–61.
63   Ross and Clark, *The Illustrated History*, p. 296.
64   Ibid., pp. 296–7.

Unionization had grown during the war and spread even to the Ford plant at Dagenham after long years of organizing. Full employment led to a situation of 'wage drift' in many factories, where local rates would rise as a result of local union pressure and labour shortages. There were a number of strikes over wages, many of them successful. By the late 1950s there were disputes especially in the docks, in the big wholesale markets such as Smithfield and Covent Garden, in the construction industry allied to the property boom, and on the buses. The London bus strike of 1958 was one of the largest post-war strikes. It went on for seven weeks, involving 53,000 workers, looking for a pay rise that would break the government pay freeze. The workers won some increase but overall suffered a defeat, leading to 10 per cent cuts in bus services and punitive redundancies. Despite support from dockers, meat porters, and meat transport drivers, the TUC refused to extend the strike and the bus workers were isolated.[65]

The 1960s saw increasing unrest over attempts by government to hold down pay and to find a way of regulating and controlling the unions. Harold Wilson's Labour government, first elected in 1964, increasingly found itself beset by problems after winning a second election in 1966. Wilson's response to this was to attack the seamen's strike which broke out in the summer of that year for a pay rise and reduced hours, demands refused by the employers. The strike became increasingly bitter as Wilson, denouncing it as Communist-led, sided with the employers in trying to crush it.

Yet a wave of working-class solidarity and support came from across Britain: in London this included the 400,000-strong London Labour Party, Port of London ship repairers, *Daily Mirror* printers, West India dock liaison committee, South London AEU, Greater London district boilermakers and dozens of local branches of unions, tenants' associations and other organizations.[66] Wilson's determination to introduce an incomes policy made a clash with the unions inevitable. Frank Cousins, the TGWU general secretary who was briefly a minister in Wilson's government, resigned over this issue in the summer of 1966. The introduction of 'In Place of Strife', the first major attempt to regulate the unions since the war, which would have introduced regulations making it harder to strike and imposing financial penalties on those who did so, led to gloves-off conflict between the unions and the Labour government, especially Barbara Castle, the ostensibly left-wing minister responsible for introducing the bill.

The revival of the Communist-led Liaison Committee for the Defence

65   Murray, *T&G*, p. 118; Widgery, *The Left in Britain*, pp. 164–5, 180–2.
66   Bodies listed in 'Not wanted on voyage', a pamphlet produced by the Hull Strike Committee, cited in Widgery, pp. 263–5.

of Trade Unions reflected rank-and-file anger at Wilson's attack on the unions. On May Day 1969 over 1 million went on strike in protest at the law, joining a huge demonstration through central London.[67] Other important strikes in the late 1960s included the Barbican strike where builders at the new upmarket development in the City entered into a major dispute which became a cause célèbre on the left. Led by the Communist trade unionist Lou Lewis, but also involving Trotskyist building work- ers, the strike was denounced by the media and government but attracted support from the newly radicalized students in London and had a pamphlet supporting it written by the left-wing journalist Paul Foot.[68]

Wilson and Castle were forced to abandon 'In Place of Strife' under pressure from the unions and in the face of growing industrial militancy. The revolt of the low-paid saw refuse workers in Hackney and nine other London boroughs out on strike unofficially in September 1969; they were supported by the TGWU, and brought out most of London. Teachers also took industrial action for the first time.[69] However, plans to place legal constraints upon the unions resurfaced when Labour was, to the surprise of many, thrown out at the general election of June 1970. The incoming Tory government under Edward Heath ushered in a decade of the most militant class struggle seen since the 1920s, the growth of union membership to its high point of over 13 million in 1979, and a strengthening of the left more substantial than anything since before the war.

THEY FOUGHT THE LAW

Heath's new Industrial Relations Act, with its own national Industrial Relations Court, helped to generalize a growing feeling of militancy within the working class and the wider left. Years of full employment and increas- ing union organization boosted this process, which coupled with rising inflation and attempts to police the unions created a potent mix, especially when added to the radical ideas which now permeated a large section of the left: women's liberation, anti-racism, gay rights, all became issues in these years. So too did did Ireland again, following the rise of the civil rights movement from 1968 onwards, and compounded by the internment of young men in Northern Ireland in 1971 followed by the shooting of thirteen unarmed demonstrators in Derry in 1972. While there were no major incidents over Vietnam, there was revulsion at US policies there and in Cambodia.

---

67   Murray, T&G, p. 134.
68   Widgery, The Left in Britain, p. 254.
69   Harman, Fire Last Time, p. 227.

Industrial action was taking off, however. The Liaison Committee for the Defence of Trade Unions (LCDTU) held a conference in November 1970 with 1,750 delegates which called a one-day strike against the laws on 8 December.[70] Half a million workers answered the call, including 200,000 in London alone, comprising dockers, printers and car workers.[71] In February 1971 the TUC organized a demonstration of 140,000 against the proposed law.[72] On the demonstration were postal workers and telephone engineers who were on strike at the time, although their national stoppage was ultimately not successful. London was part of a much wider movement, as it had been in 1911 and 1926. That same year the UCS shipbuilders occupied their yard in Glasgow, winning solidarity across Britain, and the miners struck successfully earlier in 1972, picketing coal depots and power stations in and around London, winning solidarity from workers and students.

It was against this background that dockers came into dispute with their employers in July 1972, over the issue of containerization which they feared would put paid to their jobs for good. The jobs at container depots paid lower rates and were often non-unionized. Organized through an ad hoc committee, the dockers picketed the new container depots, including one at Chobham Farm just north of the docks, and the TGWU refused to recognize the Industrial Relations Act or the court. As a result three dockers were threatened with jail, but the judges backed down, as docks came out on strike. Lord Denning later said, 'we were influenced perhaps by … the realization that there would be a general strike, which would paralyse the whole country.'[73] As the picketing continued it became clear that confrontation could not be avoided. Pickets now went to Midland Cold Storage, on land in East London owned by the Vestey family business, Union International, which had just closed down two Thameside wharves with the loss of dockers' jobs. Midland Cold Storage brought an action through the court against five pickets, who were jailed in Pentonville Prison for contempt of court on 21 July 1972. One, Tony Merrick, said: 'I am going to prison for defending the dockers' rights and the right of the working class to work.'[74]

The London docks shop stewards put a permanent picket on Pentonville, but central to victory was winning solidarity action. 'One in the dock, all out the docks' was the slogan in the port of London. An unofficial dock strike took place across the country and was almost totally solid. The

70   *Socialist Worker*, 21 November 1970.
71   Ibid., 12 December 1970.
72   Ibid., 27 February 1971.
73   Denning quoted in Harman, *Fire Last Time*, p. 245.
74   Interview in *Socialist Worker*, special edition 22 July 1972.

Pentonville picket became a hub for demonstrations, flying pickets and delegations to win support. This was not easy: the strikes were still unofficial, the law threatened financial sanctions and possibly prison. But efforts to bring out Fleet Street, initially patchy, succeeded on Saturday 22 July with action from the machine workers in the Natsopa union stopping all the Sunday papers except the *Sunday Times*. Dockers and other militants visited all the mothers and fathers of chapels (shop stewards) in Fleet Street, and by Monday the daily papers were stopped.

The main food market workers also decided to come out on the 22nd, and now many sections of industry across Britain followed suit. This was all the more remarkable given that many factories at the time closed down for annual holidays in July, and so were empty. By Monday 24 July, lorry drivers, container workers, warehousemen and ship repairers joined those already on strike. On the Tuesday, ink factories and Chiswick bus repair depots stopped for twenty-four hours. Tens of thousands marched from Tower Hill to the prison. Some building sites and London Transport buses stopped for a day on the Wednesday, while take-offs at Heathrow were paralysed. Five days after the dockers were jailed the TUC called for a one-day general strike for 31 July, although this was only under pressure from the LCDTU and the visible anger of the rank and file. They didn't need to: the judges had hastily been reconvened to put the dispute into the hands of the Official Solicitor, an obscure and little-known figure, who ordered the release of the five on a technicality. The dockers were freed that same afternoon and carried aloft through London on a victory march. One of them, Vic Turner, said many years later:

> I have said to younger people, 'unless you're prepared to stand up and be counted to defend not just your industry but your whole way of life and your whole culture, then you're not a member of the working class.' ... but to ask people to break the law. I would do it. I wouldn't ask other people to do it, you know, but ... it's a defence of what your parents and grandparents have striven for.[75]

The victory of the dockers was followed by an official strike at the docks over jobs, which ended in compromise between the union and government. Yet the release of the Pentonville Five was a great day in working-class history, and cemented the militancy which had grown over the past year.[76]

---

75 Vic Turner in interview with Geoffrey Goodman, cited in Murray, *T&G*, p. 156.
76 See ibid., pp. 153–7; Harman, *Fire Last Time*, pp. 243–7; *Socialist Worker*, special issue 27 July 1972; *Socialist Worker*, 29 July 1972.

Heath was in retreat and his law was in tatters, but the government now tried another tactic: a pay freeze which would be legally binding to stop what it deemed were 'inflationary' wage increases. Sectors such as hospital workers and civil servants struck in protest for the first time. Government legislation was politicizing groups of workers in manual trades having little tradition of militancy. Briant Colour Print, a print works in South London, was occupied by its workers in 1973 to prevent closure. On May Day 1973, the TUC called a day of action against the freeze, where 2 million struck and 100,000 demonstrated in London.[77] But while the government was unpopular, major battalions of the working class did not break through as they had done in 1972. The government, its allies and the employers were now faced with growing economic crisis, as the oil price rose rapidly in the wake of the Yom Kippur war in 1973.

There was growing talk of the threat of left extremists and of measures to deal with them. One of Heath's closest confidants, the civil servant Sir William Armstrong, became increasingly paranoid about the class struggle and talked of the need for a coalition government or even a coup. He was sent off for a rest, never to return, but he was not the only one who thought like that. There was growing fear of working-class action; building workers were imprisoned for militant picketing, and special police were being trained to take on strikers and other groups of protestors.

At the same time, the miners launched their second strike in two years over their pay claim. They were in a very strong position, with high oil prices necessitating the burning of coal stocks much faster than had been predicted. The miners seized their advantage and launched an overtime ban, then a strike which led to power cuts and a three-day week in industry. As 1974 began, the country seemed to many to be in a state of almost unprecedented crisis. Heath now gambled everything and went for an election on the issue of who ran the country. When the results were announced it was clear it wouldn't be him. Wilson was back again.[78]

Yet if industrial militancy had forced Heath out of office, Labour was keen to ensure that it didn't continue. The IRA was repealed, to be replaced with the much more union-friendly Trade Union and Labour Relations Act, and different sections of workers received large pay rises. Labour then imitated some of the policies of the Tories: the Social Contract agreed with the unions led to tight wage restraint in return for certain concessions and consultation with the unions. It was brought in by one of the leading 'left' trade unionists, now general secretary of the TGWU, Jack Jones. A veteran of Spain where he was wounded at the battle of the Ebro, he had

77　*Socialist Worker*, 5 May 1973.
78　Harman, *Fire Last Time*, pp. 261–4.

been christened James Larkin Jones after the great Irish socialist and trade unionist who fought his biggest battle against the Dublin lockout in 1913, the year Jones was born. Having helped lead the union against traditional right-wingers, he was essential in selling the Social Contract to the left, including sections of the Communist Party – the traditional leadership of the left industrially.

However, the contract was followed by a massive series of cuts in public spending at the behest of the IMF in 1976, which further slashed workers' living standards.[79] The second half of the 1970s was very different from the first, and in some cases an increasingly ugly mood grew among workers. Unemployment doubled, becoming a major political issue for the first time since the war. The strikes were now more bitter, but far fewer and not always victorious. This was true of one of the most famous and symbolic strikes of that era.

THE BATTLE OF DOLLIS HILL

Jayaben Desai was probably as surprised as anyone that she became the leader of the Grunwick strike in the late 1970s. The action at a small film processing factory in Cricklewood, North West London, was triggered following a series of grievances against their boss, who was also Asian. Matters came to a head in 1976 when a male employee was sacked for working too slowly. The mainly female Asian workforce walked out, joined the union APEX, and were on the picket lines for two years.

They were symbolic of so many things: they were women workers, they were Asian immigrants, and they had the misfortune to be fighting an intractable boss at a time when the fortunes of the labour movement in Britain were declining after its high point of the early 1970s. Their courage, symbolized by the tiny figure of Mrs Desai, wearing her sari and carrying a handbag, sparked a wave of support and solidarity across the movement. Post office workers refused to cross picket lines and for a time refused to handle all the mail. Right-wing politicians, too, treated Grunwick as a cause célèbre, and were determined to use every means at their disposal, including legal action and police repression, to break the strike.

In the summer of 1977 mass pickets were organized every morning outside the factory set among rows of terraced houses. Many people would travel across London at 5 or 6am on beautifully light summer mornings to stop the scabs going in. On one particular day there was a national mass picket when the miners, led by Arthur Scargill, turned up to stop the bus; a vicious police operation ensured that it got through. Grunwick was

---

79 Murray, *T&G*, pp. 162–6.

a turning point: even right-wing Labour politicians like Shirley Williams joined the picket line, because they understood that the future of picketing, and therefore of effective industrial action for unions, was at stake. The employers and government understood this too, and launched a huge policing operation to keep the factory open. The Special Patrol Group was used for the first time in an industrial dispute here. In total there were 550 arrests during the dispute, more than at any time since the General Strike of 1926. The strike was defeated eventually, marking the beginning of a series of defeats for organized workers.

The summer of 1977 saw the queen's Jubilee, the defeat for the fascists at Lewisham, and growing class polarization. Grunwick and Mrs Desai were an important part of this mix. The fact that Asian women would stand up for their rights and win the solidarity of white male trade unionists was important in itself, and helped to create an anti-racist culture inside the British working class. Desai's most famous saying was a criticism of the TUC. Official trade union support, she said, is 'like honey on the elbow': you can touch it, you can see it but you can't quite taste it. Jayaben Desai's failure was more heroic than most people's success.

THE THATCHER NIGHTMARE

In the 1970s the radicalization of the 1960s carried over and deepened. There were campaigns about women's and gay liberation, against racism and fascism, in solidarity with Chileans (London was host to thousands of Chilean exiles following the US-backed coup in 1973). There were campaigns over Ireland, in protest at the killings on Bloody Sunday, to get the troops out, and especially over miscarriages of justice where people were wrongly imprisoned for alleged IRA bombings. There were mass student occupations in 1976 and '77, and student leader Andy Strouthous was jailed briefly in Pentonville for defying an injunction to end the occupation at his East London college.

London became extremely polarized as the decade went on: while the left was strong, the right was also on the offensive from the middle of the decade. Ideological attacks on the post-war settlement, rises in unemployment, critiques of liberal ideas on a range of issues from education to abortion, all fuelled a more militant right wing. The National Front was a growing force. Police attacked the Notting Hill Carnival crowds in 1976, and used the SUS laws to stop and search black youth. There was a high level of racist murders. Despite the victory against the fascists at Lewisham in 1977 and the creation of the Anti-Nazi League, police and the authorities allowed the fascists to march. This policy reached its nadir in April 1979 in the heavily Asian and working-class area of Southall, when the district was effectively locked down by police in order to allow the NF to march, against the wishes of the whole community. This was followed by Blair Peach's death at the hands of a member of the already hated Special Patrol Group, forerunners of the riot police and special units. Despite cover-ups his family and friends have spent thirty years trying to get justice; a Met police report in 2010 admitted SPG responsibility, but no charges have been brought. Today in Southall, a primary school is named after him and his death is commemorated every year.

Peach's death took place during the 1979 election campaign which swept Margaret Thatcher to power. In the month leading up to this the Labour government had limped to its fractious end. Workers had launched a mass wave of strikes during the Winter of Discontent, as different groups took action to defend their living standards in the face of further income reductions. Pictures of huge piles of uncollected rubbish in London dominated the media, but the strikes also involved Ford workers, hospital workers, local government workers, lorry drivers and dockers. But unlike the earlier periods, the strikes remained fairly sectional and did not generalize politically. At least part of the reason for this lay in bitterness against the Labour government which had presided over mass unemployment and cuts in living standards.

The period of liberal ideas ushered in by the 1960s and sustained for nearly twenty years was coming to a close. But in London especially, the legacy was still fought over. A plethora of campaigns, organizations, community organizers, housing co-operatives, radical bookshops, women's centres and tenants' associations had been established in the previous two decades. They helped to shape the politics of London despite the major challenges which lay ahead.

Margaret Thatcher has to take credit for worsening London quite considerably. Her eleven-year rule, from 1979 to 1990, led to a drastic weakening of the unions, untrammelled privatization, the destruction of old communities, and the loss of many firms and jobs as manufacturing industry continued to decline. It fostered the decimation of council housing through the right-to-buy scheme (buyers then took advantage of property booms to sell the stock on), the rise of the Murdoch press, and the closure of hospitals, libraries and schools. She met resistance on many fronts: in major strikes, including by hospital workers, rail workers, printers and steel workers, and in constant protests over unemployment, privatization, and cuts. There was a revival of the Labour left around the campaign to elect Tony Benn for deputy leader of the party, which he lost by the narrowest of margins. In Ireland Republican prisoners went on hunger strike to win political rights in 1981, creating a groundswell of support in London. These and many other campaigns tried to take on Thatcher and, sometimes at least, partly succeeded.

There was a brief, spectacular resurgence of CND, following the Labour government's decision to agree to the siting of nuclear Cruise missiles in Britain – at Greenham Common in Berkshire and Molesworth in Cambridgeshire. This was in response to a major escalation of the arms race, raising the terrifying prospect of 'limited nuclear war' in Europe using these new 'battlefield nukes'. Throughout 1980 hundreds of thousands mobilized against the threat. The Labour Party National Executive Committee organized the first big demo against the missiles, and the Labour conference adopted a unilateralist position on their removal. In October 1980 the 'Protest and Survive' demo attracted at least 80,000. The following year the London demo on an international day of action was estimated at 250,000, which CND leader Bruce Kent thought 'a modest guess'.[80] Popular attention focused later on the women's peace camp at Greenham Common, but CND's activities continued throughout these years, holding meetings and launching local actions, and trying to persuade councils to become nuclear-free zones (which a number of London councils did indeed become).

RIOT CITY

Thatcher's central aim was to restore the profitability of British capitalism by cutting welfare provision, worsening labour conditions and lowering wages. In this she represented a reaction to the industrial struggles of the 1970s and a determination to break the power of the unions. As a result, unemployment rose to record levels. A People's March for Jobs in 1980 ended in London to be greeted by a major demonstration with echoes of the 1930s. Unemployment combined with police harassment of blacks and racist attacks led to riots in 1981 (and again at Broadwater Farm in Tottenham in 1985, where Constable Keith Blakelock was killed). In April 1981 a riot broke out in Brixton, home to a mixed community and one of the earliest settlements of post-war immigration in London. Rioters hijacked a bus, burnt down pubs and set cars on fire. After Brixton there were mini riots at funfairs in Finsbury Park, Wanstead, Peckham and Ealing – all relatively poor working-class areas with large Asian and black populations.

Young blacks and some whites exploded into riot across Britain in the week of 3–11 July, putting up barricades, throwing petrol bombs and looting shops. In Southall Asians fought skinheads who beat up a woman in an Asian shop. The fighting continued around the Hambrough Tavern, where the skinheads were attending a gig, and the pub was burnt to the ground. These were 'the most violent and extensive disturbances on Britain's streets

---

80   Hudson, *CND*, pp. 135–6.

since the war'.[81] The riots subsided quickly but had long-term consequences. Thatcher's policies were straining what Tories referred to as 'the
social fabric', and there were fears that this would lead to further civil unrest.

The Scarman Commission, headed by an experienced judge, investigated why the Brixton riot happened, highlighted the disproportionate
use of stop and search powers against black and minority ethnic groups,
and recommended more recruitment into the police of ethnic minorities. The riots also demonstrated the changing nature of London, which
was now much more multicultural and preserved a genuine radicalism, at
least in some inner-city areas. Hence many anti-racist whites as well as
blacks and Asians tended to be suspicious of the police and authority. Most
importantly, 1981 represented a new generation of blacks and Asians who
were demanding equal treatment in a society which acted towards them in
profoundly discriminatory and racist ways. Such was the cumulative effect
of experiences as seemingly disparate as the Deptford fire, the aggression of
the National Front, systematic police harassment, institutional racism in jobs
and education, and casual everyday racism. The mark they made on London
was permanent in creating a new and diverse working class across the city.

The most decisive of Thatcher's battles was with the miners, and was
conducted far from London. Her pit closures were meant to provoke a
strike and they did. The miners, facing the annihilation of their industry,
struck for over a year in 1984–85 in increasingly difficult conditions. They
had widespread support in London, however: groups were set up, and
demonstrations widely attended. There was a London miners' demo in
May, and one of miners' wives and Women against Pit Closures in August
1984. Delegations twinned with pits and mining villages; money and basic
supplies were collected on London streets. At Christmas, toys and food
were sent to the mining areas and parties were organized. Public meetings
and events were held in their support. Although the miners were forced
to admit defeat in March 1985, the strike taught political lessons which
many never forgot and which led to an undying hatred and contempt for
Thatcher.

THE BATTLE OF WAPPING

Fresh from her success Thatcher mounted further attacks: 1986 was her
annus mirabilis, when she closed down the GLC and supported the press
baron Rupert Murdoch in his attacks on his workforce in the print industry
– while preparing the 'Big Bang', the abrupt deregulation of City of London

81   C. Harman, 'The summer of 1981: a post-riot analysis', in *International
Socialism* 14 (Autumn 1981): 1.

financial markets that went ahead in October of that year. Murdoch, the owner of the *Sun*, *News of the World*, *Times* and *Sunday Times*, was itching to take on the print unions. He understood that he could use the introduction of computer technology to break one of the best-organized and longest-established groups of workers in London.

Jobs in Fleet Street and the London print industry were only obtainable with a union card, and union agreements controlled pay and conditions. Workers received high wages and job security, but the unions were bitterly resented by the employers, especially when the printers used their power to shut the papers down. In May 1980 the printers in Natsopa struck in support of a TUC-called day of action against Thatcher's policies – and an injunction from the *Daily Express* was simply ignored. Sean Geraghty, leader of the Fleet Street electricians, was brought before the High Court for stopping work in support of the health workers' day of action. His token fine was paid by an anonymous donor.[82] Engineers brought Fleet Street to a standstill in protest at the ban on unions at the Cheltenham 'spy centre', GCHQ. The employers were desperate to gain control. In January 1986 News International closed down its titles in Gray's Inn Road and Bouverie Street, sacked 5,500 workers and moved with a largely new workforce into what was then a rundown area of East London.

Wapping had been secretly planned for months, and the whole operation was conducted like a battle in the wider war. The new employees, quietly recruited outside London through the right-wing EEPTU electricians' union, were each asked in interview whether they would be prepared to cross picket lines. The sacked workers and their unions picketed Wapping for over a year. On Saturday nights there would be mass pickets, supported by other trade unionists who came with their banners, demonstrating in the streets around the fortified plant. There was a women's demonstration, echoing the women's demos during the miners' strike. The pickets tried to halt the lorries of the Murdoch-owned TNT road hauliers which were delivering the newly printed papers: road haulage was used to bypass the railways, which were highly unionized. One Saturday Michael Delaney, a young man celebrating his nineteenth birthday, was run over and killed by a TNT lorry leaving the plant. An inquest jury returned a verdict of unlawful killing, but no one was prosecuted.

Protestors were regularly attacked by police. One night in May, police horses led charges against the demonstrators, with many injured and arrested.[83] Murdoch could not have continued his operation without this level of policing, sanctioned by the Conservative government. The close

---

82   *Socialist Worker*, 14 August 1982 and 21 August 1982.
83   *Socialist Worker*, 10 May 1986.

relationship between the police and the *News of the World* dates from the time of Wapping, when they collaborated to ensure the papers went out.

The print unions were dealt a major blow, especially as other newspapers followed in Murdoch's wake. Defeat was not inevitable, but Murdoch had prepared for a decisive showdown. The union side fought courageously, but they were undermined by the EEPTU which helped to recruit scabs for the new plant, by the refusal of the TUC to broaden the dispute, and by the movement's defensive posture. So, even though the union-busting operation was known about in advance, there was a sense of paralysis about what to do.[84] These events helped to create the world we now live in: the weakened role of the unions (and the lower wages and worse conditions that come with it); the free-market doctrines that are supposedly unchallengeable; and the poison in the bloodstream of the body politic, as ever more powerful papers dictated to cowed politicians.

DEMOCRATIC DEFICIT

Democracy was also under threat as Thatcher proposed to abolish the GLC. London had had its own capital-wide government for nearly 100 years, first through the LCC and then expanded to the GLC and the thirty-two local boroughs from 1964. In 1981, Labour won the GLC election and Ken Livingstone, part of a new left inside the London Labour Party, became leader of the council. His most important reform was the Fares Fair policy, which reduced public transport fares in order to promote the use of tube trains and buses rather than private cars. It was very popular with Londoners for obvious reasons, and got many more people onto public transport, but was challenged by the Tory London Borough of Bromley in the High Court and defeated. Responsibility for transport was thereafter taken away from the GLC. Housing had already effectively been removed from GLC control, and Livingstone went on to challenge Thatcher over the policy of rate-capping, which curtailed local government spending by (in Thatcher's view 'profligate') Labour councils. Other councils such as Lambeth and Hackney also defied the policy, and some councillors were barred from office for failure to set a rate (local tax).

The Tories were determined to abolish the GLC and finally did so in 1986, with much talk of giving power to the boroughs. In fact many of the GLC's responsibilities passed to unelected quangos; local boroughs were instead weakened over the course of the 1980s, finding themselves

---

84 See for example *Socialist Worker*, 28 September 1985 and 21 December 1985. More generally, see J. Lang and G. Dodkins, *Bad News: The Wapping Dispute* (Nottingham, 2011).

with fewer powers, less money and more centrally imposed policy constraints.[85]

Thatcher's fall came at the height of her power: the poll tax was simply a class attack too far. Part of her plan to reform local government finance, the tax was a deeply regressive one that penalized working people and aided the rich. In the words of Thatcher's close colleague, Nicholas Ridley, the poll tax's great virtue was that 'the duke will pay the same as the dustman'. Not just dustmen, but cleaners, car workers, teachers, nurses, shop assistants and civil servants quickly realized that this was unfair. In the weeks before its introduction in April 1990, mass demonstrations at town halls across London protested at the tax and demanded that Labour councils refuse to implement it. But the defeat over rate-capping had weakened the councils, and they were urged to obey the law by the Labour leadership. So the demonstrations ended in riots again and again.

In Hackney thousands rioted, and afterwards every estate agent in a wide radius around the Town Hall had its windows smashed.[86] A huge demonstration of perhaps 250,000 assembled on 31 March at Kennington Park to march to Trafalgar Square. Organized by campaigners from the Anti-Poll Tax Federation who worked entirely outside the labour movement establishment, it was attacked by police as it reached the top of Whitehall and rioting again broke out in Whitehall and around the square. Fighting went on for hours, with mounted police moving north of the square in pursuit of demonstrators, some of whom were seriously injured. The matinee audience at the English National Opera came out to a spectacle of street fighting, baton charges, blazing cars and smashed windows. Similar scenes continued across this part of the West End until the evening. The next day when the home secretary tried to visit Soho to assess the damage he was attacked by a crowd of around 200 and another mini-riot broke out.

Amid widespread condemnation of the violence, including by some of the march organizers, even many Tories now understood that the tax was not workable. A mass campaign of non-payment began, with magistrates' courts across London overflowing as summonses were issued and some recalcitrants imprisoned. In London more than 25 per cent of the population refused to pay up. Thatcher was fatally wounded and out of office by the end of the year.

Livingstone came back, however. The Labour government under Tony Blair elected in 1997 pledged a new London government, to be known as

---

85   J. Davis, 'From GLC to GLA: London politics from then to now', in J. Kerr and A. Gibson (eds), *London from Punk to Blair*, pp. 109–15.
86   L. German, personal recollection.

the Greater London Authority. Its powers were narrower than those of the old GLC, excluding for example housing and education but including transport, police and regeneration. Instead of a council leader and council, there would be a directly elected mayor and a small assembly elected partly by proportional representation. The Tories were discredited locally and nationally, especially in Westminster which had received favoured status from the previous government, where they were able to set low rates and a poll tax, and carried out hard-line Tory policies. The council leader, Tesco heiress Lady Shirley Porter, even decanted troublesome working-class tenants out of the rich parts of Westminster, which she controlled through paying council tenants to leave their homes in marginal wards, allowing them to be bought up at market prices by those who were a likely bet to vote for Porter.[87] Livingstone, Labour MP for Brent throughout the 1990s, was the obvious candidate for the position of mayor, which Labour was near certain to win. Blair prevented his selection as Labour candidate, imposing instead another London Labour MP, Frank Dobson. Livingstone refused to accept this, stood as an independent, and galvanized a campaign of supporters, including many Labour Party members, which led him to easy victory and helped the Greens win three seats on the Assembly in 2000.

---

87   Kerr and Gibson, *From Punk to Blair*, p. 114.

Neoliberal London

I love dis concrete jungle still
With all its sirens and its speed,
The people here united will
Create a kind of London breed.

Benjamin Zephaniah

CORPORATE CITY

Modern London is today the centre for US-style neoliberal economics in Europe. The process began with a series of policies implemented under Margaret Thatcher, in particular deregulation, privatization and the phoney Lawson boom of the 1980s. The Big Bang in the City of London in 1986 accelerated this process. The successive sell-offs of public utilities and nationalized industries, the marketing of council houses, public buildings and land for property speculation, the destruction of large parts of London's manufacturing industry – all conspired to change the face of London. Levels of inequality grew as this process developed. London became a more expensive and more stressful city to live in. In 1830 the Radical William Cobbett had already described London as the 'Great Wen', a monstrous boil on the face of the country.[1] It is a powerful analogy today, when the structure of employment, the labour market, the housing market, the cost of living and transport are all grotesquely distorted.

Neoliberalism has helped shape British politics in general and the social geography of the city in particular in a way that is almost bound to lead to further social explosions. Levels of inequality and instability are as high as they have ever been in London. Grand neoliberal projects like Canary Wharf and the Olympic Park are ostentatious symbols of wealth and property in the middle of some of London's poorest areas. The accompanying

---

1   W. Cobbett, *Rural Rides* (London, 2005), p. 43.

'retail outlets' which are an inevitable part of any new building development in London are monuments to consumerism. Record levels of debt are evidence of a shopping habit which many Londoners are unable to break.

Yet neoliberal London has also created opposition to its values. Thatcher's destruction of trade unions and communities and her ideological attack on collective values created a legacy never challenged by her successors. We live with it still. But it is a legacy increasingly contested in London, where different groups of people have stubbornly resisted this path and helped to create a city with its own very different radical culture and politics. A booming economy in recent decades has attracted workers from around the world, helping to make London the diverse city that it is today. London is full of spaces where different nationalities and races, women, gays, lesbians, the disabled all began to make their voices heard, and demand that their concerns be met.

The London of most ordinary Londoners is very different from the London of the new rich. The people who work to keep the city going, who help to maintain remarkably cohesive communities, those who contribute many hours of unpaid labour to care for and improve the lives of everyone in the city, are ranged against a series of vested interests. The politicians, property developers and City of London businessmen have promoted this neoliberal London at the expense of the rest of us. The cleaners, Tube drivers, office and shop workers, students, carers, pensioners and voluntary workers have an interest in fighting for a different city. The battle between the two groups continues to decide what London's future will be.

THE NEW CITY IN THE EAST

By the time Thatcher left office, all the London docks had gone. One by one, starting with St Katherine's Dock near the Tower, all were closed and what jobs remained went to Tilbury. Left behind was a huge area of industrial wasteland. Throughout the 1970s there were various plans and consultations put forward for its development, which could have been the opportunity to create new parks and housing developments to benefit the local population. A very different course was taken and, as so often in London's history, it was driven by property developers and private profits. The London Docklands Development Corporation was set up in 1981, financed by a grant from central government and from selling land for development. It aimed to create an area which was beyond the control of the local authorities in which the land was to be developed. The LDDC had its own planning powers: this allowed it to give the go-ahead to the Canary Wharf development which became the centre of Docklands. The area became an Enterprise Zone which gave business tax breaks and rate rebates.

Despite the government's commitment to the free market and all things privatized, Docklands required huge infusions of public money to create an infrastructure and to entice businesses there. The Limehouse Link tunnel development (1993) was described as the most expensive road in Britain, costing £293 million for just over a mile of asphalt.[2] The Jubilee Line tube extension was built as a fast link between Docklands and the West End, and the Docklands Light Railway now covers large parts of the area. The LDDC spent £3,900 million public-sector money and £8,700 million private money.[3]

Canary Wharf was developed on the Isle of Dogs from the mid 1980s, with Murdoch's coup at Wapping encouraging other newspapers to move east: the geographical shift facilitated the change in printing and production methods. Big business was at first reluctant to move, but soon banks and other finance companies, assured of the necessary transport links and consumer facilities, took advantage of the cheaper rents to move to the 'new city'. Today's Canary Wharf with its skyscraper banks and newspaper offices, surrounded by acres of deluxe private housing, shows how successful developers can achieve social cleansing in what were once solidly working-class areas. Canary Wharf is protected by private security guards and in effect is a private enclave. It is home to some of the most influential and most powerful institutions in Britain: 'It contains the biggest bank, HSBC; the biggest law firm, Clifford Chance; the newspapers the *Daily Telegraph*, the *Independent* and the *Daily Mirror*, and the Financial Services Authority. And it houses many of the key operators in American and European finance.'[4]

The architecture critic of the *Guardian*, Jonathan Glancey, sums up how the heart has been taken out of the old East London with 'its thieving docks, ships from all parts of the world, the huge, hairy spiders that crept out of banana boxes', to be replaced with 'the chic and suited banality of Canary Wharf, the cheap clatter-past of the Docklands Light Railway, more boring post-modern apartment blocks than you care to imagine, and a City riverside as lifeless and as appealing as an empty fridge dumped in Barking Creek.'[5]

Local working-class people, very few of whom obtained work in the new businesses, found that their needs for decent housing were ignored

2 T. de Castella, 'The UK's last, great, expensive, short roads', *BBC News Magazine*, 27 June 2011.
3 Ross and Clark, *The Illustrated History*, p. 311.
4 A. Sampson, *Who Runs this Place: The Anatomy of Britain in the 21st Century* (London, 2005), p. 245.
5 Glancey, *Bread and Circuses*, p. 21.

while new private developments, impossible for all but the rich to afford, were being built at a rate which meant that the proportion of council housing on the Isle of Dogs had fallen from 83 per cent before the development began to 40 per cent by 1988.[6] The bitterness and resentment at the 'Fat Canary' with its high but at the same time squat-looking tower looming over the shabby tower blocks was palpable. David Widgery, an East End socialist doctor, wrote of the whole development:

> The LDDC, as usual, have done everything back to front. First they let Olympia and York build their monolith at Canary Wharf, then as the traffic jams and delays become intolerable it occurs to them that services and infrastructure, in particular road access, will be needed. So the Limehouse Link, an underground five-lane motorway of about three-quarters of a mile, has to be rammed through the main two Limehouse council estates in record time, demolishing a 500-foot tower block, obliterating 500 homes and requiring the compulsory rehousing of a further 2,000 people. All so that the journalists on the *Daily Telegraph* can get to work in time.[7]

In 1993, when at a council by-election Isle of Dogs electors voted in (temporarily) the fascist Derek Beackon, it was widely acknowledged that the development and the grievances it produced – especially over housing – played a role. Campaigners spent the next year ensuring that he was defeated in the local elections, but the issues, especially housing, became if anything more pressing.

Development elsewhere in London also continued to follow the money. Despite the property crash of the late 1980s, and the grinding to a halt of some projects, speculative building continued around all the new Tube and DLR stations, throughout the furthest reaches of Docklands. A new airport was built, and the massive Excel arena. Not just Docklands but the rest of Tower Hamlets, Hackney, and parts of Newham have seen modern blocks sprout up in every conceivable spare space, including former petrol stations and patches of industrial waste land. They join converted pubs, factories, warehouses, electricity showrooms, schools and colleges, all striving to capture the essence of city chic and 'loft living'. Around them are little enclaves of coffee bars, Tesco Metros and estate agents. But these flats have not solved the needs of ordinary Londoners. They are not for the most part designed for families, but for young childless people with high incomes. Meanwhile London council housing is in its worst state for

6   Ross and Clark, *The Illustrated History*, p. 311.
7   D. Widgery, *Some Lives!* (London, 1991), p. 155.

decades, and for the first time in 100 years there is no group of people in local or national government committed to providing high-standard, cheap housing for those who do the essential work in London. Low-paid workers are forced to live further and further from their work, and cite housing as one reason for leaving their jobs.[8]

The right-to-buy legislation of the 1980s encouraged council tenants to buy their homes at absurdly cheap prices. This combined with cuts to government building budgets was particularly devastating in London, with its already high property prices and recurrent overcrowding problem. One of the effects of the government's turn away from social housing has been to allow existing stock to decay, leaving the vast majority of estates with a distinct feeling of despair and neglect. Still, when the last Labour government pushed through a programme of transfer from councils to social housing charities, there was mass opposition from tenants across London.

THE NEW MILLENNIUM

The Millennium Dome was conceived under the Tories but delivered by the New Labour government that took office in 1997. Its celebrity opening on New Year's Eve 1999 was marred when the newly built Jubilee Line broke down under the strain at Stratford and the queen refused to link arms to sing 'Auld Lang Syne' at midnight. The Dome cost £45 million to build and a further £723 million for other costs, including its contents. Stuck on the North Greenwich peninsula 'like some washed-up jellyfish', with a McDonald's at the entrance, it symbolized for many the continuity between the old Tories under Thatcher and Major and the New Labour administration under Tony Blair.[9]

The early 1990s had seen a more radical mood emerge in London. Large demonstrations took place: in early 1991 the movement against the First Gulf War in Iraq mobilized increasing numbers. In 1994 the Tories introduced a Criminal Justice Bill which would end the right to silence for suspects and restrict the rights of young people to attend raves. An alliance of the left, civil liberties campaigners and ravers organized demonstrations, including a huge protest march to Hyde Park which only partly reached its destination when scuffles with the police broke out in Park Lane. In 1992, John Major's announcement of pit closures brought two massive processions of miners and their supporters onto the London streets within a week. Workers and residents hung out of their windows along the route of the march to wave and cheer the miners, even in cushy Kensington.

8   Glancey, *Bread and Circuses*, pp. 90–1.
9   Ibid., pp. 26–7.

These issues fed into the mood of disgust with the Tories, who were driven out by a landslide in 1997: Labour came into office for the first time in nearly twenty years. The corruption, scandal and directionless arrogance of taken-for-granted power all contributed to the Labour victory. On election night London swung heavily to Labour, most memorably when Michael Portillo unexpectedly lost his seat in Enfield Southgate to Stephen Twigg. Tony Blair, the new prime minister, neither expected nor wanted the landslide, having planned to work in close co-operation with the Lib Dems. Now he had too big a majority. Blair made it clear that his government was unlikely to deliver many of the improvements Londoners would like when he committed to remaining within Tory spending limits for two years, thus precluding expenditure on rundown public services. The insistence on pressing on with the Dome, now the project of his closest colleague, Peter Mandelson, was symbolic of this continuity. Blair's closeness to the rich and powerful was demonstrated through his intimacy with Rupert Murdoch and other businessmen, and hostility to the unions.

Meanwhile, manufacturing continued to decline. The expansion of finance in London since the Big Bang, and of retail and personal services, shifted the balance of forces towards a more non-unionized workforce. Precarious employment, low pay, temporary or fixed-term contracts, and longer hours all became common. Blair was fully in support of deregulation, seeing it as a means of increasing investment and profitability and attracting business to London. The mantra of the businesses themselves, especially the banks and finance companies, was echoed throughout local and central government. Privatization, deregulation and free markets were the answer, and nothing could be projected, created or developed without private-sector involvement.

The building of public housing slowed, schools became academies run by businesses, the arts were corporately branded and amenities ranging from parking meters to public toilets were sold off. In the boom years under Blair, development proceeded at a crazy pace: the cranes towered above London like a flock of storks. There were some prestige projects, like the 'gherkin' at St Mary Axe or the redevelopment of St Pancras, but elsewhere the developers displayed pure vandalism: the Hammersmith Palais, originally opened in 1919, one of the great wartime music venues with real historic value, was closed in 2007 to make way for yet another office block or shopping mall in Hammersmith.

None of these developments did anything to alleviate the serious crisis of housing in London. The property boom pushed prices so high that even small flats were now beyond the reach of most working people. People found that they could no longer afford to buy, and even when prizes started to fall or went stagnant with the onset of the credit crisis: the 'ultra-prime' London market remained healthy, and there was still demand for homes at over £5m.[10] The private landlord, much diminished by rent controls from the 1960s onwards, came back with a vengeance, assisted by subsidized 'buy to let' policies. Rents became so high because many people could not afford to buy. The average rent in London in 2011 was £1,360 for a two-bedroom home – nearly two and a half times the average for the rest of England. In twenty-two London boroughs, median rents cost more than 50 per cent of median local full-time earnings.[11] Scarcely any council housing was being built.

Property speculation and rocketing rents affect the wider fabric of London. Shops, markets and small businesses have all been forced to close or contract because they cannot compete with the mighty chains of stores, restaurants and coffee shops which dominate in London as they do in other cities. The working-class areas of London all once boasted their own markets. Henry Mayhew in his study of London in the mid nineteenth century devotes much space to the street markets:

> Here, and in the shops immediately adjoining, the working-classes generally purchase their Sunday's dinner; and after pay-time on Saturday night, or early on Sunday morning, the crowd in the New-cut, and the Brill in particular, is almost impassable. Indeed, the scene in these parts has more of the character of a fair than a market.[12]

Of the markets Mayhew lists, most still exist today: The Cut near Waterloo, Petticoat Lane, Whitecross Street, Leather Lane in Holborn, Somers Town, Kingsland, Hackney Road, Whitechapel.[13] Others, like Clare Market off the Aldwych have disappeared in all but name – on its site now stands the London School of Economics. The markets were the main providers of cheap food for the poor, and still remain so in many parts of London. They have also traditionally sold ingredients catering to local immigrant popu-lations, with Chapel Market stocking Greek and Italian food and Ridley Road containing a wonderful selection of Jewish, African and Caribbean stalls, as well as halal butchers.

There have been repeated battles to save them from redevelopment, such as the campaign against plans to close the Queen's Market in Newham.[14] In markets such as Shepherd's Bush, the oldest covered market in London, traders complain that councils are forcing up rents, leading to fewer stalls

10   S. O'Grady, 'House prices slip again as market faces stagnation', *Independent*, 3 September 2010.
11   L. Reynolds, *Shelter Private Rent Watch, report 1* (London, 2011), p. 3.
12   Mayhew, *London Labour and the London Poor*, p. 14.
13   Ibid., pp. 34–5.
14   See friendsofqueensmarket.org.uk.

and eventual closure, while every encouragement is given to new impersonal malls which are dominated exclusively by the big chains and supermarkets. Meanwhile the massive Westfield complex catering for upmarket customers is only five minutes away from Shepherd's Bush market. Stratford market in the East awaits the same fate, as Westfield opens there in time for the Olympics. Parking charges near markets also give an advantage to large supermarkets and malls which have free parking. New markets have sprung up in London, but they are largely farmers' markets or antiques and vintage clothing stalls: pricey goods aimed at a middle-class clientele, who combine buying fresh fish or organic vegetables with enjoying an exotic brunch. This has happened to the historic Borough Market at London Bridge, where food has been sold since Roman times, and Broadway Market in Hackney.

THE OLYMPICS

London won the bid for the 2012 Olympics in 2005. Backed enthusiastically by the Labour mayor, Ken Livingstone, it has regularly been hailed as a pathway to regeneration, jobs and housing in the east of London. It has certainly lent further impetus to the eastward shift of the city. The main stadium and Olympic village were to be built on wasteland in Stratford in the borough of Newham and thus began a massive programme of public investment in buildings, transport and publicity about the event. But the site was not quite as empty as Londoners were led to believe. It had to be cleared of its residents and workers, and of the allotments which had been so lovingly cared for by those who rented them. Most of the people who lived and worked in the designated area (once railway land in a major junction near the docks, and bordered by a canal, a river and motorways) were poor. They were clearly not the people who would be occupying the new blocks of flats which now sprang up in every space.

The new Olympic site has already required the removal or social cleansing of a range of encumbrances, including a travellers' camp, council tenants, small businesses and allotments. Sections of Hackney Marshes – a green space in one of the poorest parts of London and one of the biggest amateur football venues in London – are to be concreted over to provide coach parks for Olympic visitors. Narrowboat dwellers on the river Lea which runs along the edge of the site are threatened with eviction unless they pay mooring fees almost ten times the level which they previously paid. Sally Ash, representing British Waterways, said: 'we have to send the message that in future, living on the river will not be such a cheap lifestyle option'.[15]

---

15 I. Griffiths, 'Houseboaters being "socially cleansed" from Olympics area', *Guardian*, 9 March 2011.

The whole Olympic project is likely to cost up to £9 billion,[16] and promises to be a bonanza for property companies, retailers, security guards and hotel chains if previous Games are anything to go by.[17] The Westfield Stratford City (with its own E20 postcode) has such a role in the Olympic experience that most spectators arriving at the Games by public transport will have to go through the shopping mall to reach their destination. Likewise, those wanting to exit the 'legacy' Olympic Park on its east side after the Games are over will do so through Westfield.

Londoners are being asked to pay extra council tax to fund the extravaganza, but have received no benefits in return for this investment. Seat prices for the opening ceremony run into thousands of pounds. Tickets were oversubscribed, but those able to pay an expensive hotel package during the Games will be able to buy their way in. Super-highways are being prepared to speed politicians, businessmen and athletes along East London's congested roads, while the ticketless watch resentfully from the pavements. Meanwhile, sports and youth facilities across London are being cut as part of the government's austerity measures.

THE POLITICS OF PROTEST

London's diversity was obvious by the beginning of the Millennium. Its status as a world city was confirmed, and its population started to grow again. When the fascist nail bomber David Copeland launched attacks on Brixton, Brick Lane and the Admiral Duncan pub in the gay area of Old Compton Street, he was quite consciously attacking the diverse city which London had become and which was such anathema to him.[18] In the twenty-first century London has become once more the scene of protest around a range of issues. In this world city at the heart of the neoliberal project there were campaigns, demonstrations, meetings and events on hundreds of topics. Support for Nelson Mandela, for example, is commemorated in London streets, housing estates and colleges; he was greeted by many thousands in Trafalgar Square in 2005 where he spoke there, and gave thanks to those in Britain who had supported the struggle against apartheid. There are now statues to him in Parliament Square and at the Festival Hall.

Some protests were about neoliberalism itself: on 18 June 1999, Reclaim the Streets attracted more than 10,000 to its protests over globalization

16 'Experts debate Games bid benefits', BBC News (Scotland), 6 March 2007, bbc.co.uk.
17 J. Boykoff, 'The Anti-Olympics', New Left Review 67 (January–February 2011): 41–59.
18 N. Hopkins and S. Hall, 'David Copeland: a quiet introvert', Guardian, 30 June 2000.

and its consequences. They abseiled down Tower Bridge, had mass cycle rides, leafleted banks, trashed a McDonald's, set fire to a bank.[19] The anti-capitalist movement originated in Seattle in 1999 at a demonstration against the World Trade Organization, and spread throughout the world. Demonstrations and social forums took place in different parts of the world, always attracting large numbers of equally international participants; London hosted the European Social Forum and demonstration in 2005. On May Day 2001 hundreds of cyclists formed a 'critical mass' at King's Cross, blocking the traffic. At lunchtime a phalanx of students marched to the World Bank offices in Haymarket. In the afternoon a crowd of by now several thousand marched up to Oxford Circus where the police experimented with their now common tactic of 'kettling' – penning demonstrators in, often for hours, without food, drink, toilet facilities or warm clothes. It amounts to effective imprisonment for demonstrating. The protestors, many of them school students, were penned for six hours. The public outrage over this was substantial, and cases brought against the police went all the way to the European Court, but it was one illustration of the harsh tactics they were prepared to adopt.[20]

By far the largest movement in the first part of the twenty-first century was the anti-war movement. The events of 11 September 2001 changed politics in Britain as they did everywhere. The Socialist Workers Party called a meeting in the small hall at Friends' House a few days later which attracted around 200 and from that called, with others on the left, a meeting in the Great Hall entitled 'Stop the war before it starts'. On the night the main hall filled with more than 2,000 people, also packing two overflow rooms. There were another 500 people standing outside the building in the peace garden on its eastern side. It was noticeable that many Muslims were there, as they were the following week when an organizing meeting of 500 set up the Stop the War Coalition. The first demonstration against the Afghanistan war, launched in October that year, had been planned already by CND. But the Stop the War march on 18 November, when that war appeared effectively over, surpassed all expectations. Held during Ramadan, the organizers held an *iftar* or breaking of the fast in Trafalgar Square, where Muslims and non-Muslims shared water and dates. It marked a new level of political engagement in the left by sections of the Muslim community.

Great anti-war demos had taken place before in London – against Suez in 1956, against nuclear weapons in the late 1950s and again in the early 1980s.

---

19 J. Vidal and L. Brooks, 'Day the City turned into a battleground', *Guardian*, 19 June 1999.

20 See G. Taylor, 'Eyewitness: London, May Day 2001', in E. Bircham and J. Charlton (eds), *Anti-Capitalism: A guide to the movement* (London, 2001), pp. 369–71.

The series of post-9/11 anti-war demonstrations exceeded all of them in size, scope and diversity. It is something of an irony that London, first city of the British Empire, should now find itself at the heart of demonstrations against the new imperialism. London's diversity really shone through with people of all ages, backgrounds, religions and races coming together. The demonstration against the war on Iraq on 15 February 2003 was the biggest protest in British history. A *Guardian*/ICM poll estimated that at least one person from 1.25 million households had demonstrated on that day.[21] John Lewis in Oxford Street reported a 40 per cent drop in sales on the day. The demonstrations and movement marked a departure from their predecessors in that they were genuinely diverse, particularly attracting large numbers of Muslims, but also people from other religions and from all parts of the world. They brought together the left, the trade unions, the traditional peace movement in the form of CND, and the Muslim community through the Muslim Association of Britain, all expressing their rejection of belligerent British and US imperialism.

Hyde Park and Trafalgar Square are now known around the world as centres of protest. The demos have also asserted free speech. The Hyde Park authorities, backed by Labour minister Tessa Jowell, refused permission for the demonstration to end in the park – on the grounds that so many people would damage the grass. Stop the War refused to back down and said it would march to Hyde Park regardless of any ban.[22] The government gave in. It had to do so again when George W. Bush came to London later that year and the police threatened to close down large parts of Central London. Stop the War demanded to march where it wanted and did so, attracting 350,000 to greet Bush in what was the largest-ever weekday demonstration in London. As night fell, crowds watched the toppling of a statue of Bush in Trafalgar Square – an ironic riposte to the toppling of Saddam Hussein's statue in Baghdad, the orchestrated performance of the US invasion's military triumph. This determination to march echoed the defiant traditions of the nineteenth century.

Direct action played a big part in the movement. On Halloween thousands of students sat down in Whitehall amidst lighted, hollowed-out, Halloween pumpkins. In early 2003 school students from across London struck and walked out of their schools, as they did again on the day war broke out – when students and some workers from across London took to the streets to hold impromptu protests, such as blocking roads. Some had

---

21   Reported in A. Travis and I. Black, 'Blair's popularity plummets', *Guardian*, 18 February 2003.
22   A. Murray and L. German, *Stop the War: The story of Britain's biggest mass movement* (London, 2005), pp. 155–8.

to climb over their school gates and a number were badly treated by police, including some who were arrested.

While the movement did not stop the war, it created a mass climate of opposition to imperialism in Afghanistan, Iraq and Palestine. Disgusted at Labour's alacrity in going to war, and the lies and deceptions involved, led many to question the nature of democracy and to look for alternative politics. As a direct result of this ferment, the Respect Party was formed in 2004, winning a seat for George Galloway in Bethnal Green and Bow in 2005, and achieving some of the highest swings against Labour in Newham. The Lebanon war in 2006 saw more huge and diverse demonstrations. In 2009 Palestine erupted as Israel bombed Gaza. Massive crowds assembled in the coldest of January weather and marched to the Israeli embassy, harassed by police along the way. After the largest demo, on 10 January, police kettled young protestors trying to leave, attacked them and arrested many. The rioting lasted for hours. Those detained, many of whom were young Muslims, received prison sentences. Student occupations took place in colleges across London in support of Gaza, the first sign of a revival in the student movement which developed so spectacularly the following year.

The anti-war movement which began in 2001 has helped to create a mass solidarity movement with the Middle East and South Asia. Indignation over war and Palestine helped to create a politicized layer in London who protested and campaigned over a range of issues. The support for the Palestinians in London has been remarked on by the Israeli government, which blames it on a 'red–green alliance' of the left and the Muslim community. Right-wing columnist Melanie Phillips is so appalled by this aspect of the capital's politics that she has renamed the city 'Londonistan'.

A NEW LEFT FOR LONDON

Much that the left was used to in London thirty or forty years ago has gone: the taverns where radical printers met, the Irish pubs like the Favourite in North London with its Republican culture, the meeting halls and union offices where campaigns were won and lost.[23] But there are many new places: the inner-city churches, for example, fulfil a social function far beyond simply sharing worship. They are centres of organizing for the whole community, often addressing wider political issues such as poverty, aid for Africa, and questions of war and peace. In the past two decades in London, mosques across the capital have helped campaign over Chechnya,

---

23   For a recollection of some of these see H. Kean, 'The transformation of political and cultural space', in Kerr and Gibson, London from Punk to Blair, pp. 149–56.

Bosnia, war in Iraq and Afghanistan, Guantanamo, Kashmir, civil liberties and Palestine. Community centres such as Oxford House in Bethnal Green or Marchmont Street in Bloomsbury are regular meeting places, doubling as coffee shops, arts centres and bookshops. Friends' House, Conway Hall, and the Camden Centre hold left-wing events and meetings every week.

But politics and protest in London have changed very much in these years. The working-class giants who played such a big part in the story of London, such as the dockers and print workers, are no longer on the scene – their jobs transformed by technological change and indeed, if they exist at all, subject to worse conditions on lower pay. The big factories in West London have mostly gone. But there is a new working class in London: it reflects all the diversity and youth of the city and works on the tubes and railways, in the offices and shops, in cleaning and personal services, in restaurants. It works in schools, hospitals, job centres and council offices across the capital.

Much is made of the importance of the financial sector to London, but this should not be overestimated. It accounts for just under 332,000 jobs out of a total of more than 4 million in London, more than 100,000 of those in banks and building societies (far fewer in broking). There are similar numbers of jobs in hotels and restaurants and in transport and over half a million in wholesale and retail sales. Construction and manufacturing jobs combined amount to around 300,000. There are over 100,000 industrial cleaning jobs in the city.[24] In work as in other respects, London is a highly divided city. Over 600,000 Londoners have no qualifications, and many young people are not achieving qualifications. One in three working-age residents are out of work, and over 690,000 people claim an out-of-work benefit.[25]

While London remains a working-class city, many managers and professionals live outside and commute in. Nearly a quarter of London's higher-paid workforce are commuters.[26] Workers in new industries are frequently without a union, and many of them face conditions similar to those of their nineteenth-century counterparts. Their success or otherwise in organizing themselves will determine their future wages and conditions, and whether they can build permanent unions as the dockers and the gas workers had to do. There is no fundamental difference between today's casualized and precarious workers and those who helped to create what are still some of the most powerful unions. The difference lies in terms of organization and consciousness – whether people see themselves as part of a collective which can change society.

---

24   For these figures, see the London Skills and Employment Observatory, lseo. org.uk.

25   'The London Story', lseo.org.uk.

26   lseo.org.uk.

Recent years have shown that a new and youthful left is being formed in London. Those politicized through war, Palestine, anti-fascism and anti-racism, events in Venezuela or Bolivia, are making the connections between their own issues and the wider questions of what is wrong with the system. This radicalism is something new. Or at least it is of a kind that has been forgotten in London's history. So much that is happening today has echoes in the past, but that past has been hidden from the view of most working people by an orthodox history which stresses the role of the powerful, rather than of people like themselves. In addition, present-day radicalism is not necessarily or mainly connected with a political party, such as the Labour Party, which for much of the twentieth century had a strong and organic connection with at least sections of the London working class. That has largely gone, and certainly is in steep decline. The weakness of much of the left outside of Labour stems in part from a failure to update the old models of protest. But protest has changed, politics has changed, and the structure of the working class is different from even a generation ago.

Yet London continues to surprise us all. Who would have predicted the student demonstration which ended in a smashed-up Tory headquarters in Millbank? Or the tremendous sight of thousands of London school students flowing like quicksilver into Trafalgar Square and then leaving just as suddenly to march down Whitehall, using their mobile phones to avoid kettling? The students again joined with the half-million-strong TUC protest against the cuts in March 2011, the largest union demonstration for a generation. Who would have expected the riots which flared across London in August 2011, hitting new areas of the city like Croydon and Enfield, as well as Tottenham and Hackney which experienced rioting in the 1980s and 90s?

The changed demographic of London, fuelled by the housing crisis which drives successive generations out of their neighbourhoods, means the outer city is increasingly affected like the inner city. The riots were expressions of opposition to the consumerism, the poverty, the sheer hopelessness that affects young people in neoliberal London. Far from denoting criminality and gang warfare, as politicians claimed, they demonstrated the divisions and inequality that afflict the city.[27] As in previous riots, there was a strong element of fury at police harassment; in Tottenham, where the first riots broke out following the shooting of a black man by police, 55 per cent of defendants brought to court were black.[28]

---

27   Only 19 per cent of those arrested in London during the riots were identified as gang members, according to Home Office figures; A. Travis, 'Gangs did not play central role in riots, inquiry finds', *Guardian*, 25 October 2011.
28   Ibid.

Just two months later, who would have expected that the Occupy LSX movement – permanently encamped outside St Paul's Cathedral, having been prevented from occupying the privatized Paternoster Square – would galvanize such wide support, and trigger such a crisis in the established Anglican Church? The symbolic camp in the heart of the financial centre of one of the richest cities in the world was the physical expression of Londoners' widespread revulsion with inequality and greed.

Time and again in London the radical tradition shines through. The descendants of the London mob, the Chartists, the New Unions, the Suffragettes, the Cable Street warriors and the Pentonville dockers are all here, doing what every generation has had to do. David Widgery wrote: 'There is no physical monument to what generations of decent working-class East Enders have created and given and made and suffered.'[29] The new generation protesting across London is that living monument. London has always been at its worst when those with power and money have a free rein, and always at its best when the ordinary people assert their rights against the rich and powerful. This generation is beginning to fight for those rights.

---

29   Widgery, *Some Lives*, p. 164.

Bibliography

Ackroyd, P. *Dickens* (London, 1990)

Ackroyd, P. *London: the biography* (London, 2000)

Addison, P. and Crang, J. *Listening to Britain* (London, 2010)

Adler, G. Hudis P. and Laschitza A. (eds.), *The Letters of Rosa Luxemburg* (London, 2011)

Allan, J. *Bertholt Lubetkin and the Tradition of Progress* (London, 1992)

Allen, T. *Little Italy, The Story of London's Italian Quarter* (London, 2008)

Anderson, P. *Passages from Antiquity to Feudalism* (London, 1996)

Ashton, R. *Counter Revolution, The Second Civil War and its Origins* (New Haven and London, 1994)

Aveling, E. and Marx, E. *The Woman Question* (Leipzig, 1987)

Barltrop, R. *Jack London: The man, the writer, the rebel* (London, 1978)

Benn, C. *Keir Hardie* (London, 1997)

Bircham, E. and Charlton, J. *Anti Capitalism: a guide to the movement* (London, 2001)

Black, J. *London, A History* (Lancaster, 2009)

Bloom, C. *Violent London, 2000 years of Riots, Rebels and Revolts* (London, 2003)

Booker, C. *The Neophiliacs* (London, 1992)

Boston, S. *Women Workers and the Trade Union Movement,* (London, 1980)

Brailsford, H. N. *The Levellers and the English Revolution* (Nottingham, 1961)

Branson, N. and Heinemann, M. *Britain in the Nineteen Thirties* (St Albans, 1973)

Branson, N. *History of the Communist Party of Great Britain, 1927-1941* (London, 1985)

Branson, N. *Poplarism 1919-1925, George Lansbury and the Councillors' Revolt* (London, 1979)

Braybon, G. and Summerfield, P. *Out of the Cage* (London, 1987)

Brendon, P. *The Dark Valley* (London, 2000)

Briggs, A. *Victorian Cities* (London, 1968)

Brittain, V. *England's Hour* (London, 1941 reprinted 2005)

Brittain, V. *Testament of Youth* (London, 1978)

Bronowski, J. *William Blake and the Age of Revolution* (London, 1972)

Burn, D. *Rent Strike St Pancras 1960* (London, 1972)

Calder, A. *Revolutionary Empire* (London, 1998)

Calder, A. *The Myth of the Blitz* (London, 1992)

Calder, A. *The People's War* (London, 1992)

Challinor, R. *The Origins of British Bolshevism* (London, 1977)

Charlton, J. *It Just Went Like Tinder* (London 1999)

Cliff, T. and Gluckstein, D. *The Labour Party: a Marxist History* (London, 1988)

Cobbett, W. *Rural Rides* (London 2005)

Cole, G. D. H. *History of Labour Party since 1914* (London, 1949)

Cole, G. D. H. and Postgate, R. *The Common People 1746-1946* (London 1971)

Collette, C. *For Labour and For Women* (Manchester, 1989)

Conan Doyle, A. *The Golden Pince Nez* (London, 1981)

Conrad, J. *The Secret Agent* (Ware, 1993)
Countryman, E. *The American Revolution* (London, 1985)
Cox, J. *William Blake, The Scourge of Tyrants* (London, 2004)
Dangerfield, G. *The Strange Death of Liberal England* (London, 1970)
Dean, J. M. (ed.) *Literature of Richard II's Reign and the Peasants' Revolt: Introduction* (originally published in *Medieval English Political Writings*) (Michigan, 1996)
Donagan, B. *War in England 1642-1649* (Oxford, 2008)
Dorling, D. *Injustice: Why Social Inequality Persists* (Bristol, 2011)
Drake, B. *Women in Trade Unions* (London, 1984)
Du Noyer, P. *In the City* (London, 2010)
Earle, P. *A City Full of People, Men Women and London 1650-1750* (London, 1994)
Elborough, T. *The Bus we Loved* (London, 2005)
Engels, F. *The Condition of the Working Class in England* (Moscow, 1973)
Ensor, R. C. K. *England 1870-1914* (Oxford, 1936)
Farman, C. *May 1926, The General Strike, Britain's Aborted Revolution?* (St Albans, 1972)
Faulkner, N. *Rome: empire of the eagles* (London, 2008)
Faulkner, N. *The Decline and Fall of Roman Britain* (Stroud, 2004)
Fernbach, D. (ed.) *The First International and After* (London, 1974)
Field, N. *Over the Rainbow* (London, 1995)
Fielding, S., Thompson, P. and Tiratsoo, N. *England Arise* (Manchester, 1995)
Fishman, W. J. *East End 1888* (Nottingham, 2008)
Fishman, W. J. *East End Jewish Radicals 1875-1914* (Nottingham, 2010)
Flintham, D. *London in the Civil War* (Leigh-on-Sea, 2008)
Foot, P. *The Politics of Harold Wilson* (London, 1968)
Foot, P. *The Vote* (London 2005)
Fox, C. (ed.) *London-World City 1800-1840* (New Haven and London, 1992)
Foxell, S. *Mapping London: making sense of the city* (London, 2007)
Frank, J. *The Levellers, A History of the Writings of Three Seventeenth Century Social Democrats John Lilburne, Richard Overton, William Walwyn* (Harvard, 1955)
Froissart, J. *The Chronicles of Froissart* (translated by John Bourchier, Lord Berners)
Fryer, P. *Staying Power, The History of Black People in Britain* (London, 1984)
Fuller, K. *Champion! The London Forest Strike of 1991* (London, 1992)
Gardiner, J. *Wartime* (London, 2004)
Gardiner, S. R. *History of the Commonwealth and Protectorate,* (Aldestrop, 1989)
Gardiner, S. R. *History of the Great Civil War,* (London, 1987)
Gatrell, V. A. C. *The Hanging Tree* (Oxford, 1996)
George, M. D. *England in Transition* (London, 1962)
Gillis, J. R. *For better, for worse* (Oxford, 1985)
Gilmour, I. *Riot, Risings and Revolution* (London, 1992)
Gissing, G. *The Odd Women* (Oxford, 2008)
Glancey, J. *London: Bread and Circuses* (London, 2003)
Golden, J. *Hackney at War* (Stroud, 2009)
Grayzel, S. R. *Women and the First World War* (Essex, 2002)
Gregg, P. *Free-born John, a biography of John Lilburne* (London, 1961)
Hall, P. *Cities of Tomorrow* (London, 2002)
Haller, W. and Davies, G. *The Leveller Tracts 1647-53* (New York, 1944)
Hamilton, P. *Hangover Square* (London, 2001)
Hamilton, P. *The Slaves of Solitude* (London, 2006)
Hamilton, P. *Twenty Thousand Streets under the Sky* (London, 2004)
Harman, C. *The Fire Last Time* (London, 1998)
Harrison, S. *Sylvia Pankhurst: a Maverick Life 1882-1960* (London, 2004)
Hatherley, O. *Militant Modernism* (Winchester, 2008)
Hibbert, C. *King Mob* (Sutton, 2004)
Hill, B. *Eighteenth Century Women: An Anthology* (London, 1987)

Hill, C. *Liberty against the Law* (London, 1996)

Hill, C. *Reformation to Industrial Revolution* (London, 1967)

Hill, C. *The Century of Revolution 1603-1714* (Wokingham, 1961)

Hinton, J. *The First Shop Stewards' Movement* (London, 1973)

Hobsbawm, E. J. *Labour's Turning Point* (Brighton, 1974)

Hobsbawm, E. J. *The Age of Empire* (London, 1989)

Holmes, R. (ed.) *Defoe on Sheppard and Wild*, (London, 2004)

Holton, B. *British Syndicalism 1900-1914* (London, 1976)

Howlett, R. (ed.), *Historia Rerum Anglicarum*, in *Chronicles of the Reigns of Stephen, Henry II and Richard I, Rolls Series* 82 (London, 1964)

Hudson, K. *CND, Now more than ever* (London, 2005)

Humphries, S. *A Secret World of Sex* (London, 1991)

Humphries, S. *Hooligans or rebels? An Oral History of Working Class Childhood and Youth 1889-1939* (Oxford, 1995)

Hunt, E. H. *British Labour History 1815-1914* (London, 1985)

Hunt, T. *The Frock Coated Communist: The revolutionary life of Friedrich Engels* (London, 2009)

Inwood, S. *A History of London* (London, 1998)

Jack, A. *Pop goes the Weasel: The Secret meanings of Nursery Rhymes* (London, 2011)

Jackson, A. A. *Semi Detached London: Suburban Development, Life and Transport 1900-1939*, (London 1973)

Jacobs, J. *Out of the Ghetto* (London, 1978)

John, A.V. (ed.) *Unequal Opportunities* (Oxford, 1986)

Jones, D. *Summer of Blood, The Peasants' Revolt of 1381* (London, 2010)

Jones, W. R. D. *Thomas Rainborowe (c1610-1648) Civil War Seaman, Siegemaster and Radical* (Woodbridge, 2005)

Kapp, Y. *Eleanor Marx vol I Family Life* (London, 1972)

Kapp, Y. *Eleanor Marx vol II The Crowded Years* (London, 1976)

Keane, J. *Tom Paine, A Political Life* (London, 1996)

Kendall, W. *The Revolutionary Movement in Britain* (London, 1969)

Kent, G. *Olympic Follies* (London, 2008)

Kerr, J. and Gibson, A. (eds) *London from Punk to Blair* (London, 2003)

Kops, B. *The World is a Wedding* (Nottingham, 2008)

Krupskaya, N. K. *Memories of Lenin* (London, 1970)

Kynaston, D. *A World to Build* (London, 2008)

Lang, J. and Dodkins, G. *Bad News: the Wapping Dispute* (Nottingham, 2011)

Langford, P. *A Polite and Commercial People, England 1727-1783* (Oxford, 1989)

Laybourn, K. *The Rise of Socialism in Britain* (London, 1997)

Laybourn, K. *A Century of Labour* (Stroud, 2000)

Lewenhak, S. *Women and Trade Unions* (London, 1977)

Lewis, J. E. (ed.) *London, the Autobiography* (London, 2008)

Lewis, J. *East Ham and West Ham Past* (London, 2004)

Liddington, J. and Norris, J. *One Hand Tied Behind Us* (London, 1978)

Liddington, J. *The Life and Times of a Respectable Rebel* (London, 1984)

Lilburne, J. *An Impeachment for High Treason Against Oliver Cromwell and his son in law Henry Ireton Esquires* (London, 1649)

Lilburne, J. *The Charters of London: or the Second Part of Londons Liberty in Chaines Discovered* (London, 1646)

Lin, C. *The British New Left* (Edinburgh, 1993)

Lindley, K. *Popular Politics and Religion in Civil War London* (Aldershot, 1997)

Linebaugh, P. *The London Hanged* (London, 1991)

MacInnes, T. and Kenway, P. *London Poverty Profile* (London, 2009)

Macpherson, J. *Drawn with the Sword* (Oxford, 1996)

Manning, B. *The English People and the English Revolution* (London, 1991)

Marlow, J. (ed.) *Votes for Women* (London, 2000)

Marlow, J. *Women and the Great War* (London, 1999)

Marx, K. and Engels, F. *Collected Works* Vol. 6 (Moscow, 1976)

Marx, K. and Engels, F. *Collected Works* Vol. 14 (Moscow, 1980)

Marx, K. and Engels, F. *Collected Works* Vol. 20 (Moscow, 1980)

Marx, K. and Engels, F. *Collected Works* Vol. 22 (Moscow, 1980)

Marx, K. and Engels, F. *Collected Works* Vol.26 (Moscow, 1980)

Marx, K. and Engels, F. *Collected Works* Vol. 41 (Moscow, 1980)

Marx, K. and Engels, F. *Selected Correspondence* (Moscow, 1975)

Massey, D. *World City* (London 2007)

Mayhew, H. *London Labour and the London Poor* (Douglas-Fairhurst, R. (ed.) Oxford, 2010)

McKay, C. *A Long Way From Home,* (London, 1985, originally published in 1937)

McKibbin, R. *Classes and Cultures England 1918-1951* (Oxford, 1998)

Mearns, A. *The Bitter Cry of Outcast London* (London, 1883)

Meier, O. and Evans, F. (eds) *The Daughters of Karl Marx Family Correspondence 1866-1898* (London, 1984)

Miles, R. and Phizacklea, A. *White Man's Country, Racism in British Politics* (London, 1984)

Mitchell, J. and Oakley, A. (eds) *The Rights and Wrongs of Women* (London, 1976)

Morgan, K. O. *The People's Peace,* (Oxford, 1992)

Morton, A. L. *A People's History of England* (London, 1979)

Morton, A. L. *Freedom in Arms* (London, 1975)

Murray, A. and German, L. *Stop the War: the story of Britain's biggest mass movement* (London, 2005)

Murray, A. *The T&G Story, A History of the Transport and General Workers Union 1922-2007* (London, 2008)

Nesbit, E. *The Railway Children* (Ware, 1993)

Neville, R. *Hippie Hippie Shake* (London 1996)

Nicholson, J. *The Great Liberty Riot of 1780* (London, 1985)

Page Arnot, R. *The General Strike May 1926* (Wakefield, 1975)

Pankhurst, S. *The Suffragette Movement* (London, 1977)

Pearl, V. *London and the Outbreak of the Puritan Revolution* (Oxford, 1961)

Pearce, B. and Woodhouse, M. *A History of Communism in Britain* (London, 1995)

Pease, T. C. *The Leveller Movement* (Gloucester, Mass., 1965)

Pelling, H. *A History of British Trade Unionism* (London, 1971)

Pember Reeves, M. *Round about a Pound a Week* (London, 1994)

Perry Curtis, L. *Jack the Ripper and the London Press* (London, 2001)

Piratin, P. *Our Flag Stays Red* (London, 1978)

Plowden, A. *In a Free Republic, Life in Cromwell's England* (Stroud, 2006)

Ponting, C. *1940: Myth and reality* (London, 1990)

Porter, R. *London: a social history* (London, 1994)

Porter, S. (ed.) *London and the Civil War* (London, 1996)

Prochaska, A. *London in the Thirties* (London, 1973)

Prothero, I. *Artisans and Politics in early Nineteenth Century London* (Folkestone, 1979)

Raw, L. *Striking a Light* (London, 2011)

Reynolds, L. *Shelter Private Rent Watch report 1* (London, 2011)

Richardson, A. (ed.) *Women who Did* (London, 2002)

Robinson, D. *Chaplin: his life and art* (London, 1992)

Rosen, A. *Rise Up Women* (London, 1974)

Rosen, M. and Widgery, D. *The Chatto Book of Dissent* (London, 1991)

Ross, C. and Clark, J. *London, The Illustrated History* (London, 2011)

Rothstein, A. *The Soldiers' Strikes of 1919* (London, 1980)

Rothstein, T. *From Chartism to Labourism* (London, 1983)

Rowbotham, S. *A Century of Women* (London, 1997)

Rude, G. *The Crowd in History* (London, 1981)

Rude, G. *Wilkes and Liberty, A Social Study of 1763 to 1774* (Oxford, 1962)

Sampson, A. *Who Runs this Place: the Anatomy of Britain in the 21st Century* (London, 2005)

Sheridan, D. (ed.) *Wartime Women: a mass observation anthology* (London, 2000)

Shonfield, Z. *The Precariously Privileged* (Oxford, 1987)

Sinclair, I. *Hackney, that Rose-Red Empire* (London, 2009)

Smith, H. L. and Nash, V. *The Story of the Dockers' Strike* (London, 1889)

Soldon, N. *Women in British Trade Unions 1874-1976* (London, 1978)

Solomon, C. and Palmieri, T. *Springtime, the new student rebellion* (London, 2011)

Southern, A. *Forlorn Hope. Soldier radicals of the Seventeenth Century* (Lewes, 2001)

Stedman Jones, G. *Outcast London*, (Oxford, 1971)

Stevenson, J. and Cook, C. *The Slump, Society and Politics During the Depression* (London, 1979)

Stevenson, J. *British Society 1914-45* (London, 1984)

Stevenson, J. *The History of William of Newburgh* (1856, reprint Llanerch, 1996)

Stokes, J. (ed.) *Eleanor Marx: life, work, contacts* (Aldershot, 2000)

Stow, J. *A Survey of London: written in the year 1598* (London, 2005)

Swenarton, M. *Homes Fit for Heroes: The Politics and Architecture of Early State Housing in Britain* (London, 1981)

Taylor, A. J. P. *English History 1914-1945* (Oxford, 1992)

Thompson, D. *The Chartists* (Aldershot, 1984)

Thompson, E. P. *William Morris* (London, 1977)

Thompson, E. P. *Witness against the Beast* (Cambridge, 1993)

Thompson, E. P. *The Making of the English Working Class* (London, 1982)

Thorne, W. *My Life's Battles* (London, nd)

Thornley, A. (ed.) *The Crisis of London* (London, 1992)

Tomalin, C. *The Life and Death of Mary Wollstonecraft* (London, 1992)

Torr, D. *Tom Mann and His Times* (London, 1956)

Trotsky, L. *My Life* (London, 1975)

Vallance, E. *A Radical History of Britain* (London, 2010)

Van Houts, E. M. C. (ed. and trans.) *The Gesta Normannorum Ducum of William of Jumieges Orderic Vitalis, and Robert of Torigni*, Volume II (Oxford, 1995)

Walvin, J. *Fruits of Empire* (London, 1997)

Ward, J. T. (ed.) *Popular Movements c. 1830-1850* (London, 1980)

Webb, B. *Our Partnership* (London and Cambridge, 1975)

Weeks, J. *Sex, Politics and Society* (Harlow, 1981)

Weightman, G. and Humphries, S. *The Making of Modern London* (London, 2007)

Weinbren, D. *Generating Socialism: Recollections of Life in the Labour Party* (Stroud, 1997)

Weinreb, B. and Hibbert, C. *The London Encyclopaedia* (London, 1983)

White, J. *London in the 19th Century* (London, 2008)

Widgery, D. *Some Lives!* (London, 1991)

Widgery, D. *The Left in Britain 1956-68* (London, 1976)

Wise, S. *The Blackest Streets: The Life and Death of a Victorian Slum* (London, 2008)

Wodehouse, A. S. P. *Puritanism and Liberty, Being the Army Debates (1647-49) from the Clarke Manuscripts* (London, 1938)

Young, M. and Wilmott, P. *Family and Kinship in East London* (London, 1957)

NEWSPAPERS AND PERIODICALS

Archaeologia

Athena Review

Chronicle of the Grey Friars of London: Camden Society old series, volume 53 (1852)

Colonial Williamsburg Journal

Commonweal

Daily Herald

Daily Worker
Justice
Mercurius Militaris
Mercurius Elencticus
Military Times
Morning Star
New Left Review
New Reasoner
New Statesman
Pall Mall Gazette
Reynolds's Newspaper
Shrew
Socialist Review
Socialist Worker
Spare Rib
Guardian
Historical Journal
Impartial Intelligencer
Independent
Link
Moderate
Moderate Intelligencer
National Reformer
Newsletter
Observer
The Times
Workers' Dreadnought

WEBSITES AND ARCHIVES

Historical Collections of Private Passages of State (John Rushworth)
The Thomason Tracts (British Library)

British Library (bl.uk)
Old Bailey Proceedings Online (oldbaileyonline.org)
TUC History Online (unionhistory.info)

archive.org
brent-heritage.co.uk
british-history.ac.uk
bwtuc.org.uk
coinstreet.org
demographia.com
friendsofqueensmarket.org.uk
london.gov
lseo.org.uk
marxists.org/archive
maryonthegreen.org
pre-war-housing.org.uk
roehamptonview.co.uk
savekensalriselibrary.org
stairwaytoheavenmemorial.org

Index